·45-
#85
1987

INDUSTRIAL RELATIONS RESEARCH
ASSOCIATION SERIES

Human Resources and the Performance of the Firm

AUTHORS

Steven G. Allen	Casey Ichniowski
Brian E. Becker	Morris M. Kleiner
Richard N. Block	David Lewin
Robert L. Clark	George T. Milkovich
Ronald G. Ehrenberg	Craig A. Olson
Walter J. Gershenfeld	Paul Osterman
Harry J. Holzer	Myron Roomkin

Sidney W. Salsburg

EDITORIAL BOARD

First edition

Library of Congress Catalog Card Number: 50-13564

ISBN 0-913447-38-2

PRICE $15.00

INDUSTRIAL RELATIONS RESEARCH ASSOCIATION SERIES
    Proceedings of the Annual Meeting (Spring publication)
    Proceedings of the Spring Meeting (Fall publication)
    Annual Research Volume
    Membership Directory (every third year)
IRRA Newsletter (published quarterly)

Inquiries and other communications regarding membership, meetings, publications, and general affairs of the Association, as well as orders for publications, copyright requests on publications prior to 1978, and notice of address change should be addressed to the IRRA publication office: Barbara D. Dennis, Editor; David R. Zimmerman, Secretary-Treasurer; Marion J. Leifer, Executive Assistant.

INDUSTRIAL RELATIONS RESEARCH ASSOCIATION
7226 Social Science Building, University of Wisconsin
Madison, WI 53706 U.S.A.   Telephone 608/262-2762

CONTENTS

PREFACE

In the years following World War II, a number of scholars were concerned about the role of organizational policies and rules in determining how firms treated their employees. The conventional wisdom of that time, based on neoclassical economics, assumed that firms were price-takers in the market for labor, that is, they enjoyed little latitude in personnel practices. However, as John Dunlop, Charles Myers, Richard Lester, Lloyd Reynolds, and others recognized, there were widely varying ways in which firms treated employees and substantial differences in industrial relations practices among companies, industries, and societies.

In the 40th year of the Industrial Relations Research Association, it is appropriate that the Association should turn again to the issue of organizational practices in industrial relations. Indeed, the issue is still at the forefront of debate among and within the principal constituencies of the Association—scholars, advocates, policy-makers, and neutrals. The earlier researchers taught us that firm practices, what were then called personnel practices, were derived to a significant extent from labor market and product market considerations. Today the issues deal more with the ways in which these generic practices (now called human resources practices) contribute to or detract from the performance of the organization.

We begin this volume with the premise that firm performance and human resources were linked through policies and practices in several areas. These include compensation practices, collective bargaining and unionization, systems for dealing with employee grievances and complaints, systems of employee involvement in the workplace, practices dealing with recruitment and selection, and practices aimed at stabilizing employment and reducing turnover. Further, it seemed particularly timely to examine trade union influence over the goals of companies, that is, the so-called impact of collective bargaining on the strategic objectives of a firm. The chapters on these subjects that follow seek to examine this premise by critically reviewing published literature. However, in several instances the authors report on new work and data.

Although the objectives of the firm are often difficult to assess, each author was asked to define performance broadly and to discuss those measures of performance most appropriate to their subject. We knew from the beginning, however, that the literatures on these different subjects, which span several disciplines, have not concentrated on the same measures of performance and were not equally developed on this general question.

The editors would like to thank the following institutions for their support of this project: the University of Kansas Research Fund, the J.L. Kellogg Graduate School of Management at Northwestern University, and the School of Labor and Industrial Relations at Michigan State University.

In addition, we are deeply indebted to Barbara Dennis of the Association for her editorial assistance, encouragement, and managerial skills in bringing this project to fruition.

Morris M. Kleiner
Richard N. Block
Myron Roomkin
Sidney W. Salsburg

CHAPTER 1

Industrial Relations as a Strategic Variable

BY DAVID LEWIN°

Columbia University

During the past quarter of a century or so, the concept of business strategy has gained wide currency and attracted a veritable legion of researchers. From an initial focus on corporate-level planning, strategy research has evolved to a set of specialized studies that deal, for example, with business units, portfolios for diversified companies, mature businesses, declining businesses, new ventures, and joint ventures (Schendel and Hofer, 1979; Harrigan, 1980; Hambrick, 1980). Additionally, this research has shifted from an emphasis on strategy formulation to strategy implementation (Mintzberg, 1978; Galbraith and Nathanson, 1978; MacMillan, 1984; Yavitz and Newman, 1982).

The fascination with strategy has attracted scholars with many different perspectives and interests. Economists have studied relationships between strategy and structure (Chandler, 1962, 1977; Williamson, 1975), competitive analysis and industrial organization (Porter, 1980; Bain, 1968), and administrative behavior (Simon, 1957; Braybrooke and Lindblom, 1970). Behavioral scientists have developed organizational transformation and life-cycle models to analyze and prescribe the match of organization design to business strategy (Kimberly, Miles, and Associates, 1980; Miles and Snow, 1984). Marketing researchers have devised product life-cycle models which form the core of marketing planning (Day, 1984; Utterbach and Abernathy, 1975). Portfolio theory, which is based on concepts of risk preference, has become the centerpiece of the financial strategy literature and also appears to have been widely adopted by business organizations, especially with respect to

° The comments of John Delaney, Raymond D. Horton, Casey Ichniowski, Sanford Jacoby, Hervey Juris, Marianne Koch, Thomas Reed, Myron Roomkin, and an anonymous referee on earlier versions of this chapter are gratefully acknowledged.

acquisition and divestiture decisions (Modigliani and Miller, 1958; Roll, 1970). Even the accounting and information systems literatures have become linked to strategic business decision-making via their developing focus on and models of efficient information generation and usage (Bathke and Lorek, 1984).

Now it appears that industrial relations researchers are jumping on the "strategy" bandwagon. True, some of the 1960s literature on micro or firm-level manpower planning and modeling was nested in strategic business planning (Walker, 1969; Patten, 1971). More recently organizational behavioralists have employed strategy frameworks to analyze the personnel/human resource management function and certain of its subfunctions, such as selection and staffing, performance evaluation, compensation systems, and employee training and development (Milkovich and Glueck, 1985; DeBejar and Milkovich, 1986; Hax, 1985; Dyer, 1984). But the most recent development in this regard is the application of strategic planning notions to union-management relations and collective bargaining. Indeed, some researchers have gone so far as to claim that we now have a new theory of industrial relations, one that is grounded in the concept of strategic choice (Kochan, McKersie, and Katz, 1985).

Certainly few would decry attempts to strengthen the theoretical foundations of industrial relations, particularly because scholars from several disciplines contribute to the field and because the definition and boundaries of the field are not well settled. Further, industrial relations strategy researchers have advanced our knowledge of contemporary industrial relations through their diligent collection and imaginative analyses of new data, and they have contributed strongly to the resurgence of research interest in industrial relations. But one may nevertheless question whether and to what extent the concept of strategic choice can or does provide the lynchpin for the theoretical development of industrial relations. In fact, such questioning will be at the core of this chapter, which attempts to provide a critical assessment of contemporary research on industrial relations as a strategic variable.

To do this, the dominant conceptual models used in industrial relations strategy research are reviewed. Then empirical studies of industrial relations strategy in three areas, namely, union avoidance, collective bargaining, and labor-management cooperation are examined. These areas were selected because they have been given major attention by industrial relations strategy researchers.[1] Finally, conclusions about the validity and reliability of research on strategic industrial relations are presented, and an alternative explanation of the research evidence is offered.

Conceptual Frameworks

When the term "industrial relations theory" is used, most students of the field probably think initially of Dunlop's *Industrial Relations Systems* (1958). And they should, because Dunlop introduced his book by noting that "The present volume presents a general theory of industrial relations; it seeks to provide tools of analysis to interpret and to gain understanding of the widest possible range of industrial relations facts and practices" (p. vii).

Dunlop went on to identify the industrial relations system as the central focus of the theory; within each such system a complex of rules is created to govern the workplace and the work community. The web of rules can thus be regarded as the major dependent variable in Dunlop's framework. The major independent variables in this systems view of industrial relations include certain actors— workers and their organizations, managers and their organizations, and governmental regulatory agencies; certain environmental contexts—technology, market or budgetary constraints, and the power relations and statuses of the actors; and a certain ideology or set of shared understandings among the actors in the system. The central task of his theory, said Dunlop, was to explain why particular rules are established in a particular industrial relations system and how and when the rules change in response to changes affecting the system.

Dunlop's work unquestionably contains several major concepts, but can it be said that this theory was tested? No, it wasn't, certainly not in a formal way. The central concepts of the theory were not used to specify, construct, or operationalize dependent or independent variables. Indeed, Dunlop never refers to his concepts

---

[1] In this chapter we do not examine management, union, or joint union-management activity in the legislative arena. Such activity presumably can be analyzed from a strategic perspective, especially if it is viewed as a set of attempts to alter the environment within which unions and managements operate. However, because legislative activity is a complex subject that merits its own detailed examination, we confine ourselves to the subject of strategic industrial relations at the firm (micro) level of analysis. In this limited sense, legislative activity can be regarded as a second-order effect of the direct relationship between the parties.

as variables and in parts of his book he backs away from the notion that he was presenting a theory of industrial relations.

Empirically, Dunlop employed a wide variety of secondary sources, principally government, industry, and union reports, to describe the industrial relations systems of literally a score of countries and to identify the dominant web of rules in each of those systems. Interestingly and instructively in light of more recent industrial relations research, Dunlop concluded his qualitative study by identifying a three-fold typology of dominant industrializing "elites" in the development of industrial relations systems, thereby generalizing his theory to a transnational or world level.

Few theorists have been as ambitious as Dunlop and fewer still have received comparable attention for their work.[2] Nevertheless, *Industrial Relations Systems* cannot be said to provide a theory of industrial relations because it provides no basis for rejecting alternative hypotheses, treatments, or interpretations of the data. In short, it does not offer predictions which can be empirically confirmed or refuted, and Dunlop recognizes this when he sometimes refers to his conceptualization as a framework rather than a theory.[3]

Do any or all of these same criticisms apply to contemporary strategic-choice theory of industrial relations? To begin to answer this question, let us first consider the underlying motivation for the development of this theory. That motivation apparently stems from a belief that management as an actor in the industrial relations system has been neglected by researchers.

For example, Kochan, McKersie, and Cappelli (1984) observe that "a more realistic model of industrial relations should recognize the active role played by management in shaping industrial relations as opposed to the traditional view which sees management as reactive, responding to union pressures" (p. 2). Similarly, in assessing industrial relations developments to the mid-1980s, Strauss (1984) noted that "I begin with management, since it, rather than the union, is now the prime mover" in industrial relations (p. 2).

---

[2] See, for example, Somers (1969) and Chamberlain (1948). Also see Kuhn, Lewin, and McNulty (1983) for a comparison of Dunlop's and Chamberlain's influence on the field of industrial relations. A framework for the analysis of British industrial relations that has received considerable attention is presented by Flanders (1965).

[3] For other views of Dunlop's framework, see Singh (1976), Blain and Gennard (1970), and Wood et al. (1975).

Concentrating more narrowly on the airline industry, Cappelli (1985a) selected as the focal point of his analysis "the different business strategies chosen [by companies] to respond to . . . competitive pressures [which] play an important role in shaping the variety of labor relations outcomes across carriers through their influence on the collective bargaining environment" (p. 316).

While this preference for studying management's role in industrial relations might be thought to stem from a desire to counterbalance the strong union orientation of some industrial relations researchers, it seems instead to stem primarily from recognition of the "new" collective bargaining environment and collective bargaining outcomes, especially of the 1980s. The leading characteristics of this new environment include increased economic competition, particularly from abroad, growing substitution of capital and new technology for labor, the development of employee involvement programs and job redesign schemes intended to enhance worker commitment to the firm, largely in the nonunion sector, increased pro-employer enforcement of the labor laws by the National Labor Relations Board (NLRB) and the courts, and, perhaps as a consequence of these forces, rapidly declining rates of unionization. The leading collective bargaining outcomes in this new era include greatly reduced rates of bargained pay and benefit settlements, often referred to as "concession" bargains (Mitchell, 1982), and major declines in strike activity. Undergirding these developments, apparently, are key changes in managerial values and strategies which, according to Kochan, Katz, and McKersie (KKM, 1986), "have profoundly affected the transformation now taking place in U.S. industrial relations" (p. 9). Much the same terminology is used by Purcell and Sisson (1983) to describe the situation in Britain: "The management of industrial relations is in a state of transition . . . [T]here will be significant changes in management strategy" (p. 118).

Perhaps the clearest conceptualization of how these various characteristics can be used to inform the study of industrial relations is provided by KKM, and is shown graphically in Figure 1. These researchers describe Figure 1 as a "theoretical framework for the analysis of industrial relations" (p. 11), and their principal research thrust is to gain greater understanding of the institutional forces that determine the outcomes of labor-management interactions. Such forces, they contend, have typically been treated by other researchers, especially economists, "as a black box of random forces" (p. 16), but even when this is not the case the bulk of scholarly attention has been directed toward labor rather than management institutions.[4] Hence, KKM are most concerned with opening up the black box that is represented by the management organization in industrial relations, especially management's strategic choices and decisions.[5]

To assist this effort, KKM went on to develop a typology that features three main levels of industrial relations activity, namely, the strategic, policy, and workplace levels.[6] As shown in Table 1, each of these levels is deemed to be relevant to the three main actors in the industrial relations system—employers, unions, and government. However, and consistent with their dominant perspective, KKM are primarily interested in explaining employers' or managements' industrial relations activity. Further, while Table 1 seems to suggest that strategic choices are made only at the top level of industrial relations activity, KKM note otherwise. For example, "strategic choices that are relevant to the bottom tier are the most directly associated with the organization of work, the structuring of worker rights, the management and motivation of individuals or work groups, and the nature of the workplace environment" (p. 18). Apparently, then, the concept of strategy can be applied to and studied at each of the main levels of industrial relations activity, even though most researchers are said by KKM to have occupied themselves with mid-level collective bargaining and personnel

---

[4] These contentions apply to "modern" industrial relations research, which dates from roughly 1960. That earlier generations of scholars were primarily concerned with institutional forces in industrial relations is clearly evident from the works of Commons (1934) and Hoxie (1928).

[5] Note that model presented in Figure 1 depicts a flow from independent to intervening to dependent variables, and therefore implies that all but the final outcome variables are exogenously determined. However, variables such as managerial values and unionization may well be endogenously determined. See, for example, Bartel and Lewin (1981) and Lewin (1985). Some scholars contend that the behavior of union organizations has been neglected by industrial relations researchers. See, for example, Anderson (1977) and Lewin and Feuille (1983). Note further that Dunlop (1958) and especially Chamberlain (1948) carefully examined management's role and decisions in industrial relations. Clearly, they did not treat management as a "black box of random forces," although they did not adopt a strategic-choice perspective on management or union-management decision-making.

[6] The reader may wish to compare KKM's threefold micro-level typology with Dunlop's (1958) macro-level typology of industrializing "elites."

FIGURE 1

General Framework for Analyzing Industrial Relations Issues

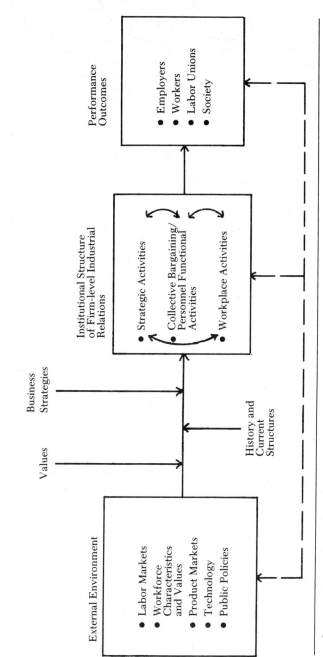

Source: Kochan, Katz, and McKersie (1986), p. 11.

TABLE 1

Three Levels of Industrial Relations Activity

Level	Employers	Unions	Government
Long-term strategy and policy-making	Business strategies Investment strategies Human resource strategies	Political strategies Representation strategies Organizing strategies	Macroeconomic and social policies
Collective bargaining and personnel policy	Personnel policies Negotiations strategies	Collective bargaining strategies	Labor law and administration
Workplace and individual/ organization relationships	Supervisory style Worker participation Job design and work organization	Contract administration Worker participation Job design and work organization	Labor standards Worker participation Individual rights

Source: Kochan, Katz, and McKersie (1986), p. 17.

policies and to have focused on process rather than strategic choices made at that level.

Despite all of this, neither KKM nor other researchers appear to offer a consistent, clear, or distinctive definition of strategy or strategic choice in an industrial relations context. Rather, propositions about strategy and descriptions of events which are claimed to reflect the strategic choices of management (and sometimes labor) abound in the literature. To illustrate, Kochan, McKersie, and Cappelli (1984) initially contend that "strategic decisions can only occur where the parties have discretion over their decisions; that is, where environmental constraints do not severely curtail the parties' choice of alternatives," and also that most of the strategy literature "focuses on the *process* of forming strategy rather than the actual *content* or *outcomes* associated with strategies" (p. 21, italics in original). Later these authors describe labor and management's "strategic choices" as a process of reactions to rapidly changing environmental conditions, especially increases in product market competition. However, more competitive market conditions would appear to lower, not raise, the parties' discretion in decision-making. In another case, Kalwa (1987) characterizes decentralization and other collective bargaining adjustments to changing product market conditions in the U.S. steel industry as "strategic choices" of the parties, but nowhere does he specifically define "strategy." Consequently, Rumelt's (1979) observation that the term "strategy" is used "idiosyncratically" in the business strategy literature seems for the present to apply to its use in the industrial relations strategy literature.

In any case, accepting Figure 1 and Table 1 as the guiding frameworks for the study of industrial relations as a strategic variable, we may ask: How have these frameworks been operationalized? For KKM, their associates, and certain other researchers, operationalization has taken the form of gathering, analyzing and attempting to integrate into the conceptual framework of Figure 1 a wide variety of primary and secondary, qualititative and quantitative data. Does the "additive" evidence produced by KKM and other researchers support the theoretical construct of industrial relations as a strategic variable or the accompanying notion of management as the prime mover of modern industrial relations activity? To address this question in greater detail, we turn in the next three sections to assessments of industrial relations strategy research that deal with union avoidance, collective bargaining, and labor-management cooperation, respectively.

Union Avoidance

Many scholars have investigated the declining incidence of unionism in the U.S., but it is the union-avoidance behavior of U.S. managers in particular that appears most likely to be labeled "strategic" by some researchers. For example, Lawler and West (1985) conclude that "employer campaign strategies impact strongly on the probability of employees voting in favor of unionization and, for the most part, these activities decrease that probability" (p. 419).

Managerial opposition to unionism in the specific context of representation elections has been studied from several perspectives and subjected to a variety of quantitative appraisals. Thus, Prosten (1979) showed that stipulated elections as a proportion of all NLRB-conducted union representation elections rose markedly during the 1960s and 1970s, and that the percentage of union wins fell precipitously as the time between petition filing and holding of an election increased. Roomkin and Block (1981) studied 45,115 union representation elections that took place during the 1970s and found a significant reduction in the proportion of union wins as the time between petition filing and the election increased; a three-month delay in the holding of an election, for example, was associated with a 10 percentage point decline in the union win rate. Seeber and Cooke's (1983) quantitative analysis supports the observation that consent elections, as opposed to stipulated elections, significantly increase a union's chances of winning a representation election.

Several studies of employer unfair labor practices as they bear upon union representation elections have also been conducted. The most common unfair practices are to discharge or otherwise discriminate against employees who form, support, or wish to join a union. Such behavior is illegal under Section 8(a)(3) of the Taft-Hartley Act. Nevertheless, 8(a)(3) unfair labor practice charges rose almost sixfold between the early 1950s and the mid-1980s.

Aspin (1966) studied 71 NLRB representation elections in which employee reinstatement was ordered and found that discharges for union activity were associated with a significantly lower union win rate. Dickens's (1983) reanalysis of Getman, Goldberg, and Herman's (1976) data drawn from 31 union representation elections showed that illegal employer campaigns reduced the proportion of employees who voted for unions by 4 percent, and that specific employer threats of punitive action against prounion workers reduced the proportion of employees voting for unions by 15 percent. Kleiner (1984) used a price theoretic choice model to estimate the probability of a firm being charged with one or more 8(a)(3) unfair labor practices during the 1970s. He found that firms that committed unfair labor practices early in the decade were more likely than other firms to commit unfair labor practices later in the decade. Cooke (1985b) tested a union representation election model on 1979 and 1980 data from NLRB region 25 (Indiana). He found that 8(a)(3) discrimination against employees reduced the probability of a union election victory by at least 17 percentage points, and that employee reinstatement was an ineffective administrative remedy for discrimination against union activists. In a prior study, Cooke (1985a) showed that 8(a)(3)-type discrimination also substantially reduced the probability of an existing union obtaining a first contract with an employer.

Clearly, these and other related studies demonstrate that illegal employer activity can "pay off" in the sense of reducing the incidence of union representation. However, this does not necessarily justify labeling such employer behavior "strategic choice." To do so overlooks several important contributing factors, including the probability that an unfair labor practice charge will be filed, the probability of the NLRB responding to the charge, the probability of a particular penalty being imposed for a violation of Section 8(a)(3), and the probability of the union's using illegal tactics to counter those of the employer—not to mention external environmental variables, such as those shown in Figure 1, that are at work in this regard.

More important, perhaps, is the fact that many other *legal* initiatives undertaken by employers influence both the probability that a union representation election will be held and the results of an election. For example, Lawler (1984) and Lawler and West (1985) found that employer use of consultants significantly reduced the chances of a union's winning a representation election. Moreover, such variables as "small group meetings" and "administration of surveys" had a large negative effect on the probability of a union victory in a representation election. This is consistent with the evidence, produced in a variety of studies, that job satisfaction is significantly negatively related to employee support for unions and to employees' voting for unions in representation elections (Getman, Goldberg, and Herman, 1976). Consequently, employers may influence both the probability of union representation elections being held and the results of such elections by "investing" in employee training and development, small group meetings, worker consultation and involvement, and periodic surveys to elicit information about organizational and workplace issues of concern to employees.

From one research perspective, the importance of these observations is to suggest that a strategic-choice model of industrial relations must be able to specify the conditions and circumstances under which some employers will undertake policies and practices to stimulate job satisfaction and positive employee attitudes, thereby reducing support for unionism ("union substitution"), and other employers will use illegal activities and tactics to reduce union support ("union suppression"). Some limited evidence about such strategic choices has recently been provided by industrial relations researchers (Fiorito, Lowman, and Nelson, 1987; Kochan, McKersie, and Chalykoff, 1986).

From another research perspective, however, this may be of small consequence. For example, while acknowledging that illegal employer behavior during representation elections lowers the probability that unions will successfully organize workers, and while admitting that the aforementioned research provides "evidence of significant problems in the current labor law that need to be remedied," KKM (1986) contend that the problems of the law and its administration are small compared to "the larger forces affecting union membership declines" (p. 78). Chief among the "larger forces," say these strategic-choice theorists, are changes in basic management values for which the clearest evidence, perhaps, comes from recent plant location and investment decisions of U.S. firms.

To substantiate this point, KKM first provide several examples of the written union-avoidance policy statements of large U.S.-based companies, including some that are partially unionized and some that previously encouraged "cooperative" unions. Then the researchers supplement the policy statements with narrative accounts of the nonunion plants opened by these and other large firms—for example, General Mills, Pepsico, Mobil Oil, Corning Glass, Pratt and Whitney, and ACF Industries—during the 1970s and 1980s. These examples are described as reflecting the basic union-avoidance strategies of company managements—strategies which ostensibly are primarily implemented by disinvesting in unionized facilities.

However, no evidence was provided by KKM to indicate specifically how other factors, such as changing work force composition or union leadership and behavior, may have influenced the incidence of plant- or firm-level unionization in these firms. Similarly, no evidence was provided to indicate what weights should be assigned to other factors—cost of capital, land costs, depreciation, taxes, product distribution channels, transportation costs, etc.—that typically influence business location decisions. Further, and perhaps most important, no evidence was provided by which to gauge the effects that competitive forces or the relative performance of union and nonunion plants and facilities in these firms may have had on subsequent business location decisions and the growth of the nonunion component of the firms. In other words, the multivariate analytical framework of Figure 1 was not applied to the cases of union avoidance and nonunion plant openings described by KKM, thereby weakening empirical support for the conclusion that these events stemmed primarily from managements' strategic choices.

A more narrowly focused study (and one relied on heavily by KKM) was conducted by Verma (1985), who examined the decisions of two large industrial firms, referred to as Firm A and Firm B, respectively, to invest in nonunion plants and disinvest in unionized plants. Over the 20-year period to 1982, Firm A not only accelerated its capital investment and employment in nonunion plants, it also shifted capital and jobs from unionized to nonunion plants. Over roughly the same period, Firm B also expanded its investment and employment in nonunion plants, but it did not shift resources and jobs from unionized to nonunion plants as rapidly as did Firm A. Verma then observed that "Firm A's management formulated and implemented a strategy of rapid disinvestment [from unionized plants] over the last 20 years," while Firm B's management chose "a relatively slow disinvestment strategy" (p. 403).

It is unclear from this analysis, however, what range of managerial behavior or choices with respect to industrial relations should be regarded as strategic. Is a firm, such as the Kroger Corporation, that chooses to maintain unionized establishments and not to open nonunion establishments behaving strategically? Does a firm, such as the Singer Corporation, that expands its unionized and nonunion facilities at comparable rates do so strategically? Is a conglomerate firm, such as Allied-Signal Corporation, acting strategically when it acquires some unionized *and* nonunion businesses or when it divests itself of other unionized *and* nonunion businesses? Is a firm that encourages its unionized employees to decertify their union somehow acting strategically, and is the occasional firm that encourages its employees to unionize also acting strategically?

Verma's research and that of KKM seem to suggest that the answer to all of these questions is yes or, in other words, that any management objective, action, or choice can be described as strategic or as reflecting an underlying strategy. But then, of course, the concept of strategy is vacuous—and, indeed, neither Verma nor KKM explicitly or operationally define the term strategy in an industrial relations context. Moreover, whereas the interview comments of managers in Firms A and B are invoked by Verma to support the two firms' respective choices of investment and disinvestment strategy, no comments of union officials are offered to clarify the unions' responses to management strategy or to illuminate union "strategies." This seems to be at odds with the notion, reflected in Figure 1 and Table 1, that interaction effects are important for understanding industrial relations processes and outcomes irrespective of whether they are strategically driven.

Another major limitation of Verma's research, and one which the author forthrightly acknowledges, is that plant-level profitability or other performance data were not available for analysis. Thus despite conducting a longitudinal study, Verma was unable to consider the extent to which union-nonunion plant performance differences contributed to the growth of nonunion plants in Firms A and B or the extent to which newly established nonunion plants subsequently outperformed older unionized *and* nonunion plants. Note that this represents a substantial departure from the business strategy literature which, while also containing conceptual and measurement limitations, usually identifies one or more end-point or outcome-type strategic objectives (for example, market share, sales growth, or profitability) of the firm (Porter, 1985). Nevertheless, Verma contends that his research evidence confirms the attainment of management's strategic objective in that "both firms clearly and formally state a policy of union avoidance in their newer nonunion operations" (p. 404).

More fundamentally, one must question the conceptual and empirical validity of treating the strategic choice of union avoidance in isolation from other strategic objectives and policies of the firm. Put differently, it should be asked: Why does the firm prefer to remain or become increasingly nonunion? Consider that the wage and benefit premiums (or rents) attributable to unionism rose markedly in the 1960s and 1970s, as reflected in a plethora of union pay impact studies (Freeman and Medoff, 1981). A related stream of research shows that unions capture a portion of firm profits (Clark, 1984; Voos and Mishel, 1986), and that both the presence of a union and strike activity have negative effects on shareholder equity (Neumann and Reder, 1984; Becker and Olson, Chapter 2 of this volume). Knowledge of these various union effects became widely diffused among unionized and nonunion employers.[7] At about the same time, behavioral science research and consultation expanded rapidly and something of a movement toward worker participation and employee involvement began to take hold (Walton, 1980). Growing international competition dramatized the wage rate/labor cost differences between the U.S. and other nations, and also underscored the seemingly greater ability of non-U.S. firms to enhance employee commitment and loyalty to the enterprise (Kochan and Barocci, 1985).

Consequently, in the 1970s U.S. companies began to invest directly and indirectly in union avoidance. Some firms did this by undertaking programs of employee participation that featured quality circles, suggestion plans, individual and group incentive systems, attitude surveys, autonomous work teams, and information-sharing programs. Often the development and implementation of these initiatives involved the use of outside consultants. Other firms pursued the goal of union avoidance by "investing" in illegal activities, such as discharging union activists and supporters and promising rewards or retribution to employees who voted against or for union representation, respectively. In this regard, the firms were "influenced" by the probabilities of government enforcement of the unfair labor practice provisions of the Taft-Hartley Act— probabilities which declined in the 1970s and 1980s, according to several researchers (Roomkin and Block, 1981; Seeber and Cooke, 1983)—and by the weak penalties imposed on employers found to have violated the act. Further and in light of the growing diversification of U.S. businesses, some companies (and their business units) have engaged in both legal and illegal union-avoidance activities.

This interpretation of the contemporary union-avoidance behavior of employers is consistent with a generalizable cost/benefit framework and with the concept of utility maximization that underlies neoclassical price theory. Following this theory, increases in economic competition can be expected to influence managerial values which, in turn, affect managers' preferences or choices of business decisions, including those pertaining to

---

[7] This conclusionary statement represents an inference drawn from the works of KKM (1986) and other researchers (e.g., Verma, 1985) who have studied managers' union-avoidance activity. Note that growing managerial opposition to unions is not consistent with the view, advanced by Freeman and Medoff (1984), that unionism has had significant positive effects on both productivity and labor costs, with the two roughly offsetting each other.

industrial relations processes and outcomes. This helps us to understand why management's dominant value orientation toward unionism, which in the U.S. has long been one of major opposition, has increasingly been translated into actual union containment and avoidance behavior, especially in the manufacturing-based stronghold of U.S. unionism where firms have winnowed unionized establishments and expanded nonunion establishments.[8]

From a research perspective, this reasoning and interpretation of the available evidence strongly suggest that the "strategic" objectives of union avoidance and disinvestment in unionized operations must be coupled with and empirically measured in relation to the "strategic" objective of improving plant, facility, or firm performance. Moreover, it may plausibly be proposed that employers' recent union-avoidance activities are as (more) consistent with a reactive behavior model as with (than) a strategic-choice model of industrial relations. Because Verma, KKM, and other scholars have not as yet conducted the type of research which permits one to reject this alternative explanation, or null hypothesis, the validity of the claim that the union-avoidance and disinvestment behavior of management supports the notion of industrial relations as a strategic variable must be questioned.

Collective Bargaining

A major impetus toward the development of strategic-choice concepts of industrial relations has come from collective bargaining settlements reached in the U.S. during the 1980s. By virtually any historical or comparative standard, these settlements have been modest and a substantial portion of them can properly be described as concession bargains (Mitchell, 1982; Cappelli, 1985b). The operative notion seems to be that business strategy decisions have been a powerful influence on these bargaining outcomes. Specifically, "management became more aggressive in requesting early contract openings, argued for decentralization of the structure of bargaining, shifted away from a strategy of promoting industrial

---

[8] It may also be argued that the market-driven "efficiency" underpinnings of management's union-avoidance behavior is a smokescreen in that such behavior stems more fundamentally from management's strong resistance to giving up its unilateral decision-making authority. This interpretation is consistent with and derives from the works of Bendix (1956), Simon (1957), and Jacoby (1985). Ironically, it may be relatively more consistent with a "strategic-choice" than a "reactive-behavior" model of industrial relations.

peace to one of emphasizing control over labor costs even at the risk of disruption in union-management relations, . . . and demanded major changes in noneconomic terms of the employment contract" (KKM, 1986, p. 112). But does the fact of diminished union bargaining power and enhanced management bargaining power in the 1980s provide support for a strategic-choice theory of industrial relations?

Consider, for example, an intraindustry study of industrial relations strategy conducted by Cappelli (1985a), who examined the early postderegulation experience in airlines. Cappelli traced the effects of the 1970s deregulation on market structure and bargaining structure in the airline industry and explicitly noted that increased competition in the industry brought about pressures for bargaining concessions in the 1980s. Further, he constructed a fourfold typology of unionized carriers based on their "product market strategies since deregulation," and he linked this typology to specific provisions and types of bargaining concessions that occurred in the airline industry during the early 1980s.

In some of these postderegulation negotiations, a few airline unions obtained job protection provisions in exchange for pay reductions and work rule modifications. Other airline unions received equity positions in certain airlines in exchange for pay and benefit reductions and work rule changes. Virtually all airline negotiations resulted in two-tier wage agreements, and a few of them provided for employee representation on company boards of directors. Cappelli also showed that most major carriers have established or joined holding companies in recent years, and that airline unions have increased their membership since deregulation. All of this is in the well-established industrial relations research tradition of examining the effects of changes in environmental variables on the process and outcomes of collective bargaining.

But does this intraindustry study enhance the conceptual or empirical underpinnings of strategic choice in industrial relations? It doesn't seem so. Consider, for example, Cappelli's observation that "the key to [a carrier's] securing concessions is whether unions are confronted with substantial unemployment at existing labor cost levels" (p. 325). Assuming generalized price stability, could this statement not apply to collective bargaining outcomes at virtually any point in time? The statement is fully consistent with the well-known Marshallian labor demand conditions and with well-known models of union wage-employment tradeoffs in bargaining (Rees, 1977; Dunlop, 1944). Specifically, if the demand for the product and thus the derived demand for labor become more elastic, the tradeoff of employment for wages is enlarged and labor's bargaining power is reduced. Cappelli clearly shows that this is what has happened in airlines, but it appears to have occurred as a reaction to a key environmental change rather than in anticipation of or as a result of strategic planning for such change. Put differently, the fact of wage and work rule concessions on the part of unions in airline bargaining during the 1980s suggests that labor and management have been responsive to environmental change but does not establish the presence of distinctively strategic underpinnings of this responsiveness.

Like Verma, Cappelli cites the comments of industry executives to support his analysis, but unlike Verma he also describes the "union response" to airline managers' supposed industrial relations strategies. However, no union officials were interviewed for Cappelli's study and no internal union organizational changes undertaken in response to new management strategies were examined or reported. While this is consistent with a research approach that views management as the prime mover in contemporary industrial relations and as a neglected object of study, it is somewhat inconsistent with the notion that private-sector labor relations feature bilateral bargaining and with the notion that organizational strategy is a salient concept generalizable to each of the main actors in the industrial relations system.

Thus, one may ask, do certain airline unions follow a "strategy" of placing top priority on obtaining membership on company boards of directors or on securing an employee stock ownership plan? Do other airline unions have different strategic priorities that give top weight to job security and skill retraining? Do certain carriers and certain airline unions share or combine jointly to formulate industrial relations strategy? More generally and following the model of Figure 1, what effects do the parties' interactions have on airline bargaining outcomes as distinct from the effects of each party's individual "strategy"? Answers to these questions are not available because the questions have not as yet been addressed by Cappelli or other industrial relations strategy researchers.[9] Rather, the bulk of Cappelli's analysis—and it is a well-informed analysis—supports the view that airline executives and union officials have reacted in some similar and a few dissimilar ways to major environmental changes. This is fully consistent with industrial relations studies and analytical frameworks provided by earlier generations of researchers (Dunlop, 1958; Chamberlain, 1948), but as with other intraindustry studies (Somers, 1980) it does not seem to support a distinctive strategic-choice theory of industrial relations.

Not only have collectively bargained pay and benefit settlements in the 1980s been smaller than were expected by practitioners or predicted by industrial relations specialists and econometricians (Mitchell and Broderick, 1987), the structure of collective bargaining has for the most part become more decentralized. The steel, trucking, rubber, automobile, and telecommunications industries provide examples of the movement from multiemployer to single-employer bargaining and from company-wide to plant-level bargaining. Such changes are claimed by both U.S. and British scholars to reflect the influence of management's strategic approach to industrial relations (KKM, 1986; Purcell and Sisson, 1983). What evidence has been produced to support this proposition?

KKM (1986) provide a narrative account of the movement away from centralized multiemployer bargaining in the U.S. over-the-road trucking industry during the 1970s and 1980s. They identify increasing economic competition, the entry of independent and unorganized drivers, and a limited form of industry deregulation emanating from legislative and administrative sources as major forces affecting the industry generally and bargaining structure in particular. This cogent account is quite consistent with quantitative, interindustry research on the determinants of bargaining structure, and it fits well with the model of Figure 1. But KKM also point to business strategy as a key influence on "the nature of changes in the structure . . . of collective bargaining" (p. 130), and they illustrate this with a case study of Schneider Transport. The study showed that through a combination of new employer-initiated training, communication, information-sharing, and pay policies adopted

---

[9] Note that KKM (1986, pp. 121–27) focus prominently on the airline industry in their discussion of the collective bargaining process and bargaining outcomes in the 1980s.

over the six-year period ending in 1982, the company was able to reduce labor costs substantially and negotiate separate labor agreements with the Teamsters' union rather than continuing to participate in multiemployer bargaining.

Unfortunately, this case approach to industrial relations strategy research is incapable of determining whether Schneider Transport differed from other firms in the industry, and thus had a distinctive "strategy"; whether in rapidly changing economic, regulatory, and union environments it was possible for any trucking firm not to adopt at least some new human resource and industrial relations policies; whether alternative industrial relations policies and practices would have led to similar changes in bargaining structure or bargaining outcomes; or whether some of the policies adopted by Schneider Transport would have had different outcomes if pursued more broadly throughout the trucking industry or other industries. Consider, for example, that Kleiner and Bouillon (1986), who conducted a cross-sectional econometric study of samples of unionized and nonunion firms, have shown that increased information-sharing with employees leads to significant increases in wages and benefits, has no effects on productivity, and brings about smaller cash flows and profits. In other words, enhanced information-sharing appears "to have reallocated firm resources from owners of capital to production workers" (p. 15). As these findings become more widely known, they should have the effect of reducing firms' information-sharing initiatives—actions which might then also be judged to meet managements' "strategic" objectives. More to the point, the case study recounted above does not permit us to conclude that business strategy significantly or independently influences bargaining structure.

In describing British industrial relations, Purcell and Sisson (1983) provide numerous examples of the diversity of collective bargaining structures, which range from highly centralized multi-employer arrangements to highly decentralized plant subunit negotiations. They point out that largely in response to the Donovan Commission report, some workplace industrial relations in Britain are being reconstructed to, in effect, raise the level of bargaining from the immediate work site to the plant or facility level. At the same time, they note that (as in the U.S.) competitive pressures are bringing about a movement away from centralized multiemployer bargaining in some industries.

Given these observations, which appear to support the view that bargaining structure is shaped by certain exogenous forces, it is surprising that Purcell and Sisson go on to claim that management strategy is a key element in the choice of bargaining level. No systematic evidence is offered to support this claim, even though Purcell and Sisson question the quantitative findings of other researchers (for example, Deaton and Beaumont, 1980), namely, that regional concentration of business, union density, and multi-unionism are positively associated with multiemployer bargaining in Britain. In fact, a full quarter-century of research in the U.S. and Britain strongly supports the hypothesis that firms and unions react to product market, labor market, regulatory, and other external forces in determining and changing the structure of bargaining (Weber, 1961; Deaton and Beaumont, 1980; Hendricks and Kahn, 1982; Koch, Lewin, and Sockell, 1987). Hence, Purcell and Sisson's conception of management strategy as a driving force behind the restructuring of bargaining in Britain—a force which they also claim will lead to bargaining "at [the] corporate level"—seems to lack empirical validation, if not theoretical justification.

Finally, both U.S. and British scholars contend that industrial relations managers, executives, and professionals have lost power and influence within their enterprises, and that this is a result of new organizational and management strategies (KKM, 1986; Purcell and Sisson, 1983). But the research methods used to study this ostensible power shift do not rule out rival hypotheses or explanations.

For example, KKM's (1986) regression analysis of 1978 and 1983 Conference Board survey data (Freedman, 1979, 1985) showed that the power of line managers increased relative to that of labor relations professionals, especially "in those firms that give a high priority to union avoidance" (p. 64), and this is interpreted to have resulted from a strategic shift on the part of senior management.[10] Note, however, that no specific variables representing management strategy or changes in strategy were included in the analysis. Further, while KKM also concluded that the power of line managers increased relative to that of "*both* labor relations and human resource management professionals" (p. 64, italics in original), no data on the power of line managers versus other functional

_____
[10] Additional analysis of these data is provided in Kochan, McKersie, and Chalykoff (1986).

managers—of marketing, finance, accounting, engineering, etc.—
were collected or analyzed. Thus, it is not possible to determine
from this work whether or not generalized intraorganizational
power shifts took place in these companies. Consider that such
generalized shifts would be consistent with the widespread white-
collar work force reductions that have occurred in U.S. firms during
the 1980s, and with the interpretation—rival hypothesis—that senior
executives have reacted to the labor and management practices of
newer domestic and established foreign companies by reducing
labor costs at the administrative and operating levels in their firms.
The same or possibly an even stronger version of this interpretation
could be applied to Britain, about which Purcell and Sisson (1983)
conclude that, due to changes in management strategy, "industrial
relations specialist managers are losing their pre-eminent position"
(p. 108). No definition of strategy, supporting data, or empirical
tests were provided to support this conclusion.

Consequently, it does not appear that industrial relations
researchers have as yet produced evidence to support a distinctively
strategic-choice theory of collective bargaining. Instead, the
available evidence can just as readily be interpreted to suggest that
labor and management in the U.S. and elsewhere have been
reacting to major environmental changes that occurred during the
1970s and 1980s.

Labor-Management Cooperation and Worker Participation

Few contemporary industrial relations phenomena have
received as much attention as those having to do with quality of
working life (QWL) and employee participation in decision-
making. Whether they take the form of quality circles, employee
involvement plans, employee membership on company boards of
directors, joint labor-management committees, employee stock
ownership plans, or QWL-improvement experiments, these
initiatives have come to be widely studied and discussed. In fact,
they have caused some casual observers to conclude that the age of
adversarial labor relations in the U.S. is in decline.[11]

Returning to the central question of this paper, is our

---

[11] For example, "The New Industrial Relations," *Business Week*, May 11, 1981,
p. 15.

understanding of new cooperative workplace arrangements enhanced by the application to them of strategic-choice concepts of industrial relations? Clearly, some students believe that the answer to this question is yes (Hanlon, 1985). Thus, Schuster (1984, 1985) examined 33 cooperative union-management programs over a six-year period and concluded that his results "demonstrate that successful cooperative strategies can change that fundamental nature of the parties' relationship . . . [M]ore [capital-intensive] or mechanized organizations have historically neglected employees, thus offering a previously unrealized opportunity available through cooperative strategies" (1985, p. 383). Similarly, Katz and Sabel (1985) described the job redesign and QWL-improvement initiatives in the U.S. automobile industry as flowing from "new product strategies" and as reflecting "new strategies of combining technology and labor" (p. 298). In much the same vein, Flaherty (1985) characterized the conversion from technological and bureaucratic control to participatory control in the British boot and shoe industry as a cycle of "employer strategy in employee relations" (p. 357). Further, Kochan and Piore (1985) claim that management's new strategies for dealing with organized workers, involving employees in work, and improving employee commitment and productivity flow from more basic changes in corporate strategies. In this regard, a study by Verma and Zerbe (1986) of three high technology firms concluded that participants in programs of employee involvement "were significantly more likely [than nonparticipants] to espouse strategic company goals" (p. 12).

These and related studies seem to demonstrate that some firms and some unions have adopted a variety of cooperative arrangements to serve their mutual interests and to provide potential long-term net advantages to both parties. Such efforts appear to reflect an integrative or win-win approach, as opposed to a distributive or win-lose approach, to labor relations (Walton and McKersie, 1965). In certain cases, labor relations have indeed become more cooperative and less adversarial, and industrial relations apparently have become a more important variable in the business planning processes of certain firms.

Moreover and from an empirical perspective, evidence has been produced that shows positive effects of worker participation and labor-management cooperation on productivity and other industrial relations outcomes. As examples, Rosenberg and Rosenstein (1980) found that group productivity in a unionized foundry increased significantly over a seven-year period following the introduction of a multidimensional program of worker consultation and participation in decision-making; Schuster (1983) showed that plant-level productivity in nine separate manufacturing sites improved significantly and employment remained stable or grew slightly over several years after the adoption of a Scanlon Plan, Rucker Plan, or plantwide productivity committee; and Katz, Kochan, and Gobeille (1983) and Katz, Kochan, and Weber (1985) showed that QWL programs introduced into selected General Motors assembly plants during the 1970s significantly enhanced the industrial relations climate, labor efficiency, and the quality of products produced in those plants. In addition, some researchers have produced case evidence to show that employee ownership and autonomous work teams introduced into unionized settings have led to positive effects on employee productivity and commitment (Granrose, Appelbaum, and Singh, 1986; Hammer, 1986; Young, 1986; Anderson, 1986).

Yet, this research evidence does not necessarily support the view that new initiatives in labor-management cooperation reflect the *strategic* choices of management and labor. To the contrary, it appears that when introducing new industrial relations policies and practices into the workplace, the parties are basically reacting to external environmental pressures and are searching for new "solutions" to labor relations problems. Consider that hardly any of the aforementioned studies provide so much as a single construct or quantitative measure of strategy—corporate strategy, business unit strategy, plant strategy, or industrial relations strategy. Instead, an organization's strategy typically is inferred from findings about the determinants or effects of one or another form of labor-management cooperation.

With so heavy a reliance on ex post facto deduction, few specific hypotheses about strategic choices among various labor-management cooperation schemes have been posed or tested. Yet, if cooperative initiatives truly reflect underlying business and industrial relations strategies, then it should be possible, for example, to predict the circumstances in which certain parties will adopt QWL or employee-involvement programs, other parties will choose gainsharing or employee-ownership programs, and still other parties will adopt autonomous work teams or quality circles. Instead, what is once again available are certain industry and case studies—studies which have been interpreted by their authors to support strategic-choice models of industrial relations, but which can just as readily be interpreted to provide contrary evidence and to support rival hypotheses.

To illustrate further, consider the U.S. automobile industry, where recent developments at the three levels of industrial relations activity shown in Table 1 have been described by Katz (1985). These developments include job redesign and QWL-improvement initiatives, the adoption of profit-sharing plans for unionized employees, and the negotiation of large scale job security and worker retraining programs. While the breadth of these efforts clearly indicates that they constitute major reforms of industrial relations policy and practice in the automobile industry, it is as plausible to conclude that the reforms have come about in response to increased product market competition and the "success" of Japanese and German automobile manufacturers, who follow industrial relations policies and practices quite different from those of their U.S. counterparts, as it is to claim that the reforms stem from new business strategies. In fact, could not such industrial relations innovations as the multiyear agreement, Supplemental Unemployment Benefits, guaranteed annual wage increase, and cost-of-living allowance, all of which emerged in the U.S. automobile industry during the 1950s when product market concentration was high, more properly be labeled "strategic choices" than the contemporary reforms of automobile workplace industrial relations?[12] This is not to denigrate the contemporary reforms but, instead, to suggest that they can more accurately be characterized as reactive rather than strategic in origin.

Additional support for this view is provided by Katz's (1985) review of the basic business decisions of U.S. automobile firms during the 1970s and 1980s. Stung by a combination of major oil shocks and increased foreign competition during the 1970s, U.S. automobile manufacturers sought to "downsize" their products and to develop products for sale in what were rapidly becoming worldwide markets. The concept of a world car represented an

---

[12] This question was suggested by an anonymous referee who reviewed the first draft of this chapter.

extension of, not a departure from, mass production principles and practices, and, when implemented, was expected to stabilize world markets.

However, as Katz notes, this "strategy" was called into question by subsequent developments, including public pressure for the reduction of automobile pollution, advances in semiconductor, computer, and construction technology, the costly inventories required to insure the flow of high quality parts, fluctuations in exchange rates, and work stoppages at various manufacturing sites. Consequently, in the 1980s, U.S. automobile producers began to shift from producing standardized cars at relatively low prices for standardized markets to producing specialty products at more varied prices for specialized markets and niches.

As Katz (1985) observes, there is nothing new in the idea of specialized markets and niches and specialty products, but the extent of competition among world automobile producers during the 1980s was new. U.S. automobile producers were spurred by this competition to reexamine their own principles of mass production; in the process, they began to experiment with quality circles, broadened job classifications, pay-for-knowledge systems, QWL-improvement schemes, gainsharing plans, and information-sharing programs. These initiatives were intended to achieve greater flexibility in and higher performance from the use of labor and equipment, and to promote modular and team production rather than standardized assembly-line production.

Katz may well be right that the move toward team production of automobiles, not just in the U.S. but worldwide, "turns the principles of mass production upside down" (p. 298). Further, his analysis supports the notion that there are systematic linkages among plant, business unit, and corporate-level industrial relations policies and practices. But fundamentally his work shows that despite their large size, well-developed business planning processes, and substantial planning staffs, U.S. automobile producers have basically been reacting to, not anticipating, changes in consumer tastes, demographic trends, and increased competition. This is vividly reflected in these firms' basic business, production, financial, and marketing decisions and practices during the 1970s and 1980s, their record of poor engineering and design planning, especially at General Motors, and their newly "cooperative" industrial relations policies and practices. Therefore the recent story of this industry, as told by Katz, cannot be said to provide strong support for a strategic-choice theory of industrial relations.[13]

But what about cooperative initiatives outside of the automobile industry? Do these initiatives and studies of them provide a stronger basis for strategic-choice models and concepts of industrial relations? It does not appear so. For example, McKersie (1985) presents a detailed account of the QWL initiation, development, and implementation process at the APEX Corporation. The account documents the existence of both corporate-level and plant-level QWL committees, reviews the formal training and development programs undertaken to impart problem-solving and team-building skills to employees, and reports survey data concerning the views of managers and bargaining-unit employees about the QWL program. Instructively, these data testify to the unease of some managers and the outright opposition of other managers to the QWL program. Certain managers (as well as some manufacturing engineering personnel) felt threatened by employee-initiated changes in work practices and job design. Additionally, some employees were concerned that the QWL program deflected attention from issues such as layoffs and job security, thereby creating tension between QWL and collective bargaining. McKersie's discussion of these employee concerns about QWL complements Goodman's (1979) analysis of the demise of a QWL-improvement effort in a mining company and is helpful for students who wish to understand the determinants and consequences of QWL-improvement initiatives.

But the same cannot be said of McKersie's characterization of the QWL process as a strategic choice of the parties, one that flowed from "the new business strategy" (p. 443). No definition of

---

[13] In December 1984, General Motors (GM) entered into a joint venture with the Toyota Corporation which provided for Toyota's takeover and operation of GM's Fremont, California, assembly plant. This venture, New United Motor Manufacture Incorporated (NUMMI), has produced some impressive results. For example, work attendance increased from about 70 percent in 1984 to about 98.5 percent in 1985; grievances declined from 50 per 100 employees in 1983 to 2 per 1,000 employees in 1985; and quality of the product, a Nova model Chevrolet, improved from the worst product in 1983 to the top rated product among *all* GM assembly plants in 1986. Yet, on the "strategic" question of just how the Japanese-managed NUMMI plant has accomplished these results, how transferable the labor relations climate and practices at NUMMI may be to other GM plants, and who will own the NUMMI operation upon expiration in 1996 of the 12-year joint venture agreement between GM and Toyota, interview data and archival evidence gathered by the author of this chapter indicate that GM executives and business planners have few if any answers and, indeed, have barely considered the questions. This example does little to support a strategic-choice perspective on GM's business decision-making.

business strategy or industrial relations strategy is offered in this narrative, no alternative "strategic" choices are considered, and no single concept or construct or strategy is operationalized or measured. Rather, the term strategy is used to label certain processes and developments in the context of a single case. Used in this way, the term strategy does not have internal or external validity.

A similar point can be made about recent accounts of "strategic bargaining" in a variety of settings—bargains that reflect one or another form of labor-management cooperation. Thus, Kochan, McKersie, and Cappelli (1984) characterize (1) a collective agreement between General Electric and the International Union of Electrical Workers (IUE) to build a factory of the future, (2) an agreement between Xerox and the Amalgamated Clothing and Textile Workers (ACTW) to provide employment continuity, and (3) joint labor-management committees in the retail food and masonry industries as strategic bargains which "build on and reinforce the sharing of information and the improved workplace relationships that have grown out of QWL processes" (p. 32). Going further, they propose that "perhaps the most significant form of strategic bargaining is found in cases where firms voluntarily recognize unions in new plants and the parties jointly agree on the design of new work systems and contractual relationships" (p. 24). In this regard, they cite General Motors' Saturn project, in which the United Automobile Workers Union is a full partner, and an agreement between Phillip Morris and the Tobacco Workers Union as relevant examples.[14]

---

[14] Once again, the case experience of General Motors hardly provides strong evidence of the "strategic" orientation of company managers. Consider that GM's Saturn Corporation, launched in early 1985, was established to develop team-oriented methods of production, product innovation, marketing, financial management, and labor relations in the manufacture of small cars—methods which the company contended would subsequently become diffused throughout GM and permit the company to leapfrog its competition, both domestic and foreign. Indeed, GM's president described Saturn as representing the vanguard of U.S. industry's return to a position of world supremacy. The reality, however, is that in late 1986 the scheduled start of production at Saturn was pushed back to 1992; GM slashed the Saturn budget by half, or from about $3.5 billion to $1.7 billion; planned production of cars was reduced from 500,000 to 250,000 annually; the plant will not be vertically integrated and won't serve as its own parts supplier, as had originally been planned; and production jobs will total some 3,500 rather than the 6,600 that had initially been forecasted (Buss and Guiles, 1986).

The point of this example is to show that, far from exercising strategic choice, GM executives and managers (and, where they have been involved, union officials) have

But does this mean that bargaining agreements or management policies *not* to recognize unions voluntarily in new plants or *not* to collaborate with organized employees on the design of new work systems are also strategic? Are there specific tests or measures by which answers to this and related questions can be derived? Can one determine what is a fully strategic industrial relations policy or labor agreement? A partially strategic policy or agreement? A nonstrategic policy or agreement? For the present, the answer to each of these questions is no, based upon the case examples and industry-level studies briefly reviewed here and found elsewhere in the literature. Moreover, even the few available econometric studies rarely provide direct measures or operational tests of industrial relations strategy or strategies of labor-management cooperation (but see Kochan, McKersie, and Chalykoff, 1986).

Note that certain other forms of labor-management cooperation and worker participation which have either been referred to briefly here or not mentioned at all, namely, employee membership on company boards of directors, continuous bargaining between union and management representatives during the life of labor agreements, and gainsharing and employee stock ownership plans, have also been described in the literature as reflecting the strategic choices of the parties (Kochan and Barocci, 1985). But in no case has an alternative choice or set of choices been modeled, measured, or tested. Once more and lacking a sense of parsimony, it appears that every choice is labeled "strategic"!

The matter of gainsharing or profit-sharing is perhaps especially instructive in this regard. There is no doubt that performance has become a more widely used criterion of pay determination in the United States, both in union and nonunion settings (Freedman, 1979, 1985; Kochan, McKersie, Chalykoff, 1986; Lewin, 1984). But despite this, and despite its vociferous support in some quarters (Weitzman, 1984), pay for performance via profit-sharing is limited to a small minority of employees. For advocates of strategic-choice theories of industrial relations and labor-management cooperation, the challenge is to offer analytical frameworks that will enable

been reacting and responding to environmental change, rather than anticipating or planning for change. This "fact" reinforces the judgment that, as important as they may be for other reasons, cooperative workplace industrial relations initiatives at GM and perhaps at other companies appear to weaken rather than strengthen strategic-choice models of industrial relations.

researchers to predict where profit-sharing will occur and to test such predictions empirically. Until that is done, the presence or absence of profit-sharing plans or other manifestations of labor-management cooperation can equally and all be regarded as reflecting the "strategic choices" of the parties.

Finally, if certain cooperative workplace industrial relations initiatives do represent the strategic choices of the parties, with management as the prime mover, how should the adversarial workplace industrial relations that prevail elsewhere be interpreted? Do these also represent the strategic choices of labor and management?

As noted earlier, researchers have documented the recent rise of union-avoidance activity among employers, and advocates of strategic-choice theory in industrial relations are well aware of this phenomenon. But it should be kept in mind that union avoidance and opposition to unions are hardly new phenomena (Bendix, 1956; Jacoby, 1985; Chamberlain and Kuhn, 1986). In a nutshell, U.S. employers have always been opposed to unionism—indeed, union win rates in NLRB-conducted representation elections have declined consistently since the early 1940s (Block and Wolkinson, 1986)—and employers have often tried to provide substitutes for unionism. These have included the American Plan, company unions, industrial psychologists, counseling and human relations programs, and other devices. In the 1930s and 1940s, as in the 1970s and 1980s, employers vigorously (and often illegally) fought unions even as they embraced concepts of worker participation and involvement in decision-making and even as they created personnel/human resource departments to protect employee rights and (ostensibly) balance company policies with employee interests.

Whether or not these industrial relations developments of previous eras should, in retrospect, be labeled "strategic" is open to question, but they bespeak a certain dualism, indeed a dichotomy, that also seems to characterize contemporary industrial relations. Simply put, the dualism is that of cooperation and adversarialism. Yes, some firms and their managements believe strongly in employee involvement, worker participation in decision-making, and team development. But other firms and their managements pursue bankruptcy filings to overturn labor agreements, purposefully withhold information about scheduled plant closings, encourage strikes to break unions and replace economic strikers with nonunion employees, and use contract labor to avoid or forestall employee unionization. A strategic-choice theory of industrial relations should be able to explain this dualism in the sense of offering testable hypotheses about the determinants of and the probabilities that cooperation or adversarialism will exist in particular labor-management relationships or at particular points in time.[15]

Indeed, if strategic-choice theory is to have meaning in an industrial relations context, then it should also be able to explain why certain firms in a particular industry, such as Eastern Airlines and Western Airlines in the airline industry, have adopted employee stock-ownership plans and employee representation on company boards of directors, respectively; why other firms, such as Delta Airlines and People Express, have vigorously pursued union-avoidance policies; and why still other firms, such as Continental Airlines and Southwest Airlines, have sought to break their unions. Similarly, a strategic-choice theory of industrial relations should be able to explain why some nonunion firms, such as IBM, that seek to remain unorganized in the U.S. sometimes adjust to the fact of unionism abroad and become partner to agreements with labor unions in other nations. In this regard, it is simply not enough to say that there are linkages among corporate level, business unit level, and plant/facility level industrial relations policies and practices, or to claim that changing managerial values constitute the lynchpin for the theory and practice of strategic industrial relations.[16] Instead,

---

[15] A study that begins to do this is Kochan, McKersie, and Chalykoff (1986). In the same vein, strategic-choice theories of human resource (HR) management policies and practices are generally unsatisfactory. Thus, HR strategy researchers have so far been unable to explain why some firms, such as those in the accounting and fast-food industries, follow policies of high employee turnover and low pay, while other firms, such as those in the aerospace and furniture industries, follow policies of low turnover and intermediate or high pay. Similarly, HR strategy researchers have not offered generalizable explanations of the growth of private company expenditures on employee training and development or of the decisions of some firms to invest in internal training and the decisions of other firms to disinvest in such training.

[16] Note, further, that some observers have described the recent report of the AFL-CIO Committee on the Evolution of Work (1985) as the blueprint for a new strategic thrust on the part of organized labor to reverse its declining position in the U.S. economy and society. Such a characterization is difficult to sustain, for the following reasons.

First, the AFL-CIO report is in no way binding on affiliated unions; indeed, the affiliates are under no compulsion even to consider the report. Second, the various recommendations offered in the report for enhancing union membership provide no specifics about the resources that would have to be committed to bring this about.

such claims must be tested on data sets obtained from more rigorously constructed research designs that pose specific hypotheses so as better to judge their validity and reliability.

An Overall Assessment

Earlier we asked if the criticisms of older theories of industrial relations also apply to contemporary strategic-choice theories of industrial relations. Based on the review and critique of industrial relations strategy research presented in this chapter, the overall answer to this question is both no and yes.

Clearly an important contribution of strategy researchers has been to open, albeit partially, the black box represented by the management organization in industrial relations. While it is well recognized that most economists have typically not modeled or investigated the inner workings of management—the theory of the firm is for the most part a stepchild of the microeconomic theory of market exchange—it is also the case that few major industrial relations theorists (with the exceptions previously noted) have closely examined managerial behavior. The early theorists' attention was directed largely toward unions as institutions, as they sought primarily to explain the behavior of union leaders and members.

The newer generation of strategy researchers has documented and, in some cases, quantitatively measured managers' union-avoidance activities, and has also shown that there are some systematic relationships among corporate, business unit, and workplace-level industrial relations policies and practices. Further, these researchers have properly called attention to (and sometimes measured) the changes in management's internal organization for industrial relations, and they have provided an impressive amount and variety of evidence showing that labor-management cooperative efforts can improve organizational climate and workplace performance. These are no small achievements, and they demonstrate some of the insights into industrial relations processes

---

Third, there is no listing of priorities among the recommendations offered in the report; each of them appears to be equally important and equally likely (or unlikely) to be implemented. Fourth, there is no mention in the report of criteria for assessing progress toward any of the goals identified therein. Fifth, no timetables are given for achieving any of the desired goals. In sum, the AFL-CIO report represents a notable introspective analysis of the labor movement to the mid-1980s and contains several provocative ideas and recommendations. However, it would do the report and its authors a disservice to claim that it represents the "strategic choices" of the U.S. labor movement (also see Lawler, 1983).

and outcomes that can be gleaned from behaviorally-oriented research studies.[17]

But it has also been argued here that this research falls short—indeed, far short—of confirming a strategic-choice theory of industrial relations. In this regard, the basic characteristics and limitations of strategic industrial relations research are summarized in Table 2. While the dominant model guiding research on industrial relations as a strategic variable seems to offer a full-blown

TABLE 2

Research Characteristics of
Studies of Industrial Relations as a
Strategic Variable

Research Dimension	Research Characteristics
Theory/Analytical frameworks	Flow models linking environmental variables to labor relations/ bargaining processes and outcomes at three levels of industrial relations activity
Concepts	Managerial values, business strategy, industrial relations strategy
Hypotheses	Few formally specified; null hypotheses not rejected; ex-post facto rival hypotheses equally plausible
Operationalization of variables	Certain process and outcome variables specified, but not managerial values, business strategy, or industrial relations strategy
Research design	Usually not specified, frequent use of case studies, some use of field studies, occasional quantitative studies of a particular process or outcome
Data sources and types	Combination of primary and secondary data, purposive samples, longitudinal data from individual company sites
Analytical methods	Archival analysis, qualitative accounts, descriptive statistics, correlation analysis, ordinary least squares regression analysis
Generalization	Quite limited due to lack of formal hypothesis testing and low validity and reliability

---

[17] For more on this point, see Lewin and Feuille (1983) and Lewin and Strauss (1988).

multivariate framework of analysis, and although the model specifies managerial values as a critical determinant of business strategy, the key variables in this model have not been operationalized or tested. An important point in support of this conclusion is that virtually none of the strategic industrial relations research poses or empirically investigates specific hypotheses. Therefore, rival hypotheses about management (and union) behavior in the new era of industrial relations are "equally plausible"; null hypotheses have not been offered, let alone rejected. This is essentially the same judgment that several scholars have reached about Dunlop's *Industrial Relations Systems* and about the analytical frameworks offered by other industrial relations theorists (Singh, 1976; Blain and Gennard, 1970; Chamberlain 1961).

Table 2 also indicates that industrial relations strategy researchers (1) rarely use or delineate an overall research design, (2) rely heavily on case studies and purposive samples, and (3) use various combinations of primary and secondary data. Consequently, it is not surprising that much of the contemporary literature on strategic industrial relations provides qualitative accounts of and descriptive statistics pertaining to managerial behavior in the areas of union avoidance, collective bargaining, and labor-management cooperation. This is not to deny that a few studies do provide quantitative assessments of the determinants and consequences of one or another of these industrial relations phenomena—although all of these quantitative studies use single equation ordinary least squares regression formats and fail to investigate more complex models in which, for example, labor-management cooperation, concession bargaining, or union avoidance are determined simultaneously with managerial values. But the more fundamental purpose of this chapter has been to show that the validity and reliability of the evidence produced by strategic industrial relations researchers is open to question. Therefore, the robustness of these empirical findings and the generalizability of the underlying analytical model that guides the research must at present be regarded as quite limited—perhaps as limited as the analytical frameworks offered by industrial relations scholars of previous eras.

Lest this be considered a particularly harsh set of judgments, recall the evidence of increased competition in the U.S. economy—well over 80 percent of the economy is now classified as competitive, compared with about 50 percent in the 1950s

(Shepherd, 1982)—and consider the proposition that competition puts pressure on managers to revise their business policies and practices, including in the area of industrial relations. Becker and Olson, among others, provide a test of this proposition; in Chapter 2 of this volume, they use a straightforward agency theory model to trace the pressures that emanated from shareholders and that were placed on managers to improve firm performance, especially managers of unionized U.S. firms that performed poorly during the 1970s. A consequence of such pressures should be an enhanced decision-making role for senior line managers and a reduced role for industrial relations and human resource professionals. As noted earlier, some researchers have produced evidence showing that such internal intraorganizational realignments of managerial decision-making power occurred during the 1980s, but these researchers insist on interpreting their findings to support a strategic-choice rather than a reactive-behavior model of management's industrial relations activity.

The reader should carefully consider the term *strategy*; it implies power and control over events, such as in determining how to deploy a military force to combat an enemy, rather than a mere accounting of events. In the economic sphere, the terms monopoly, oligopoly, and concentration refer to different degrees of authoritative control over certain functions, such as production, pricing, and distribution. But in an increasingly competitive economy or major sectors of an economy, producers experience a diminution of whatever administrative control they may previously have been able to exercise. Increasingly, business owners and managers must respond and react to external forces and attempt to match their various production, pricing, distribution, *and industrial relations* decisions to marketplace demands.

This appears to describe accurately what is happening in contemporary industrial relations. Managers of firms are reacting more swiftly to market signals and are behaving more like price-takers than price-setters. Further, such reactive behavior is spurred by the growing internationalization of product markets and is facilitated by the enhanced efficiency of information markets and financial markets. Because increasing competition typically requires numerous internal adjustments on the part of firms, it would be surprising if changes in firm, business unit, and workplace-level industrial relations policies and practices did not occur in the 1980s.

In this vein, industrial relations researchers should indeed seek to identify, operationalize, and measure the determinants and consequences of changes in industrial relations policies and practices. It is especially important to gain better understanding of how such changes affect the economic performance of the firm. But this can be done without claiming that a new breed of managers who possess values different from those of their predecessors is engaged in the strategic choice of industrial relations policy and practice. To validate this claim, researchers must be able to show how the concept of strategic choice differs from the economist's concept of choice. So far they have not done so.

Strategy is not a well-defined concept, either in general as applied to business planning (Rumelt, 1979) or in particular as applied to industrial relations. It is consistent with virtually any management action, which means that it is an irrefutable concept, and it implies a degree of power and control over external events that is decreasingly characteristic of U.S. managers, not to mention U.S. union officials. Suffice it to say that industrial relations constitute an important variable in the operations and performance of the firm. It need not be overzealously claimed that industrial relations constitute a strategic variable.

References

AFL-CIO Committee on the Evolution of Work. *The Changing Situation of Workers and Their Unions*. Washington: AFL-CIO, February 1985.

Anderson, John C. "Union Effectiveness: An Industrial Relations Systems Approach." Ph.D. dissertation, Cornell University, 1977.

Anderson, Roger L. "Implementation of the Autonomous Group Model in a Unionized Plant: The Influence of Selected Process, Design, and Contextual Considerations on Participant Support." *Proceedings of the 38th Annual Meeting, Industrial Relations Research Association*. Madison, Wis.: IRRA, 1986. Pp. 254-66.

Aspin, Leslie. "A Study of Reinstatement Under the National Labor Relations Act." Ph.D. dissertation, Massachusetts Institute of Technology, 1966.

Bain, Joe S. *Industrial Organization*. New York: Wiley, 1968.

Bartel, Ann, and David Lewin. "Wages and Unionism in the Public Sector: The Case of Police." *Review of Economics and Statistics* 63 (February 1981): pp. 53-59.

Bathke, A. W., and K. S. Lorek. "The Relationship Between Time-Series Models and the Security Market's Expectation of Quarterly Earnings." *Accounting Review* 59 (April 1984): pp. 163-76.

Bendix, Reinhard. *Work and Authority in Industry: Ideologies of Management in the Course of Industrialization*. New York: Harper and Row, 1956.

Blain, A. N. J., and John Gennard. "Industrial Relations Theory: A Critical Review." *British Journal of Industrial Relations* 8 (November 1970): pp. 389-407.

Block, Richard N., and Benjamin W. Wolkinson. "Delay in the Union Election Campaign Revisited: A Theoretical and Empirical Analysis." In *Advances in Industrial and Labor Relations*, Vol. 3, eds. David B. Lipsky and David Lewin. Greenwich, Conn.: JAI Press, 1986. Pp. 43–81.

Braybrooke, David, and Charles E. Lindblom. *A Strategy of Decision*. New York: Free Press, 1970.

Buss, Dale D., and Melinda Grenier Guiles. "GM Slows Big Drive for Saturn to Produce Small Cars in Five Years." *Wall Street Journal*, October 30, 1986, p. 1.

Cappelli, Peter. "Competitive Pressures and Labor Relations in the Airline Industry." *Industrial Relations* 24 (Fall 1985a): pp. 316–38.

————. "Plant-Level Concession Bargaining." *Industrial and Labor Relations Review* 39 (October 1985b): pp. 90–104.

Cappelli, Peter, and John Chalykoff. "The Effects of Management Industrial Relations Strategy: Results of a Survey." *Proceedings of the 38th Annual Meeting, Industrial Relations Research Association*. Madison, Wis.: IRRA, 1986. Pp. 171–78.

Chamberlain, Neil W. *The Union Challenge to Management Control*. New York: McGraw-Hill, 1948.

————. "Review" of *Industrialism and Industrial Man,* by Clark Kerr, John T. Dunlop, Frederick H. Harbison, and Charles A. Myers. *American Economic Review* 51 (June 1961): pp. 475–80.

Chamberlain, Neil W., and James W. Kuhn. *Collective Bargaining*, 3d ed. New York: McGraw-Hill, 1986.

Chandler, Alfred D. *Strategy and Structure*. Cambridge, Mass.: MIT Press, 1962.

————. *The Visible Hand*. Cambridge, Mass.: MIT Press, 1977.

Clark, Kim B. "Organization and Firm Performance: The Impact on Profits, Growth, and Productivity." *American Economic Review* 74 (December 1984): pp. 893–919.

Commons, John R. *Institutional Economics: Its Place in Political Economy*. New York: Macmillan, 1934.

Cooke, William N. "Failure to Negotiate First Contracts: Determinants and Policy Implications." *Industrial and Labor Relations Review* 38 (January 1985a): pp. 163–78.

————. "The Rising Toll of Discrimination Against Union Activists." *Industrial Relations* 24 (Fall 1985b): pp. 421–42.

Day, George. *Strategic Marketing Planning: The Pursuit of Competitive Advantage*. St. Paul, Minn.: West, 1984.

Deaton, D. R., and P. B. Beaumont. "The Determinants of Bargaining Structure: Some Large Scale Survey Evidence for Britain." *British Journal of Industrial Relations* 18 (July 1980): pp. 201–16.

DeBejar, Gloria, and George T. Milkovich. "Human Resource Strategy at the Business Level, Study 1: Theoretical Model and Empirical Verification; Study 2: Relationships Between Strategy and Performance Components." Paper presented to the 46th Annual Meeting, Academy of Management, Chicago, August 1986.

Dickens, William T. "Effects of Company Campaigns on Certification Elections: *Law and Reality* Once Again." *Industrial and Labor Relations Review* 36 (July 1983): pp. 560–75.

Dunlop, John T. *Wage Determination Under Trade Unions*. New York: Macmillan, 1944.

————. *Industrial Relations Systems*. New York: Holt, Rinehart and Winston, 1958.

Dyer, Lee D. "Studying Human Resource Strategy: An Approach and an Agenda." *Industrial Relations* 23 (Spring 1984): pp. 156–69.

Fiorito, Jack, Christopher Lowman, and Forrest D. Nelson. "The Impact of Human Resource Policies on Union Organizing." *Industrial Relations* 26 (Spring 1987): pp. 113–26.

Flaherty, Diane. "Labor Control in the British Boot and Shoe Industry." *Industrial Relations* 24 (Fall 1985): pp. 339–59.

Flanders, Alan. *Industrial Relations: What Is Wrong with the System?* London: Faber & Faber, 1965.

Freedman, Audrey. *Managing Labor Relations.* Report No. 765. New York: The Conference Board, 1979.

_____. *The New Look in Wage Policy and Employee Relations.* Report No. 865. New York: The Conference Board, 1985.

Freeman, Richard B., and James L. Medoff. "The Impact of Collective Bargaining: Illusion or Reality?" In *U.S. Industrial Relations 1950-1980: A Critical Assessment,* eds. Jack Stieber, Robert B. McKersie, and D. Quinn Mills. Madison, Wis.: Industrial Relations Research Association, 1981. Pp. 47-97.

_____. *What Do Unions Do?* New York: Basic Books, 1984.

Galbraith, Jay R., and Daniel A. Nathanson. *Strategy Implementation: The Role of Structure and Process.* St. Paul, Minn.: West, 1978.

Getman, Julius G., Stephen B. Goldberg, and Jeanne B. Herman. *Union Representation Elections: Law and Reality.* New York: Sage, 1976.

Goodman, Paul S. *Assessing Organizational Change: The Rushton Quality of Work Experiment.* New York: Wiley, 1979.

Granrose, Cherlyn S., Eileen Appelbaum, and Virendra Singh. "Saving Jobs Through Worker Buyouts: Economic and Qualitative Outcomes for Workers in Worker-Owned, QWL, and Non-QWL Supermarkets." *Proceedings of the 38th Annual Meeting, Industrial Relations Research Association.* Madison, Wis.: IRRA, 1986. Pp. 196-204.

Hambrick, Donald C. "Operationalizing the Concept of Business-Level Strategy in Research." *Academy of Management Review* 5 (October 1980): pp. 567-75.

Hammer, Tove H. "The History of the Rath Buyout: A Role Expectations Analysis." *Proceedings of the 38th Annual Meeting, Industrial Relations Research Association.* Madison, Wis.: IRRA, 1986. Pp. 205-13.

Hanlon, Martin D. "Unions, Productivity, and the New Industrial Relations: Strategic Considerations." *Interfaces* 15 (May-June 1985): pp. 41-53.

Harrigan, Katherine Rudie. *Strategies for Declining Businesses.* Lexington, Mass.: D. C. Heath, 1980.

Hax, Arnoldo C. "A Methodology for the Development of a Human Resource Strategy." Working Paper, Sloan School of Management, MIT, March 1985.

Henricks, Wallace E., and Lawrence M. Kahn. "The Determinants of Bargaining Structure in U.S. Manufacturing Industries." *Industrial and Labor Relations Review* 35 (January 1982): pp. 181-95.

Hoxie, Robert F. *Trade Unionism in the United States.* New York: Appelton, 1928.

Jacoby, Sanford M. *Employing Bureaucracy: Managers, Unions, and the Transformation of Work in American Industry, 1900-1945.* New York: Columbia University Press, 1985.

Kalwa, Richard W. "Collective Bargaining in Steel: A Strategic Perspective." *Proceedings of the 39th Annual Meeting, Industrial Relations Research Association.* Madison, Wis.: IRRA, 1987. Pp. 313-19.

Katz, Harry C. *Shifting Gears: Changing Labor Relations in the U.S. Automobile Industry.* Cambridge, Mass.: MIT Press, 1985.

Katz, Harry C., and Charles F. Sabel. "Industrial Relations and Industrial Adjustment in the Car Industry." *Industrial Relations* 24 (Fall 1985): pp. 295-315.

Katz, Harry C., Thomas A. Kochan, and Kenneth R. Gobeille. "Industrial Relations Performance, Economic Performance, and QWL Programs: An Interplant Analysis." *Industrial and Labor Relations Review* 37 (October 1983): pp. 3-17.

Katz, Harry C., Thomas A. Kochan, and Mark R. Weber. "Assessing the Effects of Industrial Relations Systems and Efforts to Improve the Quality of Working Life on Organizational Effectiveness." *Academy of Management Journal* 28 (May 1985): pp. 509-26.

Kimberly, John R., Robert H. Miles, and Associates. *The Organizational Life Cycle.* San Francisco: Jossey-Bass, 1980.

Kleiner, Morris M. "Unionism and Employer Discrimination: Analysis of 8(a)(3) Violations." *Industrial Relations* 23 (Spring 1984): pp. 234-43.

Kleiner, Morris M., and Marvin L. Bouillon. "Providing Business Information to Production Employees: Impacts on Compensation and Profitability." Working Paper, School of Business, University of Kansas and Iowa State University, 1986.

Koch, Marianne, David Lewin, and Donna Sockell, "The Determinants of Bargaining Structure: A Case Study of A.T. and T." In *Advances in Industrial and Labor Relations*, Vol. 4, eds. David Lewin, David B. Lipsky, and Donna Sockell. Greenwich, Conn.: JAI Press, 1987. Pp. 223–51.

Kochan, Thomas A., and Thomas A. Barocci. *Human Resource Management and Industrial Relations.* Boston: Little Brown, 1985.

Kochan, Thomas A., and Michael J. Piore. "U.S. Industrial Relations in Transition." In *Challenges and Choices Facing American Labor*, ed. Thomas A. Kochan. Cambridge, Mass.: MIT Press, 1985. Pp. 1–12.

Kochan, Thomas A., Harry C. Katz, and Robert B. McKersie. *The Transformation of American Industrial Relations.* New York: Basic Books, 1986.

Kochan, Thomas A., Robert B. McKersie, and Peter Cappelli. "Strategic Choice and Industrial Relations Theory." *Industrial Relations* 23 (Winter 1984): pp. 16–39.

Kochan, Thomas A., Robert B. McKersie, and John Chalykoff. "The Effects of Corporate Strategy and Workplace Innovations on Union Representation." *Industrial and Labor Relations Review* 39 (July 1986): pp. 487–501.

Kochan, Thomas A., Robert B. McKersie, and Harry C. Katz. "U.S. Industrial Relations in Transition: A Summary Report." *Proceedings of the 37th Annual Meeting, Industrial Relations Research Association.* Madison, Wis.: IRRA, 1985. Pp. 261–76.

Kuhn, James W., David Lewin, and Paul J. McNulty. "Neil W. Chamberlain: A Retrospective Analysis of His Scholarly Work and Influence." *British Journal of Industrial Relations* 21 (July 1983): pp. 143–60.

Lawler, John J. "The Influence of Management Consultants on the Outcome of Union Certification Elections." *Industrial and Labor Relations Review* 38 (October 1984): pp. 38–51.

_____. "Trade Union Strategy in a Time of Adversity." *Proceedings of the 35th Annual Meeting, Industrial Relations Research Association.* Madison, Wis.: IRRA, 1983. Pp. 40–45.

Lawler, John J., and Robin West. "Impact of Union-Avoidance Strategy in Representation Elections." *Industrial Relations* 24 (Fall 1985): pp. 406–20.

Lewin, David. *Opening the Books: Corporate Information-Sharing in Employee Relations.* New York: The Conference Board, 1984.

_____. "The Regulation of Public Sector Labor Relations: Theory and Evidence." *Journal of Labor Research* 6 (Winter 1985): pp. 77–95.

Lewin, David, and Peter Feuille. "Behavioral Research in Industrial Relations." *Industrial and Labor Relations Review* 36 (April 1983): pp. 341–60.

Lewin, David, and George Strauss. "Behavioral Studies in Industrial Relations: Symposium Introduction." *Industrial Relations* 27 (Winter 1988).

MacMillan, Ian C. "Seizing Competitive Initiative." *Journal of Business Strategy* 2 (December 1984): pp. 43–57.

McKersie, Robert B. "APEX Corporation." In *Human Resource Management and Industrial Relations*, by Thomas A. Kochan and Thomas A. Barocci. Boston: Little Brown, 1985. Pp. 441–51.

Miles, Raymond E., and Charles C. Snow. *Organizational Strategy, Structure, and Process.* New York: McGraw-Hill, 1978.

_____. "Designing Human Resource Systems." *Organizational Dynamics* 13 (Summer 1984): pp. 44–53.

Milkovich, George. "Introduction: Personnel Strategy and Evaluation." *Industrial Relations* 23 (Winter 1984): pp. 1–15.

Milkovich, George T., and William F. Glueck. *Personnel, Human Resource Management*, 4th ed. Plano, Tex.: Business Publications, 1985.

Mintzberg, Henry. "Patterns in Strategy Formation." *Management Science* 24 (May 1978): pp. 934–48.

Mitchell, Daniel J.B. "Recent Union Contract Concessions." *Brookings Papers on Economic Activity*, No. 1 (1982): pp. 165–201.

Mitchell, Daniel J.B., and Renae F. Broderick. "Flexible Pay Systems in the American Context." Working Paper No. 122, Institute of Industrial Relations, University of California, Los Angeles, July 1987.

Modigliani, Franco, and Merton H. Miller. "The Cost of Capital, Corporation Finance, and the Theory of Investment." *American Economic Review* 48 (June 1958): pp. 261–97.

Neumann, George R., and Melvin W. Reder. "Output and Strike Activity in U.S. Manufacturing: How Large Are the Losses?" *Industrial and Labor Relations Review* 37 (January 1984): pp. 197–211.

Patten, Thomas. *Manpower Planning and the Development of Human Resources.* New York: Wiley, 1971.

Porter, Michael E. *Competitive Strategy: Techniques for Analyzing Industries and Competitors.* New York: Free Press, 1980.

_____. *Competitive Advantage: Creating and Sustaining Superior Performance.* New York: Free Press, 1985.

Prosten, Richard. "The Longest Season: Union Organizing in the Last Decade." *Proceedings of the 31st Annual Meeting, Industrial Relations Research Association.* Madison, Wis.: IRRA, 1979. Pp. 240–49.

Purcell, John, and Keith Sisson. "Strategies and Practice in the Management of Industrial Relations." In *Industrial Relations in Great Britain,* ed. George S. Bain. Oxford, England: Basil Blackwell, 1983. Pp. 95–120.

Rees, Albert. *The Economics of Trade Unions,* rev. ed. Chicago: University of Chicago Press, 1977.

Roll, Richard. *Behavior of Interest Rates: The Application of Efficient Market Models to U.S. T-Bills.* New York: Basic Books, 1970.

Roomkin, Myron, and Richard N. Block. "Case Processing Time and the Outcome of Representation Elections: Some Empirical Evidence." *University of Illinois Law Review* 1 (April 1981): pp. 75–97.

Rosenberg, Richard D., and Eliezer Rosenstein. "Participation and Productivity: An Empirical Study." *Industrial and Labor Relations Review* 33 (April 1980): pp. 355–67.

Rumelt, Richard P. "Evaluation of Strategy: Theory and Models." In *Strategic Management: A New View of Business Policy and Planning,* eds. Dan E. Schendel and Charles W. Hofer. Boston: Little Brown, 1979. Pp. 196–215.

Schendel, Dan E., and Charles W. Hofer, eds. *Strategic Management: A New View of Business Policy and Planning.* Boston: Little Brown, 1979.

Schuster, Michael. "The Impact of Union-Management Cooperation on Productivity and Employment." *Industrial and Labor Relations Review* 36 (April 1983): pp. 415–30.

_____. *Union-Management Cooperation: Structure, Process, and Impact.* Kalamazoo, Mich.: Upjohn Institute, 1984.

_____. "Models of Cooperation and Change in Union Settings." *Industrial Relations* 24 (Fall 1985): pp. 382–94.

Seeber, Ronald, and William N. Cooke. "The Decline of Union Success in NLRB Representation Elections." *Industrial Relations* 22 (Winter 1983): pp. 33–44.

Shepherd, William G. "Causes of Increased Competition in the U.S. Economy, 1939–1980." *Review of Economics and Statistics* 64 (November 1982): pp. 613–26.

Simon, Herbert A. *Administrative Behavior.* New York: Free Press, 1957.

Singh, R. "Systems Theory in the Study of Industrial Relations: Time for a Reappraisal?" *Industrial Relations Journal* 7 (Autumn 1976): pp. 59–71.

Sisson, Keith. *The Management of Collective Bargaining: An International Comparison.* Oxford, England: Basil Blackwell, 1983.

Somers, Gerald G., ed. *Essays in Industrial Relations Theory.* Ames: Iowa State University Press, 1969.

_____. *Collective Bargaining: Contemporary American Experience.* Madison, Wis.: Industrial Relations Research Association, 1980.

Strauss, George. "Industrial Relations: Time of Change." *Industrial Relations* 23 (Winter 1984): pp. 1–15.

Utterback, James M., and William J. Abernathy. "A Dynamic Model of Process and Product Innovation." *Omega* 3 (December 1975): pp. 639–56.

Verma, Anil. "Relative Flow of Capital to Union and Nonunion Plants Within a Firm." *Industrial Relations* 24 (Fall 1985): pp. 395–405.

Verma, Anil, and Wilfred Zerbe. "Employee Involvement Programs and Worker Perceptions of New Technology." Working Paper No. 1167, Faculty of Commerce and Business Administration, University of British Columbia, 1986.

Voos, Paula B., and Lawrence P. Mishel. "The Union Impact on Profits: Evidence from Industry Price-Cost Margin Data." *Journal of Labor Economics* 4 (January 1986): pp. 105–33.

Walker, James. "Forecasting Manpower Needs." *Harvard Business Review* 47 (March-April 1969): pp. 152–75.

Walton, Richard E. "Establishing and Maintaining High Commitment Work Systems." In *The Organizational Life Cycle*, eds. John R. Kimberly, Robert H. Miles, and Associates. San Francisco: Jossey-Bass, 1980. Pp. 111–62.

Walton, Richard E., and Robert B. McKersie. *A Behavioral Theory of Labor Negotiations*. New York: McGraw-Hill, 1965.

Weber, Arnold R., ed. *The Structure of Collective Bargaining*. New York: Free Press, 1961.

Weitzman, Martin S. *The Share Economy*. Cambridge, Mass.: Harvard University Press, 1984.

Williamson, Oliver. *Markets and Hierarchies*. New York: Free Press, 1975.

Wood, S. J., E. G. A. Wagner, J. F. B. Armstrong, and J. E. Davis. "The 'IR System' Concept as a Basis for Theory in Industrial Relations." *British Journal of Industrial Relations* 13 (November 1975): pp. 291–308.

Yavitz, Boris, and William H. Newman. *Strategy in Action*. New York: Free Press, 1982.

Young, Karen M. "Creating the Idea of Ownership: Lessons from Employee Ownership Success Stories." *Proceedings of the 38th Annual Meeting, Industrial Relations Research Association*. Madison, Wis.: IRRA, 1986. Pp. 214–20.

Chapter 2

Labor Relations and Firm Performance

By Brian E. Becker
State University of New York at Buffalo

Craig A. Olson
University of Wisconsin-Madison

While students of industrial relations have always recognized that collective bargaining outcomes have some effect on a firm's economic position, researchers have only recently begun to investigate the nature and magnitude of this effect. Earlier research emphasis on the practice of labor relations and narrow collective bargaining outcomes (e.g., wages) is not surprising in an era of industrial relations stability. More recently, however, the erosion of private-sector unionism and unionized firms has peaked interest in the union influence on the firm's economic well-being. In addition, the recent interest in strategic industrial relations (Kochan, McKersie, and Cappelli, 1984) has focused on labor relations issues at the level of the firm and, as a corollary, the interrelationship of labor relations and firm performance. Narrowly drawn, the question is whether unions and the collective bargaining process influence profits and, if so, how much.

While the question is certainly fundamental to a thorough understanding of industrial relations, it is not an easy one to answer. For example, is there a definition of firm performance that is both conceptually sound and empirically tractable? Can a distinction be made between union effects on efficiency that might limit the magnitude of profits, as opposed to union gains that simply redistribute a particular level of profits from the firm to workers? Does any union effect on firm performance derive simply from the presence of an organized labor force, or does the effect also vary with collective bargaining outcomes and product market character-

43

istics? These questions represent the basic themes around which this chapter will be organized. We begin with a brief discussion of agency theory to motivate and frame our discussion of firm performance and labor relations. In the second section we discuss measures of firm performance, compare the relative merits of accounting versus market-based measures, and describe the conventional methodology for the estimation of union effects using capital market measures. Next we review both the accounting and capital market literature in this area. In the last section we present some of our recent research on unions, profits, and firm risk.

Agency Theory and Industrial Relations

Agency theory provides a natural framework for discussing labor relations and firm performance because it ties together the objectives of the modern corporation and what students of industrial relations consider to be the natural conflict between employee interests in job security and employer interests in economic efficiency (Barbash, 1964). Understanding this connection requires a brief overview of agency theory.

Agency theory focuses on the problems that arise whenever an individual (or principal) contracts with an agent to act on his or her behalf. The contract between the principal and agent can be implicit or explicit and may simply represent a delegation of responsibility and authority. Because the agent and principal will not normally have identical interests, the agent cannot be expected to make exactly the same decisions the principal would have made. Presumably the principal's own decisions and activities would maximize his or her own welfare, while those of the agent represent something less. Because of differences in preferences between the principal and the agent, the principal attempts to fashion a contract with the agent (implicit or explicit) that will provide the agent with an incentive to act in the principal's best interests. The costs of creating the contract, monitoring the agent's performance, and enforcing the terms of the contract are referred to as "agency costs."[1]

---

[1] Agency costs would be negligible, even where principal and agent have divergent interests, if the principal had perfect information on the agent's activities and productivity, and this information was acquired at no cost. Since the principal sets the payoffs for the transaction, under perfect information the principal would simply reward the agent based on his or her true performance.

In the modern corporation agency problems are generated by the different interests of shareholders, management, and nonsupervisory employees. In simpler forms of work organization such as the self-employed individual with no employees, no agency costs exist because the owner, manager, and employee are one and the same. Agency costs are introduced, however, when the owner hires employees. Now the owner-manager must recognize and adjust to the fact that employees will maximize their own welfare, which is not identical to the owner-manager's welfare. At this point the owner-manager will have an incentive to monitor the activities of the work force to minimize this loss. These monitoring costs are reflected in lower future profits accruing to the owner-manager than would exist had the interests of employees and employer been identical.

Additional agency costs exist in the large complex organization with publicly traded stock, the kind of firm that is often significantly unionized. Now owners (shareholders) have fully delegated the operating decisions of the firm to managers. Though managers are normally expected to act in the best interests of shareholders, the interests of managers and owners are not identical, and therefore an additional layer of agency costs is introduced. Potential agency costs in such an organization include the relationship between stockholders and the top management of the firm as well as the relationship between management and nonsupervisory labor. Contracts designed to minimize agency costs between stockholders and managers have been a topic of substantial interest to finance scholars (Jensen and Zimmerman, 1985). Agency costs associated with the divergent interests of managers and workers is an important issue in industrial relations because of the difficulties firms have measuring employee performance, designing policies to reward or penalize employees based on their performance, and then enforcing these contracts.

The distinction between the interests of shareholders, managers, and labor emphasized by agency theory is well grounded in the ideological and institutional arrangements in the U.S. industrial relations system. Two examples illustrate this point. First, the prevailing union philosophy of business unionism recognizes the different but legitimate interests of stockholders and workers. The trade union movement accepts the pursuit of profit as a legitimate firm objective. Once a profit is achieved, however, the division of this profit between workers and shareholders is subject to negotiation because of the different interests of workers and shareholders. Second, the exclusion of supervisory and management employees from coverage under the National Labor Relations Act is a recognition that management is employed to represent the interests of stockholders and this responsibility would be seriously compromised if supervisory employees were allowed to unionize. From an agency framework, this decision could be interpreted as concluding that the additional shareholder costs of monitoring "unionized" management outweighed the benefits of unionization for supervisors.

Agency Costs in Union and Nonunion Firms

In the modern employment relationship agency problems arise because most employees have better information about the nature and magnitude of their current or future effort than does the employer. Given that the interests of employees and shareholders are not identical, imperfect monitoring by the firm provides employees with an incentive to shirk and appropriate firm resources for their own use. This appropriation in most cases would simply be a unilateral "renegotiation" of the work/effort bargain by the employee. To avoid this, the firm tries to establish an employment relationship with a mix of incentives and penalties that will align the interests of labor with those of owners (shareholders). Two management strategies are possible. To the extent that the firm's business risk can be shared with labor, the workers will have an incentive to act as owners. The current support for profit-sharing and employee stock ownership plans (ESOPs) by firms is due, in part, to a belief that these plans will reduce monitoring costs (i.e., increase employee motivation to perform for the benefit of the firm) by aligning the interests of the workers with the current and future profitability of the firm. Other more common examples that help achieve this objective include internal labor markets, promotion ladders, and pay structures that compensate higher level jobs in excess of current productivity (Lazear and Moore, 1984; Lazear, 1981). A second strategy is for shareholders to accept the greater share of the firm's business risk (and associated returns) and replace incentives with closer employee supervision and control.

Labor, however, is not indifferent to these kinds of policies since in each case firms are seeking to motivate workers to further stockholder interests rather than their own. If the firm attempts to shift some of the firm's business risk to workers through profit-sharing or an ESOP, union wages and/or employment become more variable and, without a wage differential to compensate for this risk, workers are worse off (Li, 1986). Closer management supervision and control may be no more palatable for employees. Unions continually emphasize the need to avoid what might be termed "monitoring risk," namely, arbitrary performance appraisal by management. The grievance procedure, restrictions on employee discipline, and the careful delineation of jobs and their responsibilities common in many labor agreements can be viewed as constraints on what management can do to reduce agency costs. To the extent that these clauses protect workers, they also increase the agency costs incurred by stockholders and, therefore, contribute to union and nonunion differences in firm performance.

Within the union sector different institutional arrangements and practices may also produce different agency costs, and this will influence the returns to stockholders. Recent research indicates that the grievance rate and the breadth of the contract, measured by the number of pages it includes, are negatively related to labor productivity (Ichniowski, 1984a, 1984b). If the breadth of contract and the grievance rate are interpreted as proxies for the incidence and successful resolution of agency disputes, respectively, these results would be consistent with our suggested framework.

The point is that while a unionized firm will engage in more explicit negotiations over the nature of the work/effort bargain, the terms of any employment relationship are the result of the ongoing tensions between labor and the firm over the distribution of firm resources and risks. Risk-averse workers with substantial firm-specific human capital cannot diversify their income sources across several firms and are therefore interested in minimizing their risk exposure by protecting their income and job security. The owners, namely, the shareholders, hope to maximize their returns and will either seek to shift part of the firm's business risk to labor or more closely monitor workers to equalize the value of their compensation and output. The strategies chosen by firms and the response of unions to these strategies determine the effect of unions on the allocation of firm returns and the risks assumed by the various parties. The purpose of this chapter is to review prior research on these issues and introduce new evidence on the relationship between unionization and firm risk and returns.

Measuring the Impact of Labor Relations

To this point we have briefly introduced agency theory as a framework to illustrate how the continuing negotiations over the employment relationship can influence the share of the firm's resources accruing to shareholders and labor. Empirical estimation of these resource claims, however, requires a more careful discussion of the appropriate definition of firm performance and the interests of shareholders.

Accounting vs. Economic Profits

Shareholders are interested in economic profits rather than accounting profits. Economic profits focus on the stream of net cash flows that accrue to shareholders, as owners of the firm's assets, and represent revenues minus operating costs and new investments. Shareholder wealth is simply the present value of these net cash flows. Accounting profits differ from economic profits for a variety of reasons, including the fact that deductions for investment (depreciation) are made not at the time of the cash outflow, but over the life of the asset. Since shareholder wealth is determined by the present value of net cash flows rather than accounting profits, attention to the latter can misstate the former (Fisher and McGowan, 1983). Therefore, the interests of shareholders are served by maximizing price per share, not earnings per share, the former being the present value of the cash flows to the firm indexed by the number of shares of stock.[2]

In sum, the notion of firm performance is best described by attention to the present value of future cash flows to the firm rather than accounting profits in a particular period. Such a definition has

---

[2] This does not mean that investors are indifferent to accounting information, only that their interest is in accounting information that communicates changes in the expected distribution of future cash flows rather than information about changes in earnings per share. Capital market research has examined a variety of instances where managerial decisions influenced earnings per share, but not cash flow, and vice versa. Generally this work supports the proposition that investors (shareholders) react to managerial decisions that influence cash flows rather than earnings per share. See Copeland and Weston (1983) for a more detailed discussion of these issues.

the advantage of correctly focusing on the temporal distribution of profits as well as the particular interests of shareholders. Changes or differences in firm performance can, therefore, be expressed in terms of differences in shareholder wealth (the present value of future cash flows). If firm performance is measured in terms of shareholder wealth, then the impact of labor relations on firm performance must be similarly expressed in these terms. Since a firm can be viewed as a "bundle" of capital assets, firm value is a function of the expected future cash flow generated by those assets and the variance (risk) in this cash flow (Fama, 1976; Schwert, 1981).[3] Assuming capital markets are efficient, the prices of capital assets are good indicators of the present value of future profit streams associated with those assets. Operationally a measure of firm value at time t is simply the price (p_t) of an individual share of common stock at (t) times the number of shares outstanding. Changes in stock prices, therefore, can be interpreted as "an unbiased estimate of the value of the change in future cash flows to the firm" (Schwert, 1981, p. 122) and will be taken as a measure of changes in firm performance.

The prior discussion requires a caveat. To this point we have assumed that shareholders have full claim to any economic profits remaining after operating costs are covered. The value of these shareholder claims, however, will be less in a unionized firm if labor costs exceed the competitive rate. John Abowd (1987) has shown that unions can appropriate a part of these shareholder claims and reduce firm value to shareholders. In other words, unions and shareholders can be viewed as a bilateral monopoly negotiating over the distribution of the net cash flows. Therefore, stock prices (shareholder wealth) will change either as a result of new information about the size of future firm profits or the distribution of those profits between shareholders and labor.

The "Event Study" Design

One methodology for investigating the effects of labor relations on shareholder wealth is to examine what happens to stock prices

---

[3] Where the firm is entirely financed by equity, firm value and shareholder wealth are identical. If the firm is in part financed by debt, shareholder wealth represents only a part of firm value. However, because the claims of bondholders are largely fixed and they do not share the business risks of the enterprise, we will focus on shareholders' interests in this chapter.

when unexpected labor relations information is provided to investors. Since changes in stock prices reflect changes in expected future profits, price changes associated with labor relations events can be interpreted as an unbiased estimate of the effect of the event on the future profits of the firm. The validity of this methodology depends on two factors. First, the researcher must determine when new labor relations information is identified by the capital market. An "old" event or information is already capitalized into the current price of the firm and the effects of this information cannot be evaluated using this methodology. Identifying when information is "new" to investors involves identifying individual event dates or the public disclosure of information about an event.

Second, the researcher must isolate the effect of the labor relations events on stock prices from other new information that might also influence firm value. Changes in firm value, or shareholder returns (R_{it}) over a particular time period, are measured as the change in common stock prices that occurs between two points in time plus dividends paid during that period. The effects of labor relations on firm performance, therefore, will be reflected in the influence of new collective bargaining events or "information" on *future* net cash flows available to shareholders. To estimate the magnitude of these effects, one must isolate the impact of the union event (union election, strike, concession bargain, etc.) on shareholder returns during the period in which this new information became available.

The estimation procedure is reasonably straightforward and requires a simple comparison of actual shareholder returns, in light of the union event (UE), with an estimate of shareholder returns that would have occurred in the absence of such an event. The value of the union event (VUE) can then be described as:

(1) $$VUE = R_{it} - E(R_{it} \mid \text{no union event})$$

where R_{it} is observed on the day of the union event and this information is completely unanticipated by investors. If the union event increases (decreases) the value of future cash flows to shareholders, VUE will be positive (negative). For equation (1) to capture fully the impact of a union event on shareholders' equity requires that information about the event be unanticipated prior to day t and that no new information becomes available after day t.

Moreover, $E(R_{it} \,|\, \text{no union event})$ must be an accurate estimate of the expected return in the absence of a union event.

The Estimation Process: Let us first consider the estimate of $E(R_{it} \,|\, \text{no union event})$. In financial economics the conventional approach is to posit only two influences on the period-to-period returns in any sample of firms. In what is known as the market model, the only systematic influence on stock prices is the changing fortunes of the market as a whole, such that

(2) $(R_{it} \,|\, \text{no union event, market return}) = B_o + B_i R_{mt} + e_{it}$

where R_{mt} = rate of return on a value-weighted portfolio of stocks between time t and $t - 1$. The market, of course, is simply the response of all firms to changing economic conditions. The sensitivity of firm i to this overall performance is described by B_i, which represents the risk of investing in firm i relative to the market. Where $B_i = 1.00$, the changes in firm returns, on average, equal changes in market returns. The returns of firms with B_i greater (less) than 1.00 will then be proportionately greater (less) than the market return to compensate investors for assuming more (less) than the overall market risk.

Earlier we noted that one way shareholders could reduce agency costs with respect to labor would be to shift a part of the firm's business risk to labor. However, because labor is generally not risk-neutral, workers can be expected to oppose such efforts. To the extent that unions can enforce those preferences, shareholders may bear a greater share of the business risk (higher B_i) than would be expected in the nonunion firm. For example, unions have traditionally rejected profit-sharing as a substitute for part of fixed wages and fringe benefits (Oswald, 1986), reflecting the view that "wages are wages and profits are profits and never the twain shall meet" (Barbash, 1956, p. 153). We consider the possible effects of unions on the allocation of risk in more detail later in the chapter.

Beyond the influence of the market, there should be no systematic influences on firm returns in the aggregate. Were this to be otherwise, investors could regularly reap excess returns above the market average based on this information. Of course the mere fact that the market is exposed to new information does not imply omniscience or that it can *perfectly* assess the impact of these events on the firm. An efficient market simply means that investors' concern for more accurate information extends only to the point where the potential returns from greater accuracy no longer exceed the costs of acquiring it.

In the aggregate, firm returns, controlling for market variation, tend to move randomly such that e_{it} has the usual ordinary least squares (OLS) properties. Therefore, in the absence of new information affecting firm performance, the difference between expected returns and actual returns is simply due to random firm-specific events that are unanticipated by the market. Although $R_{it} - E(R_{it} | \text{no union event, market})$ may be nonzero for a particular period, $E(e_{it})$ will be zero unless significant *new* information affecting the future performance of the firm becomes available during period t. This means that unionized firms cannot be expected to exhibit systematically higher or lower risk-adjusted returns (e_{it}), since investors would simply trade the stock until the excess returns were eroded. Consequently there is no equivalent to the union/nonunion wage differential observed in traditional union wage effects studies. It is only when important new labor relations information comes to light (e.g., union election, strike, concession agreement, etc.) that $R_{it} - E(R_{it} | \text{no union event, market})$ should be significantly different from what was expected given the variance in e_{it}. Such a deviation is referred to as an excess return and is equivalent to VUE in equation (1). Each firm acts as its own control where equation (2) is estimated for a period prior to the announcement of the concession contract.

The Event Period: To consider equation (1) as an unbiased measure of VUE assumes that the market cannot anticipate the occurrence or the significance of a union event prior to the day it is announced. Relaxing these assumptions means that equation (2), which provides estimates of expected returns in the absence of a union event must be calculated over a period prior to when the union event might be anticipated. This prior period would typically cover several months of trading ending anywhere from 30 to 90 days before the event day t.

Moreover, excess returns on day t are likely to understate the total magnitude of VUE if the union event is anticipated prior to day t. In other words, if the value of the union event is reflected in price changes prior to their announcement, $R_{it} - E(R_{it} | \text{no union event, market})$ on day t will understate the total expected effect of the union event. To minimize this possibility, prediction errors over a period prior to and subsequent to the event are typically summed (cumulative excess returns, CER) for each firm. The average of the CER across *all* firms is referred to as the cumulative average return (CAR). Given the assumption that e_{it} in equation (2) is a random variable with mean zero, the sum of the prediction errors up to day t should not be significantly different from zero if the union event is largely unanticipated. To the extent that a strike or union election is anticipated by investors and affects profits, the sum of the prediction errors prior to the announcement will differ significantly from zero, and the excess returns observed on the announcement day will fall relative to what would have been observed if the market had not anticipated the union event.

Capital Market and Accounting Data

The major drawback of the event study design is its inability to evaluate differences in firm value (or profitability) that might be attributable to "old" or existing labor relations policy and practices. The methodology is useful only when new information about these policies is identified by both the researcher and the market. The methodology cannot be used to estimate firm value differentials between union and nonunion firms that are comparable to the familiar union/nonunion wage differentials (Lewis, 1986).

To overcome this problem, recent studies of union profit effects have utilized either accounting measures of profits (Clark, 1984) or Census data on price-cost margins (PCM) for establishments (Freeman, 1983; Karier, 1985; Voos and Mishel, 1986). Each of these studies finds that unions reduce profits. An important advantage of this level of analysis is that union effects within establishments or business lines that are part of a larger corporation will not be diluted by a focus on corporate profits. While these studies are useful, there are two major problems with such profit measures. First, the accounting and PCM measures may differ from an economic definition of profits. Accounting conventions dealing with issues such as depreciation, research and development, and advertising expenditures lead to a divergence between accounting measures and an economic definition of profits (Salinger, 1984). The price-cost margin from the Census data fails to allocate certain corporate expenditures to establishments, distorting the profit measure (Liebowitz, 1982). Second, these measures do not correspond to returns to capital because they do not measure either the firm's assets or the risks associated with the investments made by the firm.

Ideally a profit measure should combine both capital market data on firm value and accounting data on the asset base of the firm. Efforts along these lines (Brainard and Tobin, 1968) compare the market value of the firm with the cost of replacing the physical assets of the firm. As an example, Tobin's q ratio equals:

(Market Value of Firm)/(Replacement Value of Assets).

A highly correlated measure (Hirschey and Wichern, 1984) is the difference between market value and replacement cost of the firm's assets standardized by firm sales:

(Market Value of Firm − Replacement Value of Assets)/Sales.

Two difficulties are encountered when constructing either Tobin's q or the excess valuation measure (Lindenberg and Ross, 1981). First, total firm value equals the value of equity and debt. While the value of equity can be closely approximated using data on common stock, the value of bondholder claims is more difficult to calculate. Ignoring the value of firm debt in event studies creates a problem only if the event increases the risk of bankruptcy and, therefore, the risk exposure of bondholders. Most labor relations events are unlikely to affect bankruptcy risk so the effect of the event on stockholder wealth corresponds to the total impact of the event on firm value. Ignoring the value of debt when calculating these other measures, however, creates a more serious problem because a firm's capital structure may be correlated with unionization. Second, these measures require that the replacement value of assets be estimated. These data have only been readily available since 1976 when firms were required to report replacement values for property, plant, and equipment on their 10k reports filed with the Securities and Exchange Commission (SEC). Despite these problems, the two market-adjusted measures are superior to accounting and Census data because the market value figure is the risk-adjusted present value of all future profits of the firm and not simply a single period measure of profits that fails to account for risk and is very sensitive to measurement error (Salinger, 1984).

Two profit-unionization studies (Salinger, 1984; Connolly, Hirsch, and Hirschey, 1986) have used market-adjusted measures. Each focused on the interaction between monopoly power in the product market, unionization, and firm value. Salinger concluded that unions do capture product market monopoly rents, while Connolly et al. found no significant interaction between product market structure and unionization. They did, however, find that unions capture some of the returns to research and development and, therefore, affect R&D investment decisions.

Prior Research: Capital Market Literature

In this section we review the evidence of union effects on firm performance, based on work that uses changes in shareholder equity as a measure of profitability.[4] While this is a relatively new area, there are several studies that examine the impact of unionization and a variety of collective bargaining outcomes. In each case we will highlight the design of the study and data sources and will also discuss the results.

Union Representation Elections

Ruback and Zimmerman (1984) analyzed the marginal impact of newly organized workers on firm value by examining stock price changes during union representation election drives. As they noted, the advantage of this approach is that there is no need to control for intermediate effects on profits so that "the net effect of unionization can be measured without ambiguity" (p. 1136). The sample consisted of National Labor Relations Board (NLRB) election data from 1962 to 1980 and included 253 observations from election units with 750 or more workers. They limited their observations to firms listed on the New York Stock Exchange in order to use the monthly stock return data available from the Center for Research on Security Prices (CRSP) of the University of Chicago. The authors examined the effect of both the announcement that an election *petition* had been filed with the NLRB and the *certification* of the election results. They observed an overall average *decline* of 1.38 percent and 0.48 percent in shareholder equity in the month of the petition and certification, respectively. Only in the former case was the result statistically significant at conventional levels. In both instances the losses for shareholders were greater in firms that eventually lost the election. Declines in shareholder equity

---

[4] Detailed reviews of the accounting and price-cost margin studies can be found in Freeman and Medoff (1984) and Hirsch and Addison (1986).

attributable to the election petition were on the order of 1.10 percent for firms that eventually won and 2.41 percent for losses. Declines in the month of certification were 0.22 percent and 1.43 percent, respectively, for firms that won and lost. In neither case was the difference in effects for winners and losers statistically significant, however.

Ruback and Zimmerman also calculated the cumulative effects (CARs) on shareholders' equity over the period beginning 24 months before the petition date to 24 months after the certification. This is the best measure of the total impact of the information communicated by the union representation drive. They found that shareholder equity over this longer period declined by 1.86 percent overall (1.32 percent for winners and 3.84 percent for losers). Ruback and Zimmerman interpreted the negative effects of a union "loss" as the net influence of union-avoidance strategies and an indication that at least some support for unionization existed, given the successful petition (p. 1138). Each of the results was at least marginally significant statistically, although they could not reject the hypothesis of no difference between the effects for the winners and losers. They calculated that on a *per worker* basis, these effects represent total shareholder losses of approximately $7,000 and $46,000 for winners and losers, respectively.

Finally, they observed a not uncommon feature of capital market studies, namely, that while the overall mean of the union effects is of a particular sign, negative in this case, individual firms exhibit relatively large effects in both directions. In this study abnormal returns ranged from a 39 percent decline in shareholder equity to a 42 percent *increase*. Ruback and Zimmerman attempted to explain this variation as a function of the particular union involved in the election and the industry in which the firm was located, but with little success. However, it is this kind of effort that represents the next step for the line of research described in this chapter.

In sum, Ruback and Zimmerman found that the average marginal effect of new unionization is associated with a decline in shareholder wealth. While there are always questions in studies of this kind regarding the extent to which the market anticipated the event and therefore understated the effect, there is little reason to believe that the "true" effect is, on average, positive. It is of interest that the authors found that most of the prepetition decline in shareholders' equity for firms where unions were successful occurred early in the period. Although this could represent incredible omniscience by the market, Ruback and Zimmerman simply concluded that "firms in which unions are successful experience declines in value prior to the union activity" (p. 1145). The latter observation suggests a process by which diminishing firm performance, adjusted for the experience of other firms, might lead to management policies designed to improve efficiency and cut labor costs, with associated threats to the labor force and greater sympathy for a unionization drive.

Contract Negotiations, Firm Value, and Stockholder Wealth

The declines associated with union victories obtained by Ruback and Zimmerman might reflect market estimates of stockholder losses due to either a redistribution of the firm's cash flows from stockholders to workers or an increase in agency costs because the cost of monitoring and supervising employees increases with the presence of a union. Since a successful election signifies only a mutual duty to bargain between labor and management and does not establish the *outcome* of the bargain, there is considerable investor uncertainty about the precise terms of the agreement. Therefore it is difficult to judge precisely what union effect the market was responding to during a successful unionization drive.

A recent paper by John Abowd (1987) provides evidence of the redistributive effects of the *wage* bargain reached by the parties. Abowd posits that while shareholders have exclusive claim to economic profits (net cash flows) in a competitive labor market, the unionization of the firm introduces a competing claim for those profits. If unions can claim a portion of those profits, they can earn a premium beyond the competitive wage. The important point is that the value of the firm as measured by future net cash flows has not changed; it is just redistributed from shareholders to labor. Nevertheless, shareholder equity will fall. The opportunities for renegotiating these claims occur as part of the regular contract cycle.

The interpretation of a change in shareholder equity associated with contract settlements is not unambiguous, however. First, a new contract that conforms to investor expectations should have no effect on shareholder equity since the outcome has already been capitalized into the price of the stock. A new contract with unanticipated outcomes, however, might reflect either new information about the condition of the company and its profitability or a change in the distribution of those profits. Unfortunately, the direction of the change in shareholders' equity can be consistent with either explanation. Abowd predicts that, except under very unusual conditions, unanticipated negotiated outcomes will be reflected in a redistribution of firm value, but not in a decline in firm value. The effect of these unanticipated changes will, therefore, generally be a dollar-for-dollar redistribution or an unexpected one-dollar increase in labor costs that produces a subsequent dollar decline in stockholder wealth.

Abowd tested these predictions using a sample of nearly 4,000 contract negotiations available in the Bureau of National Affairs (BNA) *Collective Bargaining Negotiations and Contracts* for the period 1976–1984. Again, observations could be included only if the firm was listed in the relevant financial data source (CRSP and Compustat). On the basis of contract information, Abowd calculated the present value of the compensation benefits over the life of the contract as well as a predicted benefit value based on economy-wide information and prior settlement data. The predicted value corresponds to investors' expectations about the settlement based on publicly available information. The deviation of the predicted values from the actual outcomes would, therefore, represent the unanticipated changes in the contract.

Using an event period running from two months before the settlement date through the settlement month, Abowd found remarkable support for the efficient contract hypothesis and the notion that union effects reflect a *redistribution* of net cash flows rather than their level. His results indicated that the present value of unexpected settlements is reflected virtually dollar-for-dollar in changes in shareholder equity. This is not to say that unions may not affect firm value, but only that these effects may have already been capitalized and are not reflected in the ongoing negotiation process. As noted above, Ruback and Zimmerman's results could be taken as a change in firm value rather than in its distribution.

Efficient Bargains and Contract Work Rules

In addition to supporting the hypothesis that collective bargaining redistributes firm returns from shareholders to workers, Abowd's paper is consistent with models of bargaining that challenge the conventional view of restrictive union staffing and output clauses. Traditionally, the presumed effect of unions on firm productivity and performance was negative because of the restrictive contract terms included in collective agreements. The recent research by Freeman, Medoff, and their students showing a positive effect of unions on productivity in many situations has changed the maintained hypothesis motivating research in this area and stimulated substantial research on the union productivity effect. In addition to this neoinstitutional view of unions, recent work in neoclassical labor economics has posited that if collective bargaining agreements are the result of both parties seeking to develop efficient or pareto-optimal contracts, then what might appear to be "restrictive" work rules merely serve to enforce the contract in a way that enables the parties to arrive at a more efficient settlement.

In contrast to the efficient contracts interpretation, the traditional labor demand model views the elasticity of the firm's demand for labor as a fundamental constraint on the bargaining power of the union. This conclusion rests on the assumptions that unions and their members value both wages and employment, but in negotiations with employers the parties negotiate on only the wage while the employer is left to unilaterally determine employment levels conditional on the agreed-upon wage. Since the

FIGURE 1

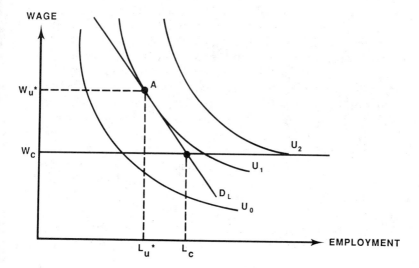

firm's labor demand curve defines employment levels that maximize profits given a particular wage, the firm will set employment after the wage is agreed upon according to the labor demand schedule.

If the union could unilaterally establish the wage in the preceding model, it would establish one that takes into account the employment effect of the wage in a manner that maximizes the utility of the union. This is easily illustrated with a graph. In Figure 1 unions positively value both higher wages and greater employment of their members, according to some preference schedule represented by a series of indifference curves, U_0, U_1, U_2, and so on. Higher levels of union utility are represented by larger numbers. If the unions could dictate the wage, they would maximize utility by setting it at the point where the union indifference curve is just tangent to the labor demand schedule (point A). Since the union-dictated negotiated wage rate (w_u^*) is higher than the competitive wage (w_c), union employment is reduced (from L_c to L_u^*). This employment loss increases as demand elasticity increases, causing the union to moderate its wage decision to reduce the employment effect of the wage settlement.

Alternatively, the efficient contracts literature begins with the notion that two parties to a transaction will agree to terms that exploit the possibilities for joint gains. Accordingly, agreements negotiated under the labor demand model are inefficient because the welfare of *both* parties could be increased if the parties establish both wages *and* employment levels during negotiations. The inefficiency of an agreement in the labor demand model is illustrated in Figure 2. In this figure isoprofit curves (curves that describe different wage and employment combinations that produce the same profit levels) are superimposed on the labor demand curve, with more profitable curves nearer the origin. Higher profit levels in this figure are denoted by higher subscripts. Point A, the wage-employment outcome predicted by the labor demand model, is inefficient because both parties would be better off if they established a wage-employment combination to the right of the demand curve at a point of tangency between an isoprofit and union utility curve. In this example, any settlement along the line segment BC (Figure 2) would make one or both sides better off without making the other party worse off.

The contract curve models predict that the parties negotiate over both wages and employment levels and reach an agreement at

FIGURE 2

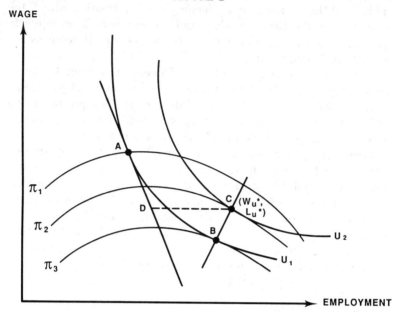

a point of tangency between the union's indifference curves and the employer's isoprofit curves. The set of points describing these points of tangency is referred to as the contract curve and describes the set of "efficient" settlements where all possibilities of joint gains have been exploited. That is, a settlement on the contract curve has the characteristic that no change in the wage-employment bargain will make one party better off without making the other side worse off.

The contract curve model creates an "enforcement" problem for the union because once the employer and the union have concluded such a bargain, the employer has an incentive to renege by providing less employment at the contract wage rate of w_u^* than the implicitly agreed upon employment of L_u^*. For example, point D on the labor demand curve horizontally to the left of (w_u^*, L_u^*) yields higher profits to the employer. The enforcement problem is particularly difficult in a dynamic economic environment because the contract curve will shift as labor demand shifts with changes in product demand. Therefore, the union must differentiate between employer requests to reduce employment because of lower demand from the employer's desire to move off the contract curve. This is difficult because of incomplete information about the demand for the firm's product and the employer's incentive to portray a decline in demand as the source of all requests for reductions in employment.

While the seemingly intractable enforcement problem has led to some skepticism about the validity of this interpretation (e.g., Farber, 1984), empirical tests of this formulation are just beginning (Abowd, 1987; Brown and Ashenfelter, 1986; Eberts and Stone, 1986; Macurdy and Pencavel, 1986). Except for Brown and Ashenfelter's paper, this research generally supports the contract curve model. Two of the studies, however, are of a single industry (newspaper publishing) and union (International Typographical Union), known to have very special industrial relations features (Lipset, Trow, and Coleman, 1956). Given the implications of this model for the interpretation of the union impact on firm performance, this controversy will undoubtedly attract considerable interest in the future. It is hoped that industrial relations scholars will contribute to this debate.

Concession Bargaining

On the basis of Abowd's work, it should follow that negotiated settlements generally perceived to be favorable to management should have a positive effect on shareholders' equity. An example would be the apparent proliferation of "concession" contracts in recent years. Despite the descriptive accounts of this phenomenon and the limited analysis of the determinants of concession bargaining and associated outcomes (Cappelli, 1983, 1984, 1985), these studies do not provide conclusive evidence on the economic impact of the concession on the firms involved.

Becker (1987) has recently examined the effects of concession bargaining on firm performance using the methodology described above. Drawing on data collected by BNA, 70 settlements referred to in published accounts as concessionary were analyzed for 1982–1983. Although event studies use each firm as its own control, Becker also collected a sample of 96 "normal" settlements during the same period. In both cases, only settlements occurring in firms included in the daily return file of the CRSP data were included in the study. The results are summarized in Figure 3 based on an event period of 90 days on either side of the settlement date. The data

FIGURE 3

Cumulative Average Residuals for 90 days (18 weeks) on Either Side of Settlement Date

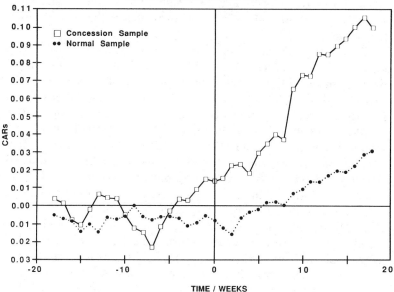

Source: Becker (1987).

show that over the first 60 days prior to the concession settlement the market does not appear to anticipate a concession settlement, but that for the last 121 days of the event period, shareholders' equity increases by more than 12 percent ($\alpha=0.001$, two-tailed test). Interestingly, the "normal" sample also shows a statistically significant increase in shareholder wealth of 3.9 percent over the last 90 days of this period. The results for the "normal" sample suggest that even where the settlement was not publicly identified as such, there seems to be a concessionary element to them.

Recall that these increases in shareholder equity could represent either an increase in firm value or simply a redistribution of value from labor to shareholders. In this case, however, the predictions are unambiguous. For example, a concession could represent new information about the profit position of the firm. Presumably the requests for concessions would be considered by investors to represent "bad news" about the future with consequent negative effects on stock prices and firm value. Alternatively, the negotiation of concessions themselves should represent good news, not about firm value, but rather about the distribution of profits between labor and shareholders. Since the results show a *positive* change in shareholder wealth, this is taken as evidence of the redistribution hypothesis.

Recall that Ruback and Zimmerman observed that firms experiencing a successful union election had also experienced declines in shareholder equity several months prior to the election drive. While they did not elaborate on the implications of this result, it suggests that firm performance might also influence labor relations events with implications for the strategic industrial relations literature. Becker (1987) examined this issue with respect to concession bargaining. He found that declines in market-adjusted shareholder returns before the 90-day pre-event period were associated with an *increase* in the likelihood of observing a concession bargain. In other words, a decline in the expected future profitability contributed to the probability of a concession settlement in the firm. Since the returns are adjusted for the market as a whole (all other firms), this implies that firm performance relative to the competition was the important influence, and management could effectively argue for pattern-breaking settlements to resolve problems not shared by other firms.

Strikes

To this point we have discussed the influence of unionism and contract negotiations generally, as well as the particular effects of concession bargaining. In each case, the evidence indicates that unions and labor relations events do influence firm performance. Next we will consider the impact of one element of the negotiation process itself, often the most visible one, namely, strikes. The relationship between strikes and firm performance is often implicit in much of the earlier strike literature since interest in this phenomenon is at least in part motivated by the apparent costs of work stoppages for the parties involved. However, as Neumann and Reder observe, "[T]he plain fact is that we do not know whether [the losses caused by labor disputes] are big or small, or even if there are any" (1984, p. 198). While they show that strikes have little or no effect on industry output, they do not examine the issue of participant costs, except to predict that these costs should be "appreciably larger than the industry cost" (p. 211).

There are two published studies that consider the effect of strikes on firm performance.[5] The first, by George Neumann (1980), actually examined the issue of strikes and profitability within the larger question of the predictability of strikes. Neumann's principal interest was to use capital market reaction to strikes and the threat of a strike as a test of competing hypotheses about the predictability of strikes. Stock market anticipation of a strike in the pre-event period would suggest that strikes are not entirely random events and indirectly that strikes are costly. Neumann's strike data were collected from reports in the *Wall Street Journal* and included the years 1967–1971 and 1974–1975. He then calculated excess returns for 14 trading days on either side of the beginning and ending dates of the strike.

Although Neumann reported no significance tests for cumulative abnormal returns over the entire strike period, he did find that shareholder equity declined significantly on two of the days in the 14-day prestrike period as well as on the day of the strike announcement. Over the entire 29-day period surrounding the strike announcement, shareholders' equity in the average firm declined by nearly 1 percent (p. 531). In short, Neumann found modest evidence that strikes are costly for shareholders and that their occurrence can at least in part be anticipated by publicly available information.

Recently, Becker and Olson (1986) examined these same issues with the benefit of improved sampling, design, and estimation procedures. They used a considerably larger sample of strikes (699) drawn from preliminary strike reports of *Current Work Stoppages*, published by the Bureau of Labor Statistics (BLS), covering the period from 1962 to 1982. In addition, they collected a sample of "peaceful" settlements taken from BNA's *Current Contract Settlements* over the period 1977–1980. The second sample, a comparison group, was used to test more accurately the hypothesis that the pre-event stock market reaction was to the strike itself and not simply to the threat of a strike in any negotiation. As Neumann observed, "There is clearly a need for an examination of the security price behavior of firms that settled rather than struck" (1980, p.

---

[5] Greer, Martin, and Reusser (1980) also examined the relationship between strikes and shareholder equity. Their study, however, includes only 91 strikes and provides no statistical tests of strike costs (CARs).

531). Finally, Becker and Olson estimated the full effects of the strikes on shareholders by calculating CARs over the *entire* strike period. They also used a wider pre- and postevent period (30 days vs. 14 days) to capture more fully any changes in shareholder wealth.

Strike Costs: Becker and Olson found that strikes have a significant impact on shareholders' equity, both economically and statistically. Across all firms the average effect was to decrease shareholder wealth by 4.14 percent. In addition, using the sample of peaceful settlements and a subsample of strikes over the same period, they were able to reject the hypothesis of no difference between the "settlement" effects represented by the peaceful sample and the strike effects represented by the two strike samples. They also calculated the dollar magnitude of these losses for four measures of strike costs: average cost per strike, average cost per striking worker, average cost per day, and average cost per 10,000 lost workdays. The dollar estimates were based on the pre-event market value of shareholder equity using information on 535 firms available in Standard and Poor's *Compustat* file.

The measures of strike costs were calculated on a weighted and unweighted basis. The unweighted estimates are the effect for the *average* firm experiencing an *average* strike, while the weighted estimates reflect the fact that smaller firms (in terms of shareholder equity) tended to experience larger strike costs (percentage loss in shareholder equity, CER).[6] Estimates of the overall percentage effect on shareholders' equity as well as industry estimates of this effect and the two versions of the dollar magnitude are reported in Table 1. They indicate that for the average firm strike costs range from $72 million to $87 million. In general, the unweighted measure shows higher average losses per strike, while in one case (cost per day) the weighted average actually shows a slight gain for shareholders.

Predictability of Strikes and Strike Costs: Becker and Olson also observed that investors consistently *underestimate* the cost of strikes during the prestrike period. There are two plausible explanations, both of which bear on the interests of the

---

[6] See Becker and Olson (1986) for a more detailed discussion of this point.

TABLE 1

Estimated Average Strike Costs to Stockholders

Industry[a]	No. of Strikes	Average Cost			
		Per Strike[b]	Per Striker[c]	Per Day[d]	Per 10,000 LWD[e]
Paper, paper containers (26)	26	−.831% [−10.09] (3.54)	−.00024% [−2.87] (5.77)	.173% [2.10] (.59)	1.029% [12.43] (3.71)
Chemicals (28)	38	−1.684 [−44.98] (−.60)	−.00222 [−59.17] (−46.28)	.657 [17.53] (11.88)	4.079 [108.9] (63.95)
Tires and rubber goods (30)	27	−2.209 [−24.65] (−20.81)	−.00447 [−49.87] (−47.47)	.198 [2.21] (5.09)	−2.152 [−24.02] (−.96)
Steel, copper, and aluminum (33)°°	44	5.156 [72.65] (122.2)	.00416 [56.64] (107.5)	−.062 [−.88] (.72)	.416 [5.86] (61.17)
Machinery and machine tools (35)°°	85	5.046 [60.21] (18.68)	.00311 [37.09] (−0.0)	−.192 [−2.29] (−2.60)	.769 [9.18] (−8.61)
Electrical products (36)°	33	6.711 [278.1] (18.39)	.00492 [210.6] (13.64)	1.963 [83.98] (−12.18)	6.824 [291.9] (−60.15)
Automobiles, trucks, and aerospace (37)	89	2.059 [43.82] (15.05)	.00010 [2.19] (−19.85)	.612 [13.02] (−15.67)	3.226 [68.66] (11.39)
Air transport (45)°°	22	14.74 [91.37] (63.31)	.00586 [36.35] (15.49)	6.038 [37.43] (27.07)	13.92 [86.26] (45.32)
Electric and gas utilities (49)°	34	4.885 [47.07] (40.11)	.00227 [21.85] (14.30)	.010 [.095] (−1.19)	.634 [6.10] (1.09)
Compustat sample°°°	535	3.686 [87.15] (72.29)	.00161 [38.15] (14.65)	.569 [13.46] (−2.10)	2.537 [59.98] (9.86)
Total sample°°°	699	4.155 [NA] (NA)	.00184 [NA] (NA)	.412 [NA] (NA)	1.798 [NA] (NA)

Notes: The first number in each cell is the percentage loss to shareholders (gains to shareholders are positive), the second figure (in brackets) is the "unweighted" average dollar loss (adjusted to 1980 dollars using the CPI), and the third number (in parentheses) is the "weighted" dollar loss.

  [a] The industry classification numbers refer to the first two digits of *Standard and Poor's* industry classification scheme. The classification of firms into industry by *Standard and Poor* is designed to match the SIC classification scheme. To correct for heteroskedasticity, the significance levels are based on a *t*-value calculated after standardizing each CER by its standard error. Because of this standardization, the *t*-values are the same across all four measures of strike activity. The formula can be found in Ruback and Zimmerman (1984).

stockholders. First, management may be understating true strike costs to enhance their bargaining position and investors are misled. Alternatively, investors may be accurately assessing true strike costs, but management pays too much attention to sunk costs and allows the strike to go beyond the point of greatest benefit to shareholders. Becker and Olson found a positive correlation between the magnitude of pre- and poststrike CERs and take this as evidence supporting the hypothesis that managers do pay attention to sunk costs. Such evidence suggests that strike costs are not entirely a function of *union* power.

Finally, Becker and Olson considered the predictability of strikes by comparing the market anticipation of the contract deadline in the peaceful sample, the strike subsample, and the overall strike sample. They show that while the market is by no means omniscient, investors do anticipate with error the occurrence of a strike. Both the strike sample and strike subsample indicate declines in shareholder equity significantly below those observed in the peaceful sample.

Public Policy Evaluations

The event study methodology can also be used to assess the potential effects of public policy changes on the distribution of cash flows between workers and shareholders. The competing claims of labor and management on the cash flows generated by the assets of the firms is illustrated in the current debate over firm decisions to terminate overfunded defined benefit pension plans. At issue is the ownership of plan assets that exceed the legal obligations of a defined benefit plan. Under existing law a firm can, with Department of Labor permission, terminate a plan, establish a trust to meet its obligation to current and future retirees under the old plan, and use the remaining assets for anything it wishes. These terminations are opposed by labor and others on the basis that workers have (or should have) a claim on these assets to increase benefits or protect them against unfavorable and unexpected events

---

^b Dollar loss figures are in millions.
^c Dollar loss figures are in thousands.
^d Dollar loss figures are in millions.
^e Dollar loss figures are in millions. LWD = lost workdays.
   * Significant at the 0.05 level, one-tailed test.   ** Significant at the 0.01 level, one-tailed test.   *** Significant at the 0.001 level, one-tailed test.
NA = not available.
Source: Becker and Olson (1986).

in the future. For example, these assets might be used to adjust benefits of retirees during periods of rapid inflation and protect real benefit levels. The resolution of this issue will determine how the claims on the cash flow of these assets are distributed between workers and shareholders.

The event methodology can also be used to assess the effect of changes in public policy on shareholder wealth when a new labor relations policy is introduced, considered, and approved by Congress, the courts, and the executive branch of government. The methodology is very similar to the studies reviewed earlier. The researcher must identify the point during the policy formulation process when key information about the content of the policy and its chances for implementation was first known to investors. This is more difficult than other labor relations events because the process of public policy formulation frequently extends over many months.

Another more technical issue that differentiates public policy event studies from other event studies is attributable to the correspondence between "event" time and "calendar" time in public policy studies. Calculation of the variance in the average excess return (AR) from the ERs from individual events typically assumes the ERs to be independent. This assumption is reasonable because the calendar dates of the events (i.e., representation election or strike) are different for each sample event. However, the event date and the calendar date are identical when the event is the formulation of public policy that may have a simultaneous effect on the value of all affected firms. In this context it is unlikely the ERs are independent across firms and failure to account for this lack of independence will likely produce biased significance tests (Schipper and Thompson, 1983; Collins and Dent, 1984; Burgstahler and Noreen, 1986).

We have recently used this methodology (Olson and Becker, 1986) to estimate the impact of the passage of the National Labor Relations Act (NLRA) in 1935 on shareholder wealth for a sample of 83 firms at greatest risk of unionization. The change in wealth for these firms is interpreted as an estimate of the effect of the NLRA on the relative power of labor and management. In other words, if bargaining power shifted toward labor as a result of this legislation, shareholder claims on the future cash flows of the firm should have fallen during the time and produced a decline in firm value.

The key NLRA events identified as having a potential impact on firm value include 14 months during the period from March 1934 through April 1937. These 14 months correspond to roughly three periods: four months in the spring of 1934 when Senator Wagner introduced and Congress considered the major precursor to the NLRA, the *Labor Disputes Act*; the four months in the spring of 1935 when Congress considered and passed the NLRA; and five postpassage months, including July 1935 when Roosevelt announced he had signed the bill and the four months when the constitutionality of the law was at issue.

The excess returns for these 14 months were calculated for 83 firms that were either described as unionized during congressional hearings or were subject to union organizing drives during the last half of the 1930s. While clearly not a random sample of publicly traded firms, we believe it does represent the group of firms most likely to be affected by the act's provisions that protect and encourage collective bargaining. The results show an average decline in stockholder wealth over the 14 months of 20 percent. This was statistically significant at the 0.05 level using a one-tail test ($t=1.84$). The results show the NLRA had a very profound effect on the balance of power between labor and management, an effect that is frequently overlooked in contemporary discussions of the weaknesses of the act.

Unions and the Allocation of Business Risk

In our discussion of the agency problem we noted that part of the implicit or explicit negotiation between the firm and labor will involve the allocation of the firm's business risk between shareholders and labor. The notion of business risk, derived from the fact that the future economic position of the firm is uncertain, consists of systematic and random components. Systematic risk represents the covariation of the firm's profits with the fortunes of all firms (the market) and is equivalent to B_i in equation (2). The random component represents the unpredictable firm-specific events that influence the profits of the firm, *independent* of the influences of the market as a whole. This latter risk, call it firm-specific risk, can be avoided by shareholders through diversification. While systematic risk cannot be avoided through diversification, in an efficient market shareholders for the most part are indifferent to changes in risk for a particular firm because they are able to adjust their overall portfolio of investments to maintain a similar risk level. Workers, on the other hand, cannot easily diversify their risk since they normally work for only one firm at a time and are, therefore, subject to the full business risk of the company.

For this reason we normally assume that workers are more risk-averse than firms and expect unions to reflect those interests by constraining management's efforts to increase labor's share of the firm's business risk. In practice labor could reduce its exposure to the firm's business risk by reducing the sensitivity of labor costs to market fluctuations. In other words, as labor costs become more and more fixed, the interests of labor approach those of bondholders rather than shareholders. Alternatively, management may attempt to shift a greater share of the business risk to labor (and away from shareholders) in an attempt to align workers' interests with those of the shareholders and therefore reduce the magnitude of agency costs.

Union effects on the allocation of risk are also important for the estimated changes in shareholder equity reported earlier. Recall that any estimate of abnormal returns is based on an expectations model like equation (2). The assumption is that B_i, or systematic risk, estimated prior to the labor relations event is unaffected by the event itself. Otherwise the estimates derived from equation (1) will be biased, depending on the direction of the change in B_i and the market return. For example, if B_i increases and shareholders now bear a greater share of the firm's business risk, the CARs will be overstated (understated) when the market is rising (falling).

Prior Research

There is virtually no published work that explicitly examines the influence of collective bargaining on the allocation of risk, though several studies test for changes in B_i to be sure that estimates of abnormal returns are not incorrect. Ruback and Zimmerman (1984) calculated abnormal returns based on pre- and postevent B_is. However, they also estimated the abnormal returns using combined B_is with similar results (p. 1141). The latter test is at least indirect evidence that shareholder risk did not change as a result of the union election drive.

Neither Neumann (1980) nor Becker and Olson (1986) tested for a change in B_i. However, in light of the time periods over which the data were collected, particularly for the Becker and Olson study, there doesn't seem to be any a priori reason to believe that the abnormal returns were estimated incorrectly. On the basis of Brown and Warner's findings (1980), Abowd simply subtracts the market returns from the firm returns over the particular period, implicitly setting B_i equal to 1.0 for all firms. While Brown and Warner show that estimates of abnormal returns are essentially equivalent with the two methods, the results offer no insights into any changes in shareholder risk. Finally, Becker (1987) explicitly tests for a change in shareholder risk as a result of concession bargaining. Publicity surrounding concession bargaining would suggest that labor is absorbing a greater share of the firm's business risk with greater acceptance of profit-sharing and gainsharing policies. Alternatively, the increased emphasis on employment security could result in a shift in risk toward shareholders in return for lower compensation and benefits. Becker's analysis, however, shows no change in shareholder risk for either the concession sample or the "normal" settlements.

New Evidence

While prior work has not shown any major influence of labor relations events on the allocation of business risk between shareholders and labor, there are instances where such effects are observed. For example, an analysis of the 1982 "Big Four" labor negotiations in the tire industry (Uniroyal, Firestone, B.F. Goodrich, and Goodyear) shows that shareholders' risk changed substantially following the settlement. Using a methodology similar to Becker's (1987), B_i is estimated over a 120-day period prior to a 180-day event period and in the last 90 days of the event period. The results, summarized in Table 2, indicate that three of the four companies had a significant *increase* in shareholder risk over this period, while Firestone experienced a decline. While suggestive, such results are quite sensitive to the fact that the labor relations event, a new contract, occurred at similar points in time for all firms. Combined with the fact that all of the firms are in the same industry, it is difficult to rule out the possibility that other events, perhaps specific to the tire industry, may have influenced the results.

In a more wide-ranging study of unions and firm financial characteristics (Becker and Olson, 1987), we have developed a data base of more than 1,000 union and nonunion firms. The data are drawn from the 1977 *Annual Return: Report of Employee Benefit*

Plan (Form 5500) as part of Treasury and Labor Department efforts to monitor the Employee Retirement Income Security Act (ERISA). The data provide estimates of the number of union and nonunion workers in company pension plans, thus identifying unionized companies and an approximate estimate of the level of organization. Company names were then matched with names available on the CRSP tapes to generate data on 692 union and 314 nonunion companies, with an average level of unionization of 43 percent in the unionized firms.

TABLE 2

Changes in Shareholder Risk (B_i) for the Tire Industry
(1982 Negotiations)

Company	Preconcession Period[a] B_i	Postconcession Period[b] B_i	Change
B.F. Goodrich	1.318 (.245)	1.58 (.218)	+.27°°°
Goodyear	.95 (.212)	1.54 (.217)	+.66°°°
Uniroyal	1.49 (.47)	2.16 (.273)	+.67°°°
Firestone	1.41 (.273)	1.21 (.241)	−.20°°°

Note: Standard errors are in parentheses.
[a] 120-day period prior to 300-day event period.
[b] Last 90 days of 300-day event period.
°°° Significant at the 0.01 level, one-tailed test.

Recall that the firm's business risk can be divided into systematic and firm-specific components. The former (B_i) is a function of the underlying variability of firm revenues and the share of that variability borne by the costs of production. In this case if labor costs in unionized firms are relatively more fixed (variable), then shareholders bear a greater (smaller) share of the business risk. Likewise, if workers in unionized firms bear a greater (smaller) share of the firm's systematic business risk, B_i in those firms would be smaller (larger).

Estimates of union/nonunion differences in B_i were calculated for each of 12 years from 1970 to 1981, controlling for industry (two-digit level).[7] Where unionization is measured as the percent of the labor force covered by a collective bargaining contract, preliminary results show unambiguously that union workers bear a *greater* share of the firm's systematic business risk than do nonunion workers. In 11 of the 12 years, B_i is *lower* in unionized firms and statistically significantly lower at conventional levels in eight of those years. The trend is illustrated in Figure 4. The differences are also economically significant, ranging from 3 to 10 percent of the nonunion levels. Over the entire period, the average B_i in unionized firms was 0.102 lower than the average nonunion B_i. Moreover there was some indication that this difference *increased* over the period. A simple regression of the B_i difference on a trend variable suggests a modest and marginally significant (one-tailed test, $\alpha = 0.05$) *increase* in this difference of 0.007 per year.

At this point we can offer only some tentative interpretations of the apparent shift in business risk from shareholders to labor in unionized companies. First, we would note that this pattern of results is consistent with the earlier agency discussion. For example,

FIGURE 4

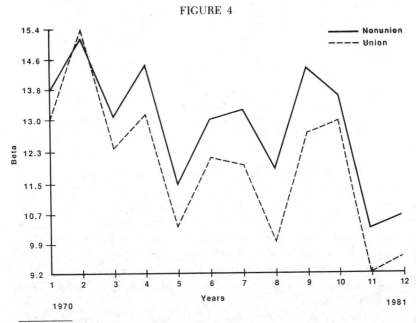

---

[7] See Becker and Olson (1987) for a more comprehensive analysis of these data.

where collective bargaining agreements limit the ability of management to monitor worker performance and act on such information, agency theory would predict that management would seek to shift greater risk to labor as an incentive to work in the best interests of the shareholders. Although wages and compensation levels are normally less flexible in unionized firms, labor costs need not be since they can be adjusted through layoffs and reductions in the work schedule. This is consistent with other research showing that unionized firms make greater use of layoffs than do comparable nonunion firms (Medoff, 1979), and by implication experience more variable labor costs.

This result also supports work summarized earlier indicating that unionized firms earn lower profits. Shareholders will accept a lower return on their investment if they bear less risk in unionized firms. Similarly, managers in unionized firms can invest in less profitable projects because the cost of capital is lower. Finally, if unionized workers do bear a greater share of their firm's business risk, agency theory predicts that they would be compensated for this greater risk exposure, assuming that labor is risk-averse. This risk premium could in part explain the commonly observed union/nonunion wage differential.

The Impact of Firm Performance on Labor Relations

Most of this chapter consists of an assessment of the impact of unions and collective bargaining on firm performance. Economic events since the beginning of the decade suggest that causation also runs in the opposite direction; the economic position of unionized firms has had a dramatic impact on the industrial relations policies pursued by many of those firms. The lower wage settlements and the change in the structure of the compensation package (i.e., greater use of profit-sharing) found in recent concession agreements were frequently the product of the deteriorating economic position of the firm involved.

The changes in the industrial relations system are, however, more fundamental than simply wage settlements below the historical trend. The theoretical model proposed by Kochan, McKersie, and Cappelli (1984) argues that the significant changes in the industrial relations system that began in the 1970s were caused by new firm policies dealing with human resource management and labor relations. Perhaps the most basic change they identify is the more active involvement of senior line management in the formulation of industrial relations policies. This change is important because it represents a new cast of management actors that have a set of values with regard to unions and collective bargaining that differ from those of many management labor relations practitioners. These different values have led to management policies designed to minimize unionization in new facilities, weaken the power and influence of established bargaining units, and strengthen the firm's human resource management capabilities at the expense of traditional labor relations activities (i.e., the negotiation and administration of labor agreements).

The more aggressive labor relations policies pursued by firms have produced substantial changes in labor relations at the firm level and, because of its apparent pervasiveness, major changes in the industrial relations system. What accounts for this change in management strategy? The three major explanations include: (1) a change in management ideology toward unions and collective bargaining; (2) greater opportunities to challenge labor because of economic, political, and work force demographic changes that have made unions vulnerable; and (3) economic pressures on the firm that have forced management to pursue more aggressive labor relations strategies to help ensure the success and survival of the firm.

Case studies supporting all three explanations can be found. The key issue is which of these explanations has had the greatest impact on management policy and, according to the theory, the U.S. industrial relations system. While we make no claim at resolving this issue, we suggest a theoretical link between the economic pressures confronting unionized firms and the greater role played by senior executives in the labor relations policies of the firm. Empirical evidence consistent with this link is summarized below along with lines of research that more directly test our hypotheses.

We hypothesize that the change in management policy over the last decade is a direct result of pressure on senior executives from shareholders of unionized companies to improve the profitability of the firms they manage. This argument is a direct application of the earlier discussion of agency theory. Stockholders hire senior management to represent their interests and then fashion implicit and explicit contracts that align the interests of senior management to the wealth-maximizing objectives of stockholders. The explicit form these contracts take includes compensation schemes such as bonuses and stock options that link executive compensation to the performance of the firm. Moreover, when firm performance is unsatisfactory, top management may be replaced, either by the current board of directors or a new board that may have come to power after a successful takeover bid. Thus, the compensation, tenure, and power of senior management depend on pursuing policies that promote the interests of stockholders.

Prior research has demonstrated that unionized firms are often less profitable than comparable nonunion firms. These losses to stockholders associated with unionization and collective bargaining explain the union-avoidance policies pursued by management. If stockholders successfully align the interests of senior management with their own, senior management will pursue policies to minimize the impact of unions when the environment makes these policies feasible. Recent evidence showing that management has been successful in reducing the union presence in the firm where bargaining is decentralized is consistent with this interpretation (Kochan, McKersie, and Chalykoff, 1986).

Opposition to unions, however, has always characterized management philosophy in this country. Thus, why the recent changes? Our research suggests that these policies are, at least in part, the result of the relatively poor performance of unionized firms during the decade of the 1970s. As a result of this poor performance, top management was forced to pursue more aggressive labor relations policies in an attempt to improve firm performance and satisfy the demands of stockholders. This conclusion is based on a preliminary analysis of the performance of approximately 1,000 firms over an 11-year period (1971–1981). Based on the capital market measures discussed above, firm performance was measured each year as the annual shareholder return to holding the stock during the year (i.e., changes in stock prices plus dividends paid out). Assuming efficient capital markets and the appropriateness of the single factor market model, the best predictor of a company's stock return for some future period is the change in market returns times the firm's beta (see equation (2)). Since all firms in the same year experience the same market return, annual firm results can be modelled as a function of beta, with the conventional expectation of a positive sign. To eliminate the influence of contemporaneous events that might influence both beta and the returns, estimated betas were calculated using returns for the preceding year.

Apart from the firm's beta and changes in the market, firm returns during the year will also change in response to new, firm-specific information that affects the future profitability of the firm. The percent of the work force unionized (U) was included to determine if there were average differences in the effect of new information on firm values based on firm-level unionization. The unionization variable was constructed using unionization data included on the 1977 ERISA filings required of pension plan administrators. This task was an extremely computer- and labor-intensive activity, and while there are undoubtedly errors in the estimates, to our knowledge these data are the only statistics available on firm-level unionization for a large sample of identifiable firms. To summarize, the following regression equation was estimated for each year from 1971 through 1981:

(3) $RET_i = B_0 + B_1(BETA_i) + B_2(U_i) + e_i$

In this simple model the union coefficient cannot be interpreted as an unbiased estimate of the *causal* effect of unions on firm values during the 1970s. While the coefficient might reflect such a relationship, it may also reflect the correlation between the impact of new information that affects profitability (positive or negative news) and the level of unionization in the firm. For example, if highly unionized industries were the recipients of particularly unfavorable news during the year, then the coefficient on the union variable would be negative. This would not necessarily mean the new information was unfavorable because these firms were highly unionized.

Our argument does not depend on unions causing the decline in firm value. Our point is simply that if, after controlling for firm risk, the performance of unionized firms fell below the performance of less unionized firms, executives in unionized firms would be under pressure to improve performance. One means of achieving this objective would be to change the firm's labor relations policies.

The union coefficients from the 12 yearly regressions are reported in Table 3. These results show that in most years the value of more heavily unionized firms declined more than what would have been expected given firm risk. The average coefficient over

TABLE 3

Coefficient on Percent of Firm That Is Unionized
in Stockholder Returns Regressions, 1971–1981[a]

Year	Coefficient
1971	−0.097378°° (0.035744)
1972	−0.096496°° (0.031343)
1973	0.062490°° (0.31712)
1974	0.074756°° (0.029339)
1975	−0.053856 (0.052383)
1976	−0.003886 (0.036888)
1977	−0.064134°° (0.027518)
1978	−0.060636° (0.036284)
1979	−0.046231 (0.051166)
1980	−0.125535°° (0.044416)
1981	−0.031309 (0.032569)
Mean, 1971–1981	−0.040201°° (0.011484)

[a] Each of the regressions also includes the firm's beta estimated from weekly returns from the preceding year.
°° Significant at the 0.05 level. ° Significant at the 0.01 level.

the entire time period was −4.02 percentage points, statistically significant at conventional levels. The declines were especially significant, practically and statistically, in the early and late years in the time period. In 1971 and 1972 the return to investors in a firm 90 percent unionized was 8.7 percentage points lower than the return in a completely nonunion firm. In 1980 the −0.1255 coefficient implies a 11.3 percentage point difference in returns between a completely nonunion firm and a firm where 90 percent of the work force is organized. This large differential is particularly significant because negotiations in 1980–1981 are commonly considered the starting point for concession bargaining.

In summary, these results indicate that investors in unionized firms earned substantially lower risk-adjusted returns relative to the returns earned by investors in nonunion firms. Given this result and the responsibility senior management has to stockholders in our economic system, it is easy to understand why unionized firms were attempting to make major changes in their general business and labor relations strategies. Additional research is needed to establish the link between unionization and firm performance reported here and the involvement of senior management in labor relations and the institution of the new, more aggressive labor relations policies identified in recent case studies.

Summary and Conclusions

The shrinking unionized sector in the American labor force and the simultaneous financial problems in heavily organized industries focuses new attention on the link between unionism and firm performance in the private sector. While the traditional locus of industrial relations research has been the bargaining process or narrow bargaining outcomes, agency theory provides a conceptual basis for extending the competing interests normally associated with the employment relationship to the level of the firm. The employee-employer conflict at the level of the job is extended to the shareholder-labor conflict at the level of the firm. Recent developments in "strategic" industrial relations reflect this shift since the greater involvement of senior management in industrial relations decisions can bring the interests of shareholders and those of labor into greater competition.

Though a consideration of the effects of labor relations on firm performance has always been at least an implicit part of industrial relations, labor research has only recently begun to focus on this question. Drawing on the competing interests of labor and shareholders as the point of departure, we have argued that it is the effects of unions and collective bargaining on shareholders' interests that represents the best measure of any influence on firm performance. Operationally this means that union effects on firm performance must be based on capital market reactions (economic profits) to labor relations events rather than on accounting profits. It was noted, however, that a capital market measure of firm performance really reflects two elements. On the one hand, firm performance is normally associated with the magnitude of profits

TABLE 4

Studies with Capital Market Measures of Union Effects on Firm Performance

Reference	Union Event	Sample Size	Effect on Shareholder Equity	Time Period	Data Source
Ruback and Zimmerman (1984)	NLRB election and certification	253 firms	Total CARs: Union loss: −1.86% Union win: −3.84%	1962–1980	NLRB monthly election reports
Abowd (1987)	"Expected" wage settlement	2,250 firms	None	1975–1982	BNA Collective Bargaining Negot. and Contracts
	"Unexpected" wage settlement	2,250 firms	Dollar-for-dollar change		
Becker (1987)	Concession bargains	166 (including 96 "normal" settlements)	CARs: +8.0%	1982–1983	BNA concession bargaining data
Neumann (1980)	Strikes	340 strikes	CARs: −1.0%	1967–1975 (excluding 1972–1973)	*Wall Street Journal* reports
Becker and Olson (1986)	Strikes	699 strikes	CARs: −4.1%	1962–1982	BLS current work stoppages (prelim. reports)
Olson and Becker (1986)	Passage of NLRA	83 firms	CARs: −20.2%	1934–1937 (14 months)	Historical accounts of legis. history & unionization drives

and efficiency. The *share* of the profit stream actually going to shareholders, however, will also be reflected in capital market reactions. Therefore, where firm performance is measured as changes in the net present value of cash flows accruing to shareholders, it is useful to distinguish between the two sources of any effect. Unions could, for example, improve the productivity of the firm through the "voice" mechanism, while capturing an even larger share of profits, with the net result being a decline in shareholder equity.

The research described in this chapter has just begun to provide some understanding of these influences. Nevertheless it seems clear that unions generally, and certain collective bargaining outcomes in particular, have a *negative* impact on capital market measures of firm performance. Initial organization drives, unexpected wage gains, and strikes all result in a loss for shareholders. Similarly, the value of earlier union gains is illustrated in the *increase* in shareholder equity associated with recent concession bargaining. The work of both Abowd (1987) and Becker (1987) supports the interpretation that these union effects are reflected in the distribution rather than the magnitude of firm profits.

Finally we report preliminary results from a study of a sample of more than 1,000 firms indicating that in the decade of the 1970s and into the 1980s unionized firms experienced relatively lower shareholder risk as well as lower risk-adjusted shareholder returns. The relatively lower shareholder risk compared to nonunion firms is interpreted as an effort by shareholders to use the allocation of business risk as an incentive for employees to work in the best interests of the firm. The result is also consistent with a risk premium for unionized workers that could in part explain observed relative wage differences. While it is not clear to what extent unions contributed to the difference in risk-adjusted returns, the existence of such a difference may well have motivated both the expanded interest by senior management in industrial relations issues during the latter part of this period, and the subsequent efforts to diminish union influence in these firms.

In sum, the influence of labor relations on firm performance remains a largely unexplored area of research. While prior work has identified an apparent link between unions and profits, we know little about the source of wide interfirm variation in these effects. Future work should also attempt to merge the micro evidence of union effects (wages, fringes, turnover, productivity) with changes in firm-level financial characteristics. Scholars with more institutional interests could usefully include the influence of financial decision-makers in future case studies. Prior work has only established that these larger effects of unions exist. The challenge for future researchers is to explain them.

References

Abowd, John M. "Collective Bargaining and the Division of the Value of the Enterprise." National Bureau of Economic Research Working Paper No. 2137, January 1987.

Barbash, Jack. "The Elements of Industrial Relations." *British Journal of Industrial Relations* 2 (March 1964): pp. 66–78.

————. *The Practice of Unionism.* New York: Harper and Row, 1956.

Becker, Brian E. "Concession Bargaining: The Impact of Shareholders' Equity." *Industrial and Labor Relations Review* 40 (January 1987): pp. 268–79.

Becker, Brian E., and Craig A. Olson. "Union and Non-Union Differences in the Allocation of Firm Risk and Return." Mimeo, 1987.

————. "The Impact of Strikes on Shareholder Equity." *Industrial and Labor Relations Review* 39 (April 1986): pp. 425–38.

Brainard, William C., and James Tobin. "Pitfalls in Financial Model Building." *American Economic Review* 58 (May 1968): pp. 99–122.

Brown, James, and Orley Ashenfelter. "Testing the Efficiency of Employment Contracts." *Journal of Political Economy* 94 (Part II, June 1986): pp. S40–S87.

Brown, Stephen J., and Jerold B. Warner. "Using Daily Stock Returns: The Case of Event Studies." *Journal of Financial Economics* 14 (March 1985): pp. 3–31.

————. "Measuring Security Price Performance." *Journal of Financial Economics* 8 (September 1980): pp. 205–58.

Brown, Charles, and James L. Medoff. "Trade Unions in the Production Process." *Journal of Political Economy* 86 (June 1978): pp. 355–78.

Burgstahler, David, and Eric W. Noreen. "Detecting Contemporaneous Security Market Reactions to a Sequence of Related Events." *Journal of Accounting Research* 24 (Spring 1986): pp. 170–86.

Cappelli, Peter. "Plant Level Concession Bargaining." *Industrial and Labor Relations Review* 39 (October 1985): pp. 90–104.

————. "Union Improvements Under Concession Bargaining." *Proceedings of the 36th Annual Meeting, Industrial Relations Research Association.* Madison, Wis.: IRRA, 1984. Pp. 297–304.

————. "Concession Bargaining and the National Economy." *Proceedings of the 35th Annual Meeting, Industrial Relations Research Association.* Madison, Wis.: IRRA, 1983. Pp. 362–71.

Clark, Kim B. "Unionization and Firm Performance: The Impact on Profits, Growth, and Productivity." *American Economic Review* 74 (December 1984): pp. 893–919.

Collins, Daniel W., and Warren T. Dent. "A Comparison of Alternative Testing Methodologies Used in Capital Market Research." *Journal of Accounting Research* 22 (Spring 1984): pp. 48–84.

Connolly, Robert A., Barry T. Hirsch, and Mark Hirschey. "Union Rent Seeking, Intangible Capital and Market Value of the Firm." *Review of Economics and Statistics* 68 (November 1986): pp. 567–77.

Copeland, Thomas E., and J. Fred Weston. *Financial Theory and Corporate Policy.* 2d ed. Reading, Mass.: Addison-Wesley, 1983.

Eberts, Randall W., and Joe A. Stone. "On the Contract Curve: A Test of Alternative Models of Collective Bargaining." *Journal of Labor Economics* 4 (January 1986): pp. 66–81.

Fama, Eugene F. *Foundations of Finance.* New York: Basic Books, 1976.
Farber, Henry S. "The Analysis of Union Behavior." National Bureau of Economic Research Working Paper No. 1502, November 1984.
Fisher, Franklin M., and John J. McGowan. "On the Misuse of Accounting Rates of Return to Infer Monopoly Profits." *American Economic Review* 73 (March 1983): pp. 82–97.
Freeman, Richard B. "Unionism, Price-Cost Margins and the Return to Capital." National Bureau of Economic Research Working Paper No. 1164, July 1983.
Freeman, Richard B., and James L. Medoff. "The Impact of Collective Bargaining: Illusion or Reality?" In *U.S. Industrial Relations 1950–1980: A Critical Assessment,* eds. Jack Stieber, Robert B. McKersie, and D. Quinn Mills. Madison, Wis.: Industrial Relations Research Association, 1981. Pp. 47–98.
_____. *What Do Unions Do?* New York: Basic Books, 1984.
Greer, Charles R., Stanley A. Martin, and Ted A. Reusser. "The Effects of Strikes on Shareholder Returns." *Journal of Labor Research* 1 (Fall 1980): pp. 217–31.
Hirsch, Barry T., and John T. Addison. *The Economic Analysis of Unions: New Approaches and Evidence.* Boston: Allen and Unwin, 1986.
Hirschey, Mark, and Dean W. Wichern. "Accounting and Market Value Measures of Profitability: Consistency, Determinants and Uses." *Journal of Business and Economic Statistics* 2 (October 1984): pp. 375–83.
Ichniowski, Casey. "Industrial Relations and Economic Performance: Grievances and Productivity." National Bureau of Economic Research Working Paper No. 1367, June 1984a.
_____. "Ruling Out Productivity? Labor Contract Pages and Plant Performance." National Bureau of Economic Research Working Paper No. 1368, June 1984b.
Jensen, Michael J., and Herold L. Zimmerman, eds. "Symposium on Management Compensation and the Managerial Labor Market." *Journal of Accounting and Economics* 7, Nos. 1–3 (April 1985).
Karier, Thomas. "Unions and Monopoly Profits." *Review of Economics and Statistics* 67 (February 1985): pp. 34–42.
Kochan, Thomas A. *Collective Bargaining and Industrial Relations.* Homewood, Ill.: Richard D. Irwin, 1980.
Kochan, Thomas A., Robert B. McKersie, and Peter Cappelli. "Strategic Choice and Industrial Relations Theory." *Industrial Relations* 23 (Winter 1984): pp. 16–39.
Kochan, Thomas A., Robert B. McKersie, and John Chalykoff. "The Effects of Corporate Strategy and Workplace Innovations on Union Representation." *Industrial and Labor Relations Review* 39 (July 1986): pp. 487–501.
Kuhn, Peter. "Wages, Effort, and Incentive Compatibility in Life-Cycle Employment Contracts." *Journal of Labor Economics* 4 (January 1984): pp. 28–49.
Lazear, Edward P. "Agency, Earnings Profiles, Productivity and Hours Restrictions." *American Economic Review* 71 (September 1981): pp. 606–20.
Lazear, Edward P., and Robert L. Moore. "Incentives, Productivity and Labor Contracts." *Quarterly Journal of Economics* 99 (May 1984): pp. 275–96.
Lewis, H. Gregg. *Union Relative Wage Effects: A Survey.* Chicago: University of Chicago Press, 1986.
Li, Elizabeth H. "Compensating Differentials for Cyclical and Noncyclical Unemployment: The Interaction Between Investors' and Employees' Risk Aversion." *Journal of Labor Economics* 4 (April 1986): pp. 277–300.
Liebowitz, S. J. "What Do Price-Cost Margins Measure?" *Journal of Law and Economics* 25 (October 1982): pp. 231–46.
Lindenberg, Eric B., and Stephan A. Ross. "Tobin's q Ratio and Industrial Organization." *Journal of Business* 54 (January 1981): pp. 1–32.
Lipset, Seymour M., Martin A. Trow, and James S. Coleman. *Union Democracy: The Internal Politics of the International Typographical Union.* Glencoe, Ill.: Free Press, 1956.
Macurdy, Thomas E., and John H. Pencavel. "Testing Between Competing Models of Wage and Employment Determination in Unionized Markets." *Journal of Political Economy* 94 (Part 2, June 1986): pp. S3–S39.

Medoff, James L. "Layoffs and Alternatives Under Trade Unions in U.S. Manufacturing." *American Economic Review* 69 (June 1979): pp. 380–95.

Neumann, George R. "The Predictability of Strikes: Evidence from the Stock Market." *Industrial and Labor Relations Review* 33 (July 1980): pp. 525–35.

Neumann, George R., and Melvin W. Reder. "Output and Strike Activity in U.S. Manufacturing: How Large Are the Losses?" *Industrial and Labor Relations Review* 37 (January 1984): pp. 197–211.

Olson, Craig A., and Brian E. Becker. "Does the NLRA Matter? Evidence from the 1930s." Unpublished manuscript, November 1986.

Oswald, Rudolph A. "Review Symposium: *The Share Economy: Conquering Stagflation* by Martin L. Weitzman." *Industrial and Labor Relations Review* 39 (January 1986): pp. 287–89.

Ruback, Richard S., and Martin B. Zimmerman. "Unionization and Profitability: Evidence from the Capital Market." *Journal of Political Economy* 92 (December 1984): pp. 1134–57.

Salinger, Michael A. "Tobin's *q*, Unionization, and the Concentration-Profit Relationship." *Rand Journal of Economics* 15 (Summer 1984): pp. 159–70.

Schipper, Katherine, and Rex Thompson. "The Impact of Merger-Related Regulations on the Shareholder of Acquiring Firms." *Journal of Accounting Research* 21 (Spring 1983): pp. 184–221.

Schwert, C. William. "Using Financial Data to Measure Effects of Regulation." *Journal of Law and Economics* 24 (April 1981): pp. 121–58.

Voos, Paula B., and Lawrence R. Mishel. "The Union Impact on Profits: Evidence from Industry Price-Cost Margin Data." *Journal of Labor Economics* 4 (January 1986): pp. 105–33.

Chapter 3

Compensation and Firm Performance

By Ronald G. Ehrenberg and George T. Milkovich[*]
Cornell University

The relationship between the compensation policies a firm pursues and the firm's economic performance is a central issue in industrial relations. Yet, while a variety of theories exist about the effects of various compensation policies, surprisingly little evidence exists on the extent to which compensation policies vary across firms and, more importantly, on the effects of pursuing alternative compensation strategies.[1] In this chapter we attempt to summarize the available empirical evidence and to lay out an agenda for future research.

The study of employee compensation has a long history in the literatures of labor economics and personnel. Wages are at the core of employment relationships; consequently, their determination is a central issue of interest in both fields. At the risk of oversimplifying to draw a contrast, economists have tended to focus on wage differentials and their correlates. Much of the work in the 1940s and 1950s examined employers' wage policies and their relationship to industry, union, regional, and occupational characteristics.[2] During the 1960s and 1970s the associations between human capital characteristics, such as age, experience, education, gender, and the like, and wage differentials were studied. Only recently has economists' focus shifted to the study of why alternative compensation policies might arise and their effects on firm performance.

---

[*] We are grateful to numerous colleagues at Cornell and to the editors for their comments on earlier drafts.

[1] Compensation-related theories come from a variety of sources; Thomas Mahoney (1979) attempts to integrate the perspectives of compensation from the economics, psychology, sociology, and personnel literatures.

[2] See Segal (1986), for example, for a discussion of the postinstitutionalist's labor market models of the 1940s and 1950s.

In contrast, the study of personnel has traditionally dealt with the techniques involved in administration of employee compensation. Much of this work focuses on comparisons of the properties of various techniques and their effects on employee work attitudes and behaviors.[3] Compensation research in the personnel literature draws heavily upon economic and psychological theories. Studies report the relationships of pay with employees' satisfaction as well as their decisions to apply, join, and remain with a firm. Further, relying heavily on motivation theories, personnel research also examines compensation's role as a reward or incentive to influence employee performance. More recently, interest has expanded to examine the effects that strategic choices in compensation policies and practices may have on firms' economic performance as well as employees' behavior and attitudes.

The effect of differences in compensation policies and practices on the firm's "bottom line" is perhaps the most important measure of their economic impact. While the literature in both fields speculates about the effects of various compensation policies and practices on firm performance, little research has been directed to assess this relationship. One reason for the lack of such research is that the data required, detailed individual compensation and performance data gathered across firms, are difficult to collect. Another reason is that a relationship between any personnel system, be it compensation, staffing, or training, and a firm's economic performance is indirect. At best, personnel policies and practices operate directly upon other more immediate variables such as employee behavior and perhaps on local plant or subunit performance. These, in turn, affect overall economic performance.

Granted, some measures employed may be considered proxies for a firm's performance. Size, measured by number of employees, assets, or sales revenues, is an example. But typically these measures are considered in terms of their effects on a firm's compensation decisions, such as its wage level and the shape of its employees' experience-earning profiles, rather than focusing on how compensation policies and changes in them affect a firm's financial performance and its value to shareholders.[4] As we shall discuss in the next section, most of the work on the direct effects of

---

[3] See, for example, Milkovich and Newman (1987) or Lawler (1971).

[4] See, for example, Brown and Medoff (1985) or Dunn (1984). We discuss the various ways firm performance may be measured below.

compensation policies has been limited to high-level executive compensation. Beyond executive pay, the plain fact is that we know very little about whether different employee compensation policies and practices affect firm performance. Speculation is rife, research rare.

At the onset, it is important to stress that compensation policies may vary on several dimensions. First, the "level" of compensation varies. From a policy perspective, the level refers to the average compensation paid by a firm relative to that paid by its competitors. Evidence suggests that firms pursue different policies; some lead, others match, and still others pay less than their competitors. Why the level of compensation should vary across firms has been the subject of considerable research by economists.[5] However, while the consequences of a firm's relative compensation level on its ability to attract, motivate, and retain a stable work force have received empirical attention, the consequences for the firm's financial performance have not been studied.[6]

Second, it is well known that the compensation structure varies across firms (Milkovich and Newman, 1987; Freeman, 1982). Structures refer to the distribution of rates or internal pay hierarchies. In some firms, the highest paid work receives over 100 times the compensation of the lowest paid and the differentials in other firms may be less than 10 times. Of importance to us are the implications of these different structures for employees' work behaviors and firm performance.[7]

A third dimension of a firm's compensation strategy pertains to the forms or the mix of various elements of total compensation. Total compensation may include base pay, a variety of incentive schemes, cost-of-living adjustments (COLAs), various forms of

---

[5] Explanations for the existence of above market-clearing wages fall under the rubric of *efficiency wage theories*; recent summaries of the literature include Katz (1986), Stiglitz (1984), and Yellen (1984). Explanations often revolve around high wage policies being used to discourage shirking in situations where monitoring costs are high. This provides one explanation of the well-known fact that wages tend to increase with establishment and firm size; see Brown and Medoff (1985).

[6] For example, recent evidence on the relationship between quit probabilities and firms' compensation levels is presented in Meitzen (1986). Earlier studies include Pencavel (1970) and Viscusi (1980). Evidence that high wages are associated with low absentee rates is presented in Allen (1984).

[7] Economists have also developed a variety of theories to explain why earnings should increase with seniority, including those based on investments in training (Becker, 1985) and those based on providing incentives (e.g., Lazear, 1979, 1981; Lazear and Rosen, 1981; Rosen, 1986).

stock options, and an increasing array of benefits. Firms differ in terms of the number of pay forms offered, the degree to which employees are offered a choice among different forms, the relative importance of each form (base wage/total compensation ratio or incentive/base wage ratio), and the proportion of the work force eligible for each form beyond the legal requirements (e.g., in some firms all employees receive profit-sharing, in others only a handful of executives are covered). Various types of employee benefits, such as pensions, may have important incentive effects that can influence employee behavior and firm performance.[8]

Fourth, policies for granting compensation increases vary among firms and, even within a firm, among occupational groups. Some firms grant increases across the board, based strictly on time worked, while others base increases on incentive mechanisms such as profit-sharing, team awards, gainsharing, or pay for individual performance. Such performance-based schemes vary widely. Some emphasize the short term (merit pay increases and bonus awards to key performers), others the long term (stock options). Some firms use subjective measure of performance (merit ratings, project completion); others use quantitative measures (units produced, return on equity, stock value). The units of analysis employed in performance measurement also vary (e.g., individual employee, work teams or cells, and unit/organization-wide). Some extend eligibility to cover all employees; others limit participation depending on the incentive plan involved. Once again, the effects of such differences on the performance of the firm are not well investigated.[9]

Finally, the *process* by which compensation is administered also differs. Administrative processes may vary on several dimensions. Among these are the extent to which pay information (rates, ranges, rationales, market data) is disclosed to employees, the nature of employee participation in the determination and administration of pay, the existence of dispute-resolution procedures, and the degree to which policy design and implementation is decentralized. Some firms have formalized job evaluation systems that aid in

---

[8] For example, Winkler (1980) shows that generous sick-leave policies may encourage absenteeism. We do not discuss the effects of another important employee benefit, pensions, in our chapter since they are the subject of Chapter 6, by Steven Allen and Robert Clark, in this volume.

[9] Theoretical models of payment by group or individual output also exist; a good survey of this literature is Lazear (1986).

determining internal pay hierarchies, while other firms allow for considerable wage flexibility across positions. Some firms operate in a unionized environment; others do not. Similarly, some allow for employee participation and disclosure in compensation decisions, while others do not. As several chapters in this volume address these latter two differences, our treatment of them will be brief.[10]

These five basic dimensions of compensation policy—the level, reflecting the competitiveness of total compensation; the structure, reflecting the internal pay hierarchies; the mix of different compensation forms; the nature of pay increases; and the process employed to administer compensation—can serve as the framework for examining the relationship between compensation and firm performance. But disentangling the effects of each of these dimensions will be a difficult and perhaps unfeasible task. It is possible that a firm's economic performance is affected by its compensation strategy in toto. If this is the case, then we need to examine a firm's behavior on these policy dimensions simultaneously rather than treating each as a discrete decision. Empirically, a firm's compensation strategy needs to be measured as a *set* of interrelated dimensions.

Once the compensation policy is focused on, the next issue is how to measure firm performance. In general, one's concern should be with a measure of the overall economic well-being of the organization. So, as we shall see below, many studies, primarily those relating to *executive* compensation, focus on the total return (dividends + capital gains) on shareholders' equity. Others focus on accounting measures, such as reported profits. Still others argue that what is relevant is how stock market or accounting measures are doing after controlling for general and industry-specific economic conditions; these studies often use relative (to other firms) industry-performance measures.[11]

As noted earlier, studies of nonexecutive employee compensation have not examined how compensation policies or practices (or changes in them) affect the overall economic well-being of an organization. The unstated premise underlying these studies is that compensation systems can directly affect variables such as

---

[10] Chapter 2, on labor relations, by Brian Becker and Craig Olson, and Walter Gershenfeld's Chapter 4 on employee participation.

[11] A more complete discussion of the measurements of firm performance is found in Chapter 2 of this volume.

employee productivity, absenteeism, turnover, and job satisfaction. The issue of the indirect effects of compensation policies and practices on more general accounting or market-return measures has been left unaddressed. It is possible that direct effects can be observed only for executive jobs where decisions may directly affect economic measures, while decisions by nonexecutive employees have at best very distant relationships to a firm's performance.

It is important to stress that a causal relationship between compensation policy and firm performance cannot be inferred directly from simple correlations of the two variables. So, for example, a positive correlation between wage levels and firm profitability might indicate that a high-wage policy causes high profits *or* that high profits provide a surplus which workers can share in the form of high wages. While some of the studies we discuss below provide correlations between firm performance and compensation policies, very few actually provide convincing evidence that compensation policy *affects* firm performance.

We begin the next section with a discussion of the evidence on the relationship between the compensation of high-level executives and firm performance. There is a substantial body of research findings here that draw heavily on both the finance and economics literature. In the following section we discuss the evidence on employee compensation and firm performance; in the main the research findings here draw heavily from the human resource and personnel literatures, although the economics literature also has something to add. The concluding section provides a summary of what we have learned from these literatures and a discussion of research issues that still need to be addressed.

Executive Compensation

Given the widely (but as we will see below, not always correctly) perceived separation between the ownership and management of corporations, concern has been expressed that corporate executives may pursue objectives such as sales maximization, growth maximization, or market-share maximization that are not necessarily in the best interests of shareholders who are concerned with short-run (accounting profits) and long-run (total stock market return) measures of the economic profitability of the corporation. Theoretical models that seek optimal ways to resolve this *principal-agent* problem—that is, ways to provide incentives for executives to take actions that are in the best interests of shareholders—always come to the conclusion that executive compensation somehow should be structured to provide such incentives.[12]

Early empirical studies of executive compensation were cross-section in nature and focused on whether, across firms, executive compensation was more highly correlated with sales or accounting profits. In the main the correlations with sales were highest suggesting, at first glance, that corporate executives' compensation was not structured in such a way to maximize stockholders' well-being.[13] However, these correlations may reflect only that large firms employ more able executives and thus must pay them more. These correlations, then, tell us little about the incentives facing any given executive at a point in time.

More recently, a number of studies have used longitudinal data and examined whether changes in top-level executives' compensation tend to be correlated with changes in the economic performance of firms.[14] The definition of economic performance varies across studies: some use accounting measures like reported profits, while others use measures of the total return on a firm's securities; some use absolute performance measures, while others use performance measures relative to other firms in the same industry (most theoretical models suggest that executive performance should be measured net of industry effects). The definition of compensation also varies: some use salaries and bonuses, while others try to include the values of stock options exercised and/or deferred payments.

Virtually all of these studies find, however, that changes in executive compensation are highly positively correlated with the economic performance measures. That is, corporate executives' compensation does seem to be at least implicitly structured in a way to provide them with incentives to maximize the economic performance of their firms. Several studies also show that relatively poor economic performance in one year is associated with a higher

---

[12] See Lazear (1986) for a survey.

[13] See Ciscel and Carroll (1980) for a survey of this literature.

[14] See, for example, Coughlin and Schmidt (1985), Kostiuk (1986), and Murphy (1985a, 1985b, 1986a, 1986b), who focus on absolute measures of performance, and Antle and Smith (1986), who focus on performance measures relative to competitors.

probability of executive turnover in later years; this further suggests that incentives that operate in the correct direction exist.[15]

Of course, to say that a *correlation* exists between executives' compensation changes and their firms' economic performance is in itself not evidence that tying their compensation to performance will lead to improved economic performance. One possibility is that corporations initially don't know what the true productivity of their executives is. However, to the extent that executives' productivity can be imperfectly *signalled* by corporate performance, relating their compensation to corporate performance is a way of "paying them what they're worth." If this is occurring, the compensation-performance nexus would reflect learning about executives' "true ability" over time, not necessarily any incentive arrangement to stimulate economic performance.[16] Furthermore, even if appropriate incentives *do* exist, it doesn't necessarily follow that they will have their intended effect.

Disentangling whether the observed correlation is due to "incentives" or "learning" is not an easy task. Murphy (1986b), in attempting to do this, used information on the state of the executives' careers (presumably learning occurs primarily at early stages) and the variability of executives' compensation over their life cycles (if learning is driving the process, an executive's variability in earnings should decline over time) and concluded that while both "incentives" and "learning" may exist, there was some evidence that "learning" effects were most important. Other

---

[15] See Benson (1985) and Coughlin and Schmidt (1985). Benson also studied the income of executives in 29 conglomerates during the 1970-1975 period and found that the annual gains (or losses) they incurred due to changes in the value of their stock holdings in their companies far exceeded their annual changes in salaries. This further ties their "fortunes" to their companies' fortunes.

Further confirmation that ownership matters comes from Lewellen, Loderer, and Rosenfeld (1985) and from Morck, Shleifer, and Vishny (1986). The former examined the abnormal stock market returns experienced by "bidder firms" in mergers from the "bid" to the "approval" date. They found these returns to be positively related to the percentage of the "bidder firm" stock owned by senior management. Thus, executives' ownership of their firms' securities helped to align the interests of stockholders and managers, at least in this case. The latter found that corporate performance (in terms of both accounting profits and stock market performance) was highest when management owns between 5 and 20 percent of the corporation's stock. They hypothesize that when small amounts are owned, managers have less incentive to pursue a profit-maximizing strategy, while when larger amounts are owned, managers may feel more secure and not work as hard.

[16] For examples of such "learning" models, see S. Freeman (1977), Harris and Holmstrom (1982), and MacDonald (1982).

studies, however, showed that the correlation of measures of performance and compensation growth were highest for better performing firms (Masson, 1971), which is at least suggestive that better incentives in executive compensation do lead to better corporate performance.

Another strand of research, which draws heavily on the finance literature, focuses on particular provisions of executive compensation agreements and examines whether adoption of such provisions is associated with abnormally high stock market returns for shareholders. For example, studies of the adoption of executive stock option plans and executive incentive compensation agreements based on short-run or long-run accounting profits measures have all shown that the announcement of the plans leads to increases in shareholder wealth.[17] At least one study (Larcker, 1983) has also found that corporate capital investments tend to increase after the adoption of long-run executive compensation (or performance plan) agreements.

At least three explanations can be given for these findings. The first is that these provisions *do* have favorable *incentive* effects and that the increases in shareholder wealth reflect anticipated increases in profits that will occur due to the adoption of the provisions.

The second is that these provisions are proposed by management and adopted by boards of directors only when management believes management will benefit from the provisions. As such, their adoption *signals* to the market that management expects good times are ahead; this would have a positive effect on shareholder wealth (since it conveys new positive information) even if no incentive effects were involved.

Finally, the provisions may be adopted for *tax* reasons. To the extent that capital gains historically have been taxed at lower rates than earned income (at least up until 1987), adoption of stock option plans may have allowed corporations to provide management with increased (or equal to preadoption) after-tax compensation levels at *lower* total costs to the corporation. If this occurred, shareholder wealth would, of course, increase.

[17] See Bhagat, Brickley, and Lease (1985), Brickley, Bhagat, and Lease (1985), and Tehranian and Waegelein (1985).

As above, disentangling which subset of these explanations is "correct" is a difficult task. A study by Bhagat, Brickley, and Lease (1985) provides some evidence in favor of the incentive hypothesis. Specifically, they found that the adoption of forms of stock-option plans that do not have tax advantages led to increases in shareholder wealth, and that boards of directors' statements often claimed that anticipated incentive effects would result from stock-option plans for executives. The former two forms of evidence, however, do not enable one to strongly discriminate between the *incentive* and *signalling* hypotheses.

To take another example, a second set of studies has analyzed "golden parachute" agreements—agreements that provide for (often substantial) compensation for a corporate executive if a change in ownership of voting stock and/or a shift in the majority of the board of directors of a corporation occurs that leads to the termination of the executive's employment. Two hypotheses have been put forth for the existence of these agreements. On the one hand, these arrangements may increase the costs of takeover bids and reduce their probability of occurring. This would make the executive's position more secure but would not necessarily be in the best interests of shareholders; in a sense it is argued that these agreements *transfer wealth* from shareholders to management.

On the other hand, one might argue that these plans help to *align the incentives* of executives and shareholders. By protecting management from harm, they encourage executives to negotiate takeovers that increase the value of shareholders' equity. This protection is particularly important in situations in which management compensation has been structured so that compensation increases with tenure, with part of this increase being a deferred reward for prior performance. Such deferred compensation schemes prove to be optimal in a theoretical sense in situations in which estimates of an executive's performance are very "noisy" but improve with his tenure.[18]

In fact, the available empirical evidence suggests that on balance the second hypothesis is the correct one (Lambert and Larcker, 1985); the adoption of "golden parachute" agreements appears to be associated empirically with favorable security market response (i.e., positive excess returns in the short-run). While such evidence cannot

---

[18] See Eaton and Rosen (1983) for one theoretical model.

disentangle the *incentive alignment* hypotheses from the hypotheses that such adoptions simply *signal* situations in which takeover bids, and hence excess returns, are likely, it is interesting that another study (Knober, 1986) found that executives' tenure-earning profiles *were* steeper in firms that had golden parachute agreements than they were in firms that did not, ceteris paribus. That is, in situations where deferred compensation appeared to be more important, golden parachutes were more likely to exist.

One must caution, however, that all of the studies that find an association between the adoption of particular provisions of executive compensation agreements and abnormally high stock market returns are drawing conclusions about the *effectiveness* of executive incentive compensation agreements from short-run changes in stock market prices. Many of these provisions are designed to encourage executives to take the long-run interests of the firm into account when decisions are made. Yet surprisingly, save for Larcker's (1983) study, it appears that these studies do not address whether the adoption of these provisions actually alters executives' decisions in any systematic way or leads to higher long-run accounting profits.

In addition to the research described above on the relationship between executive compensation and firm performance in the for-profit sector of the economy, a number of studies have examined the relationship between executive compensation and "performance" in the public and nonprofit sectors. Of course, in the absence of a profit-maximizing objective, performance is much harder to define in these sectors. Essentially, each of these studies defined what it considered to be a reasonable measure of performance and then sought to ascertain if executive compensation and/or turnover was related to this performance measure, ceteris paribus. That is, these studies asked if the compensation of executives in the public and nonprofit sectors was structured in such a way to encourage executives to try to improve the performance measure.

For example, the Ehrenberg and Goldberg (1977) study of the compensation of chief business agents of local building trades unions, who are salaried officers responsible (among other things) for negotiating contracts, found that these union leaders' salaries tended to be positively related to the relative wage advantages their members had over members of the same union in other cities and over other building trades union members in the same city. Thus, incentives appear to have existed for the business agents to try to maximize their members' wage increases.

A second study by Goldstein and Ehrenberg (1976) focused on appointed municipal government officials—specifically, city managers and police and fire department chiefs. Performance in this study was defined in terms of how well the officials were doing relative to what might be expected given the socioeconomic characteristics of the city—or, more precisely, by residuals from estimated "output equations." Positive performance for the three officials was assumed to be, respectively, lower than predicted property tax rates but higher than predicted expenditure levels (which could occur simultaneously only if the city manager was good at attracting aid from higher levels of government), lower than predicted crime rates, and better than predicted fire insurance ratings. For all three types of executives, salaries were positively correlated across areas, ceteris paribus, with the performance measures, again suggesting that some incentives for the officials to "perform" existed.

A third study of this type (Ehrenberg, Chaykowski, and Ehrenberg, 1988) focused on public school district superintendents and defined school district performance using a residual approach as above. Districts that were performing well were assumed to be those in which student test scores exceeded their predicted values, given the characteristics of the district, and where tax rates were lower than predicted, again given school district characteristics. In this longitudinal study both salary changes and the probability of moving to a better job were seen to be positively related to the performance measures. However, the magnitude of these relationships was sufficiently small that the authors concluded that no meaningful incentive to perform (as defined) existed.

While these three studies all tried to infer whether the implicit structure of executive compensation in these public- and nonprofit-sector positions provided incentives for the executives to pursue specified performance objectives, none actually examined whether the existence of these incentives did lead to improved performance. One recent study, however, was able to observe several measures of performance of local Social Security Administration offices both before and after the adoption of formal merit-pay plans that partially tied managerial salary increases to these performance measures.[19] Using a quasi-experimental design and statistical procedures to eliminate trends and cycles in the performance measures, the study found that the adoption of the merit-pay plans had no short-run effects on performance. The authors noted, however, that the system was still in its early stages and that effects might possibly be observed after it became more institutionalized and better understood.

In concluding this section, it is interesting to note that there appear to be no studies in either the private-for-profit, nonprofit, or public sectors on how the *level* of executive compensation affects economic performance. Similarly, there are no studies of how the rewards for seniority, probabilities of promotion, or salary structure across executive positions within a firm affect economic performance. That is, we do not know whether paying high salaries to attract and retain high quality executives "pays," whether offering executives rewards for seniority "pays," whether offering within-firm promotional opportunities (e.g., from vice president to president or from president to chief executive officer) "pays," and whether the compensation levels across executives within a firm are structured in such a way to encourage improved firm performance.[20]

Employee Compensation

The purpose of this section is to examine the literature pertaining to a firm's compensation policies for employees not covered under executive pay systems and the relationship of these policies to the performance of firms.

Evidence of variations in the compensation policies and practices of firms can be found in several sources. Typically the data are incomplete, collected for other purposes, or of limited use for determining any direct effects of compensation on firm

---

[19] Pearce, Stevenson, and Perry (1985). Performance measures used here include the average length of time for claims to be approved or denied, the percentage of claims approved with accurate documentation, and the percentage of postentitlement actions that took over 30 days.

[20] In fact, little attention has been given to how the relative compensation levels of top executives within a firm are set and whether the structure across executives provides proper incentives. Lazear and Rosen (1981) do present theoretical arguments as to why it may be optimal to have compensation differences across "ranks" that far exceed the relative productivity differences across the positions, but no empirical work on interfirm variations in executive salary structures has been undertaken.

performance. Sufficient signs of differences in firm's policies do exist and they are considered here in terms of the basic dimensions discussed earlier.

That differences exist in pay levels and the competitive positions among firms is well established in both the economics and personnel literatures. Reports issued by private consulting firms that survey employer practices detail differences in pay levels by characteristics of the firm (industry, revenues, work force size), job function, description, job evaluation points, and number of incumbents), and geography, and *Area Wages Surveys* conducted by the Bureau of Labor Statistics also show wide variations in wages with narrowly defined job classifications in a metropolitan area.[21]

A study by Foster (1985), who had access to a private consulting firm's survey data from aerospace companies, reported that after controlling for firm size (number of employees and revenues), substantial variations existed in the average salaries paid among these firms (e.g., the two highest paying firms paid more than 16 percent above the market average, while the average paid by the lowest two was more than 11 percent below the market average). These firms also exhibited different competitive positions for different functional specialities. For example, in one, the average pay for nine of 13 functions exceeded the market average for each function, while in another the average pay exceeded the market average in only five of the 13 functions.

These data do not permit one to distinguish whether these differences across functions reflect differential contributions of the functions to the firm's objectives or to other factors such as differences in employee age or experience distributions across functions. Whether compensation level policies tend to be occupation-specific or company-wide is unclear. It is possible that firms competing within an industry may have one policy for occupations critical to the firm's objectives and another for those less critical. Recent evidence found by Leonard (1987) tentatively agrees with the data reported above that occupation-specific as well as company-wide policies exist.

---

[21] For a brief overview of the types of data collected by the leading private compensation consulting firm, see Milkovich and Newman (1987). See any area wage survey—for example, U.S. Bureau of Labor Statistics (1985)—for a discussion of the publicly collected data.

Anecdotal accounts of different compensation policies are also available. A study of the personnel policies of large nonunion firms reports a variety of competitive policy statements about relative compensation-level positions.[22] Some firms with centralized personnel systems reportedly adhere to corporate-wide compensation policies for all business units; others report that each of their business units adopts its own competitive posture in its own market. The former seems to be most common in firms with integrated lines of business; the latter is more common in conglomerates with multiple and unrelated product lines.

The efficiency wage literature in economics suggests various reasons why some employers might set higher wages than their competitors for employees of equal quality.[23] Examples include differences in turnover costs, differences in the need for close supervision (so-called "worker shirking"), and differences in employee commitment. Evidence of different pay levels within a product market or industry is also widely available in studies of intraindustry wage differentials. Dunn's (1984) study of the effects of firm size on wage levels in the plastics industry, Groshen's (1985) study of employer effects on wage dispersion in plastics, industrial chemical, and woolen yarn industries, and Leonard's (1987) study of wages in California's high-technology sector are recent examples.

Generally these studies confirm earlier findings. For example, it is well known that differences in intraindustry wage rates are correlated with firm size. Numerous explanations are commonly advanced to explain this relationship, including (1) larger firms use more advanced technologies and require greater employee skills and discipline, (2) compensating differentials are required to offset the greater disutility of working in larger firms, (3) labor unions in larger firms have been able to appropriate some of the firm's higher profits, and (4) large firms pay higher wages to reduce employee shirking and thus supervision costs.[24] Note that these explanations imply that a firm's economic performance and the conditions it faces permit or provide economic incentives for it to adopt a particular pay posture. Unless one *tautologically* accepts these explanations as valid, however, they do *not* provide any evidence

---

[22] See Foulkes (1980) for a survey of the personnel practices of large nonunion firms.

[23] See Katz (1986) and Stiglitz (1984).

[24] See, for example, Brown and Medoff (1985) and Oi (1983).

that a firm's pay level, as part of its overall compensation strategy, actually has had any effect on its economic performance.

Some survey evidence, though limited in coverage, compares the compensation policies of high-tech firms with "traditional" firms.[25] In one study 40 percent of both the high-tech firms and the traditional firms reported following policies in which their pay levels matched those of their competition. About 20 percent in each group reported they led their competitors and the rest followed ("less than market average"). Obviously caution needs to be exercised in interpreting these data: they are based on reports of compensation managers and the mechanics used to translate a policy into practice often vary. For example, two-thirds of the firms reported they matched their range midpoints with the median rate paid in the market. However, the specific firms included in such calculation often vary, the surveys used differ, and differences in average rate paid by firms may be due to demographic differences in each firm's work force (e.g., seniority) rather than any intended competitive policy differences.

Considered together, the consultant survey information, the anecdotal accounts, the economic research, and the personnel surveys support the contention that employers' characteristics are related to the dispersion in pay level and to a firm's relative compensation position among its competitors. But we are interested in evidence on the effects of differences in relative compensation policy on firms' financial performance or shareholder value. And here the research literature is lean.

Our search of the literature yielded very few studies of the effects of different pay levels on performance measures such as compensation-to-revenue ratios, labor-cost-to-total-cost ratios, or shareholder value. One, Summers's forthcoming case study of what happened to the Ford Motor Company when Henry Ford introduced the $5/day wage in the early 20th century, found that while absenteeism, voluntary turnover, and discharges declined after the wage increase and productivity increased, these changes probably were not sufficiently large in themselves to allow one to conclude that the new policy "paid for itself." A second, Abowd's (1987) study of recent union wage settlements, found that

---

[25] See, for example, Balkin and Gomez-Mejia (1986). High-tech firms were defined as those with R&D budgets reported to be 5 percent or more of sales. A total of 105 firms were in their sample; 33 were classified as high-tech, 72 as traditional.

unexpectedly high union wage settlements were reflected virtually dollar-for-dollar in changes in shareholder value (see Becker and Olson's Chapter 2, in this volume, for more details). Thus, higher than expected wage settlements do not appear to improve firm performance. Finally, interindustry studies of the determinants of wage levels that specify that high profits cause high wages, rather than vice versa, typically do find that industry profit levels are an important explanatory variable in wage equations.[26]

A few studies do examine the effects of pay level on employee and employer recruiting and turnover behaviors. For example, some evidence suggests that establishing a relatively high pay level increases the applicant queue, permitting firms to select higher quality, and thus potentially more productive, employees. Evidence on the wage/recruitment expenditure relationship seems contradictory. One study reports that high pay levels and high recruiting costs are substitutes, while another suggests they are complements—that employers who offer relatively higher wages also exhibit relatively greater recruiting expenses (Barron, Bishop, and Dunkelberg, 1985). Thus, employers that search are more likely to pay more. But the evidence here is drawn from limited low-level occupational groups and only limited industry and firm characteristics are considered. Obviously more work is needed. Perhaps under certain conditions—critical jobs or long-term unfilled vacancies—pay levels and recruiting costs are complements, while under others they are used as substitutes.

Some evidence of the effects of pay level on job seekers' and employees' choice behavior is also available. For example, studies of the correlations between wage levels and turnover and absenteeism have already been cited. Wage levels also appear to be an important factor when job seekers have a wide range of pay levels from which to choose and higher paid workers, ceteris paribus, report they put more effort into their jobs and are more satisfied.[27] Research also exists that shows that higher military pay levels increase the flow of volunteers to the armed forces.[28]

---

[26] See, for example, Dickens and Katz (1986). As noted in the introduction, such a correlation between wages and profits provides little evidence that high wages cause high profits.

[27] See Milkovich and Newman (1987).

[28] See, for example, Brown (1985).

Another dimension of a firm's compensation strategy is its internal wage hierarchy. Wage hierarchies differ across firms in different industries that employ differing technologies. For example, breweries have relatively flat hierarchies compared to steel or automotive firms. But within an industry or firm, managers have considerable latitude in the design of wage structures. Relatively flat structures (fewer grades and wider pay ranges) tend to obscure differences in task and/or skill requirements and offer managers flexibility in deploying the work force without necessarily requiring pay changes. Greater hierarchical arrangements emphasize greater specification of work rules and skill requirements and tend to require pay adjustments more often.

Wage structures possess several characteristics, including the number of levels, the differentials between levels, and the distribution of employees among the levels. There is a tendency, especially in larger organizations, for the number of employees being paid higher wages to be less than the number paid lower wages. Several attempts to examine this feature have been reported. For example, Shaeffer (1976) used the Lorenz curve as an analog and compared the distribution of annualized salaries by cumulative percent of the work force across firms. Others analyzed the nature of the differentials between levels in the hierarchy. Simon (1957) found the functional form of differentials between hierarchical levels to be a constant proportion. The Jacques study (1961), based on the analysis of the discretionary content of work and norms ascribed to employees, reports pay ratios of 1.33 between adjacent managerial levels.

Another feature of pay hierarchies is that wages often tend to be associated with jobs rather than individual employees. Thus deploying workers to new jobs often necessitates wage changes. The alternative system of wages being tied to workers, regardless of the job performed, underlies *knowledge-based pay schemes* and *maturity curve arrangements*.[29] To date, no attempts to systemati-

---

[29] Under knowledge-based pay plans, employees' salaries increase as additional training is acquired, whether or not these skills are used on the present job. Managers may then assign workers to any task, as long as the employees possess the required skills for that task and are paid at rates for the highest skills they possess regardless of the task they actually perform. Maturity curves pay employees according to some sense of "maturity" (years-since-degree is a frequent measure), type of degree, and a performance measure. Maturity curves are frequently used for engineers and scientists whose work is on group projects where individual contribution is difficult to assess.

cally examine the effects of job-based as compared to employee-based pay structures have been initiated.[30]

There is also a tendency, at least in larger firms, for a large proportion of employees in higher paid jobs to have been promoted from lower paid jobs within the same firm and for new hires to enter at specific points in the hierarchy. Administrative procedures documented as part of internal labor markets serve to regulate these promotions and wage hierarchies (Osterman, 1984). Finally, there is some evidence that pay rates rise with seniority and experience and that the variance of earnings increases with experience and age.[31]

The literature contains many explanations for these features of pay hierarchies. Theoretically, variations in internal wage hierarchies are seen as influencing a wide array of employees' behavior.[32] These include their decisions to file grievances, invest in training, take on added responsibilities, improve their performance, turnover, form unions, and the like. But to our knowledge *no* attention has been devoted to examining empirically the effects of variations in the pay hierarchies and work force profiles on firm performances.

Recent news reports do describe cases of employers' attempts to reduce labor costs and improve productivity by modifying their pay hierarchies. They report drastic reductions in the number of levels (grades) in the pay structure as well as work force reduction schemes aimed not only at shrinking the overall work force level but at reconfiguring the distribution of employees within the structure (e.g., early retirement programs and demotions). But no systematic study of the effects of these events has been reported.

A renewed interest in wage hierarchies within firms has also occurred among labor economists. However, most of this work has been at the theoretical level; empirical research is much sketchier.[33]

---

[30] Knowledge-based pay schemes are described in Lawler (1985) and Jenkins and Gupta (1985).

[31] Earnings, experience, and age profiles have been widely researched. See, for example, Abraham and Farber (1987), Medoff and Abraham (1980), and Altonji and Shakotko (1985).

[32] For discussions of the effects of various wage differentials on employee work behavior, see Lawler (1971) and Lazear (1979, 1981, 1986).

[33] Examples of the theoretical studies include the work of Lazear and Rosen (1981) and Rosen (1986) on "rank order tournaments," Lazear's work cited above, Malcomson's (1984) work in incentives and hierarchies within internal labor markets, and Frank's (1985) rediscovery that employees value their relative position in an internal pay hierarchy as well as their absolute compensation levels.

Economists *have* found that union policies produce reductions in the dispersion at the plant level; wage dispersion within unionized firms (measured as standard deviations of the log of wages) averages one-third less than in nonunion firms (Freeman and Medoff, 1984). Considering the effects of within-firm wage differentials, this same study found that the wider the dispersion, the more likely union certification drives will be successful. Studies of this type, however, provide little direct evidence on how wage differentials influence firm performance.

We turn next to research that addresses the impact that different methods used for determining pay increases have on performance. Much of this work focuses on comparing different methods (e.g., merit versus across-the-board) rather than comparing different combinations or mixes of approaches in total compensation. For example, a recent survey by the Conference Board (Peck, 1984) reports that merit-pay plans (performance-appraisal based) are in widespread use for exempt employees. Perhaps the most telling result of the survey, which was based on responses from compensation directors, is that there were no apparent differences in the features of the merit plans between those who claimed their plans were "very successful" and those claiming theirs to be a "failure."

Typical of the research studies are those that compared employee performance in organizational units with merit pay to those in which pay increments were based on COLAs and/or seniority. In studies comparing nurses in two hospitals (one with COLA and seniority-based increases, the other with merit) and in two paper mills (one with COLA and seniority increases, the other in which a merit plan replaced a COLA/seniority plan), the employees were reported to be more productive in the merit-based units, while in another study the discontinuation of an incentive plan among welders resulted in a temporary decrease in their productivity.[34] Moreover, in a series of studies of tree planters, lumberjacks, and fur trappers, incentive-based plans were found to result in increased performance over previous levels or when compared to hourly straight-time pay with seniority-based increases

[34] See Greene (1978) and Greene and Podsakoff (1978). For a general review of the literature, see Opshal and Dunnette (1966), Lawler (1971), Kopelman and Reinharth (1982), or Nash (1980).

(Yukl and Latham, 1975; Latham and Dessett, 1978; Yukl, Latham, and Pursell, 1976).

Merit pay did not fare as well in studies in the public sector (Pearce and Perry, 1983; Pearce, Stevenson, and Perry, 1985). The most elaborate of these was the longitudinal analysis of the effects of the Federal Merit System in the Social Security Administration, which was discussed briefly in the previous section. Unit-level performance data (e.g., monthly series of types of claims processed and time to process) were collected, and while the results were not unambiguous due to court challenges that delayed the implementation of the merit plan and low merit-budget funding, the authors concluded that the merit-pay plan did not have any discernible effect on unit performance. Several reviews of merit-pay plans in public education also concluded that there is no systematic evidence that the institution of merit-pay plans for teachers led to any improvements of teaching and, more importantly, to improvements in student performance (Bacharach, Lipsky, and Shedd, 1984; Cohen and Murnane, 1985; Murnane and Cohen, 1986).

Unfortunately both the private- and public-sector studies utilize nonrigorous quasi-experimental designs and suffer from methodological and/or measurement problems (e.g., selection bias, uncontrolled variables). This leads us to conclude that we know very little about the effects of merit-pay schemes on employee performance and even less about their effects on firms' financial well-being.

It should be understood, however, just how great a gap exists between theories of pay for performance and how it actually is practiced. Personnel researchers have long recognized this gap. Many "merit-pay" schemes are underfunded, fail to offer pay increases that are meaningful to employees, and fail to establish a clear relationship between performance and pay increments. Further, only a relatively small share of most employees' compensation is contingent on performance under these plans. So the poor showing of merit-pay schemes should not come as too much of a surprise.

The gap between theory and practice appears to differ by occupation. Sales incentive plans appear to be more consistent with theory than the merit plans often used for managers or professionals. This suggests that sales jobs may offer an attractive opportunity to study the effects of various pay-for-performance approaches.

Another series of studies correlates earnings levels with previous earnings, experience, performance ratings, education, and other factors.[35] Using data collected within firms, they all reached similar conclusions—that pay level is weakly or not significantly correlated with performance rating and is more strongly related to seniority and education. For example, Medoff and Abraham (1980) reported that earnings were more attributable to experience than to performance, but they failed to report if the three firms, which provided the data, used merit-based pay. Lawler's studies (1971, 1981) reported low correlations between performance ratings and salary levels for managers in four private and three public organizations.

Correlations in these studies reveal very little about the nature of the pay-performance relationship. It is the increments in pay, not the pay level, that merit-pay plans use to affect performance. Not unexpectedly then, the correlation between the changes in pay for managers and their performance rating in one study was very much higher (0.65) than the correlation between performance and pay level (0.25) (Heneman, 1973). Obviously, none of these correlation studies sheds light on the *effects* merit pay may have on individual or firm performance. However, in spite of the failure to distinguish between pay level and changes in pay, many still refer to the weak pay-level/performance relationship as proof that merit pay does not affect performance (Milkovich and Newman, 1987).

A few studies considered the effects of the *mix* of different forms of compensation on employee performance. In one, merit pay and bonuses (individual-oriented pay increases) were found to be less effective than profit-sharing, stock ownership, and team-based bonuses (Gomez-Mejia and Balkin, 1986). Of the latter three, the team-based bonus was reported to be the most effective. This study also suffers from limitations similar to most pay-performance studies; effectiveness was measured in terms of managers' perceptions of turnover, ability to attract, and the like rather than by more objective measures. Further, the authors recognize that the study is based on a convenient sample and that data limitations did

---

[35] These studies that regress earnings or pay levels on demographic factors are reported in both the labor economics and psychology literatures. See, for example, Haire, Ghiselli, and Gordon (1967) and Medoff and Abraham (1981).

not permit them to control for different provisions in the incentive plans such as size of awards, eligibility, timing, etc.

Two other studies contrast the earnings of workers paid by the hour and those paid under a piece-rate scheme. The first found that among 183 male punch-press operators in Chicago, workers paid by the piece received approximately 7 percent more, even after controlling for differences in schooling, experience, race, and union status (Pencavel, 1977). The second used Bureau of Labor Statistics data on the earnings of over 100,000 employees in 500 firms in the footwear and men's and boys' clothing industries and found that workers paid by the piece earned approximately 14 percent more, after controlling for differences in some (but not *all*) characteristics of workers and firms (Seiler, 1984).

Unfortunately, it is difficult to interpret what these estimated differentials mean. In part, they may reflect an intended incentive effect; workers employed under piece rates may work harder, produce more, and hence get paid more. In part, they may reflect a wage premium to compensate piece-rate workers for the risk of low earnings they face during times when their productivity is low (e.g., weeks when due to physical ailments they don't produce as much as usual). In part they may also reflect that the most productive workers self-select themselves into jobs where their earnings opportunities are greatest. In the latter case, firms offering piece-rate plans potentially benefit not because the plans induce any given worker to work harder, but rather because they serve to help attract higher quality workers. Neither of these studies, however, draws any conclusions about the effects of such plans on the current profitability or stock market performance of firms.

A renewed interest in, and even popularity of, gainsharing and other productivity-sharing schemes is evident in industrial relations.[36] Widely perceived as an approach through which pay increases can successfully affect group and unit performance, proponents claim the plans hold considerable promise and even that

[36] The literature on gainsharing is burgeoning. Most of it compares the procedures and administrative aspects of various approaches. See, for example, Metzger (1980, 1984), Moore (1982), or Institute of Industrial Engineers (1983). Some make a distinction between gainsharing, in which incentives are based on team or unit-level performance improvements, or other forms such as profit-sharing (total organization financial performance), stock ownership, bonuses, and the like. A further distinction is that gainsharing schemes permit a wide definition of improvements—examples include measures of financial, production quantity and quality, accident and absentee rates, and even workplace cleanliness.

they have demonstrated success. The benefits ascribed to these plans include increases in employee and firm productivity and profitability, reduced costs, improved product quality, reduced absenteeism and tardiness, better use of capital assets, and the facilitation of employee-management cooperation, commitment, and trust.[37]

Conceptually, the notion is straightforward and appealing. As part of an overall employee relations philosophy, sharing the returns from productivity gains will engender suggestions for further improvements and motivate added performance. Typically these gains are shared in the form of bonuses and are not rolled into employees' base pay. Hence increases in compensation costs vary directly with performance levels.

Unfortunately, most of the literature on productivity-sharing is testimonial and anecdotal. The substantive empirical evaluations of gainsharing have come in two waves. The first came from the Massachusetts Institute of Technology with its historical connections to proponents such as Scanlon and Lesieur, as well as from Frost and his colleagues at Michigan State and Scanlon Plan Associates. Beyond dissertations and technical reports, little of this work has been published.[38]

More recently, the question of the effects of gainsharing and other programs was the focus of two surveys conducted in the early 1980s.[39] The New York Stock Exchange survey revealed that approximately 15 percent of all U.S. companies with 500 or more employees had some form of productivity-sharing plan and that over 70 percent of these reported that gainsharing led to improving productivity. Based on *opinion* data of this type, the NYSE Office of Economic Research concludes, "On the basis of the *evidence and the theory* (emphasis added), it appears that gainsharing can play an important role in motivating people to be more productive."

The other survey, a U.S. GAO Report (1981), concluded that "the results of productivity sharing plans suggest that these plans offer a viable method of enhancing productivity at the firm level." This conclusion was based on information obtained from interviews

---

[37] For examples of proponents of gainsharing, see Lawler (1985), Schuster (1985), and Moore (1982).

[38] For a brief review of this literature, see Bullock and Lawler (1984).

[39] See New York Stock Exchange, Office of Economic Research (1982) and the U.S. General Accounting Office (1981).

with 36 firms. However, of these, only 24 provided some financial data, only nine indicated they made *any* formal assessment of these plans, and only four could document their analyses. Nevertheless, the oft-quoted GAO results are that gainsharing improved performance by 17.3 percent at 13 firms with sales less than $100 million, and in the 11 firms with sales of $100 million or more, the average improvement was 16.4 percent. How seriously one should take these results is obviously open to question. Beyond these two surveys and some earlier evaluation studies, case descriptions of applications dominate the literature.[40]

Schuster's work (1984a, 1984b) is an exception. He reports longitudinal case studies of the effects of gainsharing schemes, the Scanlon plan, and the Rucker plan. In the most thorough study, data on productivity (measured as output per hour), employment, voluntary turnover, and suggestion rates by employees were collected on a monthly basis over approximately seven years. Based on a time-series design, the results revealed an immediate upward shift in productivity and suggestions upon implementation of a Scanlon plan, followed by a slightly positive trend thereafter. In other studies of four Scanlon and two Rucker applications, similar findings were reported.

This "plateau effect"—an abrupt positive shift in performance followed by a slight positive trend or steady performance level—is consistent with observations in the earlier descriptive literature. Schuster notes that other coincidental changes (capital improvements, new union or management leaders, etc.) may have affected productivity to a greater degree than the gainsharing schemes did. He attempts to account for these possibilities through rather exhaustive interviews of the parties involved and analysis of capital expenditure data during the study periods.

A number of monographs on profit-sharing have been published by the Profit Sharing Research Foundation.[41] Most of them describe various profit-sharing applications and their supporting philosophies. A few compare the financial performance of firms with profit-sharing to "nonprofit-sharers." In one study by Howard and Dietz (1969), financial performance measures used included *levels* and *trends* in operating income, various rates of return, earnings per

---

[40] See, for example, Goodman and Moore (1976) and Lawler (1985).

[41] See, for example, Metzger (1980).

employee, earnings per share, dividends per share, and market price per share. Nine industries were selected using a four-digit SIC classification and data were collected from COMPUSTAT tapes for the 1948–1966 period. The analyses compared the financial performance of profit-sharers with nonprofit-sharers. Profit-sharers exhibited superior performance in 50 percent of the cases and inferior performance in about 24 percent. Howard and Dietz concluded that "the financial performance of profitsharing companies was clearly superior to non-profitsharers for the nine industries as a group."

Limitations on COMPUSTAT data did not permit accounting for systematic differences beyond profit-sharing that could account for the observed performance differences. Beyond such obvious ones as capital expenditures and technological and product differences, a variety of critical compensation and personnel factors need to be considered. A few of the more obvious ones are differences in pay levels, employment levels, other incentive schemes, and whether profit-sharing was considered part of an employee's total compensation (thus placing a portion of it "at risk" in a manner similar to gainsharing) or a benefit (thus placing it along with pensions as an entitlement). Put another way, simple comparisons of mean outcomes tell us little about the effects of profit-sharing.

Our overall conclusion in this section echoes the conclusion in our summary of the executive compensation literature. It is well known that the basic dimensions of employee compensation strategies differ widely across organizations. Yet there are few rigorous studies of whether these differences make a difference. We do not know if a firm's pay position relative to its competitors, the number of pay grades it offers, pay differentials between these grades, or the profile of employees in a firm's pay hierarchy have any effect on employee behavior or the firm's economic performance.

There is evidence that individual and group-based incentive plans do affect employee performance, but it is not unambiguous. We do not know whether changes in the mix of total compensation pay off. Does it pay to shift from a base-pay system that emphasizes entitlements (emphasis on seniority, COLAs, across-the-board increases, and economic security) to a contingency-based system with emphasis on short- and long-term incentives such as gainsharing, team awards, and stock ownership? Under what conditions (e.g., state of product life-cycle, market share, etc.) might different compensation policies pay off and what are the performance implications of changing pay policies?

Considering the resources devoted to employee compensation and its management, we do not even know if the overall pay strategies adopted make any difference. That is, we simply do not know whether managing compensation pays off.

Perhaps one reason is that compensation strategies do not operate in a vacuum. Compensation is only one part, albeit an important part, of a firm's total human resources strategy. Some firms, for example, may emphasize contingent compensation while others may emphasize employment security. Disentangling the effects of one part of an overall pattern is difficult. But perhaps a more plausible reason for the dismal state of knowledge is that industrial relations researchers haven't attempted the research. It is to a suggested research agenda that we now turn.

Concluding Remarks

Our survey of the literature on the relationship between the compensation policies a firm pursues and its economic performance leads us inevitably to the conclusion that we know very little about it. Partially this is because compensation policies, by their nature, are very complex. Firms differ in terms of the level of their wage offers relative to their competitors, the returns within an occupation that accrue due to seniority, their wage structures across and within occupations, the level and mix of fringes they offer, their use of individual or group incentive pay policies, the procedures by which wage increases are granted, and the processes employed to administer compensation. Moreover, within a firm different policies may be followed for high-level executives, other managerial employees, professional employees, technical employees, office workers, and blue-collar workers, and still further distinctions are made among salaried and hourly, or unionized and nonunionized, employees. Finally, compensation policies are often established at the individual establishment level rather than at the firm level; we return to the implications of this point below.

Developing an understanding of why firms pursue different policies for various occupations instead of a single consistent policy for all employee groups is important. On the one hand, it may be that certain strategically critical occupations, such as engineers in high-technology firms or executives in most firms, have greater effects on a firm's financial performance than do other occupations. Thus variations in pay policies for critical occupations are more likely to affect firms' economic performances than policies directed at other groups. On the other hand, executive compensation usually makes up a very minor portion of total labor costs. Consequently any pay schemes that shift portions of employees' labor costs from entitlements (COLAs or seniority-based) to contingency based (gainsharing or lump-sum bonuses) seem likely to have noticeable effects on financial performance.

The vast majority of the studies we have surveyed have tended to focus on only a single dimension of compensation policy. However, a firm's economic performance is undoubtedly affected by its compensation policy in toto. Future research needs to examine a firm's policy about the various dimensions of compensation policy simultaneously rather than focusing on one policy to the exclusion of others. Empirically, a firm's compensation strategy needs to be measured as a *set* of interrelated dimensions. Developing a scheme to parameterize such a complex policy in terms of a manageable number of dimensions will not be a simple task.

Of course, one might think that one could eliminate the need for such efforts by studying how *changes* in one dimension of compensation policy affect changes in firm performance. The studies cited earlier on the relationship between the adoption of particular provisions in executive compensation agreements and performance, or those cited on the relationship between the adoption of merit pay and public-sector productivity, fall into this class. Unfortunately, the inferences one can draw from such studies depend crucially on whether *other* aspects of a compensation/industrial relations policy changed at the same time; unless other critical aspects are accounted for, causal inferences will be distorted. In addition, they depend crucially in one's ability to control for other forces besides compensation policy that might be expected to influence performance. Since adoption of a particular provision may well be influenced by other forces, this is also not always easy to do.

An argument might be made that each pay policy dimension may affect a different outcome, thus diminishing the importance of analyzing all dimensions simultaneously. The pay level of a firm, for example, may principally affect its ability to attract and retain a stable work force and the price competitiveness of its products, while a firm's policy regarding the methods by which employees are compensated (e.g., team-based incentives versus seniority) may directly affect their productivity. If such a separation of theoretical effects exists, then the need to consider simultaneously the entire pay strategy diminishes. Common sense suggests, however, that some thresholds of all pay policies may have to exist for the separate pay dimensions to have any effect. Thus, for example, merit-pay schemes may have little effect on performance if the pay level is relatively low.

The endogeneity of the adoption of particular provisions suggests another thorny issue. Not only are changes in compensation policy over time for a given firm likely to be nonrandom, but so are differences in compensation policies across firms at a point in time. There are long literatures in both economics and personnel that suggest the situations in which different compensation policies may prove optimal.

For example, the efficiency-wage literature in economics suggests that situations in which turnover costs are high, or the costs of monitoring worker productivity are high, are the ones in which above market-clearing wages and/or earnings profiles that increase with seniority may arise. The compensation literature in personnel suggests that business units that exhibit similar business strategies or operate in the same stages of product life-cycles will adopt similar compensation policies, and that these policies will differ from those of firms in the same industry in different stages or with different business strategies (Milkovich, 1987). Thus, variations in compensation policies across firms may reflect conscious decisions by firms, each trying to maximize its economic welfare.

At first glance, we appear to be left with two options. On the one hand, researchers can treat variations in compensation policy across firms as being randomly determined and ignore issues of possible simultaneity. On the other hand, researchers can acknowledge that at least some of the observed variations in firms' compensation policies are purposeful and designed to affect a firm's performance and then try to empirically model the determinants and effects of these variations. Given the latter, the effects of compensation policy on firm performance can be estimated *only* in the context of a model that treats these policies as being endogenously determined.

Our own preferences are to go the latter route. A start has already been made by some research. For example, economists have tried to see if empirical explanations exist for why the prevalence and strength of cost-of-living adjustment clauses vary across union contracts, why the fringe benefit/wage ratio varies over time and across areas, or why the probability of observing mandatory retirement provisions and above-market-clearing wages varies across individuals.[42] These types of studies have only begun to scratch the surface and much more research is needed on the determinants of compensation strategies.

We must stress, however, that pursuing this type of research will not be easy for a number of reasons. On the one hand, it is not a trivial matter to parameterize any particular compensation policy. For example, knowledge of the incentive/nonincentive pay dichotomy is probably less useful than knowledge of the magnitudes of the incentives that exist (i.e., the marginal return to the workers from altering their behaviors). Similarly, how a plan is actually administered may be quite different from what is recorded in written plan statements. The mere process of collecting data on compensation policies will require considerable efforts.

On the other hand, once such data are collected, researchers must still develop empirical models to explain variations in compensation policies. Unless such models have a good deal of explanatory power, attempts to treat compensation policies as endogenous are unlikely to lead to statistically precise estimates of the effects of compensation policies on firm performance, because of both the imprecision of the "instruments" for compensation policies that would result *and* the indirect relationship between compensation policy and ultimate financial performance.

Indeed, this problem is exacerbated by the fact that compensation policies are often set at the individual *establishment* level and are designed to affect establishment-level variables such as absenteeism, the quality of new hires, turnover, and productivity.

---

[42] See, for example, Ehrenberg, Danziger, and San (1983), Woodbury (1983), and Hutchens (forthcoming).

Yet the financial performance (stock market or accounting) measures are typically available only at the firm or corporate level.

These difficulties suggest a third option. Researchers might focus on the establishment level to estimate the effects of compensation policies on the outcomes that they are designed to directly influence, such as recruitment, absenteeism, and turnover and individual, group, and business unit performance—all in the context of models in which one attempts to control for the endogeneity of these policies. Assuming that compensation policies are shown to influence these outcomes, establishment-level data could then be used to estimate the effects of these outcomes on total costs of production and thus on underlying profitability. Related research on the effects of industrial relations type policies on establishments' costs and productivity in the automobile and paper mill industries has recently been undertaken and can serve as a starting point for these endeavors.[43] These related studies do *not* treat industrial relations variables as endogenous, however, and it is important that attempts be made to treat compensation policies as endogenous in future analyses.

Indeed, it may be that financial and stock market measures simply have too much "noise" in many situations to be useful measures of the direct effects of various compensation policies and practices. By considering only the "ultimate" performance measures and ignoring the intermediate outcomes of compensation systems, we run the risk of concluding that "nothing" matters when in fact what matters depends on the outcomes and models selected. Research on the effects of compensation policies on firm performance thus needs to focus on *both* firm-level performance measures and more intermediate-level measures.

References

Abowd, John M. "Collective Bargaining and the Division of the Value of the Enterprise." National Bureau of Economic Research Working Paper No. 2137, January 1987.
Abraham, Katharine G., and Henry S. Farber. "Job Duration, Seniority, and Earnings." *American Economic Review* 77 (June 1987): pp. 278–97.
Akerlof, George. "Gift Exchange and Efficiency-Wage Theory: Four Views." *American Economic Review* 74 (May 1984): pp. 79–83.
Allen, Steven. "Trade Unions, Absenteeism, and Exit-Voice." *Industrial and Labor Relations Review* 37 (April 1984): pp. 331–45.

---

[43] See, for example, Ichniowski (1986), Katz, Kochan, and Gobeille (1983), and Norsworthy and Zabala (1985).

Altonji, Joseph, and Robert Shakotko. "Do Wages Rise with Seniority?" National Bureau of Economic Research Working Paper No. 1616, May 1985.

Antle, Rick, and Abbie Smith. "An Empirical Investigation of the Relative Performance Evaluation of Corporate Executives." *Journal of Accounting Research* 24 (Spring 1986): pp. 1–32.

Bacharach, Samuel, David Lipsky, and Joseph Shedd. *Paying for Better Teaching: Merit Pay and Its Alternatives*. Ithaca, N.Y.: Organizational Analysis and Practices, Inc., 1984.

Balkin, David B., and Luis Gomez-Mejia. "The Relationship Between Short-Term and Long-Term Incentives and Strategy in the High Technology Industry." Mimeo, University of Colorado, Boulder, 1986.

Barron, John M., John Bishop, and William C. Dunkelberg. "Employer Search: The Interviewing and Hiring of New Employees." *Review of Economics and Statistics* 67 (February 1985): pp. 43–52.

Becker, Gary S. *Human Capital: A Theoretical and Empirical Analysis*, 2d ed. New York: Columbia University Press, 1985.

Benson, G. "The Self-Serving Management Hypothesis: Some Evidence." *Journal of Accounting and Economics* 7 (April 1985): pp. 67–84.

Bhagat, S., J. Brickley, and R. Lease. "Incentive Effects of Employee Stock Purchase Plans." *Journal of Financial Economics* 14 (January 1985): pp. 195–216.

Brickley, J., S. Bhagat, and R. Lease. "The Impact of Long-Run Managerial Compensation Plans on Shareholder Wealth." *Journal of Accounting and Economics* 7 (April 1985): pp. 115–29.

Brown, Charles. "Military Enlistments: What Can We Learn from Geographic Variation?" *American Economic Review* 75 (March 1985): pp. 228–34.

Brown, Charles, and James L. Medoff. "The Employer Size Wage Effect." Mimeo, University of Michigan, Ann Arbor, November 1985.

Bullock, R. J., and E. E. Lawler III. "Gainsharing: A Few Questions and Fewer Answers." *Human Resource Management* 5 (1984): pp. 197–212.

Cherrington, David J., H. Joseph Reitz, and William E. Scott, Jr. "Effects of Contingent and Non-Contingent Rewards on the Relationship Between Satisfaction and Task Performance." *Journal of Applied Psychology* 56 (December 1971): pp. 531–36.

Ciscel, David, and Thomas Carroll. "The Determinants of Executive Salaries: An Econometric Survey." *Review of Economics and Statistics* 62 (February 1980): pp. 7–13.

Cohen, David, and Richard Murnane. "The Merits of Merit Pay." *Public Interest* 80 (Summer 1985): pp. 3–30.

Coughlin, T., and R. Schmidt. "Executive Compensation, Management Turnover, and Firm Performance: An Empirical Investigation." *Journal of Accounting and Economics* 7 (April 1985): pp. 43–66.

Dickens, William, and Lawrence Katz. "Interindustry Wage Differences and Industry Characteristics." In *Unemployment and the Structure of Labor Markets*, eds. Kevin Lang and Jonathan Leonard. London: Basil-Blackwell, 1986. Pp. 48–89.

Dunn, Lucia. "The Effects of Firm Size on Wages, Fringe Benefits, and Work Disutility." In *The Impact of the Modern Corporation*, eds. Betty Bock et al. New York: Columbia University Press, 1984.

Dyer, Lee, and Donald P. Schwab. "Personnel/Human Resource Management Research." In *Industrial Relations Research in the 1970s: Review and Appraisal*, eds. Thomas A. Kochan, Daniel J.B. Mitchell, and Lee Dyer. Madison, Wis.: Industrial Relations Research Association, 1982. Pp. 187–220.

Eaton, Jonathan, and Harvey Rosen. "Agency, Delayed Compensation, and the Structure of Executive Remuneration." *Journal of Finance* 38 (December 1983): pp. 1489–1505.

Ehrenberg, Ronald G., Richard P. Chaykowski, and Randy Ann Ehrenberg. "Determinants of the Compensation and Mobility of School Superintendents." *Industrial and Labor Relations Review* 41 (April 1988).

Ehrenberg, Ronald, Leif Danziger, and Gee San. "Cost of Living Adjustment Clauses in Union Contracts: A Summary of Results." *Journal of Labor Economics* 3 (July 1983): pp. 215–46.

Ehrenberg, Ronald, and Steven Goldberg. "Officer Compensation and Performance in Local Building Trades Unions." *Industrial and Labor Relations Review* 30 (January 1977): pp. 188–96.

Foster, Kenneth E. "An Anatomy of Company Pay Practices." *Personnel* 62 (September 1985): pp. 67–71.

Foulkes, Fred K. *Personnel Policies in Large Nonunion Companies.* Englewood Cliffs, N.J.: Prentice-Hall, 1980.

Frank, Robert H. *Choosing the Right Pond.* New York: Oxford University Press, 1985.

Freeman, Richard B. "Union Wage Practices and Wage Dispersion Within Establishments." *Industrial and Labor Relations Review* 36 (October 1982): pp. 3–21.

Freeman, Richard B., and James L. Medoff, *What Do Unions Do?* New York: Basic Books, 1984.

Freeman, Smith. "Wage Trends as Performance Displays Productive Potential: A Model and Application to Academic Early Retirement." *Bell Journal of Economics* 8 (Autumn 1977): pp. 419–33.

Giles, Brian A., and Gerald Barrett. "Utility of Merit Increases." *Journal of Applied Psychology* 55 (April 1971): pp. 103–109.

Goldstein, Gerald, and Ronald Ehrenberg. "Executive Compensation in Municipalities." *Southern Economic Journal* 43 (July 1976): pp. 937–47.

Gomez-Mejia, Luis R., and David B. Balkin. "The Effectiveness of Individual and Aggregate Compensation Strategies in an R&D Setting." Mimeo, University of Florida, Gainesville, 1986.

Goodman, Paul S., and Brian E. Moore. "Factors Affecting Acquisition of Beliefs About a New Reward System." *Human Relations* 29 (June 1976): pp. 571–88.

Greene, Charles N. "Causal Connections Among Managers' Merit Pay, Job Satisfaction, and Performance." *Journal of Applied Psychology* 58 (February 1978): pp. 95–100.

Greene, Charles N., and Phillip M. Podsakoff. "Effects of Removal of a Pay Incentive: A Field Experiment." *Academy of Management Proceedings '78*, 38th Annual Meeting, San Francisco, August 1978.

Groshen, Erica L. "Sources of Wage Dispersion: How Much Do Employers Matter?" Mimeo, Department of Economics, Harvard University, Cambridge, Mass., December 1985.

Haire, M., E. E. Ghiselli, and M. E. Gordon. "A Psychological Study of Pay." *Journal of Applied Psychology* 51 (Part 2, August 1967): pp. 1–24.

Harris, Milton, and Bengt Holmstrom. "A Theory of Wage Dynamics." *Review of Economic Studies* 49 (July 1982): pp. 315–33.

Heneman, Herbert G. III. "Impact of Performance on Managerial Pay Levels and Pay Changes." *Journal of Applied Psychology* 58 (August 1973): pp. 128–30.

Howard, Bion B., and Peter O. Dietz. "A Study of the Financial Significance of Profit Sharing." Chicago: Council of Profit Sharing Industries, 1969.

Hutchens, Robert. "A Test of Lazear's Delayed Payment Contracts." *Journal of Labor Economics* (forthcoming).

Ichniowski, Casey. "The Effects of Grievance Activity on Productivity." *Industrial and Labor Relations Review* 40 (October 1986): pp. 75–89.

Institute of Industrial Engineers. *Gainsharing: A Collection of Papers.* Norcross, Ga.: IIE, 1983.

Jacques, Elliot. *Equitable Payments.* New York: Wiley, 1961.

Jenkins, G. Douglas, Jr., and Nina Gupta. "The Payoffs of Paying for Knowledge." *Labor Management Cooperation Brief.* Washington: U.S. Department of Labor, August 1985.

Katz, Harry C., Thomas A. Kochan, and Kenneth R. Gobeille. "Industrial Relations Performance, Economic Performance, and QWL Programs: An Interplant Analysis." *Industrial and Labor Relations Review* 37 (October 1983): pp. 3–17.

Katz, Lawrence. "Efficiency Wage Theories: A Partial Evaluation." National Bureau of Economic Research Working Paper No. 1906, April 1986.

Knober, Charles. "Golden Parachutes, Shark Repellents, and Hostile Tender Offers." *American Economic Review* 76 (March 1986): pp. 155–87.

Kochan, Thomas A. *Collective Bargaining and Industrial Relations.* Homewood, Ill.: Richard D. Irwin, 1980.

Kopelman, R. E., and Leon Reinharth. "Research Results: The Effects of Merit-Pay Practices on White Collar Performance." *Compensation Review* 14 (Fourth Quarter 1982): pp. 30–40.

Kostiuk, Peter F. "Executive Ability, Corporate Performance, and Managerial Income." Mimeo, Center for Naval Analyses, Alexandria, Va., May 1986.

Krueger, Alan, and Lawrence Summers. "Efficiency Wages and the Wage Structure." National Bureau of Economic Research Working Paper No. 1952, June 1986.

Lambert, R. A., and D. F. Larcker. "Golden Parachutes, Executive Decision-Making, and Shareholder Wealth." *Journal of Accounting and Economics* 7 (April 1985): pp. 179–204.

Larcker, D. F. "The Association Between Performance Plan Adoption and Corporate Capital Investments." *Journal of Accounting and Economics* 5 (April 1983): pp. 3–30.

Latham, G. P., and D. L. Dessett. "Designing Incentive Plans for Unionized Employees: A Comparison of Continuous and Variable Rates Reinforcement Schedules." *Personnel Psychology* 31 (Spring 1978): pp. 47–61.

Lawler, E. E. III. *Pay and Organization Effectiveness.* New York: McGraw-Hill, 1971.

———. *Pay and Organization Development.* Reading, Mass.: Addison-Wesley, 1981.

———. "Gainsharing Research: Findings and Future Directions." Technical Report T 85-1(67), Center for Effective Organizations, University of Southern California, Los Angeles, 1985.

Lazear, Edward. "Why Is There Mandatory Retirement?" *Journal of Political Economy* 87 (December 1979): pp. 261–84.

———. "Agency, Earnings Profiles, Productivity, and Hours Restrictions." *American Economic Review* 71 (September 1981): pp. 606–20.

———. "Incentive Contracts." National Bureau of Economic Research Working Paper No. 1917, May 1986.

Lazear, Edward, and Sherwin Rosen. "Rank-Order Tournaments and Optimum Labor Contracts." *Journal of Political Economy* 89 (October 1981): pp. 841–64.

Leonard, Jonathan. "Carrots and Sticks: Pay, Supervision, and Turnover." *Journal of Labor Economics* (forthcoming 1987).

Lewellen, William, Claudio Lederer, and Ahron Rosenfeld. "Merger Decisions and Executive Stock Ownership in Acquiring Firms." *Journal of Accounting and Economics* 7 (April 1985): pp. 209–23.

Locke, E. A., D. B. Feren, V. M. McCaleb, and K. N. Shaw. "The Relative Effectiveness of Four Methods of Motivating Employee Performance." In *Changes in Working Life,* eds. K. D. Duncan et al. New York: Wiley, 1980.

MacDonald, Glenn. "A Market Equilibrium Theory of Job Assessment and Sequential Accumulation of Information." *American Economic Review* 72 (December 1982): pp. 1038–55.

Mahoney, Thomas. *Compensation and Reward Perspectives.* Homewood, Ill.: Richard D. Irwin, 1979.

Malcomson, James M. "Work Incentives, Hierarchy, and Internal Labor Markets." *Journal of Political Economy* 92 (June 1984): pp. 486–507.

Masson, Robert. "Executive Motivations, Earnings, and Consequent Equity Performance." *Journal of Political Economy* 79 (November 1971): pp. 1278–92.

Meadows, E. "How Three Companies Increased Their Productivity." *Forbes* 10 (March 1980): pp. 92–101.

Medoff, James L., and Katharine G. Abraham. "Experience, Performance, and Earnings." *Quarterly Journal of Economics* 95 (December 1980): pp. 703–36.

————. "Are Those Paid More Really More Productive? The Case of Experience." *Journal of Human Resources* 16 (Spring 1981): pp. 186–216.

Meitzen, Mark. "Differences in Male and Female Job-Quitting Behavior." *Journal of Labor Economics* 4 (April 1986): pp. 151–68.

Metzger, Bert L. *Profit Sharing in 38 Large Companies,* Vols. I and II. Evanston, Ill.: Profit Sharing Research Foundation, 1976 and 1978.

————. *Increasing Productivity Through Profit Sharing.* Evanston, Ill.: Profit Sharing Research Foundation, 1980.

————. "Gainsharing Plans: What They Are, How They Compare, and the Advantages and Limitations of Each." *Profit Sharing* (December 1984).

Metzger, Bert L., and Jerome A. Colletti. *Does Profit Sharing Pay? A Comparative Study of the Financial Performance of Retailers With and Without Profit Sharing Programs.* Evanston, Ill.: Profit Sharing Research Foundation, 1971.

Milkovich, George T. "Compensation Systems in High Technology Companies." In *Management of High Techology Firms,* eds. Archie Kleingartner and Cara Anderson. Lexington, Mass.: D. C. Heath, 1987.

Milkovich, George T., and Jerry Newman. *Compensation,* 2d ed. Plano, Tex.: Business Publications, Inc., 1987.

Moore, Brian E. *Sharing the Gains of Productivity: Highlights of the Literature.* Work in America Institute Studies in Productivity. New York: Pergamon Press, 1982.

Morck, Randall, Andrew Shleifer, and Robert Vishny. "Management Ownership and Corporate Performance." National Bureau of Economic Research Working Paper No. 2055, November 1986.

Murnane, Richard, and David Cohen. "Merit Pay and the Evaluation Problem: Why Most Merit Pay Plans Fail and Few Survive." *Harvard Education Review* 56 (February 1986): pp. 1–17.

Murphy, Kevin J. "Corporate Performance and Managerial Remuneration: An Empirical Analysis." *Journal of Accounting and Economics* 7 (April 1985a): pp. 11–42.

————. "Can Theories of Wage Dynamics and Agency Explain Executive Compensation, Promotions, and Mobility?" Mimeo, University of Rochester, Rochester, N.Y., 1985b.

————. "Top Executives Are Worth Every Nickel They Get." *Harvard Business Review* 64 (March/April 1986a): pp. 125–32.

————. "Incentives, Learning, and Compensation: A Theoretical and Empirical Investigation of Management Labor Contracts." *Rand Journal of Economics* 17 (Spring 1986b): pp. 59–76.

Nash, Allen. *Managerial Compensation: Highlights of the Literature.* Scarsdale, N.Y.: Work in America Institute, 1980.

New York Stock Exchange, Office of Economic Research. *People and Productivity: A Challenge to Corporate America.* New York: New York Stock Exchange, 1982.

Norsworthy, J. R., and Craig Zabala. "Worker Attitudes, Worker Behavior, and Productivity in the U.S. Automobile Industry, 1959–1976." *Industrial and Labor Relations Review* 38 (July 1985): pp. 544–57.

Oi, Walter. "The Fixed Employment Costs of Specialized Labor." In *The Measurement of Labor Costs,* ed. Jack Triplett. Chicago: University of Chicago Press, 1983. Pp. 63–116.

Opshal, Robert, and M. D. Dunnette. "The Role of Financial Compensation in Industrial Motivation." *Psychological Bulletin* 66 (January 1966): pp. 94–118.

Osterman, Paul. *Internal Labor Markets.* Cambridge, Mass.: MIT Press, 1984.

Pearce, Jone L., and James L. Perry. "Federal Merit Pay: A Longitudinal Analysis." *Public Administration Review* 43 (July-August 1983): pp. 316–25.

Pearce, Jone L., William Stevenson, and James Perry. "Managerial Compensation Based on Organizational Performance: A Time-Series Analysis of the Effects of Merit Pay." *Academy of Management Journal* 28 (June 1985): pp. 261–78.

Peat, Marwick, Mitchell & Co. *Executive Compensation Strategies in the New England High Technology Industry.* New York: Peat, Marwick, Mitchell & Co., 1982, 1983, and 1984.

Peck, Charles. *Pay and Performance: The Interaction of Compensation and Performance Appraisal.* Research Bulletin 155. New York: The Conference Board, 1984.

Pencavel, John. *An Analysis of the Quit Rate in American Manufacturing Industry.* Princeton, N.J.: Industrial Relations Section, Princeton University, 1970.

_____. "Work Effort, On the Job Screening, and Alternative Methods of Remuneration." In *Research in Labor Economics,* Vol. 1, ed. Ronald G. Ehrenberg. Greenwich, Conn.: JAI Press, 1977. Pp. 225–59.

Redding, E. T. "Myth vs. Reality: The Relationship Between Top Executive Pay and Corporate Performance." *Compensation Review* 13 (Fourth Quarter 1981): pp. 16–24.

Rosen, Sherwin. "Prizes and Incentives in Elimination Tournaments." *American Economic Review* 76 (September 1986): pp. 701–15.

Schuster, Michael. "The Scanlon Plan: A Longitudinal Analysis." *Journal of Applied Behavioral Science* 20 (February 1984a): pp. 23–38.

_____. *Union-Management Cooperation: Structure-Process-Impact.* Kalamazoo, Mich.: W.E. Upjohn Institute for Employment Research, 1984b.

_____. "Gainsharing: Issues for Senior Managers." Mimeo, Syracuse University, Syracuse, N.Y., November 1985.

Segal, Martin. "Post-Institutionalism in Labor Economics: The Forties and Fifties Revisited." *Industrial and Labor Relations Review* 39 (April 1986): pp. 388–403.

Seiler, Eric. "Piece Rate vs. Time Rate: The Effect of Incentives on Earnings." *Review of Economics and Statistics* 66 (August 1984): pp. 363–76.

Shaeffer, Ruth G. "Comparing Staffing Patterns." *Management Review* 65 (July 1976): pp. 41–47.

Simon, Herbert A. "The Compensation of Executives." *Sociometry* 20 (March 1957): pp. 32–35.

Stiglitz, Joseph. "Theories of Wage Rigidity." National Bureau of Economic Research Working Paper No. 1442, September 1984.

Summers, Lawrence. "Did Henry Ford Pay Efficiency Wages?" *Journal of Labor Economics* (forthcoming).

Tehranian, H., and J. Waegelein. "Market Reaction to Short-Term Executive Compensation Plan Adoption." *Journal of Accounting and Economics* 7 (April 1985): pp. 131–44.

U.S. Bureau of Labor Statistics. *Area Wages Survey: Cleveland, Ohio Metropolitan Area September 1985.* Bulletin 3030-45. Washington: U.S. Government Printing Office, November 1985.

U.S. General Accounting Office. *Productivity Sharing Programs: Can They Contribute to Productivity Improvements?* Washington: GAO, March 31, 1981.

Viscusi, W. Kip. "Sex Differences in Worker Quitting." *Review of Economics and Statistics* 62 (August 1980): pp. 388–98.

Winkler, Donald. "The Effects of Sick Leave Policy on Teacher Absenteeism." *Industrial and Labor Relations Review* 34 (January 1980): pp. 207–18.

Woodbury, Stephen. "Substitution Between Wage and Nonwage Benefits." *American Economic Review* 73 (March 1983): pp. 166–82.

Yellen, Janet. "Efficiency Wage Models of Unemployment." *American Economic Review* 74 (May 1984): pp. 200–205.

Yukl, G. A., and G. P. Latham. "Consequences of Reenforcement Schedules and Incentive Magnitudes for Employee Performance." *Journal of Applied Psychology* 60 (June 1975): pp. 294–98.

Yukl, G. A., G. P. Latham, and E. D. Pursell. "The Effectiveness of Performance Under Continuous and Variable Ratio Schedules of Reinforcement." *Personnel Psychology* 29 (Summer 1976): pp. 221–31.

Chapter 4

Employee Participation in Firm Decisions

By Walter J. Gershenfeld
Temple University

The two terms most frequently associated with employee participation in firm decisions, employee involvement (EI) and quality of work life (QWL), are often considered to be synonymous. Thus, in this chapter they will be combined and treated as a single technical term, EI/QWL. However, before proceeding with our discussion we need to define the term and indicate how it will be used in our survey of studies of employee involvement.

To obtain a balanced definition of EI/QWL, it is instructive to examine the perspectives of both management and labor officials. To Glen Watts, president of the Communications Workers of America, QWL means direct participation by workers in day-to-day decision-making on the job. David Easlick, president of Michigan Bell Telephone, considers QWL a process of improving the organization by grassroots joint problem-solving and communication. Peter Pestillo, vice president, Labor Relations, Ford Motor Company, sees employee involvement as the application of common sense to the personnel process, cooperating with and seeking the ideas of employees. According to Donald Ephlin, vice president and director, General Motors Department, United Auto Workers, the purpose of QWL is to open up the relationship between the company and the union and jointly reach decisions based on impacts on people affected (Lansing Area Joint Labor-Management Committee, 1983, p. 3).

The Michigan Quality of Worklife Council (undated) makes the point that QWL is both a goal and a process. As a goal, it is the commitment of people to work improvement—a commitment to the creation of more engaging, satisfying, and effective jobs for people at all levels of the organization. As a process, QWL calls for efforts to realize this goal through the active participation of people throughout the organization.

Common definitional elements include employee participation in decision-making involving both work and the work environment and the enhancement of organizational strength and employee effectiveness and satisfaction. For our purposes here we will define EI/QWL as a structured, systematic approach to the involvement of employees in group decisions affecting work and the work environment with goals that include reducing product cost, improving product quality, facilitating communication, raising morale, and reducing conflict. Inherent in this definition are both group activity and the existence of a continuum which ranges from relatively modest worker involvement in improved communication to significant restructuring of industry in the direction of greater worker/union-management partnershp. In a sense, employee-owned plants are the ultimate in such partnerships, but they are not a focus of this chapter.

Collective bargaining topics may become involved in QWL relationships, but typical EI/QWL plans have begun with concerns other than those normally considered in collective bargaining. One exception is gainsharing arrangements. Although Scanlon, Rucker, and other formal gainsharing plans do involve employee participation, they are not the principal thrust of this chapter. Other less formal gainsharing arrangements, however, may be part of work restructuring within an EI/QWL plan and will be included in our discussion.

In part, the separation, not always verbalized, between topics for collective bargaining and those not for bargaining reflects the belief that an employer and its employees, whether or not a union is present, may have integrative and distributive concerns that can best be handled in separate forums. Over time, some relationships have merged collective bargaining topics with EI/QWL areas. In fact, some authorities believe that EI/QWL is not likely to prove lasting unless some concerns that emerge from QWL processes reach the bargaining table and impact organizational factors (Cutcher-Gershenfeld, Kochan, and Verma, 1987).

The concepts underlying EI/QWL have been with us for some time, but the terms are new and date from the 1970s. "Quality of working life" is generally attributed to Professor Louis Davis of the University of California, Los Angeles, who introduced the term in 1972. QWL was used in separate collective bargaining agreements between Chrysler, Ford, and General Motors and the United Automobile Workers (UAW) in 1973, and EI first appeared in a 1979 agreement between Ford and the UAW.

Keidel (1980) lists five major components which may be found in EI programs, along with illustrative techniques: (1) *Work Redesign*—job enlargement, job enrichment, job rotation, modular work group, autonomous work team; (2) *Pay Restructuring*—salaried work force, pay for knowledge, unit productivity sharing; (3) *Time Rescheduling*—flexible work hours, compressed workweek, job-sharing; (4) *Performance Development*—positive reinforcement, problem-solving quality circles, middle-range planning, physical redesign; (5) *Administrative Review*—information sharing, procedural change, training.

A QWL program may include most or all of the above approaches to employee involvement or only a small number of them. Obviously, some of the processes/programs are part of standard human resource activity and may not carry the EI/QWL appelation. It is when these approaches become factored into a structured and systematic group effort to include employees in decisions affecting work and the workplace that they become EI/QWL. It must be emphasized that some observers of the work scene stress the role of EI/QWL in promoting the dignity of the individual worker independent of measures of performance, and political scientists in particular are interested in whether increased workplace participation has implications for political democracy.

Now that we have defined EI/QWL and have indicated how it will be used in our discussion, we turn in the next section to a short history of employee involvement. This is followed by a consideration of the environment of QWL programs, both external and internal, and the problems involved in their installation and operation. In the remainder of the chapter we examine the evidence with regard to the success, or lack of it, of EI/QWL activity. The unionized sector is stressed, but findings from the larger nonunion sector are also reviewed.

History of Employee Involvement

Although examples abound of early ideal, though frequently unsuccessful, work societies, employee involvement is basically a 20th century phenomenon (Barthel, 1984). Turn-of-the-century efforts focused on reduction of labor-management conflict. The National Civic Federation, founded in 1900, sought to reduce industrial conflict by bringing together the "reasonable" disputants around a conference table (Rayback, 1966, p. 211). While there were some successes, the early record—and much of the later record—was of transitory organizations and approaches.

The patriotic fervor of World War I enabled the War Labor Board to establish cooperative labor-management committees numbering in the hundreds, but these virtually vanished with the end of the war. The 1920s and 1930s also saw some far-reaching cooperative efforts involving the railroad, textile, and garment industries (Cutcher-Gershenfeld, 1983). Similar in form to today's top-level joint planning committees and shop-floor quality circles, some of these efforts endured for more than a decade. Concurrently, some large employers developed the American Plan—forms of participation designed to exclude the union. Most important, the 1920s decade was the period of the Hawthorne experiments at Western Electric, which brought academic research to the fore with findings suggesting that employees who were consulted about their work were more interested in what they were doing and were more effective.

The Hawthorne experiments and other efforts led to the human relations movement with its stress on democratic leadership and improved communications. The approach was at times seized upon by employers as a union-avoidance or union-busting technique or was used in a manipulative manner. The not unexpected residue is a tradition of suspicion and hostility by some of organized labor toward cooperative endeavors (Winpisinger, 1973; Whyte, 1987).

Passage of the Wagner Act in 1935 led to a concentration on adversarial aspects of labor relations at the bargaining table, but World War II brought another round of labor-management cooperation. More than 5,000 labor-management committees were formed which aided the war effort in a variety of ways. Although many of the committees disappeared with the end of the war, some were longer lasting, particularly in the steel and West Coast longshore industries. The end of World War II also saw the formation of a national labor-management conference which succeeded in clearing the way for the postwar success of grievance arbitration. This conference, called by President Truman, was followed over the years by various national labor-management committees organized by successor presidents. The committees have had limited lasting utility.

The 1950s and 1960s brought forth an explosion in the field of organizational studies. Pioneers included Douglas McGregor, Eric Trist, Herbert Simon, and Rensis Likert. Likert (1961) reported that certain identifiable characteristics consistently differentiated the more effective organizations, in both performance and employee satisfaction, from the less effective organizations. Much European activity coalesced around the concept of looking at organizations as sociotechnical systems. The field of organizational behavior supplanted the earlier human relations area and developed strong roots in the behavioral sciences. Organizational development began to emerge with its concerns about mission clarification, team-building, and goal-setting (French, 1974). The government-sponsored *Work in America* study (U.S. Department of HEW, 1972) reported substantial worker apathy. Although questions may be raised today as to the extent to which the study was accurate, the stage was set for the current growth in employee involvement and quality of work life activity.

Institutionally, area labor-management committees (ALMCs), which began in the late 1940s in Toledo and Louisville, had a separate orientation. They concentrated on labor-management cooperation as a key to economic development in a given area. The growth of ALMCs was facilitated in the early 1970s by the government's National Commission on Productivity, which shortly after its establishment added Quality of Work Life to its title. The new ALMCs typically brought together labor and management in a geographical area that was facing difficulties in both labor-management relations and the market. They frequently adopted a two-pronged approach. First, they worked together to improve the economic climate of their region. For example, if the community had an active waterfront, management and labor might cooperate in seeking channel dredging, better wharfs, and the like. Second, they drew upon any early successes with community goals to encourage and facilitate in-plant cooperation. This type of activity led to many of the QWL programs extant today. The widely chronicled success of the Jamestown, N.Y., program became a model, and approximately 40 area labor-management committees were active recently (Leone, 1982).

The National Commission on Productivity and Quality of Work Life faded from sight in the late 1970s when it failed to receive congressional budget support. The public policy substitute was the National Labor-Management Cooperation Act of 1978. Initial government support of ALMC and QWL efforts was and still is via the Federal Mediation and Conciliation Service, which administers the act. Its work has been supplemented by the Division of Cooperative Labor-Management Programs in the U.S. Department of Labor.

Meanwhile, the first national agreements to include language on QWL were signed in 1973 following UAW negotiations with Chrysler, Ford, and General Motors. Early leaders in the effort were Irving Bluestone of the UAW and D. L. Landen of GM. An assembly plant in Tarrytown, N.Y., was selected for experimental activity, and early results were dramatically positive. Contentiousness in an assembly area was sharply diminished, and there were significant cost savings in the assembly process. EI began to spread in the auto industry, although it took an industry downturn in the late 1970s to spur the growth of EI programs. The then American Telephone and Telegraph Company followed with joint programs involving the Communications Workers of America. Michael Maccoby was associated with this effort. Two other unions with substantial early QWL interest were the United Steelworkers of America and the Oil, Chemical, and Atomic Workers. Labor-management productivity teams became a standard steel industry instrument for employee involvement. However, the industry tended to concentrate on economic measures as primary devices to effect change. Activity also grew in nonunion plants, particularly as companies experimented with work systems in new plants. Public-sector QWL programs also began to emerge (Cutcher-Gershenfeld, 1984).

Newspaper stories of worker alienation were common in this period. The General Motors plant in Lordstown, Ohio, was usually cited as the leading example. Companies such as Procter and Gamble, Shell Oil, Cummins Engine, and Steelcase built "model" plants with some formal approach to worker consultation as part of their enterprises. In addition to government and academic interest, foundation support emerged—from the Ford Foundation in particular.

Growing foreign market competition became a general public concern at about the same time as we realized that many successful European and Japanese companies were operating with greater employee participation than was true in the United States. Some analysts concluded early on, however, that European approaches to shop-floor democracy were not appropriate for the U.S. What was recommended were simpler forms of organizational change fostering employee involvement (Mills, 1978). The competitive success of the Japanese and reports by W. Edwards Deming, a U.S. quality-control expert, of Japan's excellent results with quality circles aroused interest. Quality circles are thought by many to be a Japanese innovation rather than the successful transference of an earlier American approach.

Despite a growing awareness and interest in QWL, it remained largely a pilot operation. In his key *Harvard Business Review* article in 1978, Mills noted that there were no more than 200 to 500 organizations so involved. By 1982 the U.S. Department of Labor listed QWL activity in 700 organizations (Mroczkowski, 1984). Undoubtedly the lack of systematic data collection resulted in some underreporting in earlier years, but the evidence since 1982 indicates much wider and deeper QWL activity in the U.S.

In 1982 the New York Stock Exchange conducted the broadest survey of QWL to date. The basis for the survey was stated by the Stock Exchange as follows:

> "What is American management currently doing to achieve more labor cooperation, to reduce costly adversarial tactics, to enhance the quality of production, and to raise the quality of work life? The New York Stock Exchange found many valuable case studies, but no comprehensive information. So we decided to fill this void" (Freund and Epstein, 1984, p. 119).

"Filling the void" involved a statistically representative sample of the approximately 49,000 companies with 100 or more employees—in all, a total of some 41 million employees. Table 1 shows the distribution of QWL activities among responding firms.

The study indicates that, depending on the activity, anywhere

TABLE 1

Percentage of Corporations Having Specified Activity

Activity	Total	Manu-facturing	Nonmanu-facturing
Job design/redesign	15%	9%	12%
Job enlargement	7	8	7
Job rotation	6	6	6
Formal training and instruction	25	28	22
Setting employee goals	21	22	20
Employee appraisal and feedback	23	25	22
Setting company objectives	18	18	18
Structuring plant & office space	10	11	7
Organizational structure	13	15	11
Scheduling workflow	14	15	11
Personalized work hours	9	9	10
Suggestion systems	13	13	13
Labor/management committees	8	13	4
Labor advisory groups	2	3	1
Quality circles	14	22	8
Production teams	5	9	3
Salarying blue-collar workers	2	3	1
Task forces	11	14	9
Surveys of employee attitudes	15	16	14
Financial Incentives			
Piecework	3	5	1
Group productivity	2	2	2
Profit-sharing	8	9	8
Stock purchase plans	7	10	5

Source: Freund and Epstein (1984), p. 119.

from 2 to 25 percent of American industry make use of some form of the activities listed. Manufacturing concerns are more likely than nonmanufacturing firms to be involved in such programs, nonmonetary aspects dominate monetary aspects, and larger companies are more likely to be involved in EI than are smaller firms. The 14-percent figure for quality circles is a rough median among the various activities and incentives found in American companies, but fully 53 percent of the firms listed by the New York Stock Exchange were found to have a program using some of the EI/QWL components. Verma and McKersie (1987) report that the NYSE survey, along with others by *Business Week* and the American Management Association, indicate that approximately 35 percent of all American firms make use of some type of employee-participation program.

For a 1983–1984 study of the effect of participative management on organizational performance, questionnaires were mailed to 850 firms; 125 usable replies were received, for a response rate of approximately 12.5 percent. Eighty-five percent of the respondent companies indicated that they operated with some form of industrial democracy (Carson, 1985). If we assume that non-respondents are not likely to have EI/QWL programs, we could conclude that almost 13 percent of the organizations surveyed do have such plans.

Another survey by Gerald Klein (1985) produced a similar response rate. One thousand questionnaires were mailed to employers in three states and 125 firms replied, all but 12 of whom had some type of EI. Klein's results both support the Carson study and give us pause. Although some two-thirds of the respondents mentioned quality of work life improvement as an organizational goal, Klein found that many were not comfortable with bringing lower-level managers and employees into decision-making to any greater extent.

Quality circle data indicate both substantial activity and growth. As reported in a trade union guide to QWL (Parker, 1985, p. 8):

> "In 1983, the Secretary of the International Association of Quality Circles estimated that over 135,000 circles operated at 8,000 locations in the United States, involving more than one million participants. . . .
>
> "Here are some representative figures for 1984. Westinghouse claimed 20,000 of its 140,000 employees were active in more than 2,000 circles. General Motors claimed to have approximately 3,000 groups nationwide. The United Steelworkers said there were 500 teams functioning in the steel industry. The Communications Workers estimated that in the previous two years the number of its teams went from 150 to over 1,200."

The data suggest that QWL is in a growth phase and formally operative in at least 15 percent of American organizations. The estimate is conservative and reflects the fact that some of the larger studies (for example, the NYSE survey) did not include firms with fewer than 100 employees. The Work in America Institute, an acknowledged authority in this field, estimates that as many as 25 percent of U.S. workers may be covered by EI programs. The larger percentage of workers than of organizations may reflect the fact that larger companies tend to be involved in EI/QWL programs. While the exact figure is unknown, a reasonable estimate is that QWL affects one in every five or six workers in this country, a substantial fraction.

It is not surprising to find that large organizations and especially manufacturing companies tend to lead the way in QWL activity. The data also show that many service firms are participating in QWL. Public-sector QWL activity is often reported in case-study form, so that hard data on the extent of QWL at various levels of government are not readily available, but the volume of the literature suggests that QWL is in a growth period in the public sector comparable to that in the private sector.

I turn now to the external environment for QWL, for its success or failure can best be understood with some knowledge of its context. Also, there are intraorganizational factors to consider when examining the vitality and viability of QWL, and a brief examination of that subject also follows.

External Environment for EI

Political and Economic Considerations

On the political side, both Congress and recent presidents have indicated support for labor-management cooperation. The National Labor-Management Cooperation Act is in place, and the Executive Office has frequently urged a more effective relationship between management and labor. As noted, at least two federal agencies provide funds and other support for the effort. At the same time, public policy is perceived, at least by organized labor, as supportive of a growing effort by American industry to operate on a nonunion basis or, where that is impossible, to neutralize the effects of union power (Parker, 1985). Unions have, indeed, suffered substantial membership declines, and they concentrate considerable effort on defining their difficulties and examining possible solutions. Decisions by the National Labor Relations Board and the courts, along with the traumatic dismissal of air traffic controllers, are cited by labor as illustrative of government hostility. Certainly, some confusion by labor with regard to the position of government is understandable.

An additional concern as to the role of government arises from the potential conflict between federal labor laws and labor-management cooperative activity. Section 8(a)(2) of the National Labor Relations Act makes it unlawful for an employer to dominate or interfere with the formation or administration of a labor organization or to contribute financial or other support to it. This language has been interpreted in some cases (both union and nonunion situations) to prohibit certain types of cooperative efforts or to make the employee participants ineligible for labor union representation on the theory that they have become members of management. The U.S. Department of Labor (1986) has taken a strong stand on the subject, stating: "Clearly, cooperation and problem solving offer more promise for productive labor-management relationships than the combat of the past. If our statutes and practices are an impediment to change, we must be willing to encourage a process that will ultimately benefit society as a whole."

On the economic side, the U.S. has witnessed a shift away from manufacturing and toward service industries. "Service" is a catchall term and includes a variety of high-tech activity alongside a far larger number of organizations at the lower-paying end of the labor market. When the shift to services is coupled with a younger, better-educated labor force with higher aspirations than those of the past, meeting the new workers' interest in having a say about matters affecting them becomes more important. The baby-boom numbers and their key place in today's labor market highlight the issue.

Yet another factor is that our competitive position in international markets leaves something to be desired, and this lack of an ability to compete has apparently been a motivating force driving many firms to EI. Unfortunately, concurrent high management expectations of what can be accomplished with employee involvement complicates its implementation.

The New Industrial Relations

The Massachusetts Institute of Technology (MIT) group, led by Robert B. McKersie and Thomas A. Kochan, have identified what they believe to be a significant shift in the locus of decision-making affecting the organizational approach toward employees. They identify three levels of industrial relations and human resource activity within the firm: (1) the workplace level where individuals and work groups interact with supervisors, local union representatives, and co-workers on a day-to-day basis; (2) the middle tier where collective bargaining or personnel policies are negotiated or designed; and (3) the highest level of strategy formation where long-run values, business strategies, and priorities are established (Kochan, McKersie, and Katz, 1985).

They stress that a shift has taken place away from the middle tier as the locus for organizational decision-making affecting labor relations and employee policy. The top tier with its strategic planning orientation is now in active control and depends heavily on human resource executives who have training in organizational behavior/development and who typically have broader backgrounds than some of their industrial relations predecessors.

To the extent the MIT researchers are correct—and they describe many of our most visible companies—the initiative is apparently in management's hands as it stresses nonunion operations with greater levels of participation and worker flexibility.

Top management officials are frequently quoted as supportive of EI. The *Harvard Business Review* regularly carries stories on the topic. As noted earlier, Mills's 1978 article in that journal was an important stage-setter for today's QWL. A 1982 *Business Week* article, "A Management Split over Labor Relations" (June 14, 1982, p. 19) reported on a survey of 400 high-level executives who were asked whether they would like to see a return to traditional bargaining once the economy became healthy or whether they preferred giving unions and workers a greater say in company operations if employee compensation were tied to company performance. Approximately half of the executives said they would opt for greater union and employee involvement.

A 1984 survey by The Conference Board found that a majority of executives believed that "the experience now being gained in participative management and quality-of-work-life efforts will yield a reliable alternative managerial style, necessary for the future of U.S. productivity" (Gorlin and Schein, 1984, as reported in Gold, 1986, p. 28). However, some doubts and uncertainties were expressed. These included:

"1. The participative style is too recent and too little understood; its adoption may be too abrupt in certain workplaces.

"2. Innovations, especially problem-solving groups, have a limited life expectancy.

"3. Problem-solving groups require too much time for preparation and implementation and are not worth the return in cost savings."

Another basis for management support of employee participation comes from the Japanese experience. Ouchi's Theory Z with its positive Japanese-derived approach to participation is in high regard in today's management circles. Writers are continuing to emphasize the differences between Japanese and American cultures (as well as the lack of fit of European co-determination) and to recommend that the American cooperative system should be based more on specific organizational situations (Mroczkowski, 1984).

The new industrial relations suggests that worker participation will likely exist in more nonunion firms in the future. This may consequently have a dampening effect on union participation in EI. It is also possible, however, that unions will develop a variety of distinctive and effective roles with regard to EI. In what might be termed a reverse shock effect, some unions have been driven to a more participative and flexible posture in situations where concession bargaining has taken place. In many other relationships, unions have entered into full EI/QWL partnerships with management.

The attitude toward EI/QWL is far more mixed on the union side than it is in management. Some international unions are hostile to QWL and have adopted resolutions to that effect—the American Postal Workers Union and the United Electrical, Radio and Machine Workers of America, for example. Most unions, particularly those in industries with severe economic problems, take a wary but balanced stance. They are willing to have their locals participate in QWL programs or "processes," as they frequently are called, but with substantial caveats. They may require that there be genuine information-sharing by management, no union-busting animus, and no interference with collective bargaining, and that layoffs be avoided. The International Association of Machinists and the International Union of Electronic, Electrical, Technical, Salaried and Machine Workers are examples, although the IAM makes clear that it prefers to resolve all problems through the collective bargaining process.

The UAW, the United Steelworkers of America, and the Communications Workers have been among the most active unions with joint EI/QWL programs. But even here there is considerable opposition to EI/QWL, particularly in the UAW and the Steelworkers (Kochan, Katz, and Mower, 1984, p. 175).

Internal QWL Problems

Mixed Strategy

A company that decides on a greenfields (new plant, usually nonunion) approach to expansion while courting the support of union officials for QWL programs in existing plants is inevitably going to find little interest in cooperation from the unions—except under the most dire economic circumstances. General Motors faced this dilemma more than 20 years ago when it opted for the so-called "Southern Strategy"—essentially a move southward to an economic and labor climate perceived to be more favorable to management. When interest developed in QWL at existing GM plants, the corporation had to make a decision as to which approach would predominate. The QWL approach was the choice. Certainly, other factors may have played a role in the decision, but the company recognized squarely that the decision had to be made.

Other less sophisticated organizations may seek to go down both paths at once—the mixed strategy. Most observers would have substantial doubt about the lasting value of EI in those circumstances.

Local Management and Union Positions

Stands taken by top management leaders and international unions were discussed earlier. The postures of other management and union officers, at lower levels of the organizations, also warrant consideration.

Although top management appears to be highly supportive of QWL, the same cannot consistently be said of lower level management officials. Skepticism has been known to take the form of comments by management personnel to the effect: "What are we doing, giving the workers the keys to the plant?" While it is unlikely that this is a majority position, it creates an operating problem.

This writer is familiar with one large firm where a key human resource official was asked to head up a new QWL effort in a major division. After reviewing the situation, the individual involved requested a two-year lead period to work with divisional management officials to obtain their genuine support for the QWL effort. He made it clear that without this support the program was not likely to be successful. His proviso was accepted and provides potent reinforcement for the frequently expressed maxim that top management support is essential for an EI effort.

More and more attention is being given to the lowest level of management, the first-line supervisor. The influence of first-line supervisors received what many considered a knockout blow when they were excluded from coverage under the National Labor Relations Act. Also, concern for day-to-day labor relations moved to higher level staff officials, who frequently bypassed the first-line supervisor in dealing with shop stewards. It is not surprising that first-line supervisors may see quality circles and semiautonomous work groups as new threats to their positions and status.

Janice Klein's study (1984) highlights the conflicting organizational and personal goals in the minds of first-line supervisors when QWL appears on the scene. Klein studied attitudes toward employee involvement programs in nine companies. Seventy-two percent of the supervisors thought the program was good for the company, and 60 percent believed the program was good for the employees involved. However, only 31 percent of the supervisors considered the program good for supervisors.

In other responses the supervisors made it clear that they supported the program because they had to go along if they wished to retain their jobs. The study also produced evidence that supervisors found various low-key ways to scuttle the programs. For example, one company made use of semiautonomous work teams as problem-solvers. When a team ran into snags and asked for supervisory help, the response frequently was, "It's not my job, it's the team's problem." Thus, a not unexpected finding of Klein's study is that supervisors who are told little about new quality circles and who are not invited to play any role with them see them as threats to their positions.

Management has had to learn the lesson about QWL that it has learned about many other approaches to management effectiveness. The first-line supervisor is often the implementor of the program, process, or activity or is in a position to damage or even subvert it. Just as QWL requires the support of the employee on the line, no less does it require the active support of the first-line supervisor.

The same holds true for local union leadership. Local leaders cannot be blamed for wondering whether the company is trying to wean worker loyalty away from the union through its employee participation program. New groups may be perceived as providing workers with opportunities for new allegiances. Similarly, they may have legitimate concerns over the emergence of competition from worker leaders in QWL who may choose to use their new visibility as a springboard in later union elections.

The company usually has a better opportunity than the union to prepare itself for an EI program. In many cases the local union leadership is going through an introductory education about QWL, while top management has already provided its managers with a general background. One plant which this author visited had recently established quality circles. The company and union had agreed that the quality circles were independent of the collective bargaining relationship. Shortly afterward the most senior shop steward in the plant filed a grievance. He didn't like his quality circle and felt that his superseniority was sufficient to enable him to bump into a more satisfactory group. His misconception underlines the difficulty inherent in establishing a QWL program since it may turn out to be both threatening and not fully understood.

Program Installation and Management Style

Substantial lead time is needed if an EI program is to be successful. The broad educational work that has to be done with management and union personnel was emphasized in the previous section. Here the stress is on some aspects of program installation.

A joint management-labor steering committee is usually the device employed to identify the possible approaches and potential problems. This, in turn, mandates considerable information flow up and down the line between the shop floor and the representative actors, particularly as departmental or other committees are formed. Many organizations have learned the importance of early response to some group suggestions so that a favorable track record can be used to promote the program. There are many procedural and structural problems which can be anticipated and for which practitioners have developed useful solutions. One basic issue, however, is the impact QWL has on the way in which an organization is run, and the consequential effect on program installation.

Management has traditionally operated a hierarchic organization. It is clear that there is a chain of command in most organizations, and decisions are made on the basis of conferred authority. It is true that there is a long-run need for acquiescence of the governed in many cases, but the short run, at least, is dominated by the authority structure.

Walton (1985) has referred to the change in management style as a move from control to commitment. He describes the former in these words (p. 59):

"The traditional—or control oriented—approach to workforce management took shape during the early part of the century in response to the division of work into small, fixed jobs for which individuals would be held accountable. . . . [M]anagement organized its own responsibilities into a hierarchy of specialized roles buttressed by a top-down allocation of authority and by status symbols attached to positions in the hierarchy."

He explains the commitment approach as follows:

"In this new commitment-based approach to the work force, jobs are designed to be broader than before, to combine planning and implementation, and to include efforts to upgrade operations, not just to maintain them. Individual responsibilities are expected to change as conditions change, and teams, not individuals, often are the organizational units accountable for performance. With management hierarchies relatively flat and differences in status minimized, control and lateral coordination depend on shared goals, and expertise rather than formal position determines influence."

The frequent decision to install a QWL plan in part of an organization can accentuate installation problems. For example, quality circles, with their democratic informality, operating alongside of departments with traditional management styles can create uncertainty as to just what the dominant philosophy is—the traditional or the new. The point here is that organizations (and their unions) may find it necessary or desirable to begin with a partial EI installation. They may, for example, limit themselves to quality circles. Similarly, the company may believe it appropriate to work with a limited subset of departments. In both cases an identity problem emerges that is not conducive to QWL success unless all parties understand the need for sequential installation of EI in an organization.

Relationship to Collective Bargaining

Many companies and unions start their QWL effort with the understanding that QWL activities will remain separate from collective bargaining. Aside from staying away from contractual provisions, this frequently means that the initial emphasis will be on matters affecting workplace satisfaction and product quality. To the extent that the program is successful or, conversely, that the economic status of the company requires concessions on the part of the union, particularly in workplace flexibility, the parties often find it necessary to relate the program to collective bargaining.

There is no pat formula for handling this most difficult of problems. Each set of relationships must work out its own approach. At one extreme, the cost and productivity improvements become important issues for subsequent collective bargaining. The other extreme occurs when all gains are quantified and immediate gainsharing is the normal outcome. Many other approaches are possible, but one which is beginning to receive attention is a limited form of gainsharing as a payroll add. That is, the parties may have agreed to share gains (however defined) on a 50-50 basis. The gain does not go into the base rate, but is paid as a bonus. A smaller percentage of the gain is paid for another year or two, and then the gain ceases to be paid. If the gain has lasting value, it will presumably continue to help improve the profitability of the company and can be dealt with in contractual negotiations. Also, early gainsharing is being used as a device to recoup income lost in concession bargaining.

One individual who has considered the nexus between EI/QWL and collective bargaining is Irving Bluestone, a former UAW vice president and head of its General Motors division. In an address to a QWL team at a GM plant, he said:

> "Unions have and will always have the legal and moral responsibility to protect fairly and aggressively the rights of their members. There will be a continuing need to utilize a grievance procedure and engage in collective bargaining negotiations. This is not to say collective bargaining agreements cannot be altered to meet mutually desirable objectives of the QWL process, subject of course to the bargaining process and membership ratification. At Livonia [a Cadillac engine plant], for example, the traditional wage and classification structure was altered to

accommodate the pay-for-knowledge wage system. I expect the natural progression will lead to gain-sharing programs in which the workers receive financial and other benefits as their fair share in improved performance of the enterprise" (Kochan, Katz, and Mower, 1984, p. 173).

Program Evaluation

An evaluation of EI programs is not an easy task because there are a variety of programs with distinctly different content installed under many different conditions. Thus we must recognize that we are not dealing with a set of homogeneous plans. Nevertheless, there is general agreement that appropriate measures of QWL performance include program survival, cost and productivity, quality of the program, quality of work life itself, and the industrial relations climate as well as other measures of organizational performance such as absenteeism, tardiness, turnover, safety, and overtime.

Before considering the QWL record, we should note that there are difficulties to be encountered in dealing with these listed measures:

1. Newness of programs. For practical purposes, QWL, as such, was initiated in the late 1970s and has seen its greatest growth in the 1980s. This has meant that relatively little is available in the form of substantial longitudinal data—the kind that are needed if we are to understand the long-term role of employee involvement.

2. Sources and types of data. Some data may be suspect or simply not available. Although the volume of scholarly work is increasing, much of the information on which these studies are based comes from company officials or consultants who have a vested interest in positive QWL results. Also, for whatever reasons, some companies participating in QWL studies may not make available to researchers what data they have on the full range of EI costs and cost-savings.

Many organizations may have adopted QWL programs because it was "the right thing to do," and while they may have costed-out specific improvements, they have not attempted a general cost/benefit analysis, particularly in a program's early stages. Indeed, in some cases companies have made the point that early quantification of results could be a deterrent to success.

True cost data are not easy to come by. Not only are we concerned about the time of company personnel assigned to QWL and the expense of consultants, supporting staff, materiel, and employee clock hours, but an appropriate portion of executive (and union official) time should be allocated to the program.

3. Indirect effects. In many cases new patterns of cooperation have to overcome deep-seated lack of trust. While positive changes will show up in some performance measures, the type of employee and union trust that would create a climate for future work-rule flexibility and more effective bargaining may not be picked up in the program evaluation.

4. Theoretical confusion. Many studies, particularly the early ones, adopted what has been called the human relations notion that a satisfied worker is a productive worker. The empirical evidence for this belief is weak, and the other point of view—that productive employees, for whatever reason, are satisfied employees—if anything, has better standing. Yet many organizations have relied on attitude surveys for their QWL evaluations—as examples, AT&T, its spinoffs, and the Communications Workers of America. It should be noted, however, that these organizations are now using a broader range of measures to evaluate their well-established QWL efforts.

One operating problem with attitude surveys is that a single study at a particular point in time tells us little. If we find that 60 percent of the employees are satisfied with their supervisory relationship or corporate communication, we need to know how that figure changes over time to understand the effect of ongoing programs.

Another illustration of theoretical confusion is the simplistic conclusion that a decline in the number of grievances filed is an indication of QWL success. As most practitioners know, what underlies the grievance rate must be analyzed in order to identify possible reasons for the change. For example, a reduction in the number of grievances may be unhealthy and reflect softness on the part of first-line supervision. An increase may be healthy if it mirrors voice not available to previously frightened employees.

During the course of this study, the author interviewed a number of company and union officials at various plants. Much of what they had available on program evaluation was anecdotal, but the company officials involved were becoming increasingly aware that more refined program evaluations were necessary for the future of their employee involvement programs.

An obvious conclusion is that current evaluations of QWL programs are weak and often flawed. The difficulties listed above suggest that we must approach evaluating EI's effects on firm performance with considerable care.

Outcomes

Program Survival

QWL programs have high mortality rates. Given the nature and scope of problems associated with the introduction of these programs, it is not surprising that the data indicate lack of longevity as a common outcome. If a program gets past the initial stage, plateauing frequently takes place—that is, the program achieves a measure of success but is unable to proceed beyond a given level of participative activity.

Paul Goodman (1980) provides us with a good review of EI activity in the 1970s. At the end of the decade he studied plans known by him to be at least five years old and found that at least 75 percent of them were no longer functioning. He noted that this finding was in line with earlier research and cited work by Walton (1975).

Personnel associated with the Survey Research Center of the University of Michigan analyzed eight public- and private-sector projects originating between 1973 and 1978 and found that all eight had been terminated by 1984 (Cammann et al., 1984). Parker (1985), in his trade union guide to QWL, quotes James O'Toole and D. L. Landen as finding high mortality rates. O'Toole, who was closely associated with the formulation of the government's *Work in America* study, described the results of the experience as "one of a brief leap forward followed by prolonged backsliding." Landen, who has been active in the QWL world, including an important role with the Michigan Quality of Work Life Council, estimates that two-thirds to three-fourths of QWL programs fail (Parker, 1985, p. 132). Schuster (1984) studied 10 plans over a four- to seven-year period and found that only three of the plans had survived beyond six years. Noteworthy was the fact that those three plans remained successful after eight, 12, and 17 years (Gold, 1986, p. 31). Rankin (1986) estimated that approximately 40 percent of EI/QWL plans last for two or three years or less. These reports of relatively low survival rates are particularly significant when it is realized that some programs are undoubtedly operative in name only.

Why did so many plans remain at a plateau or fail outright? Conference Board researchers found the following characteristics contributing to a lack of success (Gold, 1986, pp. 45–46):

"1. The units with poor records were those in which there were severe management problems and poor profitability prior to the new plan.

"2. Union participation was either not invited early enough or was not invited at all.

"3. Real commitment from management (plant and/or corporate) was not communicated or proved.

"4. Training for managers, advisers, facilitators, and participants was insufficient.

"5. Line managers and supervisors did not fully accept their new roles in the participatory environment.

"6. People were not convinced that gains in productivity would not lead to layoffs."

On the union side, one study reported that union officials found the principal reasons limiting the growth of participation programs to be layoffs, management efforts to change work rules or practices, and supervisory resentment or resistance (Kochan, Katz, and Mower, 1984, p. 146).

A large number of existing EI/QWL plans were established in the 1980s, and it is too early to determine their long-term survival and success rates. Nevertheless, it is important to remember that the parties have had a chance to study other plans as well as the literature and to observe the problems associated with EI plans that failed. It is to be expected that plans newly established in the 1980s can benefit from the experience of their predecessors.

Our knowledge of organizational theory and behavior is helpful in the establishment and maintenance of QWL plans, but predictive certainty as to the degree of effectiveness will likely remain difficult to achieve. One reason for the severe limitations on that score is that we are dealing with values ranging from those associated with interpersonal relationships to those connected with the economic and political organization of society.

During the time they are functioning, even failed programs

often report positive results when measured by organizational effectiveness and/or employee satisfaction. The juxtaposition of lack of longevity of QWL programs with worthwhile utility levels suggests that program burnout may be a factor to be considered in trying to improve program success, or even survival. It is not surprising that the parties often report burnout as a problem. It may be that parties who are not ready to move beyond a certain QWL level at a given time can benefit from a jointly agreed-upon suspension of the program until conditions permit its resumption. Alternatively, they might choose simply to slow the pace of QWL activity for a while. Some parties, such as Xerox and the Amalgamated Clothing and Textile Workers Union, have traced plateauing to lack of contractual support and have negotiated employment security provisions and preferences for many forms of participation, not just quality circles (Cutcher-Gershenfeld, Kochan, and Verma, 1987). We are in a position to apply our increasingly deeper knowledge of QWL to the monitoring of ongoing plans.

While the early demise of many EI plans is known, we have very little information about what lasting effects the programs might have had on the organizations involved. It would be worthwhile to examine the "failed" programs to determine if there has been a residue of increased employee participation and trust with consequential effects on organizational performance and employee attitudes.

The performance of EI is examined in the section that follows. Since various studies have emphasized different aspects of organizational performance and/or employee attitudes, the reporting and analysis are facilitated by concentrating on study outcomes regardless of the mix of variables studied. As will be seen, in toto the analysts cover the range of relevant variables.

Other Outcomes

Symptomatic of many research results, a review by Locke and Schweiger (1979) found that worker satisfaction increased with participation in approximately 60 percent of 43 studies, but productivity improvement was associated with a participation program in only 20 percent of 46 cases.

A substantial examination of QWL during the 1980s has been proceeding at the Massachusetts Institute of Technology. While the work is continuing, three reports chronicle a cross-section of early findings (Katz, Kochan, and Gobeille, 1983; Kochan, Katz, and Mower, 1984; Katz, Kochan, and Weber, 1985). Longitudinal data have been emphasized—the study by Katz, Kochan, and Gobeille covered 18 plants during the period 1970–1979. Kochan, McKersie, and Katz (1985, p. 269) summarized the findings in their presentation at the annual meeting of the Industrial Relations Research Association in 1984 as follows:

"1. Quality of worklife (QWL) processes and other participatory processes diffuse slowly across organizations and rarely have diffused to the point where all, or even a majority of, workers participate in the QWL process on a continuous basis.

"2. QWL processes appear to be successful in improving the level of trust and motivation of employees for a period of time. The maintenance of these attitudinal improvements on a continuing basis, however, depends on the extent to which QWL programs are either reinforced or jeopardized by events that occur at higher levels of collective bargaining and strategic decision-making. Major layoffs, management demands for concessions, conflicts over union avoidance or recognition in nonunion facilities, etc., can all threaten the continuity of improved workplace relations, slow or stop the diffusion of the QWL process, and lower the contributions of QWL to organizational performance.

"3. The independent contributions of QWL to organizational performance, at least as measured by such things as labor costs and product quality, are rather marginal. However, QWL processes that include modifications in the organization of work have had a more significant positive impact on costs, productivity, employment, member satisfaction with union performance, and other performance measures."

Later work by the MIT group has reinforced No. 3 above. Based on a study of nine firms and 15 local or national unions, Cutcher-Gershenfeld, Kochan, and Verma (1987, p. 28) stated: "Our overriding conclusion is that stand-alone employee involvement processes have a low probability of being sustained over time in organizations. We have observed few examples where participation has been sustained and diffused in collective bargaining relation-

TABLE 2

How Corporations Rate the Productivity
of Specific Activities (in percents)

Activity	Very Success-ful	Somewhat Successful	Unsuccessful	Too Early or No Response
Job design/redesign	26%	48%	1%	26%
Job enlargement	25	42	1	33
Job rotation	24	43	1	32
Formal training and instruction	37	40	0	23
Setting employee goals	32	40	1	28
Employee appraisal and feedback	28	45	1	27
Setting company objectives	40	31	0	29
Structuring plant & office space	33	32	0	35
Organizational structure	26	43	1	30
Scheduling workflow	29	37	0	33
Personalized work hours	44	32	0	24
Suggestion systems	13	49	14	25
Labor/management committees	16	55	9	21
Labor advisory groups	0	66	0	35
Quality circles	28	29	1	43
Production teams	32	36	3	29
Salarying blue-collar workers	67	15	0	18
Task forces	34	35	1	29
Surveys of employee attitudes	22	47	3	28
Financial Incentives				
Piecework	60	17	3	20
Group productivity	18	58	2	24
Profit-sharing	26	47	3	20
Stock purchase plans	14	47	15	24

Source: Freund and Epstein (1984), p. 160.

ships without leading to or being associated with more fundamental structural changes in the labor-management relationship."

The New York Stock Exchange study (Freund and Epstein, 1984), referred to earlier, provides us with a broad range of management opinions on QWL effectiveness; the results are summarized in Table 2. Data underlying these opinions are unavailable. Nevertheless, these evaluations, collected in 1982, show management as believing in general in the efficacy of a variety of QWL processes. When the "very successful" and "somewhat successful" categories are combined, no process or activity has less than a majority of respondents reporting some degree of success. Although none of the respondents rated labor advisory groups as "very successful," they did consider the activity "somewhat successful." The overall results indicate general satisfaction with a selection of EI activities, but these evaluations must be tempered with the realization that firms with EI/QWL plans tend to be supportive of their programs.

Another study of 101 industrial firms (Carson, 1985) found that those with participatory management have higher value-line financial ratings and better industrial relations. The industrial relations findings were based on five factors (see Table 3). Thirteen of the 14 value-line financial ratings, shown in Table 4, were found to be more favorable in the participatory firms.

The results are correlative and the measures have undoubtedly been affected by many externalities. Nevertheless, the positive association of healthy industrial relations and economic performance measures with participatory management is, at the least, encouraging to organizations considering a new EI/QWL program or an expansion of an existing one.

Sophisticated evaluation techniques have been used in some studies reported here. Miller and Monge (1986) utilized meta-analysis which considers the strength of effects between variables and corrects for systematic error. They concluded that participation affects both satisfaction and productivity, but the effect of participation on satisfaction is greater than its effect on productivity. They also report that findings are affected by research settings and organizational factors.

Many EI/QWL reports involve either a single firm or a small number of organizations. With the exception of the outright failures,

TABLE 3
Industrial Relations Compared for Responding Firms

	Firms Reporting Better Than Industry Average[a]	
Measure	Participative (85)	Nonparticipative (16)
Employee turnover	2.64	2.50
Absenteeism	2.47	2.44
Accidents	2.76	2.81
Grievances	2.78	2.63
Pay and benefits	2.47	2.13
Total labor relations measures reported as better by participative firms: 4		

Source: Carson (1985), p. 47.
[a] Based on a 1–5 scale with 1 being poor and 5 being very good.

TABLE 4

Financial Performance Ratings of Responding Firms

Measure	Average Rating Reported by Firms	
	Participative (85)	Nonparticipative (16)
Financial strength	57.18	54.06
Stock price stability	53.33	44.69
Price growth persistence	53.41	47.50
Earnings predictability	50.00	58.44
Sales per share	124.42	96.06
Cash flow per share	9.58	7.25
Earnings per share	5.96	4.75
Average annual price/earnings ratio	13.07	12.75
Average annual earnings yield percent	9.02	9.38
Net profit ($ in millions)	210.84	147.44
Net profit margin (percent)	6.74	5.81
Net worth ($ in millions)	1294.72	901.50
Percent earned total capital	14.13	13.94
Percent earned net worth	16.59	15.63

Total financial ratings reported as higher by participative firms: 13

Source: Carson (1985), p. 48.

ratings of the impact of EI on organizational performance range from highly favorable to cautious optimism.

In the latter category is Richardson's (1985) six-year study of four companies in mature industries—steel, copper, chemicals, and ore. He reported (p. 43):

"The experiences of the four firms described in this article demonstrate that productivity improvement and cost reduction through employee involvement are possible in theory but are hard to achieve and sustain in practice. If successfully implemented, however, the returns can be substantial in both economic and social terms for both the company and its employees. Still, the initiative involves substantial risk, and may end in failure if it is not well managed."

Richardson went on to stress that the commitment of top management was far and away the most critical factor in the success of a program. One result of the study, which he characterized as potentially surprising to observers, is the extent to which companies and unions were able to work together on tough cost objectives. He noted (p. 43):

> "The successful companies in this study, however, found that employees and unions understand the economic reality and are willing to accept fewer jobs, so long as they are secure and as long as necessary terminations allow employees to leave with dignity. Those who remain can have pride in their contributions to the competitiveness of the operation. From the firms described here, it appears that what is needed is a little imagination, good no-frills management, and a genuine willingness to communicate and cooperate."

Richardson elected to deal with four industries known to be in serious economic difficulty. The fact that there was some success to report for the effect of EI on firm performance in these industries as well as a clear direction for an effective future role for EI is a positive finding. The potential for realistic labor-management cooperation in cost reduction is also significant.

Three single-plant studies are illustrative of favorable EI productivity findings. In the first, Rosenberg and Rosenstein (1980) examined the records of 262 meetings of workers, supervisors, and managers at a unionized foundry over the period 1969–1975. An index of participative activity was prepared and compared with an index of productivity. The authors conclude (p. 367):

> "The results of the statistical analysis performed strongly support the hypothesis that an increase in the level of the conduct and content of group participative activity is associated with an increase in group productivity. The research findings also appear to support the mediating effect of monetary rewards. The effect of group productivity improvement appears to have been enhanced by a productivity-related monetary reward. However, further analysis of variance corroborates the conclusion that group participative activity, the monetary reward notwithstanding, was the principal indicator of change in productivity."

Rosenberg and Rosenstein suggest that their results are supportive of the human resource model which perceives participation, by increasing worker influence and self-direction, as leading to productivity which, in turn, reinforces the desire and ability to participate further. This is as contradistinct to the human relations model which stresses participation itself as providing the direct motivation for productivity improvement.

A second study (Cornell, 1984) examined variables influencing QWL and job performance in a bank encoding task. Cornell concluded (p. 377): "An important finding was that the variables which contributed to job satisfaction were different from those which led to productivity. . . . The productivity results indicated that operators who are satisfied with the organizational context (i.e., co-workers, supervision, job security and compensation) are more productive. . . ."

EI is concerned with improving satisfaction in both the job and the organizational context. When it succeeds in altering the organizational context positively, from the viewpoint of the worker, the Cornell study indicates that productivity is enhanced. The basic thesis that productivity can be improved through worker participation is supported by the Cornell study, but it also suggests that we need to know more about the precise mechanism involved.

Not all programs that terminate are unsuccessful. Illustrative is a program at Bethlehem Steel's shipbuilding facility in Beaumont, Texas. Both problem-solving teams and semiautonomous work teams were utilized. The U.S. Department of Transportation (1986) reports (p. 1): "The process at the Beaumont Yard was brief, lasting only seven months, due to a rapid business turn down. During this short period of time the program generated annual savings of 125,000 manhours, with a return of 3:1 over cost."

Management's interest in EI as a vehicle for improving firm performance is apparently increasing, albeit that EI programs exist at a minority of American employers. Mohrman and Ledford (1985), who studied the diffusion of QWL, concluded (p. 414):

"An ever increasing number of American businesses are keenly interested in human resource practices that may be able to increase both performance and adaptability by more fully tapping the potential of their workforce. Many companies no longer view such practices as curious innovations practiced in some corner of the company, but see them as key ingredients to profitability or even survival. A wide variety of approaches to increasing employee involvement are being attempted."

One student of EI, Mroczkowski (1984), mindful of the European emphasis on formal industrial democracy as opposed to the more informal worker participation in the U.S., raises an important concern. He wonders whether the largely nonunion, and possibly paternalistic, American approach can survive (p. 60):

"With the labor relations scene divided into 'unionised' and 'non-unionised' sectors, change programs in the U.S. are suspended between the management-dominated paternalist and the collective bargaining perspective. There is evidence that both approaches have yielded some benefits. The question remains however if in the long run the benefits of participative management can be maintained within the purely paternalistic mode which appears to be preferred by more U.S. organisations so far, or whether the logic of genuine labor-management partnership will ultimately bring about an increase in power sharing based on negotiation."

With regard to workplace attitudes toward workplace issues after an EI experience, the Kochan, Katz, and Mower (1984) study in five automobile plants found the effects of participation to be largely positive (see Table 5). Almost three-quarters of the respondents believed that worker morale, supervisory relationships, productivity, and quality were improved by worker participation; they rated the impact of worker participation as having a "somewhat positive effect" or a "very positive effect." More than 60 percent of the union officers reported that there had been cost improvements. The least positive scores were associated with their appraisal of union members' views of the union and its officers. Here too, however, the number of positive responses exceeded the negative ones.

The data suggest that while union officers may have some questions about QWL because of their concern regarding the effect of such programs on the union, their beliefs that the programs have had a healthy effect on workplace issues are stronger. While it is difficult to generalize on the basis of these limited findings, they indicate that there are strong positive reasons for union association with QWL, particularly when organizational viability is involved.

Also, Verma and McKersie (1987) note that EI programs enhance worker identification with the firm and its goals. They

TABLE 5

Effects of Participation on Workplace Issues

Activity	Very Negative	Somewhat Negative	No Effect	Somewhat Positive	Very Positive
Worker morale/job satisfaction	2.8	12.0	13.0	54.6	17.6
Worker-supervisor relations	0.0	14.7	17.4	56.2	17.1
Productivity	3.8	5.7	17.1	56.2	17.1
Product/service quality	3.8	4.7	17.0	34.0	40.6
Labor costs	4.7	5.7	28.3	50.0	11.3
Job security	11.1	13.9	36.1	26.9	12.0
Member-committeeman relations	1.9	18.5	24.1	42.6	13.0
Member satisfaction with union	6.5	25.9	27.8	31.5	8.3
Grievance rate	1.9	4.7	29.0	38.3	26.2
Union officer-plant management relationship	1.9	4.7	15.1	49.1	29.2
Absenteeism	2.8	7.4	48.1	34.3	7.4
Safety and health	2.8	2.8	39.4	44.0	11.0
Union member-officer relationship	4.7	11.2	34.6	39.3	10.3
Membership identification with union	5.6	17.6	39.8	29.6	7.4

Source: Kochan, Katz, and Mower (1984), p. 136.

point out that, to the extent the union is a co-sponsor of the plan, EI can help reinforce identification with the union as much as with the firm.

Gerald Klein's (1985) study makes a final major point about management's interest in employee involvement as a continuing phenomenon. Management is usually the instigator or the triggering force for an EI program. Also, management usually carries the major part of the ongoing expense of the program. Thus, management's attitude toward continuation of well-established QWL programs is important.

Klein's results, reported in Table 6, show both high levels of management satisfaction with various types of activity and strong interest in maintaining the programs. Although some of the respondent numbers were small for particular activities, it is striking that the smallest percentage of management reporting likelihood of program continuation for any one activity is 83.3 percent. Given the

TABLE 6

Satisfaction with Fully Operational
Programs and Likelihood of Continuation

Activity	Level of Satisfaction with Program to Date[a]	Likelihood of Program Continuation—Percent[b]
Productivity teams n=4	6.50	100.0
Semiautonomous groups n=6	6.17	93.3
Worker involvement programs n=12	6.17	83.3
Workplace study groups n=2	6.00	92.5
Profit-sharing n=28	5.97	98.7
Organization development programs n=18	5.94	96.4
Bonuses paid on unit productivity n=25	5.72	97.6
Other productivity improvement programs n=7	5.71	91.4
Quality circles n=12	5.67	89.6
Communication program n=51	5.64	96.5
Cost reduction program n=34	5.36	93.4
Employee suggestion systems n=44	5.09	91.1
Labor-management productivity committees n=3	5.00	85.0

Source: Gerald Klein (1985), p. 68.

[a] Seven-point scale from "very satisfied" (7), "moderately satisfied" (4), to "very dissatisfied" (1).

[b] Scale based on 10 percent increments.

large number of EI program failures, it is encouraging to find that programs which have apparently successfully resolved program-design obstacles and achieved an established status are highly regarded by management. The nature of the satisfaction responses also indicates that managements are pleased with the programs not just for their intrinsic value in relationship improvement, but that they also find the programs making a substantial contribution to organizational effectiveness.

Conclusion

Employee involvement takes many forms in the United States, ranging from single entities such as quality circles alone to a variety of broad-based programs. American programs are largely nonideological as compared with some of their European counterparts. While the move toward EI/QWL has historic roots going back to at least the turn of the century, the current movement has been with us only since the late 1960s. Fully operational EI/QWL plans are found in a minority of American organizations, but their numbers are increasing and may now be in 10–15 percent of such organizations and affect approximately 15–20 percent of American workers, both union and nonunion.

We have learned much about the installation of EI programs, including the need to have the support of top management, to integrate the first-line supervisor into the activity, and to meet the needs of the union and its membership when EI is introduced.

Research data show that established EI programs typically increase worker satisfaction with the job and the organizational context across a wide variety of organizational types. Although dramatic, single-case, cost or productivity improvements are frequently cited, organizational productivity improvements, as measured by a varied group of indicators, have been present in less than half of most large-scale studies. At the same time it must be emphasized that it is rare for EI/QWL programs to be associated with any diminishing in organizational performance. Satisfactory institutional arrangements for the difficult reward-sharing and collective bargaining interfaces are still in the early stages of development. The desirability of stand-alone EI programs evolving into collective bargaining issues and affecting the organizational environment is becoming increasingly clear.

Relatively positive findings for existing programs are juxtaposed with a high rate of program failure. The outlook for future programs is an improved success rate, however, based on the lessons we have learned about EI/QWL program installation and support. Management satisfaction with outcomes in well-established plans and growing worker interest in affecting workplace decisions are factors affecting EI/QWL growth. The mixed posture of unions toward EI/QWL is likely to continue, but the prevailing union approach is expected to be a cautious acceptance of EI/QWL when satisfactory survival and growth ground rules can be established. Thus, continuing EI/QWL activity in the short run may be expected in both union and nonunion settings.

No single model of EI has emerged as dominant, nor do we have any agreed-upon approach to EI program evaluation. As with many other social programs, evaluations in this area are becoming more sophisticated, but researchers still face the difficult task of sorting out long-term missionary effects from the more readily quantifiable short-term results. Another difficulty with evaluations is that EI/QWL programs may have a variety of goal emphases. Nevertheless, as we continue to experiment with employee involvement in the decade ahead, it is reasonable to expect that program evaluation will receive increased attention.

It must be remembered that significant numbers of organizations and employees involved in EI/QWL are a product of the 1980s. Substantial longitudinal data likely to emerge in the next decade will be important in determining the extent to which formal employee involvement activity becomes a standard organizational concern in both union and nonunion environments. The ability of employee involvement programs to survive economic stress at the organizational level will also be watched closely.

References

Barthel, Duane L. *Amana*. Lincoln: University of Nebraska Press, 1984.

Cammann, Courtlandt, Edward E. Lawler III, Gerald E. Ledford, and Stanley E. Seashore. *Management-Labor Cooperation in Quality of Worklife Experiments: Comparative Analysis of Eight Cases*. Report to the U.S. Department of Labor, Survey Research Center, University of Michigan, March 1984.

Carson, S. Andrew. "Participatory Management Beefs Up the Bottom Line." *Personnel* 62 (July 1985): pp. 45–48.

Cornell, Paul T. "Variables Influencing QWL and Job Performance in an Encoding Task." In *Human Factors in Organizational Design and Management*, eds. H. W. Hendrick and O. Brown, Jr. North Holland: Elsevier Science Publishers, 1984. Pp. 373–77.

Cutcher-Gershenfeld, Joel E. "QWL: An Historical Perspective." *The Work Life Review* 2 (September 1983): pp. 16–24.

_____. "Labor-Management Cooperation in American Communities: What's in It for the Unions?" *Annals of the American Academy of Political and Social Science* 473 (May 1984): pp. 76–95.

Cutcher-Gershenfeld, Joel E., Thomas A. Kochan, and Anil Verma. "Recent Developments in Employee Involvement Activities: A Matter of Erosion or Transformation." Paper presented at the 1987 Pacific Rim Labor Policy Conference, Vancouver, June 15–17, 1987.

French, Wendell. *The Personnel Management Process*, 3d ed. Boston: Houghton-Mifflin, 1974.

Freund, William C., and Eugene Epstein. *People and Productivity*. Homewood, Ill.: Dow Jones-Irwin, 1984.

Gold, Charlotte. *Labor-Management Committees: Confrontation, Cooptation or Cooperation?* Key Issues No. 28. Ithaca, N.Y.: ILR Press, Cornell University, 1986.

Goodman, Paul S. "Realities of Improving the Quality of Work Life." *Labor Law Journal* 31 (August 1980): pp. 487–94.

Gorlin, Harriet, and Lawrence Schein. *Innovations in Managing Human Resources.* Report No. 849. New York: The Conference Board, 1984.

Hanlon, Martin D. "Unions and the QWL Movement." *QWL Review* 1 (Fall 1981): pp. 8-13.

Katz, Harry C., Thomas A. Kochan, and Kenneth R. Gobeille. "Industrial Relations Performance, Economic Performance, and QWL: An Interplant Analysis." *Industrial and Labor Relations Review* 37 (October 1983): pp. 3-17.

Katz, Harry C., Thomas A. Kochan, and Mark R. Weber. "Assessing the Effects of Industrial Relations and Quality of Work Life Efforts on Organizational Effectiveness." *Academy of Management Journal* 28 (September 1985): pp. 509-27.

Keidel, Robert W. "Quality of Working Life in the Private Sector: An Overview and a Developmental Perspective." Washington: U.S. Office of Personnel, 1980.

Klein, Gerald D. "Productivity Improvement and Quality of Work Life in the Delaware Valley." Working Paper No. 9, Rider College, Lawrenceville, N.J., October 1985.

Klein, Janice A. "Why Supervisors Resist Employee Involvement." *Harvard Business Review* 62 (September-October 1984): pp. 87-95.

Kochan, Thomas A., Harry C. Katz, and Nancy R. Mower. *Worker Participation and American Unions: Threat or Opportunity.* Kalamazoo, Mich.: W.E. Upjohn Institute for Employment Research, 1984.

Kochan, Thomas A., Robert B. McKersie, and Harry C. Katz. "U.S. Industrial Relations in Transition: A Summary Report." *Proceedings of the 37th Annual Meeting, Industrial Relations Research Association.* Madison, Wis.: IRRA, 1985. Pp. 261-76.

Kochan, Thomas A., Harry C. Katz, and Robert B. McKersie. *The Transformation of American Industrial Relations.* New York: Basic Books, 1985.

Lansing Area Joint Labor-Management Committee, Inc. *QWL/EI.* Lansing, Mich.: The Committee, 1983.

Lawler, Edward E. III, and Susan R. Mohrman. "Quality Circles After the Fad." *Harvard Business Review* 62 (January-February 1985): pp. 64-71.

———. "Education, Management Style and Organizational Effectiveness." *Personnel Psychology* 38 (Spring 1985): pp. 1-26.

Leone, Richard D. "The Operation of Area Labor-Management Committees." Washington: U.S. Department of Labor, 1982.

Likert, Rensis. *New Patterns of Management.* New York: McGraw-Hill, 1961.

Locke, E. A., and D. M. Schweiger. "Participation in Decision-Making: One More Look." In *Research in Organizational Behavior*, Vol. 1, ed. B. M. Staw. Greenwich, Conn.: JAI Press, 1979. Pp. 265-339.

Michigan Quality of Work Life Council. "QWL, A Goal and a Process." Duplicated. Troy, Mich.: undated.

Miller, Katherine I., and Peter R. Monge. "Participation, Satisfaction and Productivity: A Meta-Analytic Review." *Academy of Management Journal* 29 (December 1986): pp. 727-53.

Mills, Ted. "Europe's Industrial Democracy: An American Response." *Harvard Business Review* 56 (November-December 1978): pp. 143-52.

Mohrman, Susan A., and Gerald E. Ledford, Jr. "The Design and Use of Effective Employee Participation Groups: Implications for Human Resource Management." *Human Resource Management* 24 (Winter 1985): pp. 413-27.

Mroczkowski, Tomasz. "Is the American Labor-Management Relationship Changing?" *British Journal of Industrial Relations* 22 (March 1984): pp. 47-61.

Parker, Mike. *Inside the Circle.* Boston: South End Press, 1985.

Rankin, Tom. "Integrating QWL and Collective Bargaining." *Work-Life Review* 5 (July 1986): pp. 14-18.

Rayback, Joseph G. *A History of American Labor.* New York: Free Press, 1966.

Richardson, Peter S. "Courting Greater Employee Involvement Through Participative Management." *Sloan Management Review* 26 (Winter 1985): pp. 33-43.

Rosenberg, Richard D., and Eliezer Rosenstein. "Participation and Productivity: An Empirical Study." *Industrial and Labor Relations Review* 33 (April 1980): pp. 355–67.

Schuster, Michael H. *Union-Management Cooperation.* Kalamazoo, Mich.: W.E. Upjohn Institute for Employment Research, 1984.

Turban, E. "Do Quality Circles Pay?" *Training and Development Journal* 39 (June 1985): pp. 10, 12.

U.S. Department of Health, Education, and Welfare. *Work in America.* Washington: U.S. Government Printing Office, 1972.

U.S. Department of Labor, Bureau of Labor Management Relations and Cooperative Programs. *U.S. Labor Laws and the Future of Labor-Management Cooperation.* Washington: 1986.

U.S. Department of Transportation, National Shipbuilding Research Program. *Problem Solving Teams in Shipbuilding.* Washington: November 1986.

Verma, Anil, and Robert B. McKersie. "Employee Involvement: The Implications of Noninvolvement by Unions." *Industrial and Labor Relations Review* 40 (July 1987): pp. 556–68.

Walton, Richard E. "The Diffusion of New Work Structures: Explaining Why Success Didn't Take." *Organizational Dynamics* 3 (Winter 1975): pp. 3–21.

————. "From Control to Commitment in the Work Place." *Harvard Business Review* 63 (March-April 1985): pp. 57–74.

Whyte, William F. "From Human Relations to Organizational Behavior: Reflections on the Changing Scene." *Industrial and Labor Relations Review* 40 (July 1987): pp. 487–500.

Winpisinger, William. "Job Enrichment: A Union View." *Monthly Labor Review* 96 (April 1973): pp. 54–56.

Chapter 5

Grievance Procedures and Firm Performance

By Casey Ichniowski and David Lewin
Columbia University

Why are grievance procedures worth studying? One reason is that the procedures may affect worker turnover and productivity, and thereby affect firm performance. Second, labor and management in both union and nonunion settings have been experimenting with new forms of grievance procedures, and these experiments may be generating new patterns of workplace dispute resolution. Third, characteristics of individuals, organizations, and the environment can influence the structure, scope, use, and effectiveness of contemporary grievance procedures. Ultimately, research on all these issues is needed to build a positive theory of grievance procedures that will provide a more systematic framework than is presently available for thinking about the role of the grievance procedure in the workplace.

Of the numerous questions that can be posed about grievance procedures, the most widely studied appears to be: What are the determinants of grievance activity? Empirical studies have found that there are a number of factors that may influence grievance filing—the community (Derber et al., 1965), technology (Kuhn, 1961), size of establishment (Peach and Livernash, 1974), urbanization (Stern, 1976), employee sex and race (Freeman, 1980; Ashenfelter, 1972), supervisory relations (Fleishman and Harris, 1962; Stagner, 1962; Weissinger, 1976), management policies (Slichter et al., 1960), and union structure (Anderson, 1979; Bok and Dunlop, 1970).

One theme shared by much of the existing literature on grievance filing and resolution is that the grievance handling process is a direct extension of the collective bargaining process (Kuhn, 1961; Chamberlain and Kuhn, 1986). Therefore, prescriptions found in the literature on grievance procedures often reflect values in the United States system of collective bargaining—values which emphasize industrial peace and direct determination of terms of employment by labor and management. For example, "effective" grievance procedures have been described as ones in which grievances are settled quickly (Thomson, 1974; Thomson and Murray, 1976), as close to their sources as possible (Slichter et al., 1960), and by experienced grievance handlers and negotiators (Begin, 1971). A number of recent studies have measured the effectiveness of grievance procedures by examining several dimensions of grievance handling and resolution. For example, Anderson (1979), Briggs (1984), Lewin (1983, 1984), and Lewin and Peterson (forthcoming) have developed multidimensional measures of grievance procedure effectiveness which include grievance filing rates, speed and level of settlement, arbitration rates, and perceived equity of settlement.

Still, the majority of research focuses heavily on the determinants of grievance filing and resolution while often ignoring the outcomes or consequences of grievance systems. Direct tests of the assumptions that underlie the studies of determinants of grievance activity are rarely performed. For example, to what extent are dimensions of grievance procedures such as the filing rate and speed of settlement important concerns of labor and management? Do these factors actually affect worker satisfaction, turnover, or productivity? Therefore, the major question to be addressed in this chapter is: What are the consequences of grievance procedures, especially their effects on firm performance?

In addressing these questions, we begin by reviewing the historical development of grievance procedures and then consider the factors that lead labor and management to adopt these procedures. We conceptualize the decision to implement a grievance procedure as part of a larger set of decisions concerning the systems of communication and dispute resolution between labor and management. These decisions are framed in a compensating wage differentials model in which there is a tradeoff between voice mechanisms and other aspects of the compensation package. Then we review published and in-process research that examines the relationships between grievance procedures and three specific measures of firm-level performance—employee turnover, strikes, and establishment or firm productivity. Here we distinguish the effects that the availability of grievance procedures have on the three performance measures from the effects that the use of procedures has on performance.

The Historical Evolution of Grievance Procedures[1]

While grievance procedures in unionized settings, especially those ending in third-party arbitration, are generally thought to have emerged around the time of World War II under the encouragement of the War Labor Board, there is ample evidence that some form of grievance procedures existed in the U.S. in the late 1800s and early 1900s. For example, a national bargaining agreement in the stove industry in 1891 explicitly established grievance machinery for the resolution of workplace disputes arising during the term of the labor agreement (Chamberlain and Kuhn, 1986). This agreement did not include a provision for grievance arbitration, but other agreements negotiated around the turn of the 20th century did so. The Industrial Commission of 1902 commented on this phenomenon in its final report:

> "While this local collective bargaining as to the general conditions of labor is seldom carried on by any very formal system, a large proportion of the local agreements themselves provide more or less formal methods of conciliation and arbitration, as regards minor disputes concerning the interpretation of their terms, usually by joint arbitration committees. Such committees are either temporary—being chosen by the parties to a particular dispute—or, somewhat less commonly, they are permanent, being chosen by the parties to the agreements as such, and having authority to settle all disputes arising during their term of office. Such permanent committees are found especially in those trades where both employers and employees are strongly organized." (Industrial Commission, 1902)

In the same year, an award issued by the Coal Strike Commission, which had been appointed to settle a particularly bitter labor conflict, led the anthracite industry to adopt a procedure to resolve workplace disagreements. While the new

---

[1] This is a selective rather than an exhaustive historical review. For additional accounts, see Chamberlain and Kuhn (1986), Jacoby (1986), and Lewin and Peterson (forthcoming).

procedure applied to all anthracite mines and provided a high-level board to settle disputes under terms of the award, it did not provide for grievance settlement at the mine sites themselves. In 1912, however, the anthracite coal industry's grievance procedure was extended to the work site when a multistep grievance procedure was established that incorporated informal discussion, a local grievance committee, a preliminary board of conciliation, a full board of conciliation, and, as the final step, decision by an umpire on a case-by-case basis.

The early record on this industry's grievance procedure is surprisingly well documented. During the 10-year period ending in 1923, 253 cases primarily involving wage issues were taken to boards of conciliation. Of these cases, the boards refused to hear five; 32 were settled by the parties prior to board hearings; 89 were withdrawn by grievants, perhaps indicating that informal settlements were reached; 78 decisions were rendered by the boards; and 49 disputes were submitted to and ruled on by umpires. Charges of discrimination against workers for union activity made up the second largest category of grievances in the anthracite industry during the 1914–1923 period.

Probably the best known grievance procedure in existence during the early 20th century was the one established in the 1911 labor agreement between Hart, Schafner, and Marx (HSM) and the Amalgamated Clothing Workers Union—a procedure that subsequently spread throughout the clothing industry and to the unionized portions of the millinery and hosiery industries. The HSM agreement followed the Protocol of Peace created by Louis Brandeis and others in 1910 to settle a strike in the women's garment industry.

Both the Protocol and the HSM agreement declared that the employer retained the right to discipline and discharge employees. However, certain due-process protections were afforded to employees. As examples, all suspended workers were notified of charges against them within a specified time period; written records of disciplinary actions were maintained; workers could appeal disciplinary actions to an arbitration board and could not be penalized for doing so; each party was required to submit written statements to the board; and board decisions were rendered in writing. Because the burden of proof in cases brought under this procedure was on the employer, and because the arbitration board had the power to reinstate employees to their jobs, this agreement was instrumental in establishing a worker's property in the job—a principle which clearly ran counter to the then prevailing notions of private property ownership and employment-at-will in the labor market. Subsequent experience with grievance handling and arbitration under an agreement between the Cloak, Suit, and Skirt Manufacturers' Protective Association and nine locals of the International Ladies' Garment Workers' Union extended and developed the concept of property in the job.

Still, grievance procedures, particularly those culminating in arbitration, were far from common in the United States during the early 20th century. The anthracite and clothing industry "cases" are notable because they were unusual. Unionized employees, who accounted for only about 10 percent of the U.S. work force at that time, generally did not have access to grievance procedures during the early part of the century, so that the concept of property in work was quite limited.

However, at about the same time certain nonunion employers were establishing personnel departments and procedures that to some extent also recognized the principle of property in work. Perhaps the foremost of these was the National Cash Register (NCR) Company, which in 1901 created a Labor Department to implement new labor policies. Some of the more notable of those policies provided that no employee could be dismissed without prior approval of the department; employees were permitted to appeal discharges to the department which possessed the authority to settle disputes between foremen and employees; the department formulated disciplinary rules and held weekly meetings with foremen and employees to explain and discuss the rules; and foremen were required to follow company rules rather than exercising their own authority in discharge matters. While clearly motivated by a desire to eliminate unions (the company in short order became an open-shop employer), NCR management's labor relations policy was a forerunner of current employment practices in those nonunion companies that explicitly recognize the concepts of property in work and due process in the employment relationship.

During the 1920s and 1930s recognition and development of policies rooted in the principle of workers' property rights advanced in American industry, but only sluggishly and fitfully. Although a number of grievance procedures and personnel departments were established, they were abandoned in some sectors and strongly opposed in others. While the human relations movement of the late 1930s and early 1940s spurred more active development of personnel departments, it was the War Labor Board of World War II that gave a large boost to the adoption of grievance procedures, at least in unionized settings. The procedures insisted on by the Board had, in its judgment, been distilled from "the best practices of employers and unions developed through years of collective bargaining and trial and error" (Bureau of Labor Statistics, 1948). These called for multistep grievance procedures culminating in third-party arbitration, which were to be formally written into labor agreements.

These "instructions" of the War Labor Board seem to have been followed. In 1944, arbitration provisions were common in some industries, such as steel refining, textiles, petroleum, and aircraft, where over 80 percent of all collective bargaining agreements contained such provisions. Arbitration was less common in other industries. Only 40 percent of all automobile industry labor contracts in 1944 provided for grievance arbitration. Of 1,254 collective bargaining agreements in 14 industries analyzed by the Bureau of Labor Statistics (BLS) in 1944, 73 percent provided for arbitration (U.S. BLS, 1944). This percentage grew to 83 percent in 1949 (U.S. BLS, 1950), 89 percent in 1952 (U.S. BLS, 1966), and 94 percent in 1962 (U.S. BLS, 1966). While these figures indicate that grievance procedures and arbitration provisions became common features of U.S. collective bargaining agreements by the 1950s, the scope of these provisions varied considerably from contract to contract and often did not cover all disputes arising under the contracts (U.S. BLS, 1966).

Employers challenged the authority of decisions reached through arbitration, but a series of Supreme Court decisions consistently supported, or deferred to, the decision-making authority of grievance arbitration. *Textile Workers* v. *Lincoln-Mills*[2] allowed for court enforcement of arbitration awards. Three Supreme Court decisions of 1960, known as the Steelworkers

[2] See 353 U.S. 448, 40 LRRM 2113 (1957).

Trilogy,[3] further protected grievance arbitration decisions by holding that, while the court could review whether or not an issue was arbitrable, it would not consider specific merits of a given arbitration decision. These rulings also indicated that where there are questions about arbitrability, courts should favor arbitration over court procedures for settling industrial disputes. Finally, these decisions formally recognized that grievance arbitration is the quid pro quo for a no-strike clause in a collective bargaining agreement.[4] With these protections, grievance procedures and arbitration provisions became even more common features of U.S. collective bargaining agreements. In 1977, 98.5 percent of all U.S. contracts had grievance procedures and 96.5 percent provided for arbitration (U.S. BLS, 1977).

Despite the widespread adoption of grievance procedures in U.S. collective bargaining agreements, the dramatic decline in unionism since the mid-1950s means that fewer unionized workers are covered by grievance procedures today than at almost any time since the end of World War II. Moreover, it is not clear whether the absolute number of unionized workers covered by grievance procedures is larger or smaller than the number of workers covered by grievance-like due-process and appeal systems that are currently used by many nonunion companies. For example, a recent Conference Board report showed that a majority of large U.S. companies have adopted some kind of grievance-like system for nonunion personnel (Berenbeim, 1980). A subsequent Conference Board report indicated that management's primary objective in adopting a grievance procedure was to maintain the nonunion status of its work force (Freedman, 1985). Other studies support the conclusion that many nonunion employers have adopted formal systems for handling employee grievances. For example, in one sample of nonunion firms that were involved in union organizing drives which subsequently led to collective bargaining agreements, Freeman and Kleiner (1987) found that 38 pecent had a "formal" grievance procedure at least one year before the start of the organizing drive, and in another sample of nonunion firms that did

---

[3] *Steelworkers* v. *American Mfg. Co.*, 363 U.S. 565, 46 LRRM 2414 (1960); *Steelworkers* v. *Warrior & Gulf Navigation Co.*, 363 U.S. 574, 46 LRRM 2416 (1960); *Steelworkers* v. *Enterprise Wheel & Car Corp.*, 363 U.S. 593, 46 LRRM 2423 (1960).

[4] For a more complete discussion of court decisions affecting grievance procedures and arbitration provisions, see Lewin and Peterson (forthcoming), Ch. 2, and Kochan (1980), pp. 387–89.

not face union organizing drives, an even larger proportion, 52 percent, had formal grievance procedures. Even if these figures overestimate the proportion of nonunion firms that maintain grievance procedures, they clearly indicate that formal due-process and appeals systems are not strictly the province of unionized workplaces.

The Decision to Implement a Grievance Procedure

This brief summary of the evolution of grievance procedures in the United States raises a set of questions about the decision to implement such a procedure. An obvious pattern in this evolution is that grievance procedures, especially those ending in third-party arbitration, are more common in the union than in the nonunion sector. A simple theoretical explanation for this is that unions force employers to agree to grievance procedures by exercising their bargaining power. In the same vein, the existence of grievance procedures in the nonunion sector can be attributed to the threat of unionization, as nonunion employers seek to keep unions out of their firms by instituting grievance-like procedures.

While this line of reasoning is appealing, it is too simple to account for several other aspects of the historical development of these procedures. For example, if unions obtain grievance procedures by exercising their bargaining power, they should be less common in those sectors where unions have relatively little power. Yet empirical evidence does not support this proposition. Moreover, there have been no reports of the modification or removal of grievance procedures from contracts in industries such as automobiles, steel, or airlines which have experienced widespread pay and benefit concessions during the 1980s. If the cost of implementing and maintaining a grievance procedure is inherently low, this would help to explain why unionized employers would be more willing to agree to a grievance procedure than a wage increase in a labor contract, but it would not explain why employers are generally less likely to implement a grievance procedure in nonunion settings. Thus, while union bargaining power may be one important determinant of the decision to adopt a grievance procedure, a richer theoretical explanation of the costs and benefits of grievance procedures is needed to understand the evolution and dynamics of grievance procedures in union and nonunion settings.

The proposition that employers, employees, and, in unionized settings, the representatives of employees care about the existence and dimensions of grievance procedures is a useful starting point for the theoretical discussion. This proposition can be modeled more formally within a "compensating differentials" framework. Where a grievance procedure or a specific feature of a procedure imposes relatively small costs on or even generates net benefits for employers, grievance procedures or specific provisions of the procedure are more likely to be adopted. Employees who find that the benefits of a grievance procedure are particularly large will have a correspondingly high level of demand for a procedure. Within this framework, the price that an employee would be willing to pay for a procedure is measured by the wages the employee is willing to forgo in return for the implementation of the procedure. When a grievance procedure imposes costs on an employer, the employer will have to be compensated in the form of a lower wage bill before agreeing to implement the procedure.

In developing this framework more fully below, we consider the costs and benefits that grievance procedures create for employers and employees. Next, employer and employee characteristics that affect the magnitude of these costs and benefits are considered. We then discuss whether employer and employee differences help account for the greater reliance on grievance procedures in the union sector and we also consider whether this framework provides any insight into its historical evolution. At the end of this section we use the theoretical discussion to speculate about how certain contemporary developments in labor-management relations, such as the erosion of the employment-at-will doctrine, might affect the evolution of grievance procedures in the future.

Several functions served by grievance procedures could potentially be valued by employees and employers. First, a grievance procedure is inherently a system of communication between employees, their employers, and any union representatives. Such a system can provide valuable information to employers and a degree of voice about how the firm is run to employees or their representatives. This voice can be used to develop, modify, or interpret informal guidelines or formal rules for the norms of employee and employer behavior. These formal and informal guidelines may extend to the administration of due process and discipline when one party allegedly violates the norms.

It would be misleading to conceptualize the decision to

implement a grievance procedure as simply a dichotomous choice. Mechanisms other than grievance procedures ranging from simple suggestion box programs to work stoppages can serve as communication systems in the workplace, and these systems will vary by the extent to which employees are given an effective voice in the determination of various workplace issues. In this way, specific features in formal grievance procedures and grievance-like appeal systems help determine the degree of voice that employees have in determining rules of the workplace and methods for adjusting complaints. For example, union and nonunion grievance systems that include a provision for binding arbitration by a neutral third party should significantly reduce management's ability to make decisions unilaterally and should increase the extent of employee voice. Similarly, other features will affect how employers and employees will value the grievance procedure. Is the system simply a "suggestion box" program? Will employees be guaranteed access to higher levels of management beyond their immediate supervisors on a confidential basis? The specific decision to implement a "formal" grievance procedure thus can be conceptualized as part of a larger set of decisions that determines the extent of employee voice in the workplace and the degree to which management's property rights to make decisions are shared with employees.

We use Figure 1 to develop the compensating differentials framework for analyzing grievance and grievance-like communication systems. In this figure, the extent of employee voice is measured along the horizontal axis. Moving to the right on this axis corresponds to mechanisms and procedures providing greater degrees of employee voice. To understand the decision to implement a formal grievance procedure or to incorporate a specific provision such as arbitration in the procedure, the employer's and employee's valuation of such voice mechanisms must be considered.

The Employer's Perspective

In this framework, management will be indifferent among those wage rate–degree-of-voice combinations that generate the same level of profits.[5] A particular employer may have isoprofit curves

---

[5] Wage rate refers to all aspects of the compensation package other than voice mechanisms.

FIGURE 1

Employer and Employee Valuation of Voice Mechanisms

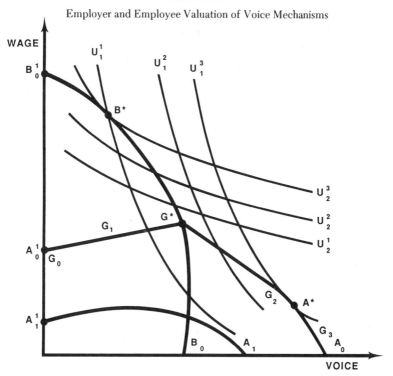

such as $A_0^1 A_0$ and $A_1^1 A_1$ in Figure 1. The $A_1^1 A_1$ curve corresponds to higher levels of profits than the $A_0^1 A_0$ curve since the latter curve has higher wage rates for a given level of employee voice. In mapping out an isoprofit curve, an employer considers the costs and benefits of various types of voice mechanisms. For example, if G_0 in Figure 1 corresponds to no mechanism of any kind, it seems likely that an employer may find that certain voice mechanisms are associated with net benefits and would therefore be able to pay higher wages and maintain the same level of profitability. For example, G_1 to the right of G_0 may correspond to a procedure for generating efficiency-improvement ideas from the work force. If such a procedure were successful in generating ideas that the employer would not have considered on his own, the employer could pay for such a scheme and keep the same level of profits. Programs that, on net, are costly to the employer would lie to the right of G_1. For example, guaranteeing access to higher levels of management would require more time of better paid managers and executives and would correspond to a point like G_2 if the plan did not generate sufficient benefits to offset these costs. Adding a provision for third-party arbitration would correspond to a point like G_3 for many employers, since there may be particularly large costs associated with diminishing the firm's ultimate decision-making authority (Bendix, 1956; Jacoby, 1986). The slope of the isoprofit line at any point represents the incremental change in the wage that must result to compensate the manager for implementing a mechanism that marginally increases the extent of worker voice.

Not all employers, however, will value grievance procedures or certain provisions of those procedures equally. Various characteristics of the employer will determine the magnitude of the costs and benefits of various types of procedures and therefore cause the isoprofit curves of different employers to have different shapes. For example, in firms where management is far removed from the production process and the work force possesses decidedly more information about the technology of operations, the employer will probably receive a larger benefit from information obtained through a voice mechanism than would managers who are more directly involved in their production processes.

Another characteristic of firms that could affect the magnitude of costs and benefits provided by a grievance procedure or other employee voice mechanisms is the nature of work rules and practices. Where work rules and practices are explicit, specific, and subject to little change, the cost to management stemming from any loss of decision-making authority because of features of a grievance procedure may not be particularly large. However, where work rules and practices are more flexible and provide only broad limits on the norms and standards of employer and employee behavior, employees might file more grievances if a formal procedure were implemented, since the standards for judging acceptable behavior may be complex and unclear. This high level of grievance filing in turn imposes additional costs on the firm. Moreover, procedures with binding third-party arbitration could be particularly costly for employers that operate with less well-defined work rules, since arbitration decisions may reduce the desired level of flexibility by setting precedents for future cases.

Grievance procedures and other voice mechanisms can also serve as a substitute for other methods of resolving points of contention between an employee and an employer. Various empirical applications of Hirschman's exit-voice theory (1970) to the analysis of union effects on turnover consistently show markedly lower quit and discharge rates for union workers than for nonunion workers.[6] From the employer's perspective, a grievance procedure could be particularly beneficial when the costs of turnover are high. Especially in tight labor markets, managers stand to benefit from reducing employees' reliance on the exit option to resolve workplace conflict.

Another mechanism for workers to resolve conflict is a work slowdown or stoppage. Grievance procedures should reduce workers' reliance on this mechanism. Therefore, where the probability of a work stoppage is high, management will have a larger incentive to implement a grievance procedure. In considering the relationship between work stoppages and grievance procedures, the costs of a stoppage or slowdown (as distinct from the probability of a work stoppage) should also be considered. Where such costs are inherently high, grievance procedures (even in nonunion firms) will be more beneficial to the employer. For example, where customer loyalty is low and ready substitutes for a company's product exist, a work stoppage that halts production can be especially costly. Similarly, where it is difficult to produce for inventory in anticipation of a work stoppage, employers will find a grievance procedure that reduces work stoppages especially attractive. In other sectors, where the cost of interrupting work in certain essential services is high, such as hospitals and police and fire protection, the potential benefits of grievance procedures will be large.

Differences in the willingness of employers to implement grievance procedures can be represented in Figure 1 with differences in the slopes of isoprofit curves. Consider employer A, who because of either the nature of the product (an essential service or a service with many substitutes) or the nature of the workplace (featuring a distinct separation between management and the production process or explicit work rules) finds that the relative cost of providing workers with voice mechanisms is low. Employer A's

---

[6] See Freeman and Medoff (1984) for a review of these studies.

isoprofit curve representing a normal rate of return may correspond to $A_0^1 A_0$. Here the relatively gradual slope of the isoprofit curve indicates that, because voice is relatively low cost, the employer requires only small wage reductions for increases in worker voice. Alternatively, employer B may find that, because of the characteristics of his product market (ability to produce for inventory or the existence of few substitutes) or the nature of his workplace (featuring undefined work rules), worker voice is more costly. Employer B's normal profit isoprofit curve may be represented by $B_0^1 B_0$. The steep slope reflects the large wage reductions necessary to induce employer B to implement a worker-voice mechanism. The envelope curve of employer A and employer B's isoprofit curves, represented by $B_0^1 G^* A_0$, is the wage-voice locus offered to employees. For points to the left of G^*, employees would not choose to work for firm A, since at comparable levels of worker voice firm B offers higher wages than firm A. Similarly, for points to the right of G^*, employees would choose to work for firm A, since for comparable levels of worker voice firm A offers higher wages than firm B. Therefore, in the eyes of the worker, firm B is a high-wage low-voice employer, while firm A is a low-wage high-voice employer.

The Employee's Perspective

The employee's willingness to pay for grievance procedures or other kinds of voice mechanisms must also be considered before a final decision about these procedures can be made. Among other things, an employee's utility is a function of wages and voice; indifference curves map an employee's preferences for wage-extent-of-voice combinations. As with employers' preferences, the magnitude of the wage-voice tradeoff will depend on how employees value greater degrees of participation in decision-making processes in relation to the alternatives of quitting or striking in response to differences with their employers.

There will, of course, be differences in the tastes of individuals for participation. For example, certain individuals who are more interested in stable employment (e.g., older workers or those with families) will probably pay a relatively higher price for a procedure that reduces the need to quit than will other individuals. One can represent the preferences of these employees by the set of indifference curves U_1^1, U_1^2, U_1^3. Here, the steep slope of the indifference curves represents the large wage loss the worker is willing to tolerate for increased voice. Alternatively, workers employed in occupations with tight labor markets will not find voice a particularly valuable job characteristic. The preferences of these employees can be represented by the indifference curves U_2^1, U_2^2, U_2^3. Again, the relatively gradual slope of these curves reveals that these employees will tolerate only small wage reductions in return for increased levels of voice.

When faced with the wage-voice locus of exchange offered by employers, the more stable worker will maximize his utility by choosing employment with firm A at A°. The worker who has the larger set of external labor market opportunities will maximize his utility by working for firm B at B°. Thus, this particular framework is helpful in explaining why the mechanisms for worker voice differ across firms and in identifying the factors that affect firm and employee decisions concerning the wage-voice tradeoff. In addition, once the framework is placed in a dynamic context, one can consider certain economy-wide factors that may cause shifts in the wage-voice locus offered by employers or changes in the slopes of the indifference curves of employees. This type of analytical framework may be particularly useful for explaining historical changes in the extent of voice mechanisms at the workplace.

Unionism and Grievance Procedures

Following this framework, the fact that grievance procedures, particularly those with arbitration mechanisms, are more common in the union than the nonunion sector can be explained not just by union bargaining power, but also by the possibility that the "price" of a grievance procedure may be lower in unionized settings. Consider that unionism is defined by a formal collective bargaining contract; because terms and conditions of employment are legitimate subjects of bargaining, labor contracts typically provide for a set of written work rules. The labor agreement will also clarify the boundaries of the issues that may be subjects of discussion within the grievance procedure. Similarly, the issues that have not been formally agreed upon and that may eventually be resolved by arbitration decisions should be fewer in union than in nonunion environments. In contrast, nonunion employers will need to specify the range of issues subject to the grievance-like procedure as well as the accepted set of standards for filing a grievance.

Another factor that may contribute to the relatively greater incidence of grievance procedures in unionized settings is that the organization of workers may increase the probability of a work stoppage. The benefits of a grievance procedure will therefore be greater for employers in unionized settings. While union bargaining power undoubtedly has allowed organized employees to obtain higher wages and a greater degree of those voice mechanisms that are costly to employers than nonunion employees receive, other changes that accompany unionization may also make voice mechanisms such as grievance procedures less costly in unionized settings. For these reasons, union firms may more closely resemble firm A in Figure 1, while nonunion firms may more closely resemble firm B.

The Theoretical Framework and Historical Developments

The historical development of grievance procedures can now be considered within the theoretical framework described above by considering factors that may have caused changes in the wage-voice combinations offered by employers or in the preferences of employees for voice mechanisms. Various aspects of the historical evolution of grievance procedures are consistent with the framework. For example, Jacoby (1986) found that nonunion employers began to experiment with grievance procedures during World War I, when labor markets were tight. With higher costs of turnover in tight labor markets, employers' isoprofit curves became less steep as they offered higher wages for a given level of voice in attempting to reduce turnover. Equilibrium levels of voice will, of course, be higher in tight than in loose labor markets. Once unemployment rates rose after World War I, this experimentation waned.

The emergence of grievance procedures, particularly those with arbitration provisions, during the time of the War Labor Board can also be understood within this conceptual framework. During the wartime period of the early 1940s, the costs of work stoppages in the form of lost production implied threats to national security. If the government were willing to pay a premium for timely production or if employers themselves internalized the higher costs of work stoppages as part of the war effort, isoprofit curves would become flatter, indicating that firms were prepared to offer a greater degree of voice at a given wage level in order to obtain and maintain industrial peace. Moreover, given that firms' ability to increase wages was limited by wartime controls, it became even more important for employers to offer other job characteristics valued by employees. Finally, the willingness of employees to strike during the war period may have also declined, and this coincided with an increased government demand for settling differences with employers through grievance machinery.[7]

The Theoretical Framework and Contemporary Developments

What factors may account for the apparent recent increase in the use of complaint and appeals systems in the nonunion sector? This development cannot be attributed to an increase in the threat of unionization, given the secular decline in private-sector unionization since the mid-1950s. Rather, nonunion grievance procedures may be emerging as production technologies become increasingly complex and are also perhaps better understood by workers than by managers. It is also possible that younger cohorts of workers who are increasingly better educated exhibit a greater desire for voice and participation in the workplace than did earlier generations of workers. Further, a change in the legal environment surrounding employee relations may also be responsible for the observed increase in nonunion grievance procedures. Specifically, court decisions in several states are eroding the employment-at-will doctrine and management's ability to discharge employees (Heshizer, 1984). Decisions which hold that certain statements made in personnel manuals constitute enforceable, implicit employment contracts may increase the incentive for employers to

---

[7] What the framework presented here does not account for is that the grievance procedures and arbitration provisions remained in place after wartime production. The forces associated with World War II that made grievance procedures more attractive to employers and employees should have diminished after the war. A useful extension of the theoretical model, therefore, may be to incorporate the cost of removing a procedure after it is implemented. Such a cost may correspond to a type of training cost in that the existing set of managers and employees would have to learn how to resolve issues under some new procedure. Note also that recent work by Knight (1986) suggests that, within an existing grievance-arbitration procedure, the parties "learn" from prior experience and subsequently adjust their grievance handling behavior. Knight further implies that the grievance procedure itself may be modified over time.

implement grievance procedures.[8] For example, an employee who goes to court to appeal a dismissal can impose significant legal costs on an employer, so that the costs of production absent a voice mechanism (or a specific procedure for redressing discharges) have increased. These decisions also give employers an incentive to clarify and formalize certain work rules, namely, those pertaining to the grounds for dismissal. Therefore, the formalization of rules and guidelines for employer and employee behavior should reduce the barriers to implementing a nonunion grievance procedure.

The Economic Consequences of Grievance Procedure Availability

In developing the previous discussion of why grievance procedures might be implemented in the firm, several mechanisms through which the procedures may affect firm performance were suggested. Costs to the firm obviously include those associated with administering the procedure. Furthermore, decisions that reduce the firm's ability to terminate employees whose performance it finds unacceptable will increase the costs to the employer. Benefits to the firm may include reductions in turnover or work stoppages. Grievance procedures may also improve firm performance directly through an increased flow of information concerning the production process. In this section, we review the sparse literature dealing with the effects of grievance procedure availability on turnover, strike activity, and overall firm productivity. The subsequent section considers whether different patterns of *use* of grievance procedures are associated with different levels of firm performance, as indicated by these same three measures.

Turnover

No study directly compares turnover rates in unionized firms that have grievance procedures with turnover rates in nonunion firms that do or do not have grievance-like procedures. Instead, the literature that deals with the effects of grievance procedures on turnover consists of studies which compare turnover in union and nonunion settings, but which do not specifically incorporate data on the presence or absence of a procedure. These studies consistently

---

[8] See, for example, *Woolley* v. *Hoffman-LaRoche*, 491 A.2d 1257, 119 LRRM 2380 (1985), and *Weiner* v. *McGraw-Hill, Inc.*, 57 N.Y.2d 458, 457 N.Y.S.2d 193, 118 LRRM 2689 (1982).

find that voluntary and involuntary turnover (other than layoffs) are significantly lower in unionized settings after controlling for the effects of wages and other factors. They attribute this result to the increase in employee voice provided by grievance procedures in unionized firms. The consistency of the finding of lower turnover in unionized environments provides persuasive support for this hypothesis. Longitudinal investigations that track the tenure of the same individuals in union and nonunion establishments (Freeman and Medoff, 1984) address the particular concern raised in the theoretical model presented in the previous section—that employees who prefer stable employment relationships will move to firms with grievance procedures. Nevertheless, an investigation that directly incorporates data on any grievance procedures in nonunion firms would address an important issue raised by the studies of the union effect on turnover. In particular, it has been argued that the estimated union/nonunion turnover differentials may not only indicate that grievance procedures serve to lower turnover rates, but may also mean that the grievance procedures that do exist in the nonunion sector do not give employees an effective voice (Freeman and Medoff, 1984, pp. 107–109). Therefore, it is important to test directly whether grievance procedures in nonunion settings reduce turnover to the same extent as they do in unionized settings, or whether nonunion grievance procedures are inherently less effective voice mechanisms than union grievance procedures.

While no study directly tests this hypothesis, Spencer (1986) investigated whether an index derived from the number of employer-employee voice mechanisms in an organization is correlated with turnover. A new analysis of these data, which focuses on the effects of grievance procedures on turnover in union and nonunion organizations, has been provided by Spencer and is presented here. Specifically, the following equation is estimated:

$$TURNOVER = a + \beta_1\ UGRV + \beta_2\ NUGRV + \beta_3\ X + \epsilon$$

where $TURNOVER$ = the ratio of the number of registered nurses who quit to the total number of registered nurses; $UGRV$ = a dummy variable for hospitals with unionized nurses, all of which have grievance procedures; $NUGRV$ = a dummy variable for hospitals with nonunion nurses, all of which have grievance

procedures; and $X =$ a set of other controls that could influence
turnover rates. While Spencer's sample is limited to cross-section
data and turnover rates are simple aggregate averages for the
hospitals he studied, the opportunity to compare turnover rates in
unionized organizations with grievance procedures to turnover
rates in nonunion organizations with and without grievance
procedures is unique.

TABLE 1

The Effects of Grievance Procedures
on the Voluntary Turnover Rates of Registered Nurses
in Union and Nonunion Hospitals[a]
(*t*-statistics in parentheses)

	Number of Observations	
	106	95
Union grievance procedure	−15.53° (2.5)	—
Nonunion grievance procedure	−14.48° (2.6)	—
Union grievance procedure with arbitration	—	−17.19° (2.6)
Nonunion grievance procedure with arbitration	—	−17.41°° (2.9)
Nonunion grievance procedure without arbitration	—	−15.44°° (2.7)
R^2	.18	.21

°° Significant at the .01 level, two-tailed test.

° Significant at the .05 level, two-tailed test.

[a] Other control variables are: average hourly wage rate in the hospital; fringe
benefit expenditures per worker hour; county unemployment rate; number of beds
in the hospital and in the county; minority employment in the hospital; and grievance
filing rate.

When the turnover equation is estimated, the parameters in
Table 1 are obtained. The column (1) specification compares the
voluntary turnover rates of registered nurses in three kinds of
hospitals: (a) hospitals with unionized nurses (all of whom are
covered by a grievance procedure); (b) hospitals with nonunion
nurses but where formal grievance procedures exist; and (c)
hospitals with nonunion nurses where grievance procedures do not
exist (the omitted group). The coefficients in column (1) show that
turnover rates are significantly lower in union and nonunion

hospitals with grievance procedures than in nonunion hospitals without grievance procedures. The −15.53 and −14.48 percentage point coefficients are large effects in this sample, since the average annual voluntary turnover rate for the entire sample is 21.13 percent.

In column (2), the turnover equation is reestimated, but the "nonunion with grievance procedure" category is divided into two subgroups: (a) those nonunion hospitals with a grievance procedure ending in arbitration, and (b) those nonunion hospitals where the grievance procedure does not include third-party arbitration. Note that all the unionized hospitals that provided information on the final step of the grievance procedure indicated that the final step was arbitration. The sample size is 95 rather than 106 hospitals, since 10 nonunion hospitals and one union hospital did not report information on the final step of the grievance procedure.

Nonunion hospitals with either type of grievance procedure experience significantly lower turnover than those nonunion hospitals without grievance procedures. Interestingly, the turnover rates in the nonunion hospitals with and without third-party arbitration are not significantly different from the turnover rates in the unionized hospitals. These results suggest that nonunion establishments can implement grievance procedures that effectively lower employee quit rates, and also that a provision for arbitration by an outside neutral is not necessary to achieve lower turnover rates.

Clearly, these estimates could be improved by longitudinal investigations of turnover rates (i.e., analysis of turnover before and after grievance procedures are instituted in union and nonunion settings) or by more extensive controls for differences in employee and employer characteristics. More comprehensive samples would also improve our understanding of the effects of grievance procedures on turnover. However, as the only available data set that contains information on turnover rates, union status, and grievance procedure characteristics, the results obtained from analysis of this sample are noteworthy. In particular, the results do not support the claim that nonunion grievance procedures—including those without arbitration—are less effective in reducing turnover than grievance procedures in unionized organizations.

Strike Activity

According to the theoretical model presented earlier, the availability of grievance procedures, particularly those ending in arbitration, should reduce strike activity. The fact that a no-strike policy is commonly exchanged for arbitration of grievances has often been cited in industrial relations literature. Mills (1986) observes, for example, "The procedure that has evolved to resolve these various [labor relations] problems is for management to accept binding arbitration of grievances in return for a no-strike pledge by the union" (p. 277). Reynolds (1982) notes that "a properly constructed grievance procedure capped by arbitration should in principle render work stoppages unnecessary during the life of the agreement" (p. 410).

On the one hand, historical evidence seems to support this view. Wildcat strikes in the manufacturing sector, which were common during the 1930s and 1940s, became rare occurrences by the 1950s and 1960s. Certainly the spread of formal grievance procedures was an important contributing factor to this decline, although growing legal restraints on and challenges to wildcat strikes were also a major contributing factor. By the early 1980s, a sample of managers of large U.S. companies who were surveyed by The Conference Board reported that "wildcat strikes during the contract" were far and away the least important labor relations outcome to their firms (Freedman, 1979, 1985).

On the other hand, there is virtually no systematic evidence available from studies that actually compare strike rates where grievance procedures are and are not available. Some light is shed on this issue by Brett and Goldberg (1979), who analyzed wildcat strikes in bituminous coal mining during the mid-1970s, a time when they were increasing. Brett and Goldberg did not directly test for the effects of grievance procedure availability. However, they did examine certain determinants of strike activity and concluded that "management at low-strike mines appears to be more accessible to miners than management at high-strike mines, and there is less friction between foremen and miners at low-strike than at high-strike mines" (p. 475). Since all mines had grievance procedures, these findings suggest that the availability of grievance procedures by itself is not sufficient to eliminate wildcat strikes. Factors related to the nature of the grievance procedure and how the procedure is used also determine wildcat strike activity.

Robust tests of the relationship between grievance procedure availability and wildcat strikes have not been performed. In unionized settings, like the coal mines investigated by Brett and Goldberg, grievance procedures are such a common feature of collective bargaining agreements that unionized settings without grievance procedures are practically unobservable. Systematic data on strike activity in nonunion firms are not available. A study that surveyed a large number of union and nonunion firms and specifically tested whether the level of wildcat strike activity in union firms is lower than the level of strike activity observed in nonunion firms without grievance procedures would provide a more definitive assessment of this relationship than currently exists.

Productivity

Our review of the literature found no study that linked the availability of various kinds of grievance procedures directly to measures of overall firm productivity or profitability. Again, studies that estimate union/nonunion differentials without specific reference to the availability of a grievance procedure may provide some insight on this issue. Since this somewhat controversial literature has been surveyed elsewhere (for example, Freeman and Medoff, 1984, pp. 165–169; Addison, 1982), we will not replicate those reviews here. However, it is worth citing the studies that specifically consider whether grievance procedures are responsible for any estimated difference in the productivity of union and nonunion firms or workers.

As suggested above, grievance procedures may contribute to firm performance through their effects on turnover and worker experience. In their industry-level study of union productivity differentials, Brown and Medoff (1978) found that differences in turnover rates between union and nonunion workers accounted for only one-fifth of the overall union productivity differential. In a longitudinal investigation of six cement plants, Clark (1980) found that grievance procedures were introduced in all plants following the unionization of employees, so that an estimated union productivity differential of approximately 6 percent might have been attributable to the effects of grievance procedures. However, the productivity differential in this study was estimated in a model that controlled for differences in worker quality; therefore, if grievance procedures are partly responsible for the union productivity effect in Clark's sample, they must enhance productivity through mechanisms other than improved worker quality. Clearly, a study that directly estimates the effects of grievance procedures on productivity would contribute to a better understanding of grievance procedures. In particular, a study designed to estimate these effects with and without controlling for differences in turnover rates would be especially useful.

The Economic Consequences of Grievance Procedure Usage

The limited evidence on average differences in measures of firm performance between firms with and without grievance procedures was reviewed in the previous section. However, variation may also exist in the performance of workers or firms within each of these categories. Among firms that have established grievance procedures for employees, firm performance may vary depending on how grievances are handled and processed within the procedure. Therefore, in this section, we consider how the three indicators of firm performance discussed above—turnover, strike activity, and productivity—are influenced by the actual use of grievance procedures.

Turnover

No study compares turnover rates across organizational grievance procedures that differ according to the rate of grievance filing, speed of settlement, perceived equity of settlement, reliance on arbitration, or other procedural characteristics. However, Lewin and Peterson's (1987; forthcoming) analysis of workers in four unionized organizations and Lewin's (1986, 1987) analysis of workers in three nonunion firms compared the turnover of workers who do and do not file grievances.

Lewin and Peterson investigated turnover rates in one production, one clerical, and two service work forces, all of which were unionized. Lewin examined turnover of employees in three nonunion firms that had formal complaint procedures, one of which provided for arbitration by a neutral as the final step and the other two ended with a final decision by top-level management. Both studies performed multivariate analyses of the determinants of voluntary turnover. Among the possible determinants of turnover was a variable indicating whether or not the worker filed a grievance in the prior (baseline) year. In all seven union and non-union work forces, individuals who filed a grievance or complaint in the baseline year had a significantly higher probability of quitting by the end of the following year than did individuals who did not file grievances.

These studies also explored the relationships between turnover and other aspects of grievance procedure activity. Specifically, for all union and nonunion work forces, subsequent voluntary turnover was always higher for groups of individuals whose grievances were ultimately decided in the employer's favor than for those whose grievances were decided in the employee's favor.[9] This empirical relationship appears to be consistent with the reduction in turnover associated with grievance procedure availability discussed in the previous section. Specifically, without an appeals mechanism, employees with grievances have no avenue for raising complaints; they will behave as if they had lost their grievances. If employees who do not have their positions upheld in grievance cases are more likely to quit, and if, where a procedure exists, grievances are not always decided in the employer's favor, then turnover should be lowered by the availability of a grievance procedure.

Strike Activity

As noted earlier, grievance procedures are commonly claimed to reduce the incidence of strikes. It should be easier to construct samples to test the relationship between use or characteristics of a procedure and strike activity than it is to develop samples for testing the relationship between grievance procedure availability and strike activity. Unfortunately, there are very few empirical studies of the relationship between grievance procedure usage and strike activity.

A study of several unionized steel mills in the early 1970s (Peach and Livernash, 1974) suggested that a problem-solving type of relationship between labor and management may reduce the frequency of grievances which, in turn, may reduce the incidence of strikes. Another study of unionized coal mines, also conducted in the early 1970s, concluded that miners with grievances were more

---

[9] This comparison of turnover rates was limited to subsets of all grievance (complaint) filers who appealed their grievances to one of the last two steps. Outcomes of grievances settled at earlier steps of the procedure were unknown.

likely to conduct a wildcat strike than to pursue grievance settlement to higher stages of the grievance procedure (Dix et al., 1972). However, these studies only assert these hypotheses. Empirical tests of these relationships that control for other possible determinants of strike activity were not performed.

Brett and Goldberg's study (1979) cited above investigated the relationship between grievance filing and wildcat strike activity in two high-strike and two low-strike bituminous coal mines during the mid-1970s. They find evidence that workplace problems are resolved effectively at the local level—that is, at steps one and two of the grievance procedure—in low-strike but not in high-strike mines. However, this seemed to have resulted as much or more from employee avoidance of formal grievance filing as from the use of the grievance procedure. Attitudinal variables and management's willingness to discuss grievances informally were the most important determinants of workplace grievance settlement at these mine sites.[10]

Brett and Goldberg also tested the hypothesis that miners had greater confidence in the "nonlocal" steps—that is, steps three and four (arbitration)—of the grievance procedure at low-strike than at high-strike mines. This hypothesis was not supported by qualitative or statistical analysis. In fact, in both the high-strike and low-strike mines, workers perceived the grievance procedure to be too slow, arbitrators to be biased, and union representatives to be less skilled than management representatives at grievance-handling.

Brett and Goldberg's findings suggest that certain characteristics of grievance procedures in coal mining signal "distressed" grievance procedures (Ross, 1963)—procedures that appear to raise, not lower, the incidence of strikes. To determine if such distress in grievance procedures could be reduced, Brett and Goldberg (1983) conducted a subsequent field experiment in grievance mediation over two six-month periods in two districts of the United Mine Workers of America. The results of this experiment showed that 89 percent of the 153 grievances taken to mediation were resolved without going to arbitration. This "success rate" was not significantly affected by whether one or both parties initiated grievance mediation, but was significantly affected by the parties'

---

[10] It should be noted that these researchers did not have data on step two grievance settlements, which would have allowed further tests of the relationship between settlement of grievances at early steps of the procedure and strike activity.

willingness to negotiate over the definition and processing of grievances. Other outcomes of the experiment included significant cost savings (compared to arbitrated settlements) and significantly faster grievance settlements.

However, the results of these two studies should not be overgeneralized. Besides being limited to four mine sites, the first study provided no data on actual grievance filing rates. Hence, no formal test of the relationship between grievance filing and strike activity was performed. The second study, which the authors accurately describe as experimental, involved intentional manipulation of key variables (for example, the cost of mediation) so that threats to external validity cannot be overlooked. Moreover, despite finding a high strike level co-existing with a high arbitration rate in their first study, Brett and Goldberg's second study did not address the effects of grievance mediation on strike activity or strike proneness.

As with the relationship between grievance procedure availability and strike activity, there is no study which systematically examines the effects of grievance filing, processing grievances through higher level steps, or outcomes of grievance settlement on strike activity. Despite the fact the grievance procedures and their usage are commonly asserted to be important determinants of strike activity, we simply do not know very much about the effects of actual grievance procedure usage on strike activity in U.S. industrial relations.

Productivity

Four studies have considered how a direct measure of firm efficiency or productivity varies with different levels of use of a grievance procedure. Three studies (Katz, Kochan, and Gobeille, 1983; Katz, Kochan and Weber, 1985; Ichniowski, 1986) analyzed firm-level data, and the fourth (Norsworthy and Zabala, 1985) was an industry-level investigation. While the specific productivity measures and determinants varied across the studies, each incorporated a grievance filing rate variable as one possible determinant of productivity. In all of the studies, this variable was defined as the number of written grievances filed per employee or per employee-hour, so that informal discussions between grievants and foremen-supervisors were not considered.

Despite differences in the definition of the dependent variable and in other aspects of the research designs in these four studies, they reached a common conclusion: increases in the grievance filing rate reduce (increase) the productivity (cost) index. Table 2 summarizes the magnitude of the relationships in the three plant-level studies.[11] While each study has certain limitations which may reduce confidence in its findings, the consistently negative relationship between productivity and grievance filing suggests that the results are robust. However, two of the plant-level studies as well as the industry-level study referred to above were limited to data drawn from automobile manufacturing. Absent further empirical studies, the extension of these results to other settings depends on the confidence one has in the theoretical interpretation of the grievance-filing–productivity relationship. In this regard, the theoretical rationales presented in these four studies do not convincingly account for all of the reported empirical results.

One explanation for the grievance-filing–productivity relationship offered in two of the studies is that a "displacement effect" is involved; that is, when more time is devoted to grievance handling, less time is devoted to production tasks. However, the magnitude of the productivity loss appears to be too large for this explanation to account for all of it.[12]

Another proposition is that the effect may be a reduction in worker effort when employees feel they are being treated inequitably, since alleged violations of a collective bargaining agreement should signal inequitable treatment (Ichniowski, 1986). However, Norsworthy and Zabala (1985) found that unresolved grievances were not significantly related to costs. While this finding may still be consistent with an equity-based explanation in that employees may no longer perceive inequity to exist once the grievance is being processed, it is questionable whether mere grievance filing is more of an indicator of inequitable treatment than is an unresolved grievance.

---

[11] Because Norsworthy and Zabala estimated the effect of grievance filing in a translogarithmic cost function, their study did not report a single independent effect of grievance filing on industry cost. Due to the confidentiality of their data, the authors could not supply the information necessary to calculate this effect with the levels of other control variables held constant.

[12] See, for example, Ichniowski (1986).

TABLE 2

Effects of Grievance Filing on Firm Performance

Dependent Variable (Performance Index):	Sample		
	(1) 18 General Motors Plants 1970–1979 Difference Between Actual Labor Hours and "Standard" Hours of Production	(2) 25 General Motors Plants 1970–1980 Difference Between Actual Labor Hours and "Standard" Hours of Production	(3) 11 Paper Mills 1976–1982 Tons of Paper Produced
Change in Performance Index from 1 standard deviation increase in grievance filing	− 6.7%	−2.1%	− 1.5%
Change in Performance Index from an increase in grievance filing from average rate to maximum rate	−15.9%	−6.0%	−11.7%
Change in Performance Index from a decrease in grievance filing from average rate to minimum rate	+ 5.0%	+3.3%	+ 1.1%

Sources: (1) Katz, Kochan, and Gobeille (1983); (2) Katz, Kochan and Weber (1985); (3) Ichniowski (1986).

Finally, Katz, Kochan, and Weber (1985) suggest that a high rate of grievance filing reflects an inability of labor and management to resolve conflict. However, in Ichniowski's (1984) investigation of paper mills, the use of the arbitration mechanism had either a positive or no significant effect on productivity. High rates of arbitration usage seem to be a more direct indication of an inability to resolve conflict quickly and informally than are high rates of grievance filing.

In light of the finding discussed earlier that grievance filing is associated with higher employee turnover, it might be argued that this is the underlying cause of the grievance-filing–productivity relationship. However, a careful examination of the methodologies used in the four studies that estimate a grievance-filing–productivity relationship suggests that the estimated relationship is independent of any effect of grievance filing on turnover. In Norsworthy and Zabala's study, for example, the industry quit rate was a control variable, so that an effect of grievance filing on productivity was observed independent of any increased voluntary turnover that was associated with grievance filing. Similarly, in the paper mill investigation (Ichniowski, 1984), the coefficient on the grievance filing rate variable remained significant and negative after a set of turnover rate variables was included as a possible determinant of productivity.

The significant inverse relationship between grievance filing and productivity provides empirical support for the assumption that higher filing rates are a signal of less effective grievance procedures. This finding is particularly notable because the counterargument has been made that low grievance filing rates are a sign of ineffective procedures. For example, workers may not file grievances if they fear retaliation from management or if management's power dominates that of the union (Slichter, Healy, and Livernash, 1960). Clearly, however, additional research is needed in order to understand the observed inverse relationship between grievance filing and productivity and in order to determine if this relationship can be generalized to other settings. The range of explanations provided in the studies reviewed here may be part of a more complex model of how grievance procedure usage affects firm performance. While grievance procedures can provide certain benefits to employees and employers (such as those associated with reduced turnover), many different messages will be transmitted through these voice mechanisms. All of the messages may not contain useful information, but all of them must be processed. Research that attempts to extend this small set of studies may be able to incorporate indicators of grievance procedure usage beyond the filing rate to uncover how different types of messages transmitted through the grievance procedure affect firm performance.

Conclusion

Some important conclusions emerge from this review and assessment of the literature on grievance procedures and firm performance. First, there is fairly robust evidence that grievance procedures substantially reduce employee turnover—although the most recent research shows that knowledge of "who prevails" in grievance settlement is critical to an understanding of the turnover consequences of grievance procedures. Second, grievance activity seems to have a dampening effect on firm productivity—an effect that is independent of any reductions in work force experience that are associated with increased turnover.

Perhaps the most obvious conclusion to be drawn from this review is that in many areas there is very little research that directly assesses the effects of grievance procedures on firm performance. Clearly, the major limiting factor is the lack of publicly available data sets that include indicators of firm performance and characteristics of firms' grievance procedures or appeals systems. Industrial relations scholars who have the opportunity to assemble such data and extend research in this area should borrow from the strengths of the process-oriented literature rooted in the management and behavioral science traditions and the less extensive set of studies of how grievance procedures affect economic outcomes.

Analyses of the effects of grievance procedures on economic outcomes provide important tests of the assumptions underlying the process-oriented literature about which facets of grievance procedures matter to employers and employees. However, the process-oriented literature should help guide the ways in which researchers use grievance procedures and attributes of those procedures to measure the degree of employee voice. In particular, if various aspects of grievance procedures and appeals systems matter to employers and employees, then the compensating differentials framework described in this chapter would be useful for developing testable hypotheses about grievance procedures. Unfortunately, existing empirical tests of compensating differentials between wages and virtually any aspect of employment packages are seriously plagued by methodological problems, including difficulties in measuring aspects of employment packages accurately. It would be particularly difficult to measure the "extent of employee voice" in operationalizing the suggested compensating differentials framework.

However, some measures will be better than others. Simple union/nonunion dichotomies are less accurate than ever before in measuring the existence of a formal appeals system given the recent growth of these systems among nonunion firms. In the same vein, measurement of employee voice based on the availability of a grievance procedure, appeals system, or arbitration mechanism could be refined by incorporating indicators of how employees and employers actually use a given system. For example, there may be important differences in how much voice employees have under a given grievance procedure depending on how frequently employees use the procedure, the level at which the parties resolve their differences, and the decisions or outcomes of grievances. Finally, research on the economic consequences of the availability and use of grievance procedures and appeals systems should consider models in which indicators of economic performance and measures of grievance procedure availability and use are both determined by characteristics of employees and firms because it is likely that grievance procedure availability and use are not exogenous to the economic characteristics of firms or employees. Any progress that contemporary industrial relations scholars can make in these areas would provide a much more complete answer to the question: What difference do grievance procedures make?

References

Addison, John T. "Are Unions Good for Productivity?" *Journal of Labor Research* 3 (Spring 1982): pp. 125–38.

Anderson, John C. "The Grievance Process in Canadian Municipal Labor Relations." Paper presented to the 39th Annual Meeting, Academy of Management, Atlanta, August 1979.

Ashenfelter, Orley. "Racial Discrimination and Trade Unionism." *Journal of Political Economy* 80 (May/June 1972): pp. 435–64.

Begin, James P. "The Private Grievance Model in the Public Sector." *Industrial Relations* 10 (February 1971): pp. 21–35.

Bendix, Reinhard. *Work and Authority in Industry: Ideologies of Management in the Course of Industrialization.* New York: Harper, 1956.

Berenbeim, Ronald. *Non-Union Complaint Systems: A Corporate Appraisal*. Report No. 770. New York: The Conference Board, 1980.

Bok, Derek, and John T. Dunlop. *Labor and the American Community*. New York: Simon and Schuster, 1970.

Brett, Jeanne M., and Stephen P. Goldberg. "Wildcat Strikes in Bituminous Coal Mining." *Industrial and Labor Relations Review* 32 (July 1979): pp. 465–83.

————. "Grievance Mediation in the Coal Industry: A Field Experiment." *Industrial and Labor Relations Review* 37 (October 1983): pp. 3–17.

Briggs, Steven. *The Municipal Grievance Process*. Los Angeles: Institute of Industrial Relations, University of California, Los Angeles, 1984.

Brown, Charles, and James L. Medoff. "Trade Unions in the Production Process." *Journal of Political Economy* 86 (June 1978): pp. 355–78.

Chamberlain, Neil W., and James W. Kuhn. *Collective Bargaining*, 3d ed. New York: McGraw-Hill, 1986.

Clark, Kim B. "The Impact of Unionization on Productivity: A Case Study." *Industrial and Labor Relations Review* 33 (July 1980): pp. 451–69.

Derber, Milton, W. Ellison Chalmers, and Murray Edelman. *Plant Union-Management Relations*. Urbana: Institute of Labor and Industrial Relations, University of Illinois, 1965.

Dix, Keith, Carol Fuller, Judy Linsky, and Craig Robinson. *Work Stoppages in the Appalachian Bituminous Coal Industry*. Morgantown, W. Va.: Institute for Labor Studies, 1972.

Fleishman, Edwin A., and Edwin F. Harris. "Patterns of Leadership Behavior Related to Employee Grievance and Turnover." *Personnel Psychology* 15 (January 1962): pp. 43–56.

Freedman, Audrey. *Managing Labor Relations*. Report No. 765. New York: The Conference Board, 1979.

————. *The New Look in Wage Policy and Employee Relations*. Report No. 865. New York: The Conference Board, 1985.

Freeman, Richard B. "The Exit-Voice Tradeoff in the Labor Market: Unionism, Job Tenure, Quits, and Separations." *Quarterly Journal of Economics* 94 (June 1980): pp. 643–73.

Freeman, Richard B., and Morris Kleiner. "Union Organizing Drive Outcomes from NLRB Elections During a Period of Economic Concessions." *Proceedings of the 39th Annual Meeting, Industrial Relations Research Association*. Madison, Wis.: IRRA, 1987. Pp. 41–47.

Freeman, Richard B., and James L. Medoff. *What Do Unions Do?* New York: Basic Books, 1984.

Heshizer, Brian. "The Implied Contract Exception to At-Will Employment." *Labor Law Journal* 35 (March 1984): pp. 131–41.

Hirschman, Albert O. *Exit, Voice, and Loyalty*. Cambridge, Mass.: Harvard University Press, 1970.

Ichniowski, Casey. "How Do Labor Unions Matter?" Ph.D. dissertation, Sloan School of Management, MIT, 1984.

————. "The Effects of Grievance Activity on Productivity." *Industrial and Labor Relations Review* 40 (October 1986): pp. 75–89.

Industrial Commission. *Final Report of the Industrial Commission*. Washington: The Industrial Commission, 1902.

Jacoby, Sanford M. "Progressive Discipline in American Industry: Origins, Development, and Consequences." In *Advances in Industrial and Labor Relations*, Vol. 3, eds. David B. Lipsky and David Lewin. Greenwich, Conn.: JAI Press, 1986. Pp. 213–60.

Katz, Harry C., Thomas A. Kochan, and Kenneth R. Gobeille. "Industrial Relations Performance, Economic Performance, and QWL Programs: An Interplant Analysis." *Industrial and Labor Relations Review* 37 (October 1983): pp. 3–17.

Katz, Harry C., Thomas A. Kochan, and Mark Weber. "Assessing the Effects of Industrial Relations Systems and Efforts to Improve the Quality of Working Life on Organizational Effectiveness." *Academy of Management Journal* 28 (September 1985): pp. 509–26.

Knight, Thomas. "Feedback and Grievance Resolution." *Industrial and Labor Relations Review* 39 (July 1986): pp. 585–98.

Kochan, Thomas A. *Collective Bargaining and Industrial Relations.* Homewood, Ill.: Richard D. Irwin, 1980.

Kuhn, James W. *Bargaining in Grievance Settlement.* New York: Columbia University Press, 1961.

Lewin, David. "Theoretical Perspectives on the Modern Grievance Procedure." In *New Approaches to Labor Unions, Research in Labor Economics,* Supp. 2, ed. Joseph D. Reid, Jr. Greenwich, Conn.: JAI Press, 1983. Pp. 127–47.

————. "Empirical Measures of Grievance Procedure Effectiveness." *Proceedings of the 1984 Spring Meeting, Industrial Relations Research Association.* Madison, Wis.: IRRA, 1984. Pp. 491–99.

————. "Conflict Resolution in the Nonunion High Technology Firm." In *Human Resource Management in High Technology Firms,* eds. Archie Kleingartner and Cara Anderson. Lexington, Mass.: D.C. Heath, 1986. Pp. 137–55.

————. "Nonunion Dispute Resolution: A Theoretical and Empirical Analysis." *Journal of Conflict Resolution* 31 (September 1987): pp. 465–502.

Lewin, David, and Richard B. Peterson. "Behavior Outcomes of Grievance Activity." Working Paper, Columbia University Graduate School of Business, October 1987.

————. *The Modern Grievance Procedure in the United States.* Westport, Conn.: Quorum, forthcoming.

Mills, Daniel Quinn. *Labor-Management Relations,* 3d ed. New York: McGraw-Hill, 1986.

Norsworthy, J. R., and Craig A. Zabala. "Worker Attitudes, Worker Behavior, and Productivity in the U.S. Automobile Industry, 1959–1976." *Industrial and Labor Relations Review* 38 (July 1985): pp. 544–57.

Peach, David A., and E. Robert Livernash. *Grievance Initiation and Resolution: A Study in Basic Steel.* Boston: Graduate School of Business Administration, Harvard University, 1974.

Peterson, Richard B., and David Lewin. "A Model for Research and Analysis of the Grievance Procedure." *Proceedings of the 34th Annual Meeting, Industrial Relations Research Association.* Madison, Wis.: IRRA, 1982. Pp. 303–12.

Reynolds, Lloyd G. *Labor Economics and Labor Relations,* 8th ed. Englewood Cliffs, N.J.: Prentice-Hall, 1982.

Ross, Arthur M. "Distressed Grievance Procedures and Their Rehabilitation." In *Labor Law and Industrial Change,* Proceedings of the 16th Annual Meeting, National Academy of Arbitrators, ed. Mark L. Kahn. Washington: Bureau of National Affairs, Inc., 1963.

Slichter, Sumner, James J. Healy, and E. Robert Livernash. *The Impact of Collective Bargaining on Management.* Washington: Brookings Institution, 1960.

Spencer, Daniel. "Employee Voice and Employee Retention." *Academy of Management Journal* 29 (September 1986): pp. 488–502.

Stagner, Ross. "Personality Variables in Union-Management Relations." *Journal of Applied Psychology* 46 (September 1962): pp. 350–57.

Stern, Robert N. "Intermetropolitan Patterns of Strike Frequency." *Industrial and Labor Relations Review* 29 (January 1976): pp. 218–35.

Thomson, Andrew W. J. *The Grievance Procedure in the Private Sector.* Ithaca: New York State School of Industrial and Labor Relations, Cornell University, 1974.

Thomson, Andrew W. J., and Victor F. Murray. *Grievance Procedures.* Lexington, Mass.: Lexington Books, 1976.

U.S. Bureau of Labor Statistics. *Arbitration Provisions in Union Agreements.* Bulletin No. 780. Washington: U.S. Government Printing Office, 1944.

————. *Termination Report of the National War Labor Board.* Washington: U.S. Government Printing Office, 1948.

————. *Characteristics of Labor-Management Contract Provisions.* Bulletin No. 1022. Washington: U.S. Government Printing Office, 1950.

————. *Characteristics of Major Collective Bargaining Agreements.* Bulletin No. 1425-6. Washington: U.S. Government Printing Office, 1966.

————. *Characteristics of Major Collective Bargaining Agreements*. Bulletin No. 1957. Washington: U.S. Government Printing Office, 1977.

Weissinger, William J. "The Determinants of Grievance Rates: A Case Study." Master's thesis, New York State School of Industrial and Labor Relations, Cornell University, 1976.

Chapter 6

Pensions and Firm Performance

By Steven G. Allen*
North Carolina State University and
National Bureau of Economic Research

and Robert L. Clark*
North Carolina State University

Pension benefits represent a form of deferred compensation that a worker receives after he retires from a firm, provided he has met certain age and service requirements. The magnitude of these benefits depends on the nature of the employment contract and whether the worker and the firm have fulfilled the obligations of that contract. In this chapter we examine the role of pensions as a form of compensation and how pensions are used as a component of personnel policy. Such a review requires a clear understanding of how future pension benefits are evaluated by workers and financed by firms. Having determined these concepts, we can assess the influence of pensions on firm performance. Pensions are strictly regulated by the federal government and so our examination will include a brief review of current regulations and how they temper the impact of pensions on firm performance.

Our examination of pensions begins with a brief overview of the growth and development of the employer pension system in the United States. This includes a discussion of the distribution of pensions by worker and firm characteristics. In the second section, specific plan characteristics are described and their importance is discussed. Next we present several alternative rationales for why

* Stan Liebowitz gave us useful advice on the measurement of profit rates. We have received helpful comments from Richard Ippolito and the University of North Carolina Human Resource Economics Workshop and excellent research assistance from Linda Shumaker and Myra Ragland.

workers and unions want pensions as part of their compensation. In the fourth section we describe competing models of the pension contract and develop predictions for the effect of pensions on compensation and performance. The impact of pensions on employee behavior is considered from a theoretical perspective in the fifth section, and the sixth section is an assessment of the evidence concerning the impact of pensions on firm performance. We report our conclusions in the final section and discuss some areas where further research would be useful.

Growth, Development, and Patterns of Employer Pensions

While public pensions in the United States are as old as the republic (dating to benefits for Revolutionary War veterans), private pensions first appeared in the late 19th century. Greenough and King (1976) credit the American Express Company with establishing the first formal employer pension in 1875. Early pensions were generally found in railroads, banking, and public utilities. Prior to World War II, growth in pension coverage was slow; however, in the immediate postwar period there was a rapid increase in the number of employers offering pensions and the number of workers covered by a pension. The proportion of wage and salary workers in the private sector covered by an employer pension grew from 25 percent in 1950 to over 50 percent in 1984. Most of this growth occurred prior to 1975. In the last decade, coverage rates have changed only modestly. The proportion of covered workers actually fell from 56 to 52 percent between 1979 and 1983 (Andrews, 1985). Growth in coverage and increases in benefits raised the percentage of payroll going to pensions from 1 percent in 1950 to 6 percent in 1980 (Fields and Mitchell, 1984).

Ippolito (1986a) estimates that in 1984 there were 788,000 pension plans, of which 744,000 covered fewer than 100 participants. Allowing for duplicate coverage, these plans contained 57.5 million active participants and 8 million annuitants. Public employees have always been more likely to be covered by an employer pension than have private-sector workers. Currently, more than 90 percent of state and local workers and all federal workers are covered by an employer pension (Munnell, 1979).

How can the observed pattern of development of pensions be explained? Several factors may have stimulated the surge in pension coverage after World War II. A comprehensive assessment of the economic rationale for the existence of pensions is provided in subsequent sections of this chapter. However, it is useful to point to several changes that occurred during the 1940s which may have provided the impetus to increased pension coverage. First, the 1942 amendments to the Internal Revenue Code clarified and expanded tax treatment of pensions and precluded the establishment of pension funds limited to corporate officers (Greenough and King, 1976). Second, wartime stabilization policy made it easier to increase fringe benefits than base wages. Third, in 1949 the U.S. Supreme Court ruled in the *Inland Steel* case that pensions were a proper subject for collective bargaining.[1] This action removed a constraint that limited unions' abilities to achieve pension coverage for their members and may have altered union attitudes toward seeking pension benefits (Allen, Melone, and Rosenbloom, 1984).

Are there similar specific events that might explain the slowdown in the growth of the coverage rate in the past decade? In 1974 the Employee Retirement Income Security Act (ERISA) was enacted, imposing a sweeping new set of regulations on the use and funding of pensions. In addition, a number of subsequent modifications of the pension laws have raised the administrative costs of pensions and reduced the range of permitted pension contracts. Some writers have speculated that restrictions on the use of pensions may partially explain the slowing in the growth of pensions. However, Ippolito (1986b) concludes that ERISA had only a small effect on plan terminations.

In addition to the new regulations, the growth in pension coverage may have slowed simply because workers who were most likely to desire pensions were already covered. Relatively high current coverage rates among high-wage workers, unionized workers, and employees in large firms imply that further extension of pension coverage may proceed more slowly in the future.

Patterns of Pension Coverage

The odds that any individual will be covered by a pension plan on his job vary tremendously with both personal and job characteristics. The most up-to-date information is reported in the pension supplement to the May 1983 Current Population Survey (CPS). We restrict the sample to full-time private wage and salary

---

[1] 336 U.S. 960, 24 LRRM 2019 (1949).

workers. Those who have jobs that are covered by collective bargaining agreements are much more likely to be included in a pension plan than are nonunion workers. The coverage rate for private-sector workers is 82 percent for union versus only 44 percent for nonunion workers, as shown in Table 1. Union contract

TABLE 1

Determinants of Pension Coverage, 1983 CPS[a]

	Percentage Covered by Pension	Marginal Impact on Pension Coverage Probability from Probit Equation ($\times 100$)
Union contract coverage		
Nonunion	44.1	—
Union	82.2	26.3
Establishment size		
Less than 25	27.8	—
25–99	51.1	2.4°
100–499	68.9	4.7
500–999	77.6	9.6
1000 or more	85.9	10.2
Company size		
Less than 25	17.1	—
25–99	36.7	15.1
100–499	54.6	26.5
500–999	62.7	31.1
1000 or more	79.7	45.2
Industry		
Agriculture, forestry, fisheries	11.3	4.0°
Mining	74.0	14.4
Construction	35.9	−11.0
Durable manufacturing	72.2	9.2
Nondurable manufacturing	64.7	6.2
Transportation and utilities	70.8	2.2°
Wholesale trade	52.1	11.6
Retail trade	31.7	−3.5°
Finance, insurance, real estate	58.8	10.7
Services	39.6	—
Occupation		
Executive, administrative, managerial	60.2	—
Professional specialty	61.6	0.1°
Technicians & related support	60.0	−3.0°
Sales	42.6	−6.0

[a] Sample is limited to private wage and salary workers between the ages of 16 and 64 who usually work more than 35 hours per week. The estimates in the second column are probit estimates of the derivative of the probability function evaluated at the means of the independent variables. All of the above variables were included in the probit equation.

Estimates with a significance level *below* the 95 percent level are indicated with an asterisk (°).

TABLE 1 (*Continued*)

Determinants of Pension Coverage, 1983 CPS[a]

	Percentage Covered by Pension	Marginal Impact on Pension Coverage Probability from Probit Equation ($\times 100$)
Administrative support, including clerical	55.8	3.4°
Private household service	0.0	—
Protective service	37.7	−17.7
Other service	27.6	−8.9
Precision production, craft & repair	57.4	−1.3°
Machine operators, assemblers & inspectors	59.5	−4.7°
Transportation & material moving	53.7	−3.6°
Handlers, equipment cleaners, etc.	47.2	−3.4°
Farming, forestry & fishing	11.1	−17.2
Region		
Northeast	57.5	7.8
North Central	58.0	10.9
South	47.5	5.0
West	47.4	—
Sex		
Female	45.6	—
Male	56.8	3.4
Marital Status		
Married, spouse present	57.6	2.9
Other	42.2	—
Age		
16–24	26.0	—
25–34	50.5	13.4
35–44	61.2	20.4
45–54	62.2	24.3
55–64	62.8	24.0
Years of schooling		
Less than 9	43.6	—
9–11	44.4	1.8°
12	52.0	7.8
13–15	52.0	7.0
16	57.2	4.8°
More than 16	66.6	10.1
Average hourly earnings		
Less than $4	13.2	—
$4–$5.99	31.8	17.6
$6–$7.99	51.8	28.6
$8–$9.99	63.2	32.9
$10–$14.99	73.3	37.4
$15 or more	79.4	41.2

Estimates with a significance level *below* the 95 percent level are indicated with an asterisk (°).

coverage is correlated with a number of other personal and job characteristics which, in turn, are also highly correlated with pension coverage (e.g., wages, industry). In order to gauge the net effect of union contract coverage, we estimated a probit equation for pension coverage which included all of the variables in Table 1. The probit results showed that, other things equal, those covered by union contracts have a 26.3 percentage point higher probability of being covered by a pension than nonunion workers.

The size of the workplace (establishment) and the size of the company, especially the latter, are also important correlates of pension coverage. In establishments with fewer than 25 workers, only 28 percent of the work force is covered by a pension plan. Coverage rates jump to 51 percent in establishments with 25 to 99 workers and reach 86 percent in establishments with 1,000 or more workers. The share of workers covered by a pension in companies with fewer than 25 workers is a paltry 17 percent. This percentage also rises with size, reaching 80 percent in firms with 1,000 or more employees.

These two size measures are obviously correlated, so it is reasonable to ask which matters the most. According to the probit analysis, the resounding answer is company size. Other things equal (including company size), there is only a 10 percentage point difference between pension coverage probability in companies with fewer than 25 employees and those with 25 to 99 employees. This widens to a 45 percentage point difference between companies with fewer than 25 employees and those with 1,000 employees or more.

The pattern of pension coverage across different age groups suggests that over time workers gradually sort themselves into jobs with pensions. Only about a quarter of workers between ages 16 and 24 are covered by pensions. Pension coverage rises to 50 percent for those between 25 and 34; it is slightly above 60 percent for all older workers. Other things equal, the odds of being covered are 13 percentage points higher for 25–34-year-olds and 20 to 24 percentage points higher for 35- to 64-year-olds than for 16–24-year-olds. Although patterns within a cohort over time may be quite different from the across-cohort patterns, they suggest the possibility that if a worker is not covered by a pension by the time he reaches the 35–44 age group, given the low turnover rates among older workers, there is a good chance he never will be covered.

Because of the favorable tax treatment of pensions, it should come as no surprise that pension coverage is also strongly correlated with average hourly earnings. The coverage rate for workers earning less than $4 an hour is a mere 13 percent in contrast to coverage rates above 70 percent for those earning $10 an hour or more. Most of this difference cannot be explained by other factors, as indicated by the probit results.

Workers with jobs in mining, manufacturing, and transportation and utilities have higher pension coverage rates than those in other industries. However, much of the difference in coverage rates across industries can be explained in terms of other factors such as firm size, earnings, and collective bargaining coverage. For instance, the probit results show that workers in wholesale trade have a 12 percentage point greater probability of being covered by a pension than service industry workers, holding all other factors constant. The difference between workers in durable manufacturing and services turns out to be even smaller (9 percentage points), despite the fact that the raw, unadjusted coverage rate for durable manufacturing (72 percent) is much higher than that for wholesale trade (52 percent).

Table 1 also indicates that pension coverage rates are lower for persons in service occupations (compared to blue- or white-collar occupations), lower for those living in the West, higher for men, higher for married workers, and higher for high school and college graduates. The magnitude of these differences is relatively small in relation to the differences in pension coverage associated with union contract coverage, company size, age, average hourly earnings, and industry.

Significance of Pension Benefits and Funds

The growth of pensions over the past four decades has increased their importance in a number of areas. First, pensions have grown as a source of income for older Americans. Ippolito (1986a) estimates that the mean initial pension annuity for 1984 beneficiaries was $6,360, representing 23 percent of their final earnings. A U.S. Department of Labor study (1985) reports that the replacement rate rises with the level of final earnings. Replacement rates for 1978 retirees rose from 14 percent for those with earnings less than $6,000 to 20 percent for those with earnings between $10,000 and $11,999 and to 25 percent for retirees with between $14,000 and $19,999 in final earnings. A total of $70 billion was paid to retirees in pension benefits in 1984. Over the past quarter century, pension benefits have come to represent an increasing proportion of retiree income.

Second, pension funds represent a growing proportion of invested funds in the United States. Ippolito (1986a) estimates that 1984 pension assets totaled $1 trillion. These funds represented 22.8 percent of all corporate equity and 49.9 percent of all corporate bonds. The dramatic rise in pension funds is shown by comparing these values to their 1950 rates. In 1950, pensions held less than 1 percent of corporate equity and only 13.1 percent of all corporate bonds. Another measure of the size of pension assets is that in 1981 pension assets per worker were equal to $10,907, which represented 75 percent of annual earnings.

Pension Plan Characteristics

Pension plans are of two basic types: defined contribution and defined benefit. Within a particular plan type, pensions differ in their plan formulas, vesting requirements, maximum benefit provisions, Social Security integration, age of normal and early retirement, reductions for early retirement, and benefit increases associated with delayed retirement. In this section we examine these diverse characteristics among pensions and indicate how these differences affect behavior at the workplace.

Types of Pension Plans

Of the two basic types, defined contribution plans are by far the most common, representing 71 percent of all plans in 1984. However, these plans tend to be provided by relatively small employers and, as a result, they cover less than 20 percent of all

TABLE 2

Percent Defined Contribution Coverage Among Pension-Covered Workers, 1982

Pension Plan Size (Participants)	Union	Nonunion
1–99	12.9	63.1
100–999	4.3	31.2
1,000–10,000	3.6	11.2
Greater than 10,000	0.7	4.9
Total	2.0	22.4

Source: Ippolito (1986b), Table 4.

pension participants. Table 2 shows this greater incidence of coverage by defined contribution plans among small employers. Sixty-three percent of pension participants in nonunion plans covering fewer than 100 participants are in defined contribution plans. This compares to a defined contribution coverage rate of only 12.9 percent for small union plans and 0.7 percent for large union plans. The greater use of defined contribution plans among small employers is attributable to lower administrative costs, plus the tremendous costs of compliance with government regulations they would face with the alternative defined benefit plans (Smeeding, 1983; Mitchell and Andrews, 1981).

In a defined contribution plan, the firm promises to contribute a fixed amount of money to an individual's pension account at specified regular intervals. In some plans workers will also be allowed or even required to make contributions. The funds are invested by the plan and accumulate throughout the worker's life. The benefit at retirement is determined by the size of the individual's pension fund at that time. The worker bears all of the risk related to the rate of return on the invested funds. However, he does not risk losing pension benefits if he leaves the firm prior to retirement or if the company goes out of business, terminates the pension, or fires the worker. Property rights are clearly defined; the funds in defined contribution plans belong to the worker. These plans have no impact on turnover, except for the simple fact that workers covered by such plans have more total compensation than other workers if all other variables (including cash earnings) are held constant. They also have no effect on retirement decisions, except to the extent that workers face liquidity constraints and are unable to use their benefits as collateral (in which case they may have to postpone retirement). The key factor to recognize is that there are no bonuses or penalties associated with the choice of retirement age in defined contribution plans.

Defined benefit plans are much more common among large employers and, as a result, almost 80 percent of pension participants are covered by defined benefit plans. These plans are more complex than defined contribution plans and federal regulations tend to be more restrictive. In a defined benefit plan, the worker is promised a benefit upon retirement based on plan generosity, years of service, and, in some cases, earnings. The firm must set aside sufficient dollars to provide for these future benefits. The rate of firm contributions is regulated by the government. As we will explain in detail below, a worker who leaves prior to the retirement age will lose benefits relative to the worker who remains with the firm. Thus, in these plans the worker bears risks associated with plan termination, his own desire to quit, and potential firing by the firm. However, the firm bears all risks concerning the rate of return on the pension fund. The use of these plans to influence turnover and retirement is explored later in this chapter.

Plan Characteristics

Several plan characteristics that play a critical role in determining benefit levels are described below, as are their economic effects and the frequency of their use. It should be noted that much of the discussion is relevant only to defined benefit plans.

Benefit Formula: Defined benefit plans typically use one of three types of formulas. According to the 1983 Employee Benefit Survey of Medium and Large Firms (EBS), the one most frequently used is the terminal earnings formula which determines benefits by multiplying years of service by an average of the earnings for the final three or five years and a generous parameter. Plans using this type of formula cover 54 percent of all participants. The career-earnings formula is similar, except that the salary average is based on all earnings with the firm rather than just the three or five final years. These plan formulas cover 14 percent of participants. Dollar-amount formulas provide a fixed dollar amount to all retirees or multiply years of service times a fixed dollar amount. These formula types cover 28 percent of participants.

Earnings-based formulas are used more frequently by plans covering professional workers and in noncollectively bargained plans. Obviously, these plans allow for a variance in pension benefits that reflects earnings. Dollar-amount formulas are used more frequently in plans covering production workers and unionized workers. These formulas tend to reduce the variance of the benefit distribution relative to the earnings distribution and to flatten the age-compensation profile of union workers relative to nonunion workers (Allen and Clark, 1986).

Vesting: Vesting pertains to the portion of a worker's specified benefit to which he is legally entitled upon leaving the firm. Prior to 1987, regulations allowed firms to select one of three vesting rules: 100 percent vesting of accrued benefits after 10 years of service, 25 percent vesting of accrued benefits after five years of service with additional vesting accruing each year until the worker is 100 percent vested after 15 years, and 50 percent vesting of accrued benefits when age and service add up to 45 with 100 percent vesting five years later. Almost all companies adopted the 10-year 100-percent vesting rule (Schulz, 1985). Tax legislation in 1986 altered vesting standards; choices are now either 100 percent vested after five years or graded vesting, with a worker being 50 percent vested after three years and accruing additional vesting each year until he is 100 percent vested after seven years.

If a worker leaves prior to being vested, he will receive no retirement benefits. Even if the worker achieves 100 percent vesting, there is still a penalty for leaving the firm, which we will describe in detail below.

Postretirement Increases: If pension benefits are not increased after retirement, their real value will decline in the presence of inflation. Until recently, it was widely believed that pension benefits were fixed in nominal terms. Surveys of large firms indicate that less than 5 percent of private plans automatically increase benefits in response to inflation. The lack of automatic adjustments does not necessarily imply that no postretirement increases are granted. Approximately two-thirds of large plans provided one or more ad hoc increases during the last half of the 1970s (King, 1982). Allen, Clark, and Sumner (1986) report that between 1973 and 1979 average benefits for persons already receiving benefits in 1973 increased by 24 percent during a period when the Consumer Price Index rose by 63 percent.

Table 3 shows that benefit increases were larger and more prevalent in collectively bargained plans. The method of benefit increase also varied by collective bargaining status (Allen and Clark, 1986), with bargained plans being more likely to use methods that provide the largest percentage increases to those with the lowest benefits.

Maximum Benefit Provisions: Pension plans often incorporate specific rules to set a maximum benefit. Such provisions are incorporated into pension plans covering 42 percent of participants represented in the 1983 EBS sample firms. The most prevalent rule is to limit credited service to a specific number of years. This type of limitation is used in plans covering 31 percent of participants; the limit is usually 30 years or more. Terminal-earnings plans are much more likely to include such limits than plans with other types of benefit formulas. Eleven percent of participants are in plans that limit benefits either to a maximum percentage of terminal or career earnings or to a maximum flat-dollar amount.

Social Security Integration: Firms are permitted to reduce pension benefits by including the worker's Social Security benefit as part of total pension benefits or costs. Just over half of all participants in the EBS were in plans that integrated pension benefits with Social Security benefits. Smaller plans are more likely to be integrated (President's Commission on Pension Policy, 1980). Until 1987, Internal Revenue Service regulations allowed two types of integration: the excess method and the offset method. The excess method allows firms to provide greater benefits based on earnings above the Social Security taxable earnings limit than on earnings below this limit. In an excess plan which does not consider years of service, the pension benefit based on earnings above the specified limit could not exceed 37.5 percent of the plan benefits based on earnings below that level. Plans could set this compensation limit no higher than the current year's Social Security taxable earnings limit. Most plans set the limit well below the allowable amount and tended not to have adjusted this earnings amount as the Social Security earning limit rose (Urban Institute, 1982).

TABLE 3

Postretirement Increases in Pension Benefits

	Union		Nonunion	
	Percent Awarded Increase	Benefits as Percent of 1973 Benefit	Percent Awarded Increase	Benefits as Percent of 1973 Benefit
1973	45.0	100.0	25.6	100.0
1974	59.6	105.6	31.6	101.3
1975	62.2	110.3	35.6	105.1
1976	52.6	114.7	19.1	108.9
1977	60.4	119.4	42.9	110.3
1978	65.6	123.2	11.4	117.2
1979		128.6		118.5
Change 1973–1979		28.6		18.5

Source: Clark, Allen, and Sumner (1986), p. 196.

The offset method allows a certain portion of the retiree's primary insurance amount (PIA) to be subtracted from the pension benefit. Prior to 1987, the offset could not exceed 83.33 percent of the worker's PIA. Most surveys indicate that integrated plans did not use the maximum possible offsets. In offset plans, the most frequently used percentage is 50 percent of the PIA. It remains to be seen how plans will adjust to the 1986 tax changes governing Social Security integration.

Retirement Age and Gains for Continued Employment: Pension plans specify an age of normal retirement, which is the time that a worker can retire and receive full pension benefits as provided by the pension formula. In recent years the age of normal retirement has been lowered in many plans. In the EBS sample, only 36 percent of the participants were covered by plans using 65 as the normal retirement age. Another 33 percent were in plans that specified ages between 60 and 64 and 11 percent were in plans with specified ages between 55 and 59. Approximately 18 percent of plans had no age requirement; eligibility in these plans depends solely on length of service.

Virtually all defined benefit plans allow for retirement prior to the normal retirement age at reduced benefits. In most plans, the reduction in benefits is less than the actuarial equivalent of the normal retirement benefit.

After the 1978 amendments to the Age Discrimination in Employment Act, firms were unable to mandatorily retire workers prior to the age of 70. Thus, workers could continue to work past the normal retirement age. However, firms were able to erect strong pension incentives for older workers to retire at the normal retirement age. First, relatively few of them provided any actuarial increase in benefits for work past the normal retirement age and, as a result, pension wealth might fall after this point. Second, in 1985 approximately half of all participants were covered by plans that did not continue to credit years of service and earnings after the date of normal retirement. Thus, the pension was fixed in nominal terms at the normal retirement age. The worker could continue on the job but could lose that year's pension benefits.

Legislation enacted in 1986 has altered both the mandatory retirement and the pension accrual regulations. For most firms, mandatory retirement is now entirely forbidden as a firm personnel policy regardless of the age of the worker. In addition, firms providing a pension cannot discontinue wage and service accruals at a specified age. These changes reduce the ability of firms to provide incentives for older workers to retire.

Why Do Workers and Unions Want Pensions?

Pension coverage has expanded through the labor force and the magnitude of pension benefits has increased in response to the actions of various labor market agents striving to maximize their objective functions. To understand the development of the pension system, we must determine who the players are, what their objectives are, and how pensions can help them achieve their objectives. These negotiations are conducted in a changing regulatory environment which alters the incentives associated with the use of pensions.

The primary agents in bargaining concerning pensions are workers, firms, and unions. Workers seek to maximize total compensation for a given amount of labor supply or effort. Firms seek to maximize profits. The objectives of unions tend to be more complex and may include reducing income inequality, providing economic security for workers and retirees, and raising wages and benefits. In the remainder of this section we examine how pensions help workers and unions achieve their primary objectives. Later we will analyze how pensions affect firm performance.

Worker Utility and the Desire for Pensions

Economic theory assumes that individual workers attempt to maximize utility subject to their personal budget constraint. A simplified version of this maximization process has the worker's utility as a function of total compensation and the amount of labor supplied. Compensation may come in many forms other than current cash, such as job safety, comfort on the job, and all types of employee benefits including pensions.

For the purposes of this part of the discussion, assume that the firm is a neutral agent and is willing to sell the worker any type of benefit at a price that is equal to the firm's cost of acquiring this benefit. The worker pays for each benefit by receiving less in cash compensation. Theoretically, this compensating differential would allow the worker to buy the desired amount of any benefit offered by the firm. The worker would purchase benefits until the marginal utility of this benefit was equal to the marginal value of a dollar of cash spent on other goods and services (Rosen, 1974). With no taxes or other governmental interference, benefits would be bought only if the firm could buy these goods at a lower cost than the worker could purchase them in the market or if the benefit were tied to the job and could only be bought from the firm.

Neither of these explanations for the existence of fringe benefits seems to apply in the case of pensions. Today there are financial intermediaries which give individuals access to a wide spectrum of investment opportunities; workers are not required to save through a pension to gain access to financial markets. The diversity of investment opportunities available to individuals also makes it unlikely that the expected rate of return to pension funds is greater than the expected rate of return that an individual investor could receive.

During the early development of the pension system these conditions may not have prevailed. Prior to the development of large mutual funds, small investors may have been unable to obtain widespread diversification. Therefore, capital market regulations and institutions may have played a role in the initial growth of pensions. Even today there may remain differences in transactions costs associated with individual investments versus investment through a pension fund. Despite this potential offset, it seems highly unlikely that the widespread pension coverage in today's economy can be explained in terms of lower transactions costs.

A much more convincing rationale is the tax status of pensions in comparison to current earnings. Firms with qualified plans make tax-deductible contributions to a pension fund that is used to provide future benefits to current workers. The value of these contributions is not viewed as current compensation to the worker and therefore is not subject to the individual income tax in the current period. The return to assets in these funds is also not taxable. Instead, benefits are taxed when they are received and the expectation is that the worker will be in a lower tax bracket at that time. Prior to the advent of Individual Retirement Accounts, workers had no other form of savings that received such preferential tax treatment.

Pension contributions by firms are also exempt from Social Security and unemployment insurance payroll taxes. For the worker the value of pension contributions permanently escapes the employee's share of the Social Security tax, although the resulting lower earnings means that future Social Security benefits will also be lower. Given today's benefit structure, the expected loss in benefits will be less than the savings from reduced taxes and the worker's lifetime income will rise.

As a result of the differential tax treatment, workers could increase total compensation by agreeing with the firm to establish a pension plan. The value of a pension plan is dependent on the prevailing tax rate. Thus, as tax rates rise, more workers would be expected to request their firms to institute a pension. The tax effect is also an important determinant of the distribution of plans across workers in any given year. High-wage workers are much more likely to be covered by a plan than are low-wage workers, as shown in Table 1.

Union Objectives and the Use of Pensions

Unions have played an important independent role in the expansion of pension coverage and the development of certain pension characteristics. Historically, unions have consistently exerted pressure on both employers and governments to provide economic security for older workers through private pensions and Social Security. Private pension plans became much more widespread after the 1949 *Inland Steel* decision made pensions a permissible topic for collective bargaining. Even today workers who are covered by collective bargaining agreements are much more likely than other workers to receive a pension when they retire.

Despite the difficulties associated with defining union objectives in precise terms, it is quite clear that pensions can help achieve many possible union objectives. First, the preferences of older, more senior workers receive much more weight in determining the terms of the employment contract under unionism. These workers prefer a compensation package with lower wages and higher retirement income, holding the cost of the package constant. As a result, the package becomes more likely to contain a pension along with other provisions which increase the income and economic security of older workers. Second, pensions can be used to compress the distribution of total compensation among union members. Allen and Clark (1986) show how the choice of benefit parameters can reduce pension inequality among workers.

Third, pensions can serve the interests of union officers. Albert Rees (1962) argues that by obtaining a new benefit for their members, union leaders can gain much more credit for innovation than they would if they had obtained a wage increase of equal value. In cases where the union has some control over the pension plan, the scope of authority of the leadership is significantly greater as well. Fourth, unions have an organizational advantage in certain aspects of pension administration. For instance, unions often administer plans in industries with small employers or short job durations. Without unions there probably would not be very many workers covered by private pensions in the construction industry. Unions also monitor plan behavior so that employers do not renege on explicit or implicit contracts. Finally, higher wages place union members in higher marginal tax brackets, thereby increasing the demand for all forms of tax-free or tax-deferred compensation, including pensions.

What Is the Pension Contract?

The influence of pension plans on firm performance depends on the nature of the pension contract and how this contract is evaluated by the worker and the firm. Two models of pension contracts have been developed in the economics literature. The first is based primarily on the work of Bulow (1982), who derived the value of pensions under a strict legal or explicit contract. This model assumes that a worker considers only the value of benefits that a firm is legally required to pay if the worker were to leave the firm at the end of the current period. The model clearly applies to defined contribution plans and many contend that it applies to defined benefit plans as well. The second model, developed in recent work by Ippolito (1985a, 1986a) and others, allows for the existence of implicit long-term employment contracts and focuses on the role of defined benefit plans in such contracts. This model assumes that a worker views the employment contract as an implicit promise by the firm to retain the worker (subject to performance requirements) until retirement and to pay a benefit based on final pay.

These models yield different predictions concerning incentives for the worker to quit and incentives for the worker to provide a high level of job performance and to minimize risks of being fired. In addition, these theories of the pension contract predict alternative patterns of life-cycle compensation. In this section, each of these models is examined in detail and the corresponding relationship with firm performance is assessed. The final objective of this section is to analyze the role of collective bargaining in models of the pension contract.

The Explicit Contract View of Pensions

The basic premise of the explicit contract model is that workers act as if the employment contract is for only one period. Of course, if both parties are agreeable, employment may be continued on a period-by-period basis. Since the worker knows that he may be terminated at the end of the current period, he is unwilling to accept any compensation that is contingent on his remaining with the firm for an extended period of time. This type of contract implies that the worker will value future retirement benefits on the basis of work to date and will consider only benefits that the firm is legally required to pay.

Under explicit employment contracts, a worker faces no loss in future benefits if he quits his current job. As a result, pensions cannot be used to reduce turnover or encourage a higher level of job performance. Despite the lack of a capital loss associated with leaving a job, pensions still represent an important component of compensation and will affect the growth rate of earnings of a worker covered by a pension. In addition, coverage by a pension alters the cash wage offer necessary to entice a worker to leave his present job. To elaborate on these effects, we briefly discuss the evaluation of pension wealth and the related concept of annual pension compensation.

The expected present value of future pension benefits, pension wealth, is determined by finding the discounted value of a life annuity beginning at retirement. The magnitude of the annual flow is governed by the pension formula and the individual's own work history. The most frequent form of benefit formula is one where the benefit is determined by multiplying the number of years of service by a fixed percentage of the worker's average earnings during the final years of employment. Pension wealth is calculated by using the worker's current years of service and salary average along with the prevailing benefit formula. These values, along with assumptions concerning survival probabilities and the market interest rate, are sufficient to calculate pension wealth for any worker.

Pension compensation is the change in pension wealth resulting from continued employment. From the above discussion, one can see that pension wealth rises due to an additional year of service and to any increase in earnings. Mathematical derivations of pension compensation are found in Bulow (1982), Clark and McDermed (1986a), and Kotlikoff and Wise (1985). These studies illustrate that if earnings are rising with tenure, pension compensation grows more rapidly than earnings.

The explicit contract literature assumes that in each year a worker is paid total compensation equal to the value of his output. With perfect capital markets, the cost to the firm of funding pension benefits is the same as the value that the worker places on these benefits. If there are not other forms of compensation, the wage plus pension compensation will equal the worker's output. With pension compensation growing more rapidly than earnings, pension compensation will increase as a proportion of total compensation as the worker continues on the job. This lifetime pattern of compensation is shown in Table 4.

TABLE 4

Earnings and Pension Compensation by Age and Tenure[a]

Age	Tenure	Earnings	Pension Compensation	Total Compensation	
				Percent Earnings	Percent Pension Compensation
30	10	$ 7,743	$ 321	96.0	4.0
35	15	8,891	456	95.1	4.9
40	20	10,174	663	93.9	6.1
45	25	11,606	957	92.4	7.6
50	30	13,189	1,374	90.6	9.4
55	35	14,914	1,969	88.3	11.7
60	40	16,753	2,820	85.6	14.4
64	44	18,262	3,767	82.9	17.1
65	45	22,796	−106	100.5	−0.5
70	50	30,118	−3,814	114.5	−14.5

Source: Clark and McDermed (1986a), pp. 341-61.

[a] The analysis is based on a defined benefit plan with an earnings-based formula. Salary average is computed over the last five years of earnings and the generosity parameter is 1.0 percent per year of service.

Under the explicit contract model, pension wealth and pension compensation are zero until the worker is vested in the pension plan. After vesting but still during the early working years, pension compensation is small in both absolute terms and as a percentage of total compensation. If the worker remains on the job, pension compensation grows rapidly and may reach 30 to 50 percent of total compensation during the final working years prior to retirement. This increase in pension compensation produces a corresponding growth in pension wealth to which the worker is legally entitled.

Although there is no loss in pension wealth if the worker leaves his job, pensions still affect the wage offer from a competing firm that is necessary to entice the worker to leave his current job. A competing firm that has no pension must offer a cash wage equal to the worker's current earnings plus pension compensation. Even if the competing firm has a pension that is identical to the one on the worker's current job, the wage offer must exceed current earnings. This follows because pension compensation will be lower on the new job, either because the worker will not be vested or because he will have fewer years of service on the new job.

This discussion would seem to indicate that under the explicit contract model, pensions would tend to reduce turnover by raising the reservation wage at other firms. This is an incorrect inference. Since the model assumes a spot market with all firms willing to pay total compensation equal to the worker's marginal product, competing firms are willing to pay the higher cash wage solely because they are not providing as much pension compensation.

Several important predictions can be derived from this model. First, there is no pension loss from leaving the job, so pensions should not reduce quit rates. For the same reason, pensions cannot be used as a personnel policy to encourage reduced worker malfeasance. Second, workers covered by pensions should have a flatter wage-earnings profile than workers who receive their entire compensation in cash. In addition, Bulow (1982) has shown that earnings should exhibit discrete jumps at several times, associated with large changes in pension compensation. For instance, at vesting, pension compensation goes from zero to hundreds of dollars. Assuming no similar increase in the value of the worker's output takes place, wages must adjust in the opposite direction. There should be no ad hoc postretirement increases in benefits for workers covered by an explicit contract. For the most part, these predictions are contradicted by the available evidence.

The Implicit Contract View of Pensions

An alternative to the single-period contract described above is a long-term employment contract that requires future payment for current labor services. Terms of such contracts may be either explicit, as in formal contracts, or implicit. In a series of recent papers Lazear (1979, 1981, 1983, 1985) and Malcomson (1984) have pointed out how implicit labor contracts can be used to modify worker behavior and improve firm performance. Pensions can be an important component of these contracts. The key factor in the use of pensions in an implicit contract is the difference in the implied value of pension wealth if the worker remains with the firm until retirement and the actual value of the pension if the worker leaves prior to fulfilling the terms of the contract.

Firms and workers may enter into an implicit contract in order to reduce labor turnover and increase the level of worker productivity. These objectives are accomplished by imposing a wealth loss on workers who quit the firm prior to the end of the contract or who are fired due to shirking on the job. The wealth loss is produced by assuming that the worker is paid at each period total compensation equal to his output; however, the value of the compensation is conditional on the worker's continuing to meet the terms of the contract.

Pension compensation comprises the conditional component of total compensation. In this model, pension wealth is based on the worker's expectation that he will remain with the firm until he retires. As such, the expected pension benefit is based on his projected final earnings. The difference between the calculation of pension wealth using the implicit contract method and the explicit contract model is the use of projected final earnings instead of current earnings to determine the value of current pension wealth. The use of projected earnings will produce a higher estimate of pension wealth.

In an implicit contract, the worker receives pension compensation based on the change in pension wealth as calculated using projected earnings. In this case, pension wealth increases only because of additional years of service. Pension compensation will be greater than under the explicit contract early in life, but will not rise as rapidly with years of service. Ippolito (1985a) has shown that under certain conditions pension compensation will represent a constant proportion of total compensation throughout work life.

The worker is assumed to pay for a pension conditional on remaining with the firm until retirement. If he leaves the firm, his actual pension will be considerably smaller than the pension he was paying for in the form of reduced earnings. Thus, termination of the employment contract imposes a capital loss on the worker. This capital loss equals the difference between pension wealth based on projected earnings and pension wealth under the legal method. Formulas for calculating the capital loss are reported in Ippolito (1985a) and Allen, Clark, and McDermed (1986).

The existence of this potential loss will make the worker less likely to quit and more likely to perform at a level that will not tempt the firm to fire him. The value of this capital loss rises during the early work years and then begins to decline as the worker approaches the age of retirement. An example of this effect is shown in Table 5. For many workers, the loss in pension wealth associated with quitting may represent half of annual earnings or, with high rates of inflation, perhaps as much as a full year's earnings (Ippolito, 1985b, 1987; Allen, Clark, and McDermed, 1986).

TABLE 5

Lifetime Compensation (Projected Earnings Method): Manufacturing, Professional, and Administrative Workers, 1,000 or More Employees[a]

Age	Tenure	Earnings	Pension Compen- sation	Total Compen- sation	Pension Wealth	Pension Loss From Leaving
25	0	8,839	1,161	10,000	0	0
35	10	11,866	1,573	13,439	15,728	8,921
40	15	13,744	1,835	15,580	27,529	13,727
45	20	15,912	2,150	18,061	42,990	18,029
50	25	18,398	2,540	20,938	63,492	20,833
55	30	21,231	3,042	24,273	91,259	20,416
60	35	24,428	3,711	28,139	129,870	13,661
64	39	31,448	222	31,670	173,174	0
65	40	32,809	−188	32,620	181,514	0
70	45	43,873	−6,057	37,816	227,394	0

Source: Allen, Clark, and McDermed (1986a).

[a] The analysis is based on the average plan in manufacturing for professional workers. The plan is a defined benefit plan with an earnings-based formula. Average salary is computed over the last five years of earnings and the generosity parameter is 1.53 percent per year of service.

The implicit contract model generated several predictions concerning earnings and worker performance. First, workers covered by a pension should be less likely to quit and should be more willing to provide a high level of effort to reduce the probability of being fired. Second, the rate of growth of earnings for workers covered by a pension should be approximately the same as the growth of earnings of similar workers not covered by a pension. Available evidence seems to support the latter prediction (Clark and McDermed, 1986b; Mitchell and Pozzebon, 1986; Ippolito, 1985a); evidence on turnover will be examined in detail later.

The Pension Contract Under Collective Bargaining

The impact of unionism on any pension contract, whether explicit or implicit, hinges on the decision-making process within the union and how various groups exert their influence on the determination of the bargaining agreement. In the simple "monopoly union" framework, there is only one prediction about union impact: pension plans should be more generous in all respects. This means higher initial benefits, larger increases in benefits after retirement, earlier eligibility for benefits, and fewer restrictions on participation and vesting.

Public-choice models recognize the conflicts within the union concerning the division of monopoly rents. Despite the well-known difficulties involved with specifying the political mechanisms at work, two of the most tractable public-choice approaches yield the prediction that the pension contract will be tilted in favor of older workers. Freeman (1985) has shown formally that in a median voter approach, the pension contract will be written to match the preferences of inframarginal workers, whereas in a nonunion setting it will be written to match the preferences of the marginal worker.

The inframarginal worker is likely to be older and more attached to the firm than the marginal worker. As a result, the union firm is more likely to have a pension plan and that plan is likely to have provisions which older, less mobile workers will find attractive. Freeman argues that unions are more likely to adopt a defined benefit rather than a defined contribution plan and that union plans will have stricter provisions for eligibility and portability. Under both of these provisions, persons who leave the firm subsidize those who stay. The political dominance of older workers in union politics need not result from median voter characteristics; autocracy rather than democracy may very well be a better rationale. This approach still yields the same answer to pension issues as the median voter approach—more pensions under unionism and the adoption of pension contract provisions favorable to older workers.

Unions can also change the terms of the pension contract so as to redistribute income within and across cohorts of workers. This objective serves union interests by promoting worker solidarity and eliminating compensation cost differences as a basis for competition among employers. Standard wage rate policies help reduce income differences between older and younger workers and between skilled and unskilled workers. Their counterpart in the pension contract is the use of benefit formulas which give all workers either the same flat benefit or the same dollar amount of benefits for each year of service. Pension benefits are very rarely based on earnings in a plan covered by collective bargaining. Allen and Clark (1986) show that the impact of both earnings and years of service on pension benefits within a cohort of retirees is much smaller for union than for nonunion beneficiaries. In addition, unions equalize pension wealth across cohorts by giving proportionally larger postretirement increases to those who have been retired the longest.

Regardless of whether the pension contract is implicit or explicit, these considerations lead us to expect that collectively bargained plans will differ from nonbargained plans. A difficulty that arises in many types of implicit contracts is that in certain situations one party stands to gain from violating the contract. For instance, postretirement adjustments seem to be part of an implicit contract under which firms reduce uncertainty about the plan's rate of return and the impact of inflation in return for lower wages or lower benefits. Firms have an incentive to renege on such a contract because the worker pays for the insurance but has no legal title to claim postretirement increases promised by the firm. In general, one would expect that firms would weigh the short-term gains from breaking the agreement against the reputational costs. Even if a firm currently faces large reputational costs for breaking implicit contracts, there still is a chance that the reputational costs will become smaller at some point in the future.

These difficulties decrease the probability that certain types of implicit contracts will be written without some form of outside enforcement. Unions can play an important role in this regard. As long as it is in the interests of the union, it can raise the cost of violating such implicit agreements well above the cost of a diminished reputation. Since both sides recognize this, it becomes easier to write such contracts in a collective bargaining situation.

Ippolito (1985c) has argued that the pension contract plays a completely different role under collective bargaining—that of a bond which the union posts to guarantee the survival of the firm. With fixed investments in physical and human capital, the firm faces the risk of a "holdup" by the union (in the form of higher wage demands or lower productivity) when it starts to receive the returns from those investments. Without some insurance against this possibility, the firm will be unable to attract capital and provide jobs for union members. Ippolito claims that underfunded pension plans provide this insurance. Under this setup, should the union ever decide to stage a holdup, its members would lose the portion of their pensions which had not been funded and which was not insured by the Pension Benefit Guaranty Corporation (PBGC). All parties gain from such an arrangement because holdups become unlikely, allowing the firm to make profits and the union members to collect rents.

Ippolito's model predicts that union members are more likely to be covered by pension plans than are nonunion workers and that such plans are more likely than nonunion plans to be underfunded. This also means that defined contribution plans will not be adopted under unionism because such plans are by definition always fully funded. The role of past service credits for older workers in this framework is to make them more concerned about the financial well-being of the firm. The prediction about underfunding is the distinctive feature of this model.

In a subsequent paper, Ippolito (1986b) argues that virtually all systematic underfunding in private pension plans in the United States is attributable to underfunded plans covering unionized participants. He claims that the union tendency to "hold up" firms and the response of firms to underfund plans was one of the principal reasons for organized labor's support for passage of ERISA, including the insuring of pension benefits through the PBGC, and he concludes that the resulting system provided large transfers to unionized workers. This follows from the tendency toward underfunding and the fact that the overall probability of plan-sponsor failure during 1978 through 1983 was 1.4 percent, while the probability of failure for firms that were 100 percent unionized was almost 200 percent higher. PBGC data show that almost 95 percent of the monies transferred through the pension insurance system have been claimed by union participants.

Participants covered by the United Automobile Workers and the United Steel Workers of America received 63 percent of these transfers.

Pensions and Employee Behavior

The characteristics of the pension contract outlined above have predictable consequences for certain types of employee behavior. It has long been recognized that pensions should and do reduce employee turnover. In the explicit contract framework, the observed correlation between pension coverage and low turnover occurs because workers who are vested in their pensions receive more compensation than other workers, other things equal. In the implicit contract approach, pensions reduce turnover by imposing a tax on workers who leave the firm. This tax can be imposed through vesting rules which prevent workers who leave the firm before a given number of years from receiving a pension. It can also be imposed through benefit formulas based on final earnings. For instance, consider a case where a worker earns $20,000 after 20 years and $40,000 after 40 years in the labor market and is covered by a pension plan which will annually pay him 1.5 percent of final earnings for each year of service when he retires. If he stays at the same job throughout this period, his annual benefit will be $24,000 (.015 x 40 x 40,000). However, if he switches jobs after his 20th year, his benefit will be only $18,000 (.015 x 20 x 20,000 + .015 x 20 x 40,000). Recognizing this, the worker becomes less likely to leave the firm because the benefit formula rewards those who stay. The incentive to stay is even greater in periods of rapid inflation because benefits are based on historical earnings unadjusted for inflation.

In addition to the direct incentives which vesting and earnings-based benefit formulas provide for any employee to stay with the firm, these pension characteristics will also influence the type of employee which the firm is able to attract. Consider the following simple example. Suppose there are two types of workers with quit probabilities p and q, respectively, with $p > q$. These differences could arise from expected differences in mobility costs. A firm which must invest a great deal in worker-specific training will want to attract the worker with the lower quit probability. This can be done by setting up a compensation schedule which includes a pension with delayed vesting and an earnings-based formula. This will simultaneously discourage the p-applicants and encourage the *q*-applicants. The result is a set of employees with lower initial odds of leaving the firm. Ex post, whenever these employees consider leaving the firm, the financial incentives created by vesting and the benefit formula will discourage many of them from doing so. This argument is presented formally and with several interesting extensions in Viscusi (1980, 1985).

As a form of deferred compensation, pensions can also be used as part of a scheme to discourage workers from shirking. Lazear (1979, 1981) has shown how deferred compensation results in workers being paid less than their marginal product during their initial years with the firm and more than their marginal product in their final years. The underpayment in the initial years is equivalent to the posting of a bond for good performance. Workers who shirk must forfeit the bond as well as the ability to collect the returns to the bond in the future. This compensation scheme benefits workers because they end up with higher productivity over their lifetime and thus with more income. Lazear shows how the combination of a pension payable upon retirement and an age-earnings profile which is steeper than the age-productivity profile produces this result.

One problem which arises when firms adopt payment systems where workers receive more than their marginal product in their later years is that they have an incentive to stay with the firm too long. "Too long" in this context means that if the worker was actually paid his marginal product rather than a premium above his marginal product, he would choose to retire or work elsewhere. Lazear (1979) shows that mandatory retirement results in more efficient separation decisions by removing this adverse incentive. Pensions can also be used to encourage workers to make efficient separation decisions by acting as a form of severance pay, as shown in Lazear (1983). If the provisions for early retirement benefits are sufficently generous, pension compensation (the change in pension wealth attributable to staying an extra year with the firm) becomes negative, making total compensation (earnings plus pension compensation) equal marginal product and thereby eliminating the incentive to stay "too long."

This can explain the frequent use of "sweetened" early retirement benefits in companies which must reduce employment, especially if the cost of the sweeter benefits is less than the cost of layoffs (e.g., difficulties in attracting workers in the future, higher payroll taxes). Typically, firms will offer a retirement "window"— a short time period during which workers can retire under special terms. These programs often add years to a person's age and job tenure for the purpose of calculating pension benefits.

Pensions also encourage certain types of behavior which are detrimental to the firm. It is not inconceivable that pensions may reduce turnover too much. The pension loss associated with leaving a firm will keep some workers in jobs that they do not like and for which they are not well suited. This is especially likely in companies where opportunities for individual advancement turn out to be less than what employees expected.

There is also usually very little connection between pension benefits and worker performance. Pension wealth depends on either length of service or length of service and earnings. In the former case, performance affects pension wealth only to the extent that the pension discourages the worker from engaging in behavior for which he would have been dismissed. In the latter case, the pension-performance connection depends entirely upon the linkages between earnings and performance. Unless those linkages are quite strong, the rational worker will regard pension compensation as a fixed element in the compensation package, just like health insurance and paid holidays.

By reducing the pay differentials across different jobs within an organization, pensions limit the ability of managers to use those differentials to obtain skills needed for advancement or to use the pay system to reward certain types of behavior. For instance, Allen (1981) uses a simple labor-supply model to show how an increased share of employee benefits in the compensation package creates an incentive for excessive absenteeism.

Thus, the overall impact of pensions on employee behavior has both desirable and undesirable consequences for the firm. Firms with pensions should have lower turnover rates, which will save them the costs of finding and training replacements. Early retirement benefits can also be used to encourage people to leave the firm when their marginal product has fallen below their earnings. There is some risk, however, that turnover may fall too much and that many workers in the middle of their careers may stay in jobs which they do not like for fear of losing future pension benefits. Workers covered by pensions will be less likely to shirk, for fear of getting fired and losing some of the pension wealth they would have received if they had not lost their job. This is offset by the fact that the risk of getting fired is about the only linkage between pension compensation and worker performance.

Regulatory Environment

The overall impact of pensions on firm performance will be influenced by regulation. Most pension regulations deal with purely financial matters which can be ignored in the present context. Nonetheless, certain of them constrain the choices made by workers and firms and thus influence outcomes. At the most obvious level, pensions would be a much less popular form of compensation if they were not tax-exempt. Beyond that, the Employee Retirement Income Security Act of 1974 (ERISA) contains certain provisions which are likely to be relevant. First, ERISA sets minimum vesting standards. Under past regulations, most firms chose to provide complete vesting after 10 years of service. It is doubtful that this has much effect on turnover in light of the very low rates of turnover among workers with 10 or more years of service who are not covered by pensions (Allen, Clark, and McDermed, 1986). Second, ERISA makes it difficult for firms to restrict pension coverage to particular individuals. This probably has some impact on firms which are just on the margin of having a pension plan. Third, ERISA imposes limits on underfunding of pension plans and requires firms to pay for plan-termination insurance. This would limit the ability of firms to use pensions to stop union holdups.

Evidence of Pensions and Firm Performance

Pensions are most likely to influence employee behavior by raising productivity and by influencing labor mobility. The impact of pensions on the overall financial well-being of the firm depends on the monetary value of these effects. It also depends upon how pensions affect the overall size of the compensation package. If there is not a dollar-for-dollar tradeoff (after taxes) between pensions and other forms of compensation, then firms with pensions will have higher labor costs than firms without pensions *and* firms with pensions will be at a competitive disadvantage, unless there is some offsetting productivity or cost differential in their favor. We begin this section by summarizing previous evidence and reporting some new evidence on compensating wage differentials for pensions. Then we report the first evidence regarding the impact of pensions on productivity levels, productivity growth rates, and profitability. This direct evidence is inconclusive. To gain further insights, in the final part of this section we summarize evidence on indirect mechanisms through which pensions can affect productivity such as turnover, retirement, and absenteeism.

Compensating Wage Differentials for Pensions

Testing for wage-pension tradeoffs has always been a very tricky business. The data sets that are usually employed by economists report wages or earnings, but they do not report pension compensation. This latter variable can be reported only by employers and even here it is not clear theoretically which concept (legal or projected earnings) of pension compensation should be used. There is a further problem with reverse causality. Workers with high earnings are also in high tax brackets and thus should want a larger share of their income in the form of pension compensation. Anyone who puts wages on the left-hand side and estimates pension compensation on the right-hand side of an ordinary least squares (OLS) equation should not expect glowing referee reports. This problem is further exacerbated by the fact that in defined benefit plans with earnings-based formulas, pension compensation is a direct function of earnings. Last, it is very difficult to hold all other relevant factors constant. The critical omitted variables include other forms of compensation as well as a set of variables which will, in effect, hold either employee utility or firm profitability constant so that a true wage-pension tradeoff can be estimated.

A few studies have developed procedures which overcome some of these problems; their estimates are summarized in Table 6. Of the six studies, only two contain any evidence that wages drop by the amount of pension compensation; Schiller and Weiss (1980) got this result for the 45-54 age group in a 1969 sample which matched a U.S. Labor Department file of pension plan characteristics (including benefit formulas) with a Social Security earnings history file for males in those companies whose benefits were vested, and Smith (1981) estimated a compensating differential for nonuniformed government workers in a sample of 58 cities and counties in Pennsylvania in 1976. Schiller and Weiss's results for other age groups provide little in the way of additional confirmation. They find a weak negative tradeoff between wages

TABLE 6

Previous Evidence on Wage-Pension Tradeoffs

Study	Sample	Key Results
Direct tests		
Schiller and Weiss (1980)	1969 Labor Dept. private pension file match with SSA earnings histories; males in defined benefit plans	Coefficient of legal method pension compensation in log earnings equation is −1 for 45–54 age group but no wage-pension tradeoff for other four age groups
Smith (1981)	1976 Pennsylvania nonuniformed government workers in defined benefit plans	Coefficient of legal method pension compensation in log earnings equation is −1
Smith and Ehrenberg (1983)	200 firms providing pension and earnings data to Hay Associates	Earnings difference across Hay Point levels within firms uncorrelated with either difference in pension value or difference in pension costs
Indirect tests		
Ehrenberg (1980)	1973 data on police and firefighters	Entrance pay and maximum earnings inversely related to ratio of benefits to earnings for police; no correlation for firefighters
	1974–75 data on police, firefighters, and sanitation workers	Average annual earnings uncorrelated with ratio of benefits to earnings
Clark and McDermed (1986a)	1971–75 Retirement History Survey; full-time males	Earnings significantly higher for those working past age of pension eligibility to offset drop in pension compensation
Mitchell and Pozzebon (1986)	1983 Survey of Consumer Finance; private nonagricultural wage and salary employees	Log hourly wage significantly higher for those covered by either defined benefit or defined contribution plans

Source: Mitchell and Pozzebon (1986).

and pensions for the 26–34 and 35–39 age groups, a weak positive tradeoff for the 40–44 age group, and no tradeoff for the 55–64 age group; all of these estimates are very imprecise. The only other study to test directly for compensating wage differentials by putting pension compensation on the right-hand side of the equation is Smith and Ehrenberg (1983), which found no evidence of a wage-pension tradeoff. The other three studies found no evidence that pensions reduce wages.

One limitation that all of these studies face is that they use individual characteristics as proxies for worker productivity. With industry data, one can include productivity directly as a right-hand side variable. This is done in Table 7, where the log of average hourly earnings for workers in 3-digit manufacturing industries in the May 1983 CPS are regressed on a set of standard control variables (hours, age, schooling, union, establishment size, tenure, marital status, race, and sex) and then a productivity measure (value added per hour) is added to the equation. In the first model, average hourly earnings are 38 percent higher in industries where all workers are covered by pensions than in industries where no workers are covered by pensions. This earnings difference drops to 35 percent when the productivity variable is added to the model. Thus, adding productivity to the set of right-hand side variables

TABLE 7
Log Average Hourly Earnings Equation Estimates

Sample and Pension Variable	Additional Controls	Pension Coverage Coefficient (S.E.)
3-digit manufacturing industries, 1983 Annual Survey of Manufacturers		
Percentage participating in pension plan	List 1	.319 (.079)
Percentage participating in pension plan	List 1, log of value added per hour	.301 (.077)
Full-time private wage and salary workers, May 1983 CPS:		
Participates in pension plan	List 2	.174 (.009)
Employer provides pension plan	List 2	.146 (.009)

List 1: Average weekly hours, average age, average years of schooling completed, percentage covered by union contracts, percentage in small establishments, percentage with less than one year of service, percentage married, percentage white, percentage male

List 2: Age, years of schooling completed, union contract coverage, sex, marital status, establishment size, firm size, region, industry, occupation does not yield any new insights. Equations estimated over full-time private wage and salary workers in the May 1983 CPS produce sharply lower estimates of the wage premium that workers with pensions receive (16 to 19 percent). This suggests that aggregation may be contaminating the estimates obtained from industry data, but it is clearly not creating enough bias to reverse the direction of the estimate.

In summary, the empirical evidence on wage-pension tradeoffs is quite clear. Most estimates of compensating wage differentials for pension coverage show that wages do not drop dollar-for-dollar with increases in pension compensation. Firms with pensions pay higher compensation to their current workers. Thus, the empirical studies suggest that firms must have higher productivity or receive some cost-savings elsewhere in order to survive in markets with firms that do not have pensions. Of course, another plausible explanation is that these studies have been unable to estimate accurately the true pension compensating wage differential. A final conclusion on the magnitude of any compensating differential awaits better theory or better data.

Pensions, Productivity, and Profits

As pointed out in the previous section, pensions can potentially increase productivity by reducing turnover and shirking and by producing efficient retirement decisions. These positive effects may be offset by excessively low turnover rates, higher absenteeism, and the weaker linkage between performance and pay that is generated by many pension plans. To determine whether pensions do have any impact on productivity, we merged data for 3-digit manufacturing industries from the 1983 Annual Survey of Manufacturers (ASM) with pension coverage data for those industries from the May 1983 CPS. The production function is assumed to be Cobb-Douglas with constant returns to scale. The productivity measure is the log of value added per hour. It is regressed on the log of the capital/labor ratio and the fraction of workers in each industry who participate in an employer- or union-sponsored pension plan, along with a set of 20 binary variables indicating 2-digit industry. We also included a set of six additional control variables: ratio covered by union contracts, ratio in establishments with fewer than 25 employees, ratio with less than one year of service with their employer (new hires), average years of schooling, and average age.

After experimenting with a variety of specifications, we found that the impact of pension coverage on productivity varied with union contract coverage, average age, and the share of employees who are new hires. Thus, we added interaction terms between each of these variables and pension coverage. To estimate the impact of the size of pension benefits on productivity, we also included an interaction term between pension coverage and the log of average hourly earnings. The results are reported in Table 8 with and without the interaction terms.

In the specification without interaction terms (column 1 in Table 8), productivity is 25.3 percent lower in industries with high pension

TABLE 8
Productivity Equation Estimates, 1983 ASM 3-digit Industries

	(1)	(2)
$\ln(K/L)$	.427 (.037)	.424 (.037)
Ratio covered by union contracts	−.078 (.207)	1.742 (.905)
Ratio in establishments with fewer than 25 people	−.360 (.217)	−.462 (.219)
Ratio with less than one year of service	−.173 (.446)	4.448 (2.127)
Average age	−.001 (.010)	.102 (.042)
Average years of schooling completed	−.027 (.034)	−.056 (.042)
Average weekly hours	.034 (.016)	.031 (.016)
Ratio covered by pension	−.292 (.242)	5.865 (2.757)
Pension ° average $\ln(w)$		.358 (.344)
Pension ° union		−2.463 (1.190)
Pension ° new hires		−5.974 (2.884)
Pension ° age		−.142 (.059)
R^2	.789	.807

coverage rates, but the impact of pension coverage is not statistically different from zero. In fact, productivity is uncorrelated with most variables in the model, except for the capital/labor ratio and average weekly hours.

The results for the specification containing the interaction terms show a much more complex relationship between productivity, pension coverage, and the other right-hand-side variables. The impact of pension coverage on productivity clearly varies with average hourly earnings, union contract coverage, average age of workers, and the share of workers who are new hires. Pensions are more likely to have a positive impact on productivity in industries with high earnings, a small share of workers covered by union contracts, a small ratio of new hires to employment, or a large share of young workers. At the across-industry means of these variables, productivity is 35.3 percent lower in industries where all workers are covered by pensions than in industries where no workers are covered. Pension coverage is correlated with greater productivity in industries where union contract coverage is below 12.6 percent, where fewer than 6.8 percent of all employees are new hires, and where coverage age is below 35.4 percent. (The across-industry means of these variables are 30.5 percent, 14.1 percent, and 38.5 percent, respectively.) On balance, these results show that in the average industry pensions have no effect on productivity, but pensions are associated with higher productivity in nonunion industries with low new-hire rates, high wages, and younger workers.

A related measure of firm performance is productivity growth. In most studies of productivity growth by economists, the focus is on the impact of such variables as research intensity, concentration ratios, and collective bargaining. The impact of human resources policies on innovative activity has not been carefully explored. To the extent that pensions help mold long-term economic security among the work force, they may also encourage innovation.

The U.S. Department of Labor calculates productivity growth indexes for a set of 4-digit industries where output can be measured in physical units. The ratio of the 1983 to the 1972 values of the productivity index was regressed on pension coverage to estimate the impact of pension coverage on productivity growth; the results are shown in Table 9. Pension coverage data from the beginning of the period are unavailable. To establish the robustness of the

TABLE 9

Productivity Growth Equation Estimates, 4-digit Industries 1972–1983[a]

	(1)	(2)
Constant	.763 (.181)	.884 (.223)
Pension coverage 1983	.317 (.316)	
Pension coverage 1979		−.026 (.424)
Percentage union 1973–75	−.039 (.298)	.164 (.344)
Change in percentage union 1973–75 to 1984	−.764 (.530)	−.649 (.553)
Concentration ratio 1972	.344 (.157)	.417 (.157)
Change in concentration ratio 1972 to 1982	1.288 (.499)	1.226 (.500)
R&D intensity	1.160 (.576)	1.187 (.583)
R^2	.234	.222

[a] Standard errors appear in parentheses

findings, we constructed pension coverage rates by 3-digit industry from the 1979 as well as the 1983 May CPS. Also included as control variables were percentage union members in 1973–1975, the change in unionization between 1973–1975 and 1984, the 1972 four-firm concentration ratios, the difference between the 1982 and the 1972 concentration ratio, and the ratio of R&D used by the industry to value added. The sample consists of 73 industries.

When pension coverage in 1983 appears on the right-hand side of the equation, 1972–1983 productivity growth is 32 percentage points greater in industries where workers are covered by pensions than in industries where workers are not covered. However, this estimate is barely larger than its standard error. Further, when 1979 coverage rates are used instead, there is no correlation between pension coverage and productivity growth. Productivity growth is faster in industries which are concentrated, in industries where concentration ratios are rising, and in industries with high ratios of R&D to output. Pension coverage does not seem to affect productivity growth.

The final indicator of the impact of pensions on firm

performance which we examined was profitability. This variable can be measured in the 1983 ASM data in two different ways. Profits equal value added less depreciation, total payroll (including benefits and social insurance), and rental capital. The estimated rate of return on assets equals profits divided by the gross book value of capital at the end of the year. The price-cost margin equals profits divided by value added. Both variables were regressed on the same set of control variables that were used in the productivity-level equations in Table 8; the results are reported in Table 10.

TABLE 10

Rate of Return and Price-Cost Margin Equation Estimates, 1983 ASM 3-digit Industries[a]

	Rate of Return on Assets		Price-Cost Margin	
	(1)	(2)	(3)	(4)
$\ln(K/L)$	−.407 (.085)	−.426 (.086)	−.004 (.016)	−.009 (.015)
Ratio covered by union contracts	−.368 (.477)	.855 (2.134)	−.117 (.089)	.446 (.377)
Ratio in establishments with fewer than 25 people	−.355 (.499)	−.438 (.516)	.052 (.093)	.010 (.091)
Ratio with less than one year of service	.742 (1.027)	7.273 (5.017)	.212 (.191)	2.827 (.887)
Average age	.007 (.024)	.136 (.100)	−.004 (.004)	.048 (.018)
Average years of schooling completed	−.045 (.078)	−.106 (.100)	−.004 (.014)	−.011 (.018)
Average weekly hours	.066 (.037)	.062 (.037)	.007 (.007)	.006 (.006)
Ratio covered by pension	.129 (.557)	6.978 (6.504)	.119 (.104)	3.198 (1.150)
Pension ° average $\ln(w)$		.827 (.813)		.202 (.144)
Pension ° union		−1.818 (2.809)		−.803 (.497)
Pension ° new hires		−8.725 (6.805)		−3.482 (1.203)
Pension ° age		.181 (.140)		−.073 (.025)
R^2	.635	.650	.642	.690

Industries with high pension coverage rates seem to have the same profit rates as industries with low coverage rates. In the specifications without pension interactions (columns 1 and 3), each profit measure is 12 to 13 percentage points higher when all workers are covered by pensions than when none are, but neither estimate is significantly different from zero. When the interaction terms with pension coverage are added in columns 2 and 4, the average rate of return on assets is 4 percentage points lower in the average industry if it has full pension coverage than if it has no pension coverage, whereas the price-cost margin is 8 percentage points higher if it has full pension coverage. Neither estimate is statistically significant. Except for the age interaction in the rate-of-return equation, the signs of the interaction terms in both profit equations are the same as in the productivity equations. Thus, the profit equations also indicate that pensions are more likely to enhance firm performance in nonunion industries with relatively few new hires and a younger work force.

Profit rates should be lower in industries with high coverage rates if pensions raise labor costs but do not raise productivity. Why are these results contradictory? The first suspect is always the data, in this case the ASM data used to estimate the productivity and profit equations. In the data's defense, we note that there was a very strong positive correlation between productivity and the capital/labor ratio and that the coefficient of the capital/labor ratio was always near capital's share of output in manufacturing (all coefficients were between .42 and .44). Perhaps the pension coverage rates from the CPS contained too much measurement error, but restrictions on the sample to industries with more than 30 observations for each 3-digit industry cell did not affect the results. This leads us to believe that the data are not the problem.

Another possibility is the empirical model. We used pension coverage but could not take into account variation in the size of pension compensation across different industries. Based on our studies of pension benefit formulas across different industries, we find it hard to believe that this is contaminating our results. Benefit parameters do not vary all that much among manufacturing firms with common formula types. Differences in other pension characteristics, such as age of eligibility for early or normal benefits, may be important in this regard, but study of any of these questions awaits better data.

One final way to resolve this contradiction is to examine variables which are believed to affect productivity, although the exact magnitude of their impact is unknown. We do this in the final part of this section, focusing on the evidence on pensions and turnover.

Indirect Evidence on Pensions and Productivity

All of the available evidence shows that pensions reduce turnover. Mitchell (1982) tested the effect of pension coverage on quits and job changes using the longitudinal sample from the 1973 and 1977 Quality of Employment Surveys. She found that men were 10 percent less likely to quit if they were covered by a pension plan. Pension coverage had a smaller and statistically insignificant effect on quits among females. Job changes were much less likely to occur among males and females covered by a pension. Taking into account the simultaneity between wage offers and quits, Mitchell (1983) obtained similar results: pension coverage lowers the quit rate for males but has no significant effect on the quit rate for females. The impact of pensions on mobility has also been studied by McCormick and Hughes (1984), using a United Kingdom data sample. They also found that pensions reduce mobility.

This still leaves open the question of why pensions reduce mobility. One factor which has always been thought to be important is vesting. A worker who is considering leaving a company may remain with the firm longer than he would otherwise in order to receive a pension. The impact of vesting on turnover depends on how much pension wealth is obtained at vesting. The available evidence indicates that for most workers this gain is fairly small. Looking across 1,183 plans in the Bureau of Labor Statistics 1979 Level of Benefits survey, Kotlikoff and Wise (1985) show that the gain in pension wealth when vesting occurs at age 40 ranges between 5 and 37 percent of salary. At their intermediate wage and interest rate assumptions, the gain is 14 percent. For most workers this amounts to a few thousand dollars. This will be of critical importance to a worker with nine years of service who can move from zero to full vesting by staying an additional year. It is not likely to have much effect on workers with less than five years of service, the group where turnover is most likely to take place. The only empirical evidence on this issue comes from a study, done by Schiller and Weiss (1979), of persons covered by 133 pension plans.

They found that stricter vesting requirements were associated with *higher* exit rates. Thus, both theory and evidence indicate that vesting is not likely to explain why pensions reduce turnover.

There are three other possibilities. First, lower mobility rates for workers covered by pensions may merely reflect a higher overall level of compensation. Most studies include either actual or imputed wages as control variables, so it should be no real surprise that they find a negative correlation between pension coverage and mobility. Workers covered by pensions have higher total compensation than other workers, ceteris paribus. A second possible explanation is that pension benefit formulas are structured so that there is a capital loss for those leaving the firm. As noted above, this can happen only if the pension is part of an implicit labor contract. Under the legal or explicit contract interpretation of the value of pension wealth, there is no penalty for turnover. The final possibility is that the lower mobility observed among workers covered by pensions reflects the use of pensions as a sorting device. Workers who expect to stay with a firm are attracted to firms which provide pensions; those who do not intend to stay prefer a different compensation structure.

One can distinguish between these three explanations by focusing on the coefficients of pension coverage, pension compensation, and the capital loss associated with mobility. Under the first explanation, once pension compensation is added to the model, pension coverage should no longer be correlated with mobility. If it is only greater compensation that ties workers to jobs with pensions, then the pension compensation variable will be a much more accurate measure of the extra value of those jobs than is the coverage dummy. The validity of the second explanation depends on the correlation between the capital loss and turnover. If the third explanation is correct, then the coverage dummy will still be a good predictor of turnover, but pension compensation and the capital loss will be uncorrelated with turnover.

Allen, Clark, and McDermed (1986) examined the validity of each of these explanations by estimating length-of-service and mobility equations over three different data sets; the results are summarized in Table 11. In every data set pension coverage is a very strong predictor of length of service and turnover, even when the pension compensation and the capital loss variables are included in the model. Also, except for the years-of-service equations

TABLE 11

Evidence on the Impact of Pension Coverage, Pension Compensation,
and Pension Capital Loss on Years of Service, Job Change Probability,
and Quit Probability

Sample and Dependent Variable	Results		
	Pension Coverage	Pension Compensation	Pension Loss
May CPS 1979-1983; survival rates across 100 pension/age/industry/occupation cells	Survival rates are 35-47 percentage points higher		
May 1983 CPS; years of service	Years of service increases by 34 to 49%	Years of service increases by 5% with each dollar	Positively correlated with years of service
1975–1982 PSID household heads under 55; job change probability	Reduces job change probabilities for all four age groups	No effect in any group	Reduces job change probabilities for 45-54 year olds; no effect on other age groups
1975–1982 PSID household heads under 55; quit probability	Reduces quit probabilities for 25–34, 35–44, 45–54 age groups	No effect in any group	No effect in any group
1975–1982 PSID household heads under 55; hazard for additional years of service on 1975 job	Additional years of service 28% higher	No effect	Additional years of service 22% higher for $10,000 loss
1971–1981 NLS older men; job change probability	Reduces job change probability by 11 to 16 percentage points	No effect	No effect
1971–1981 NLS older men; quit probability	Reduces quit probability by 8 percentage points	No effect	No effect

Source: Allen, Clark, and McDermed (1986a).

estimated over the May 1983 CPS (all spells in progress), pension
compensation has no effect on mobility or length of service. Both of
these findings clearly contradict the first explanation.

The results for the capital loss variable vary across each sample.
In both the CPS and the Panel Study of Income Dynamics (PSID),
the capital loss was strongly related to years of service. It was
correlated with lower job-change probabilities for workers between

the ages of 45 and 54 in the PSID. However, the capital loss had no effect on mobility for workers under the age of 45 in the PSID, nor did it have any effect on mobility in the National Longitudinal Survey (NLS) sample of older men.

A likely explanation for the negative findings on mobility for younger workers is that the mean of capital loss of pension wealth per year of remaining work life is rather small. It is $36 for workers covered by pensions who are less than 25 years old; $143 for those between ages 25 and 34; and $335 for those between 35 and 44. In contrast the average loss for workers between ages 45 and 54 is $590. Thus the loss may not have very much effect on workers under 45 because the loss is not very big.

This rationale does not apply to the workers in the NLS sample, where the mean loss per year of remaining work life is $1,270. The key factor here is probably the very low mobility rate in the sample. The average age of workers in the sample in 1971 is 56 and only 17 percent of them change jobs over a 10-year period. Among those covered by pensions, the mobility rate is an even smaller 9 percent. Thus the capital loss may have little effect on mobility because a negligible proportion of older workers covered by pensions change jobs.

The results also support the self-selection argument. Self-selection is clearly not the only factor, as the capital loss results indicate. Yet neither the capital loss variable nor the pension compensation variable can account for the lower turnover observed among younger workers covered by pensions. Self-selection is the only remaining explanation for this group.

An estimate of the impact of this decline in turnover on productivity can be obtained by using the result of Brown and Medoff (1978) that a decline of the log of the annual quit rate equal to one results in an 11 percent increase in productivity. Based on the PSID sample means, it seems reasonable to us that pensions reduce turnover from about 4 percent per year to 2 percent. This translates into a log change of −0.69 which is associated with a productivity increase of about 7.6 percent.

In addition to turnover, indirect evidence on the effect of pensions on productivity can be obtained from studies of work attendance and retirement. Allen (1981) found in a sample of 41 paper and box manufacturing plants that a 10 percent increase in monthly pension benefits per year of service is associated with an increase in the absence rate of 0.2 percentage points (the mean absence rate was 2.5 percent). This evidence is consistent with the theory that workers consider income from benefits as exogenous in making labor-supply decisions and that increases in exogenous income reduce the number of hours which employees desire to work.

The survey article by Mitchell and Fields (1982) indicates that most studies find that higher pensions tend to encourage earlier retirement. Further evidence in support of this conclusion appears in more recent studies by Fields and Mitchell (1984) and Allen and Clark (1986).

The implications of these findings for productivity are not clear. Some studies have indicated that the effect of age on productivity is insignificant prior to age 60 or older. When productivity begins to decline (whether due to changes in technology, depreciation of human capital, or changes in mental or physical abilities), this need not translate into a drop in job performance. Older workers may be able to adjust by having lower absence rates, lower turnover rates, or increased quality of work. Reviews of studies concerning the age-productivity relationshp are provided by Clark and Spengler (1980), Kreps (1977), and Riley and Foner (1968). In examining productivity by age, it is also important to recognize that only workers who remain employed are included in the measured population. The least productive workers may have already quit or been fired, in which case earlier retirement of the remaining workers may not be in the firm's best interest. Much needs to be learned about these issues.

Observations and Conclusions

The role of pensions as a form of compensation and as a method of achieving personnel objectives has received substantial attention by economists over the past decade. The rapid growth and now widespread use of employer-provided pensions suggest that offering a pension as a form of compensation does not adversely affect the economic performance or the profitability of firms. Coverage rates vary significantly across industrial and occupational groups; however, no sector has 100 percent coverage or zero coverage of workers by pensions. Thus, firms with and without pensions coexist side-by-side in many different types of markets.

We have presented the first empirical evidence that the rate of profits among firms is not affected by the existence of a pension. Obviously, pensions cost the firm money, but if they do not reduce profits, then there must be some compensating offsets either through a reduction of other labor costs or through an increase in productivity. A brief review of existing studies of compensating wage differentials attributable to pensions yields inconclusive results. At best, we can conclude that there is no empirical basis for arguing that wages or other forms of compensation decline in the presence of a pension. This does not necessarily imply that there are no compensating wage differentials for pension benefits; it merely means that there is presently little empirical evidence of such differentials. We provide the first estimates of the direct effect of pensions on labor productivity and are unable to find any significant effect of pension coverage on productivity within industries while holding constant average worker and firm characteristics.

If all of these findings are correct, how do firms offering pensions compete with firms that do not provide this form of compensation? There are two possibilities. First, the evidence seems to indicate that the answer is indirect productivity effects. Instead of being neutral sellers of pensions to workers, firms use pensions to achieve personnel objectives. These objectives are to reduce turnover during most of the employee's work life and to increase retirement rates among older workers. Lower turnover means fewer resources are devoted to hiring and training new workers. It increases the proportion of workers with a greater amount of job tenure and on the average this raises labor productivity. Earlier retirement among older workers may reduce average salaries and also may affect average productivity of workers. The second possibility is that the empirical results are misleading, particularly those on compensating wage differentials.

These changes in the age-tenure composition of the labor force and their effect on productivity are not captured in the productivity regressions discussed above. It seems likely that they provide the solution to our puzzle. Furthermore, these effects may provide an explanation for the pattern of pension coverage across firms. Firms with greater costs of turnover should be more likely to offer pensions. Firms in which workers suffer greater productivity declines with advancing age should be more likely to offer pensions. Since these are different objectives, some firms may wish to discourage turnover but not encourage earlier retirement. These firms should have different plan characteristics than firms which seek to encourage early retirement.

Many of the conclusions concerning pensions and firm performance are quite tentative and must await further confirmation. Past studies have been hindered by a lack of data that relate plan features and the characteristics of sponsoring firms to worker characteristics. The 1983 Survey of Consumer Finance may be helpful in this regard, but it does not allow the researcher to determine the productivity and profitability of the firm. We anticipate continued progress in the estimation of the effect of pensions on mobility and retirement decisions. A greater knowledge of these effects and a better understanding of the link between age, tenure, and productivity would significantly increase our understanding of the relationship between pensions and firm performance. It would be useful to have a theory of the optimal age structure of a firm and how pensions can be used to achieve this objective.

One element of the relationship between pensions and firm performance which this study has not addressed is the impact of the financial status of the pension plan. Studies of market valuation done by Feldstein and Seligman (1981), Feldstein and Morck (1983), and Bulow, Morck, and Summers (1985) all indicate that the stock market treats net assets in a pension plan as if they were part of the corporate balance sheet. In other words, underfunded pension plans translate into a lower market value of the firm's stock, with the decline in market value equal to the funding liability.

The recent decline in interest rates and the accompanying bull market have put most pension plans on excellent financial footing. A growing number of plans are being terminated with the excess assets reverting to the firm. In most cases, a new pension plan is created after a termination which preserves the legal pension wealth of both participants and annuitants. It remains to be seen whether their wealth under the implicit contract interpretation of the firm's pension promises will also be preserved and, if not, what impact this will have on employee behavior.

References

Allen, Everett, Joseph Melone, and Jerry Rosenbloom. *Pension Planning.* Homewood, Ill.: Richard D. Irwin, 1984.

Allen, Steven. "Compensation, Safety, and Absenteeism: Evidence from the Paper Industry." *Industrial and Labor Relations Review* 34 (January 1981): pp. 207–18.

Allen, Steven, and Robert Clark. "Unions, Pension Wealth, and Age Compensation Profiles." *Industrial and Labor Relations Review* 39 (July 1986): pp. 502–17.

Allen, Steven, Robert Clark, and Ann McDermed. "Job Mobility, Older Workers and the Role of Pensions." Final Report for U.S. Department of Labor, Contract No. J-9-M-5-0049, October 1986.

Allen, Steven, Robert Clark, and Daniel Sumner. "Postretirement Adjustments of Pension Benefits." *Journal of Human Resources* 21 (Winter 1986): pp. 118–27.

Andrews, Emily. *The Changing Profile of Pensions in America.* Washington: Employee Benefit Research Institute, 1985.

Brown, Charles, and James Medoff. "Trade Unions in the Production Process." *Journal of Political Economy* 86 (June 1978): pp. 355–78.

Bulow, Jeremy. "What Are Corporate Pension Liabilities?" *Quarterly Journal of Economics* 97 (August 1982): pp. 435–52.

Bulow, Jeremy, Randall Morck, and Lawrence Summers. "How Does the Market Value Unfunded Pension Liabilities?" National Bureau of Economic Research Working Paper No. 1602, April 1985.

Clark, Robert, and Joseph Spengler. *The Economics of Individual and Population Aging.* New York: Cambridge University Press, 1980.

Clark, Robert, Steven Allen, and Daniel Sumner. "Inflation and Pension Benefits." In *The Handbook of Pension Statistics 1985*, eds. Richard Ippolito and Walter Kolodrubetz. Chicago: Commerce Clearing House, 1986.

Clark, Robert, and Ann McDermed. "Earnings and Pension Compensation: The Effect of Eligibility." *Quarterly Journal of Economics* 101 (May 1986a): pp. 341–61.

_____. "Labor Contracts, Pension Plans, and Lifetime Earnings." Unpublished paper, North Carolina State University, 1986b.

Ehrenberg, Ronald. "Retirement System Characteristics and Compensating Wage Differentials in the Public Sector." *Industrial and Labor Relations Review* 33 (July 1980): pp. 470–83.

Feldstein, Martin, and Randall Morck. "Pension Funding Decisions, Interest Rate Assumptions, and Share Prices." In *Financial Aspects of the United States Pension System*, eds. Zvi Bodie and John Shoven. Chicago: University of Chicago Press, 1983. Pp. 177–210.

Feldstein, Martin, and S. Seligman. "Pension Funding, Share Prices and National Savings." *Journal of Finance* 36 (September 1981): pp. 801–24.

Fields, Gary, and Olivia Mitchell. *Retirement, Pensions, and Social Security.* Cambridge, Mass.: MIT Press, 1984.

Freeman, Richard. "Unions, Pensions, and Union Pension Funds." In *Pensions, Labor, and Individual Choice*, ed. David Wise. Chicago: University of Chicago Press, 1985. Pp. 89–122.

Greenough, William, and Francis King. *Pension Plans and Public Policy.* New York: Columbia University Press, 1976.

Ippolito, Richard. "The Labor Contract and True Economic Pension Liabilities." *American Economic Review* 75 (December 1985a): pp. 1031–45.

_____. "The Economics of Pensions and Mobility." Unpublished paper, 1985b.

_____. "The Economic Function of Underfunded Pension Plans." *Journal of Law and Economics* 28 (October 1985c): pp. 611–51.

_____. *Pensions, Economics and Public Policy.* Homewood, Ill.: Dow Jones-Irwin, 1986a.

_____. "A Study of the Regulatory Impact of ERISA." Unpublished paper, 1986b.

_____. "Why Federal Workers Don't Quit." *Journal of Human Resources* 22 (Spring 1987): pp. 281–99.

King, Francis. "Indexing Retirement Benefits." *The Gerontologist* 22 (December 1982): pp. 488–92.

Kotlikoff, Laurence, and David Wise. "Labor Compensation and the Structure of Private Pension Plans." In *Pensions, Labor, and Individual Choice*, ed. David Wise. Chicago: University of Chicago Press, 1985. Pp. 55–85.

Kreps, Juanita. "Wage, Work and Income." *Southern Economic Journal* 44 (April 1977): pp. 1423–37.

Lazear, Edward. "Why Is There Mandatory Retirement?" *Journal of Political Economy* 87 (December 1979): pp. 1261-84.

————. "Agency, Earnings Profiles, Productivity, and Hours Restrictions." *American Economic Review* 71 (September 1981): pp. 606–20.

————. "Pensions As Severance Pay." In *Financial Aspects of the United States Pension System*, eds. Zvi Bodie and James Shoven. Chicago: University of Chicago Press, 1983. Pp. 57–90.

————. "Incentive Effects of Pensions." In *Pensions, Labor, and Individual Choice*, ed. David Wise. Chicago: University of Chicago Press, 1985. Pp. 253–82.

Malcomson, James. "Work Incentives, Hierarchy, and Internal Labor Markets." *Journal of Political Economy* 92 (June 1984): pp. 486–507.

McCormick, Barry, and Gordon Hughes. "The Influence of Pensions on Job Mobility." *Journal of Public Economics* 23 (February-March 1984): pp. 939–56.

Mitchell, Olivia. "Fringe Benefits and Labor Mobility." *Journal of Human Resources* 17 (Spring 1982): pp. 286–98.

————. "Fringe Benefits and the Cost of Changing Jobs." *Industrial and Labor Relations Review* 36 (October 1983): pp. 70–78.

Mitchell, Olivia, and Emily Andrews. "Scale Economies in Private Multiemployer Pension Systems." *Industrial and Labor Relations Review* 34 (July 1981): pp. 522–30.

Mitchell, Olivia, and Gary Fields. "The Effect of Pensions and Earnings on Retirement: A Review Essay." In *Research in Labor Economics*, Vol. 5, ed. Ronald G. Ehrenberg. Greenwich, Conn.: JAI Press, 1982. Pp. 115–55.

Mitchell, Olivia, and Silvana Pozzebon. "Wages, Pensions and the Wage-Pension Tradeoff." Unpublished paper, Cornell University, 1986.

Munnell, Alicia. *Pensions for Public Employees.* Washington: National Planning Association, 1979.

President's Commission on Pension Policy. *An Interim Report.* Washington: November 1980.

Rees, Albert. *The Economics of Trade Unions.* Chicago: University of Chicago Press, 1962.

Riley, Matilda, and Ann Foner. *Aging and Society*, Vol. I. New York: Russell Sage Foundation, 1968.

Rosen, Sherwin. "Hedonic Prices and Implicit Markets." *Journal of Political Economy* 82 (January/February 1974): pp. 34–55.

Schiller, Bradley, and Randall Weiss. "The Impact of Private Pensions on Firm Attachment." *Review of Economics and Statistics* 61 (August 1979): pp. 369–80.

————. "Pensions and Wages: A Test for Equalizing Differences." *Review of Economics and Statistics* 62 (November 1980): pp. 529–38.

Schulz, James. *The Economics of Aging.* Belmont, Cal.: Wadsworth, 1985.

Smeeding, Timothy. "The Size Distribution of Wage and Nonwage Compensation: Employer Cost versus Employee Value." In *The Measurement of Labor Costs*, ed. Jack Triplett. Chicago: University of Chicago Press, 1983. Pp. 237–77.

Smith, Robert. "Compensating Differentials for Pensions and Underfunding in the Public Sector." *Review of Economics and Statistics* 63 (August 1981): pp. 463–68.

Smith, Robert, and Ronald Ehrenberg. "Estimating Wage-Fringe Trade-Offs: Some Data Problems." In *The Measurement of Labor Costs*, ed. Jack Triplett. Chicago: University of Chicago Press, 1983. Pp. 347–69.

Urban Institute. "Financial Retirement Incentives in Private Pension Plans." Report submitted to the U.S. Department of Labor, Washington, 1982.

U.S. Department of Labor. *Findings from the Survey of Private Pension Benefit Amounts*. Washington: U.S. Government Printing Office, 1985.

Viscusi, W. Kip. "Self-Selection, Learning-Induced Quits, and the Optimal Wage Structure." *International Economic Review* 21 (October 1980): pp. 529–46.

_____. "Nontransferable Pensions as a Mobility-Reduction Device." In *Pensions, Labor, and Individual Choice*, ed. David Wise. Chicago: University of Chicago Press, 1985. Pp. 223–48.

Chapter 7

Hiring Procedures in the Firm: Their Economic Determinants and Outcomes

By Harry J. Holzer
Michigan State University and
National Bureau of Economic Research

Hiring procedures in the firm usually consist of two sets of activities. One set involves the *recruitment* of applicants, and the second involves the *screening* and *selection* from among applicants. Recruitment activities often include the solicitation of referrals from current employees or other employers, posting "help-wanted" signs, placing ads in newspapers, and obtaining referrals from a variety of other sources (e.g., state or private employment agencies, schools, community agencies, etc.). Screening activities often include reviews of written applications, interviews, physical examinations, cognitive/dexterity tests, and reference checks. Probation periods can also be considered part of the screening process.

These hiring procedures have been discussed and analyzed at great length in the personnel/human resources literature, but have not received much attention from labor economists in recent years. This apparent neglect is surprising since economists have produced a voluminous literature on job search and job matching in the past two decades. Recent search models have emphasized search by employers as well as employees and the problem of finding jobs for which individuals are best suited in terms of their productivity. However, these models rarely focus on the specific activities that constitute search by employers; rather, they deal primarily with the time and resources a firm spends in a search, or with reservation (or minimally acceptable) productivity levels. Little empirical work has been done on any part of the employer search process.

This lack of attention to hiring procedures by economists is also surprising given their potentially important economic effects. For a given amount of resources devoted to hiring procedures, the choice of recruitment and screening strategies may help to determine the length of time it takes to fill a job—that is, the *duration* of the vacancy—as well as the characteristics of the individual who ultimately fills the slot and thus his/her performance there. Not only are these effects important from the point of view of a firm which presumably is trying to maximize its profits, but they also will have major implications for unemployment and the distribution of job opportunities in the labor force. Thus, both efficiency and equity considerations imply a need for economists to explore these issues.

In this chapter I hope to expand our knowledge of the economic determinants and effects of hiring procedures in the firm. I have three principal aims: (1) to review and assess the literature on hiring procedures in labor economics and personnel/human resources; (2) to provide an economic framework within which hiring procedures can be analyzed and which might bridge the wide gulf that currently exists between labor economics and personnel/human resources on this topic; and (3) to provide empirical evidence on the determinants and effects of these procedures. The evidence is based on data from a 1982 phone survey of about 3,500 firms nationwide that was developed by the National Center for Research on Vocational Education and administered by Gallup, Inc.

Analysis of these data shows that recruitment choices by firms appear to have important effects on both job performance and demographic characteristics of those hired. In particular, referrals from current employees and other employers produce new hires with higher performance ratings and less turnover than do other recruitment methods. However, these strategies are less likely to produce employees who are young, female, and with less experience—groups that apparently have fewer "connections" among current employees or have greater difficulty obtaining information and references from them. The reliance of employers on referrals may therefore be detrimental to those who are already at some disadvantage in the labor market. In a sense, these recruitment strategies may be creating an "efficiency-equity" tradeoff by the firms who use them.

The remainder of this chapter is divided into four sections. The first is a review of both the labor economics and personnel/human resources literatures which are relevant to hiring procedures. While the effort expended on this topic has been greater in the latter area, the economics literature provides some institutional perspectives as well as some recent theoretical work that can be extended to deal with hiring procedures. One such model that deals with employer search is developed in the second section, and the implications of this model for both determinants and outcomes of hiring procedures are discussed.

The third section then presents empirical evidence on these procedures. Equations are estimated which attempt to explain both the choices of procedures and their effects on perceived performance, turnover, and demographic characteristics of employees. Other outcomes such as vacancy durations are also considered. The fourth section is a summary of the findings and the implications for future research.

A Review of the Relevant Literature

Two distinct bodies of literature are relevant for any discussion of hiring procedures in the firm: the contributions from labor economics and those from personnel/human resources. While studies in the latter area are frequently directed at the practitioner rather than the academic, a good deal of academic research is worthy of note.

Of course, the fields of labor economics and labor relations (personnel) were not always as distinct as they are today, and much of the work done in the 1940s and 1950s by labor economists has been influential in both areas as they developed independently since the 1960s.[1]

Labor Economics

Lloyd Reynolds made important contributions to the study of hiring procedures in his 1951 classic, *The Structure of Labor Markets*. In that volume he stressed the limited information which potential employers and employees have about each other in the labor market. Certain informal methods of recruitment, such as

---

[1] For a discussion of how labor relations has evolved out of labor economics, see Dunlop (1977).

those that rely heavily on current employees for dissemination of information to friends and relatives, might provide more accurate insight to the employer at a lower cost than would other approaches. This theme would again be emphasized by Albert Rees (1966). When he compared the "informal" with the more "formal" recruitment methods, such as the State Employment Service, he found that the former was often preferable in terms of information. In his view, the Employment Service seemed to lack interest in the job-referral portion of their assignment and that those referred were often stigmatized as low-skilled employees. This was Rees's response to critics who chided employers for not relying more heavily on formal recruitment methods and who advocated greater public expenditures on these mechanisms.

As for empirical work in this area, early papers by Malm (1954, 1955) contained survey information on recruitment sources and their effectiveness. More recent work by Reid (1972) for the United Kingdom and by Datcher (1983) for the United States confirmed the earlier findings that referrals by current employees generated a pool of new hires with higher productivity and/or lower turnover. Various reports by the Bureau of National Affairs (BNA) and the U.S. Department of Labor made available a broader range of data on employers' use and the perceived effectiveness of these and other recruitment strategies.[2]

A somewhat different strand of literature that generated interest in these issues among economists began with Clark Kerr's "The Balkanization of Labor Markets" in 1954. The notion that markets for particular occupations and in particular localities were "Balkanized" (or segmented) implied that competition for various jobs was highly imperfect and that access to many attractive jobs would be limited by information and location as well as skills. The central role of personnel "rules" as opposed to market forces for determining employment outcomes was stressed by Kerr and many who followed him.

Among the latter, Doeringer and Piore (1971) extended this notion with their work on internal and dual labor markets. If

---

[2] The relevant Department of Labor publications are *Recruitment, Job Search, and the United States Employment Service* (1976) and *The Public Employment Service and Help-Wanted Ads* (1978). The Bureau of National Affairs (BNA) reports results of its Personnel Policies Forum in *Selection Procedures and Personnel Records* (1976) and *Recruitment Policies and Practices* (1979).

training, promotion, and other activities were handled internally by firms, then access to such "internal" markets becomes the crucial determinant of job opportunities for various groups and individuals. Recruitment and screening procedures of firms determine this access. Furthermore, certain procedures (e.g., recruitment through employee referrals, screening through interviews and tests, etc.) may create disadvantages for minorities (or women) which block their entry into "primary" markets and leave them disproportionately in "secondary" markets.[3] Thus, the firm's hiring procedures can have distributional implications as well as the effects on employee performance discussed above. While the empirical work on internal and dual labor markets has been controversial,[4] the notion that hiring procedures may create discrimination problems seems relatively uncontested.

The institutional features of labor markets and limited competition have received less attention in recent years as labor economists have concentrated on the formalization of models and market forces. An important area that is relevant here is job search. Beginning with Stigler (1962) and developing with seminal pieces by Mortensen (1970) and McCall (1970), the search literature grew rapidly during the ensuing decade as efforts were made to explain cyclical and secular unemployment trends. Search models focused almost exclusively on the activities and choices of individual prospective employees—namely, their reservation wage (lowest acceptable wage) and search effort.[5] However, the past five years has seen the development of search models that incorporate employer behavior as well. These models, including those of Pissarides (1984) and Albrecht and Axell (1984), often posit that employers consider recruitment and selection time, advertising expenditures, reservation productivities, and sometimes wages. However, the exact procedures by which applicants are generated and productivities are inferred are usually left unspecified.

As for empirical work, a series of papers by John Barron, John

---

[3] Doeringer and Piore (1971), pp. 137–47. The designation of the young as a disadvantaged group that has difficulty obtaining employment in the primary sector appears in Osterman (1980), pp. 151–54.

[4] For a review and critique of the empirical evidence of dual labor markets, see Cain (1976). For more recent evidence, see Dickens and Lang (1985).

[5] For a review of the early literature on employee search, see Lippman and McCall (1976).

Bishop, and their colleagues stand alone as attempts to test some implications of these employer search models. Not only have they focused on employers' total search time and time per applicant,[6] they also have considered how specific recruitment procedures affect applicant flows and employer profits.[7] The empirical evidence reported below, using the same data, extends their work.

A few other economic models should be mentioned before moving on to the personnel literature. The early 1970s saw the development of several models that sought to explain discrimination in a way that did not depend on employer tastes, as did Becker's (1971) model.[8] These include the statistical discrimination or screening models of Arrow (1973) and Aigner and Cain (1977), as well as Spence's signalling model (1973). All of them emphasize that race, sex, or even education may be viewed as proxies for true productivity, which is itself too costly to measure. Although some of these models have been criticized for not allowing for employer learning over time, they do suggest that procedures which are cost-effective from the employer's point of view may work to the disadvantage of individuals with particular characteristics.[9] Such a possibility is considered below.

Finally, there are some other recent economic models of personnel issues. Work by Lazear (1979) and others suggests that it may be optimal for employers to create earnings profiles over time that deviate from productivity profiles.[10] These models essentially depict the operation of internal labor markets in which firms and workers have long-term attachments. Furthermore, the recently popular implicit-contract and efficiency-wage models of business cycles similarly imply long-term attachments and wages deviating

[6] For employer search models that seek to explain total time spent recruiting and screening as well as time per applicant, see Barron, Bishop, and Dunkelberg (1985).

[7] In Barron, Bishop, and Hollenbeck (1983) we find analyses of how specific recruitment procedures affect applicant flows to the firm as well as firm profits.

[8] For critiques of neoclassical discrimination theory, see Marshall (1974) and Cain (1976).

[9] In Spence's (1973) models, individuals respond to how firms interpret signals in a way that may tend to verify those signals. For instance, blacks may underinvest in human capital because of the low returns they face, thereby validating their original belief. Thus the learning problem of Arrow's (1973) model is avoided.

[10] In Lazear's (1979) models, the deviation of wages from market-clearing levels arises from a worker's incentive to shirk and the employer's construction of an upward-sloping wage profile that induces the worker to supply effort until retirement.

from market-clearing levels.[11] All of these models suggest that the process by which some individuals are chosen for these long-term arrangements, while others are not, may be crucially important for understanding the performance of individuals in these firms and the distribution of jobs among people.

Personnel

Unlike the models of the labor economists, the personnel research has focused on the effects of specific recruitment and selection procedures. Some models have also been developed which are close to those of economists in capturing firm considerations in the hiring process. Several researchers have considered the effects of different recruitment channels on the ultimate performance of employees hired. Recent contributions include papers by Breaugh (1981), Schwab (1982), Taylor and Schmidt (1983), and Hill (1970). Most continue to find that employee referrals generate individuals with higher perceived performance and/or lower turnover, though the exact effects may also depend on additional factors such as morale among the employees and their closeness to those being referred.

Theoretical models have also been developed which attempt to capture the benefits and costs of various recruitment strategies and selection mechanisms from the employer's point of view. Often called "utility" models, they incorporate the effects of various methods on both the mean and variance of value generated by employee services, employee turnover, costs and accuracy of predictions generated by such mechanisms, etc. Boudreau and Rynes (1985) is a recent example of such work.

Another major strand of this literature reviews the results of tests for the validity or reliability of selection procedures. These issues are of interest to employers seeking cost-effective hiring procedures, as well as to minorities and other groups whose performance as predicted by various selection techniques may be relatively low. In fact, Supreme Court interpretations of the Equal Employment Opportunity Act require employer validation of tests and other selection procedures which may have negative effects on the

---

[11] For a recent survey of implicit contract and efficiency wage models, see Stiglitz (1984).

employment of members of any minority group.[12] Reviews or analyses of selection technique validity have been done by Lilienthal (1980) for reference checks, Karren (1980) for the selection interview, and Globerson (1968) for the probationary period. Their results, especially for reference checks and interviews, show questionable validity and suggest that validity might be increased by the introduction of standardized formats and structure as well as training of the personnel officers.

Other researchers have sought to define or clarify the criteria for "fairness" in cases where either test performance or test validity differs across racial groups. Steffy and Ledvinka (1986) have run simulations of employment outcomes using a variety of equal opportunity definitions, while Hunter and Schmidt (1982) and Schmidt et al. (1973) have questioned the evidence on the differential validity of various tests across racial groups.

Although the studies cited are noteworthy, little has been done to analyze the differential effects of recruitment procedures on racial, gender, and age groups. Furthermore, a wide gap remains between the perspectives of the economics and personnel literatures on these issues. The economists' search models might specify total time or resources allocated to hiring, but specific hiring methods and their economic effects are rarely considered. On the other hand, the studies in the personnel literature provide evidence on specific methods but rarely present a broader framework within which to analyze them. Even the utility models in this literature do not go beyond the perspective of the employers to capture features of the labor market that influence their choices, such as skill levels of the labor force, or reflect them, such as the well-being of minorities or women within the labor force. Nor do these models fully capture the tradeoffs facing the employer in terms of vacant jobs and newly hired workers with varying degrees of skill.

Thus a need exists for models on this issue which bridge the gap between labor economics and personnel by incorporating contributions which each area has made to the analysis of hiring procedures. A need also remains for more empirical evidence on how these procedures are chosen and on their effects on both the firm and the

---

[12] The need for employers to validate selection procedures in cases of possible racial discrimination was established by the Supreme Court in its ruling in *Griggs* v. *Duke Power Co.*, 401 U.S. 424, 3 FEP Cases 175 (1971).

labor force. It is hoped that the work reported in the next two sections is a step toward meeting these needs.

An Economic Model of Firm Hiring Procedures

Outlined here is an employer-search model in which the firm chooses its hiring policies and a reservation level of perceived productivity in the job applicant when hiring for a particular vacancy. The firm maximizes its expected profits in the following manner:

$$(1) \qquad \max E\,(Profit\,)_t = P_{Hire,t} \; {}^*\; E\,(Profit \mid Prod^r)$$
$$+ (1 - P_{Hire,t}) \; {}^*\; E\,(Profit\,)_{t+1} - C_{Hire,t}$$

where $E\,(Profit\,)_t$ is the expected (discounted) profit stream which flows from the job at time t; $P_{Hire,t}$ is the probability of hiring someone to fill the position during this period; $Prod^r$ is the reservation (i.e., minimum acceptable) level of productivity chosen by the firm; and $C_{Hire,t}$ is the cost of the hiring procedure used by the firm during that period.

Equation (1) posits that the firm incurs hiring costs during this period and faces two options: hiring an individual with productivity at least as high as $Prod^r$ and thus benefiting from a stream of profits that begin in this period, or not hiring anyone who meets the minimum standard and thus facing the same problem during the next period. The value of each option is weighted by the likelihood of that option occurring, once the hiring costs have been incurred.

In this formulation, the likelihood of hiring someone to fill the vacancy in this period should depend on the quality and number of applicants, the likelihood that an offer will be made, and the likelihood that it will be accepted.

The number and quality of applicants should depend on the characteristics of the local labor supply (such as skill mix), the wage and training policies already chosen by the firm, and the number of times each of several recruitment procedures is used. The likelihood of making an offer depends on the distribution of productivities available to the firm among its applicants as well as the firm's reservation productivity. The firm's ability to accurately gauge the productivity of its applicants will depend on the number of times each of several selection procedures is used. The likelihood of the offer being accepted then depends on the applicant's own reservation wage and the distribution of wages available to him or her in the local market.

If the vacancy is filled, the expected stream of profits that the new hire generates will depend on the product price for output produced, the wage paid, and the expected productivity of the individual.

Finally, the cost of hiring procedures should depend on the unit costs of using each recruitment method and each selection method as well as the number of times each of these methods is used. The unit costs, in turn, should reflect salaries of personnel department employees and the time-intensities of the methods as well as the direct costs incurred in each activity (e.g., cost of advertisements, etc.).

The intuition behind the model is that there is a tradeoff between the costs of using various hiring procedures and the benefits they generate in terms of filling a vacancy and hiring an individual with high expected productivity. The costs and benefits of using a particular procedure will vary across firms and industries as well as across jobs within a firm. For instance, recruiting through employees is a low-cost method which, according to the claims made in the literature (e.g., Reynolds, 1951; Rees, 1966; Breaugh, 1981; Schwab, 1982) should generate applicants in whose productivity the employer can be confident. However, this method may not be the most expedient for jobs that require more education or skills. In such cases the higher costs of newspaper ads, professional employment agencies, etc., may be justified. Legal constraints (from Equal Opportunity policies, for example) may also lead the firm to rely on these more costly mechanisms. The choice of a recruitment method may also be affected by firm characteristics such as size and union status, since large and/or unionized companies might generate a large applicant flow independently of the hiring activities they undertake. In these cases, a sufficient number of applicants for low- or medium-skill jobs might be produced by direct walk-ins. The skill level needed for the job should also determine a firm's willingness to use the State Employment Service and the screening mechanisms (interviews, probationary periods, etc.) it selects.

It should be noted that there are similar costs and benefits related to the wages and training procedures the company chooses to offer, since high wages and the availability of training might attract more and/or better qualified applicants. However, in the proposed model these longer-term decisions are taken as given in the short run.[13] Once chosen, the wages and training that accompany a job should also influence recruiting and screening strategies. It is possible that high wages and the availability of training might serve as substitutes for hiring procedures by generating a large number of high quality applicants, as suggested above. On the other hand, if high wages and training reflect the skill needs of the job, they may serve as complements for strategies that are more useful in screening applicant quality.

Choosing reservation productivity also entails a tradeoff. The choice of a higher level decreases the probability of hiring an individual during an early period and thus postpones the stream of profits which filling the job can generate. But a higher reservation level also leads to a higher expected level of productivity and profits when the vacancy is filled.

Once the hiring procedures and reservation productivities are selected, a number of expected outcomes are also determined. Two important ones—the expected productivity and profit generated by the new hire—have been noted above. Others include the expected duration (in number of periods) of the vacancy and the total time spent in recruiting and selection. The former is the reciprocal of the probability of hiring in this period, while the latter is the sum of hours spent on each method.

It should be remembered that this model assumes profit-maximizing behavior on the part of firms and full information with regard to the benefits of different methods and the characteristics of local markets which determine them. Yet the possibility remains that firms may engage in hiring procedures that, from their standpoint, are not totally optimal. Learning over time should move them toward adopting more optimal behavior, but may not completely eliminate some of the discrepancies (especially from nonprofit-maximizing behavior on the part of personnel department employees).

---

[13] The exogeneity of wages and training in the short run can be justified by thinking of them as being embodied in contracts or bureaucratic practices that are not easily changed. For firms that are either unionized or "wage-takers" in competitive labor markets, the assumption of exogenous wages can be sensible as well. However, alternative (and more complicated) models can be developed in which wages and training are chosen simultaneously with hiring procedures.

We also note that the outcomes listed above represent the firm's point of view and might be classified as "efficiency" outcomes by an economist. A different category, "equity" outcomes, should also be of concern.[14] In particular, the proportions of minorities, women, and young people hired for various jobs can be viewed as socially important outcomes of a firm's search choices. These proportions may be influenced by hiring procedures simply because different groups in the population find different methods of search more or less productive and more or less costly, given their own characteristics. For instance, evidence that young blacks are particularly disadvantaged in the use of friends and relatives and of direct applications as walk-ins appeared in Holzer (1987). The disadvantage related to the use of friends and relatives might be traced to a variety of causes—among them the absence of employed individuals in welfare homes, past discrimination which has led to the underrepresentation of blacks in many fields, and the generally high unemployment rates in many black neighborhoods. Women, the young, and other minorities may face similar problems.

However, the disadvantages facing particular groups usually will not be internalized by a firm, even if it is not explicitly discriminating. If the "signals" used by employers reflect their own misperceptions of ability and, therefore, have discriminatory content, the problems are exacerbated. Thus, both the efficiency and equity outcomes of a firm's choices of hiring procedures must be considered in any analysis of these issues.

Empirical Evidence on Hiring Procedures

In the presentation of empirical evidence on the hiring procedures of firms, we consider two types of issues: (1) the determinants of a firm's hiring activities, and (2) the effects of these activities on observed outcomes, incorporating both efficiency and equity effects. The data used for the analysis are part of a 1982 survey of 3,500 firms, designed by the National Center for Research on Vocational Education and administered by Gallup, Inc., which was a followup of a 1980 survey that was part of the government's analysis of the Employment Opportunity Pilot Project. Both surveys, and especially the latter, focused on the firm's recent

---

[14] A different category of equity concerns obviously involves the distribution of economic rewards between the firm (stockholders) and its workers. This set of outcomes should reflect various market forces as well as bargaining power within the firm. However, hiring procedures should not have any direct effect on this issue.

vacancies and hiring procedures as well as on the characteristics and performance of some recently hired employees.[15]

Of particular interest here, the 1982 survey asked what recruiting activities the firm had undertaken in the past 10 days, including soliciting referrals from current employees, posting "help wanted" signs, contacting the State Employment Service, placing ads in newspapers, etc. The survey then inquired about the number of phone calls, visits, and applications it had and how many vacancies it had filled during that time period. Information on other characteristics of the firm (size, union status, industry, sales volume, turnover rates, etc.) was also solicited.

Another section of the survey asked about the firm's most recently hired employee and various characteristics of that individual, such as age, sex, and relevant work experience. Other questions concerned the individual's performance on the job—whether the person was still employed, whether he or she had been promoted, and the employer's perception of the individual's productivity on the job at various points in time. For this last item, the employer was asked to rate performance on a subjective scale of zero to 100. (For comparative purposes, the same questions were asked about a "typical" employee.) Additional information was gathered on the procedure by which the newly hired employee was recruited, the use of a probationary period and a reference check in screening the applicant, the percentage of applicants interviewed, the total time spent recruiting and screening, and the duration of the vacancy (both planned and total).

With this information we can present summary data and equations for choice of hiring procedures as well as for the effects of these choices. In particular, we provide estimates for the following general equations for the lth firm and the ith individual:

$$(2) \qquad RM_{jl}, SM_{kl} = f(X_l, W_l, TR_l) + e_{RS,l}$$

$$(3) \quad Prod_{il}, Turn_{il}, Prom_{il} = f(X_l, W_l, TR_l, X_{il}, RM_{jl}, SM_{kl}) + e_{PT,l}$$

$$(4) \qquad X_{il} = f(X_l, RM_{jl}, SM_{kl}) + e_{x_x,l}$$

$$(5) \qquad DV_l = f(X_l, RM_{jl}, SM_{kl}) + e_{P,l}$$

$$(6) \qquad TRS_l = f(X_l, RM_{jl}, SM_{kl}) + e_{T,l}$$

---

[15] The decision to go with the 1982 followup rather than the original survey was based on the broader range of recruitment variables available in the former.

where RM_{jl} and SM_{kl} represent the hiring procedures mentioned above, the X_l represent firm characteristics, W_l and TR_l are choices of wages and training by the firm, $Turn_{il}$ represents whether the newly hired individual has left the firm, $Prom_{il}$ is whether the individual has been promoted, $Prod_{il}$ is the employer's subjective performance rating of the individual, X_{il} are individual characteristics (age, sex, experience), DV_l is vacancy duration, and TRS_l is total time spent recruiting and screening. The productivity variable appears in absolute form as well as relative to that of the "typical" employee (i.e., new hire productivity minus "typical" employee productivity), since the latter term would remove the tendency of some managers to rank all of their employees higher or lower than average.

Equations (2) can be interpreted as employer-choice estimates, based on the model presented earlier (equation (1)), while equations (3)-(6) estimate the various effects of those choices. In particular, equations (3) assess the efficiency outcomes and equations (4) the equity outcomes, while equations (5) and (6) estimate other outcomes that are closely linked to employer choices of hiring procedures and their costs to the firm. The overall model is recursive, with choices affecting outcomes but not vice versa.[16]

Table 1 presents summary evidence on the use of hiring procedures by firms. Part A shows the percentages of all firms with at least one vacancy within the past 10 days who used each of the major recruiting methods during that period. Part B shows the

---

[16] This theoretical model predicts that the expected distribution of productivities facing a firm will affect its choices: i.e., *expected* outcomes rather than *actual* outcomes help determine a firm's choices. Thus, the choices can be entered in the equations for actual outcomes without having to worry about their endogeneity. Controls for expected outcomes can be found in variables such as size, union status, wages, etc., which partly determine the pool of individuals applying to the firm.

A few other econometric issues should be briefly noted here. One problem with the outcome equations involves *self-selection*—that is, the tendency of firms to choose hiring policies precisely because they are trying to maximize the dependent variables. This implies that the policy variables are not chosen randomly and estimates of their effects are biased. Though more formal methods are available for dealing with this problem (see Willis and Rosen, 1979), we use the determinants of the hiring procedures from equations (2) as additional controls in the outcome equations to deal with this problem informally.

A related problem involves *sample-selection*—that is, the omission from the sample of those not hired. This could cause biased estimates of the effects of age, experience, or sex on the outcomes of equations (3). Unfortunately, without data on the characteristics of those omitted from the sample, little can be done here. The results reported below must be interpreted with this limitation in mind.

TABLE 1

Use of Recruiting and Screening Methods

A. Last 10 Days—Firms with vacancies:	
Percentage of firms using:	
Announcements to current employees	.528
Help-wanted signs	.142
Newspaper ads	.372
Employment Service	.201
Union/private agency	.218
Other	.259
B. Most recently hired employee	
recruited through:	
Current employee (friend/relative)	.359
Walk-in	.186
Newspaper ad	.132
Employment Service	.026
Other employer	.070
Friend/relative of employer	.076
Other	.150
Screened through:	
Physical exam	.085
Probationary period	.639
Interview	.830
Reference checks	.518

Note: All means are weighted by sample weights.

percentages of firms that recruited their most recent employee through each method and used each of the screening mechanisms in the hiring process. All means are weighted by sample weights to correct for the oversampling of large, low-wage firms in these data.

The results show announcements to current employees as being the most frequently used recruiting method, followed by newspaper ads. These frequencies are lower in most categories than those that have previously appeared in the Bureau of National Affairs (BNA) reports (1976, 1979). For instance, the 1979 BNA survey on recruitment reports more than 90 percent of the companies using employee referrals, over 80 percent using walk-ins, and over 60 percent using the Employment Service. However, the participating companies in that survey were highly nonrandom, with an overrepresentation of large firms in manufacturing. The questions in the BNA survey also dealt with general hiring (i.e., over all jobs and time periods) rather than with specific vacancies in a particular period. Still, the relative rankings in the two surveys are quite similar.

Our results also show that more than 43 percent of the new

employees are recruited through friends or relatives of either the employees or the employer. Direct walk-ins and newspaper ads together account for over 30 percent, while the Employment Service provides only about 2.5 percent.

It is important to remember that the frequencies in Part A reflect only the employer's frequency of use for each method, while those in Part B reflect both use and effectiveness in generating an acceptable employee—that is, all of the factors that are part of equation (1). The high fraction of recently hired employees generated through friends and relatives in Part B thus suggests that both its effectiveness and relative use are greater than other methods. In addition to being a low-cost recruiting method, referrals by friends and relatives appear to supply employers with information about applicants that they regard as reliable, as argued decades ago by Reynolds (1951) and Rees (1966). Whether or not these impressions are borne out by employee performance will be analyzed below.

It is also noteworthy that the Employment Service generates far fewer employees than one might expect from its frequency of use. In this case a low-cost recruiting method seems to be effective in only a limited number of cases. This, too, is consistent with the observations of Rees and others. But the low-cost method of direct walk-ins and the higher cost method of newspaper ads generate substantial numbers of employees.

As to screening methods, we see that about five out of every six employers use interviews. Despite questions about their validity that have been raised in a number of studies, employers seem to regard the interview as an important source of information about prospective employees. More than half of the firms surveyed use probationary periods and reference checks, while only about one in 12 uses physical exams. These numbers are substantially lower than comparable figures in the BNA surveys (the 1986 selection report shows over 90 percent of the firms checking references and 76 percent giving physical exams). But, again, the relative rankings are quite similar.

Tables 2 and 3 present estimates for equations (2), in which recruiting and screening methods used for the most recently hired employee appear as the dependent variable. Independent variables include industry dummies, employer size, percent of employees unionized, number of openings available in that position, education

TABLE 2
Equations for Recruitment Method for Last Employee Hired

Industry	Current Employee	Employment Service	Newspaper Ad	Walk-In	Employer Fr./Rel.	Other Employer
Manufacturing	-.011 (.034)	.032* (.013)	-.063* (.023)	.059* (.032)	-.007 (.018)	-.028* (.017)
Transportation, comm., utility	.005 (.055)	-.030 (.021)	-.026 (.037)	.095* (.052)	.020 (.042)	.005 (.027)
Agriculture	-.318 (.335)	-.027 (.089)	-.126 (.158)	.281 (.218)	-.071 (.124)	.433* (.115)
Construction	-.006 (.043)	.013 (.016)	-.066* (.029)	.080* (.040)	-.008 (.023)	-.013 (.021)
Mining	.015 (.079)	-.028 (.030)	-.070 (.053)	.147* (.074)	.020 (.042)	-.008 (.039)
Wholesale and retail trade	.005 (.024)	-.003 (.009)	-.037* (.016)	.064* (.022)	-.003 (.012)	-.014 (.012)
Size	-.020* (.005)	.004* (.002)	.003 (.003)	.010* (.005)	-.004 (.003)	-.002 (.002)
Percent union	.010 (.010)	.002 (.004)	-.002 (.007)	.002 (.010)	.003 (.006)	-.006 (.005)
Number of openings	.000 (.004)	-.000 (.001)	.002 (.003)	.004 (.004)	-.002 (.002)	-.002 (.002)
College education	-.124* (.041)	.012 (.015)	.068* (.027)	.007 (.037)	-.021 (.021)	.017 (.020)

Notes: Size of firm measured in hundreds of employees. Hours of training measured in hundreds of hours. Omitted industry is the service sector (including financial services).

Equations estimated using ordinary least squares. Standard errors appear in parentheses and asterisks represent significance at or about the 90 percent level. These notes apply also to Tables 3, 4, 5, and 6.

TABLE 2 (Continued)
Equations for Recruitment Method for Last Employee Hired

Industry	Current Employee	Employment Service	Newspaper Ad	Walk-In	Employer Fr./Rel.	Other Employer
High school education	-.038 (.032)	.010 (.012)	.049* (.022)	-.007 (.030)	-.010 (.017)	.007 (.016)
Current wage of employees in this position	.008* (.004)	-.0015 (.0014)	.002 (.003)	-.019* (.003)	.001 (.002)	.008* (.002)
Hours of training	-.020 (.024)	-.003 (.009)	.001 (.016)	.002 (.022)	-.002 (.013)	-.009 (.012)
$\bar{R}^2$	.016	.010	.011	.024	.003	.023
N	2153	2153	2153	2153	2153	2153

Notes: Size of firm measured in hundreds of employees. Hours of training measured in hundreds of hours. Omitted industry is the service sector (including financial services).

Equations estimated using ordinary least squares. Standard errors appear in parentheses and asterisks represent significance at or about the 90 percent level. These notes apply also to Tables 3, 4, 5, and 6.

dummies of the individual hired (which presumably reflect skill requirements for the job), current wage of employees in that position, and the individual's total hours of training.[17] These variables are chosen to reflect exogenous characteristics of the job, firm, and industry that should determine the firm's ability to generate applicants through each recruiting method, given the qualifications it requires. The wage and training variables, in particular, may be picking up part of the required skills beyond the education level. They also represent alternative, long-run policies to attract skilled labor, which may be complementary with or substitutable for the hiring policies analyzed here.

The results in Table 2 for the recruitment procedures provide only a very limited explanation of firm choices (as shown by the $\bar{R}^2$s). Much of the unexplained variation may be accounted for by differences in the jobs for which these individuals were hired or differences in the firms themselves. Still, some interesting findings emerge. There are few significant industry effects for use of current employees, which implies that their use is very widespread across industries. This is consistent with the previously stated belief that employers find this method low in cost and high in ability to generate useful information. However, referrals are used less frequently (or successfully) by larger firms and in recruiting to fill jobs that require a college education. In these cases, presumably more formalized personnel policies are employed and/or the jobs require that applicants have more specific skills than those who might be referred by current employees.

The Employment Service is used most frequently by manufacturing firms and for low-wage jobs, consistent with the findings by Rees (1966) and others about the perceived quality of these applicants. Newspaper ads are used most often, and direct walk-ins least often, by companies in the omitted service and finance category. Newspaper ads are the choice of firms seeking college-educated applicants, while direct walk-ins are used mostly by large firms to fill low-wage jobs. The higher cost of newspaper

---

[17] The exact wage variable used here is one for a "typical employee in this position with two years' experience." Such a variable seemed less endogenous with respect to hiring policies than would a variable for the wage of the individual under consideration. However, estimation involving different wage measures produced few differences in outcomes. Also, the training variable used here involved total hours of formal training over the first three months for the newly hired person. Again, other training variables produced outcomes similar to those listed above.

TABLE 3

Equations for Screening Methods Used
for Last Employee Hired

Industry	Proba-tionary Period	Physical Exam	Reference Check	Interview
Manufacturing	.090° (.034)	.104° (.023)	−.019 (.037)	−.034° (.021)
Trans., comm., utility	.031 (.055)	.157° (.037)	.050 (.058)	−.074° (.032)
Agriculture	.243 (.312)	−.068 (.211)	.444 (.337)	.066 (.187)
Construction	−.180° (.042)	−.081° (.029)	−.180° (.046)	−.112° (.025)
Mining	−.220° (.080)	.504° (.054)	.029 (.087)	−.070 (.048)
Wholesale & retail trade	−.003 (.024)	−.002 (.016)	−.022 (.025)	−.042° (.014)
Size	.013° (.005)	.021° (.003)	.018° (.005)	.003 (.003)
Percent union	−.015 (.010)	.002 (.007)	.002 (.011)	.008 (.006)
Number of openings	−.003 (.004)	.002 (.003)	−.005 (.004)	.002 (.002)
Number of applicants per opening	.002° (.001)	.000 (.003)	.003° (.001)	.0010° (.0003)
College education	.014 (.041)	−.036 (.028)	.065 (.044)	−.008 (.024)
High school education	.030 (.032)	.010 (.022)	.126° (.035)	.023 (.019)
Current wage of employees in this position	.001 (.004)	.015° (.003)	.015° (.004)	−.003 (.002)
Hours of training	.047° (.025)	.000 (.017)	.056° (.026)	.017 (.015)
$\bar{R}^2$	.038	.135	.057	.027
N	1946	1946	1946	1946

Note: All equations estimated using ordinary least squares.

advertising thus appears to be worthwhile for those seeking
specialized and skilled employees, while the low cost of using direct
walk-ins makes this method worthwhile in filling positions requiring
less skill and for firms that are likely to attract many unsolicited
applicants by virtue of their size. All of this is consistent with the
model proposed in the previous section.

The results in Table 3, on determinants of screening methods, show that manufacturing firms, large firms, and firms where the jobs require long periods of training make extensive use of probationary periods. Firm size and the training effects, as well as high wages, also appear important for reference checks. In both cases the cost of time-intensive screening methods may be more easily borne by large companies and are more necessary for jobs in which high wages and training will be invested. These screening devices thus appear to be somewhat complementary with the other, longer-term personnel choices.

Physical examinations are used primarily for jobs requiring less education but paying higher wages, especially in mining, manufacturing, and the utilities. Low-skilled but physically demanding jobs are likely to be in these categories. Since most firms use interviews, this screening method shows few significant determinants (except for a low level of use by construction contractors).

Overall, the results summarized in the first three tables show that firms use a variety of hiring procedures and that their choices at least partly reflect some of the underlying characteristics of jobs and firms in terms of skills needed and applicants available. Still, the low explanatory power of the equations estimated indicates that a great deal of unexplained variation in firm behavior remains.

In Tables 4 and 5 we turn to estimates of equations (3) and (4) for, respectively, efficiency and equity outcomes. Table 4 presents results for four dependent variables: perceived productivity in the first two weeks of employment, both absolutely and relative to the "typical" worker in the job, and dummy variables for whether the individual is still with the firm and whether the new employee has received a promotion. Explanatory variables include the recruitment and screening procedures (with the "other methods" category omitted from the mutually exclusive set of recruitment dummies) as well as the underlying characteristics of firms and jobs which appear as determinants of these choices. Two versions of each equation are estimated: one with and one without the demographic characteristics of age, sex, and experience in the position (measured in months) appearing as independent variables. While these characteristics may be related to performance outcomes and should therefore be analyzed and controlled for, they may also be the channels through which hiring procedures affect performance. In

TABLE 4
Equations for Efficiency Outcomes of Using Hiring Methods

	Productivity		Relative Productivity		Still with the Firm		Received Promotion	
	(1)	(2)	(1)	(2)	(1)	(2)	(1)	(2)
Recruitment:								
Current employee	2.25 (2.05)	1.26 (1.99)	1.77 (1.44)	1.28 (1.42)	.052° (.035)	.050 (.035)	-.032 (.037)	-.025 (.037)
Employment Service	-1.28 (3.70)	-2.45 (3.63)	.867 (2.62)	.383 (2.58)	.045 (.054)	.039 (.064)	-.018 (.068)	-.006 (.068)
Newspaper ad	2.36 (2.55)	.136 (2.31)	1.74 (1.82)	.367 (1.80)	.038 (.044)	.026 (.045)	-.068 (.047)	-.050 (.047)
Walk-in	3.01 (2.13)	2.34 (2.08)	1.06 (1.51)	.742 (1.49)	.002 (.037)	.000 (.037)	-.025 (.038)	-.021 (.039)
Employee friend/rel.	3.58 (2.91)	2.80 (2.85)	1.37 (2.06)	1.08 (2.03)	.023 (.051)	.022 (.050)	-.007 (.053)	-.002 (.053)
Other employer	5.24° (3.10)	3.22 (3.04)	2.92 (2.20)	1.60 (2.17)	.063 (.054)	.052 (.054)	-.050 (.057)	-.034 (.057)
Screening:								
Probation period	-4.26° (1.47)	-3.77° (1.44)	-1.62 (1.05)	-1.32 (1.03)	-.036 (.026)	-.034 (.026)	.040 (.027)	.036 (.027)
Physical exam	2.13 (2.14)	2.10 (2.10)	.353 (1.51)	.607 (1.49)	.008 (.037)	.011 (.037)	-.036 (.039)	-.036 (.039)
Interview	-5.12° (2.55)	-4.70° (2.50)	-.288 (1.85)	.049 (1.81)	-.061 (.045)	-.058 (.045)	-.036 (.048)	-.040 (.048)
Reference	-3.01° (1.44)	-3.61° (1.42)	-.547 (1.027)	-.912 (1.011)	.021 (.025)	.017 (.025)	.076° (.027)	.082° (.027)

TABLE 4 (*Continued*)

Equations for Efficiency Outcomes of Using Hiring Methods

	Productivity		Relative Productivity		Still with the Firm		Received Promotion	
	(1)	(2)	(1)	(2)	(1)	(2)	(1)	(2)
Personal characteristics:								
Age	—	.258* (.077)	—	.074 (.055)	—	.002* (.001)	—	−.004* (.001)
Sex (Male = 1)	—	1.276 (1.369)	—	−.501 (.978)	—	−.022 (.024)	—	.007 (.026)
Experience in position previously	—	.064* (.013)	—	.052* (.009)	—	.024 (.023)	—	−.025 (.024)
$\bar{R}^2$	.039	.082	.016	.052	.016	.020	.027	.035
N	1618	1618	1576	1576	1703	1703	1699	1699

Note: Equations also include determinants of hiring policies from previous tables as independent variables.

TABLE 5

Equations for Equity Outcomes
of Using Hiring Methods

	Age	Sex (Male = 1)	Previous Experience
Recruitment:			
Current employee	1.49°	.084°	7.36°
	(.725)	(.034)	(4.33)
Employment Service	2.579°	.056	4.71
	(1.336)	(.063)	(7.96)
Newspaper ad	3.290°	−.053	19.33°
	(.917)	(.043)	(5.44)
Walk-in	.889	.023	4.41
	(.760)	(.035)	(4.53)
Employee friend/relative	1.02	.069	1.88
	(1.04)	(.049)	(6.20)
Other employer	2.86°	−.026	17.57°
	(1.13)	(.053)	(6.66)
Screening:			
Probationary period	−.527	.000	−4.81
	(.532)	(.025)	(3.17)
Physical exam	.760	.129	−3.20
	(.769)	(.036)	(4.39)
Interview	−.920	.048	−4.18
	(.924)	(.043)	(5.57)
Reference	1.20°	−.035	5.75°
	(.522)	(.024)	(3.11)
$\bar{R}^2$	.069	.184	.092
N	1805	1834	1734

Note: Equations also include determinants of hiring policies from previous tables as independent variables here.

the latter case, one would want to compare the results of these equations to see how personal characteristics affect the findings on hiring procedures.

Recruitment through current employees is seen to have a positive effect on employee performance for all measures except promotion. However, these effects are generally only marginally significant and occur primarily in equations where personal characteristics are not included. The inclusion of personal characteristics in the perceived productivity equations lowers the effect of hiring procedures in a manner which indicates that a substantial part of the latter's effects works through the former. A similar pattern emerges for employees who are recommended by other employers.

In spite of the low significance levels, these results are fairly consistent with those of several studies mentioned above and thus provide some support for the claims frequently made in the literature about the quality of information on applicant qualifications that is obtained from these sources. Their extensive use in hiring (as documented in Table 1) thus appears expedient from the employer's viewpoint.

It is possible that employers view these job candidates as being more productive simply because they had good references, though this would not explain the higher tendency of these individuals to stay with the firm. It is also possible that those who have friends and relatives working for the firm perform better because of a supportive social environment. This latter possibility is not, however, inconsistent with the general observation that they do perform better than other new hires once on the job.

As for screening procedures, we find generally positive effects for probation periods and reference checks on promotion, but surprisingly negative effects on most other outcome measures. Interviews also have a quite negative effect in most cases. The effects are much smaller in the relative productivity than in the absolute productivity equations, indicating that there may be a good deal of subjective measurement error on the employer's part. Still, the persistence of negative effects in several cases may reflect either some statistical bias (e.g., omitted control variables that are positively correlated with performance) or a failure on the part of employers to select the best procedures (perhaps because of limited information, etc.). A different version of the latter hypothesis, which would be fairly consistent with the results of validation studies cited above, is that selection procedures are being used without sufficient structure or training of the personnel officials involved. Perhaps more refined measures of selection activities would show better results. In any event, the interpretation of the results here remains problematical.

Among the personal characteristics, we note that age and job-specific experience have positive and generally significant effects on all outcomes except promotion. Sex, however, is not significant. The results on age and experience are consistent with much that has been written in economics using the human capital framework, which suggests that individuals acquire important skills from working on the job.[18] Yet the possibility remains that there may be discriminatory biases in judgment with regard to the young and inexperienced (as well as women).

In Table 5 we present the results for equations in which those characteristics are themselves the dependent variables. The independent variables are thus identical to those of the first specification in Table 4. Recruitment methods are shown to be important determinants of the demographic characteristics of workers hired. In particular, recruitment through current employees is likely to generate employees who are older, more experienced, and likely to be male, relative to the omitted category of "other methods" (which include schools, community agencies, professional publications, etc.). Recruitment through other employers has similar effects on age and experience, as does the use of newspaper ads. However, the latter has a marginally negative effect on the likelihood that the new employee is a male.[19]

As before, the effects of screening methods on demographic characteristics are a bit less clear. The use of references raises the age and experience of new hires, but lowers the probability of the individual being male. Few of the other screening methods have consistent, significant effects on the demographic outcomes.

Taken together, the results in Tables 4 and 5 indicate that recruitment methods may necessitate some tradeoff between productive efficiency and demographic equity. Specifically, recruitment through current employees produces individuals who have higher perceived productivity and lower turnover. But these employees are less likely to be members of groups that are generally regarded as being disadvantaged—that is, the young, females, and inexperienced workers. Age and experience show some direct relationship to our measures of performance in Table 4. In fact, they appear to be a primary channel through which recruitment methods affect our performance measures. However, no such effect appears to hold for an employee's sex.

---

[18] A long literature in labor economics suggests that productivity may rise and turnover fall with age or experience due to greater investments by older workers in firm-specific human capital. Well-known examples of this literature include Mincer (1974).

[19] The finding that newspaper ads are effective for recruiting women is consistent with findings that appear in the 1979 BNA survey.

The last finding, combined with inferences from previous work (Holzer, 1987) that blacks are at a disadvantage when firms rely on informal search methods, suggests that a cost-effective technique by which employers often choose their most productive employees can have unintended negative effects for certain demographic groups. The evidence here on women may indicate that the negative effects are strictly a consequence of their weak "connections" with or references from those holding jobs rather than their own lower productivity. Since employers do not take this possibility into account when making employment decisions, fewer qualified women are hired. Furthermore, there may not be any reason for these effects to diminish with time unless the contacts available to the disadvantaged groups improve if and when their employment status rises. Thus, the discriminatory wage and employment differentials of the past may well persist as employers maintain hiring policies that are expedient from their point of view.

This finding, if true, raises important questions for policy-makers concerned with equity across demographic groups. While it makes little sense to attempt to restrict hiring procedures which appear to generate positive outcomes, a mandatory use of techniques which are more successful in recruiting qualified minorities and women may be appropriate. Of course, such mandates are standard parts of many current Equal Employment Opportunity programs. Furthermore, the BNA reports suggest that community agencies and advertising are the recruiting techniques that managers perceive to be most successful for hiring minorities and women, respectively.

Before concluding, we should briefly consider the estimates of equations (5) and (6) for two more outcomes: vacancy duration and hours spent recruiting and screening. These outcomes are useful as measures of the costs to employers of various recruiting methods, since vacancy duration captures forgone profits and time spent by personnel officials represents direct costs to the firm.

Two measures of vacancy duration are considered here: total duration and duration "needed" (defined as total duration minus planned duration—that is, the time before the new employee was "needed" on the job). Table 6 presents estimates of recruiting and screening methods on these outcomes. These equations also include the determinants of these hiring procedures as controls.

The results show that use of current employees and direct walk-

TABLE 6

Equations for Duration of Vacancy
and Time Spent Recruiting/Screening

	Duration of Vacancy: Total	Duration of Vacancy: Time "Needed"	Hours Spent Rec./Screening
Recruitment:			
Current employee	−8.88° (2.26)	−5.71° (2.00)	−4.67° (1.89)
Employment Service	−2.70 (4.24)	−3.94 (3.78)	−1.26 (3.52)
Newspaper ad	−5.69° (2.85)	−6.18° (2.54)	5.25° (2.38)
Walk-in	−8.35° (2.37)	−5.85 (2.10)	−5.17 (1.97)
Employee friend/ relative	2.07 (3.28)	−1.81 (2.91)	−1.84 (2.72)
Other employer	−2.56 (3.53)	−1.33 (3.15)	−1.87 (2.96)
Screening:			
Probation period	1.49 (1.66)	.768 (1.47)	1.43 (1.38)
Physical exam	−.122 (2.40)	.029 (2.13)	1.93 (2.00)
Interview	9.17° (2.86)	4.59° (2.53)	6.81° (2.38)
Reference	3.53° (1.63)	3.20° (1.44)	3.00° (1.35)
$\bar{R}^2$	.085	.042	.172
N	1877	1842	1894

Note: Equations also include determinants of hiring policies from previous equations as independent variables here. Durations and hours measured in hundreds.

ins significantly lowers the duration of a vacancy and time spent recruiting. These estimates thus confirm our belief that these methods have the lowest cost in terms of direct resources or forgone profits. They also make the reliance on current employees to be even more cost-effective than was previously thought. Newspaper ads also lower duration but increase time spent on recruiting and screening, thereby reducing one cost but raising another.

As for screening effects, it appears that interviews and reference checking increase the duration of the vacancy as well as the time spent recruiting and screening. Probationary periods also have positive effects, though these may be due to a correlation with unobserved variables rather than any direct causation. Thus, the time-intensive nature of many of the screening methods used by firms becomes apparent. In light of these findings, the general lack of observed returns to their use, detailed in Table 4, becomes an even greater mystery.

Conclusion

This chapter has been a report of my investigation of the economic determinants and outcomes of hiring procedures used by firms. The need for such an investigation was made apparent by a review of the literature in both labor economics and personnel/human resources. The former was composed of older and traditional institutional studies of these issues which had never been modeled and analyzed very thoroughly. However, the recently formulated search models did provide a framework within which specific procedures could be analyzed. The personnel literature contained in-depth analyses of many hiring procedures and issues surrounding their use. But these analyses often lacked a framework that went beyond the perspective of the employer to capture relevant features of the labor market.

An attempt was therefore made to outline an employer search model in which firms choose specific recruiting and screening procedures in order to maximize profits. Each procedure involved costs and benefits that varied across jobs and firms. Once chosen, these procedures would help determine "efficiency" outcomes for the firm, such as employee productivity, as well as "equity" outcomes, such as the demographic mix of employees hired.

Empirical evidence was presented on the use of these procedures and on their effects on outcomes. The results showed that the most frequently used recruiting procedure was announcing vacancies to current employees. The use of other recruiting and screening procedures was shown to be determined in part by observable characteristics of the firm and the job, such as industry, size, education/skill level needed for the job, and wages offered.

As for effects on outcomes, the use of current employees to recruit applicants produced workers who had higher perceived productivity and lower turnover than did other recruiting methods. However, the new hires so generated also were older, more experienced, and more likely to be male. At least the last of these effects had no observable relationship to outcomes and therefore appears to be an equity cost of using this method. Results for the use of different screening methods were less clear. Finally, equations that incorporated vacancy duration and time spent hiring showed the use of current employees and direct walk-ins to be the least costly to the firm in terms of forgone earnings and direct costs, while the various screening methods generally appeared to be most costly.

It should be stressed that these results are of a fairly general nature. They are not refined measures of the use of various procedures, especially screening methods. Certain statistical flaws also were not totally eliminated. Yet it is hoped that these results will stimulate more research by both economists and labor relations specialists on a topic of considerable importance.

References

Aigner, Dennis, and Glen G. Cain. "Statistical Theory of Discrimination in Labor Markets." *Industrial and Labor Relations Review* 30 (January 1977): pp. 175–87.

Albrecht, James W., and Bo Axell. "An Equilibrium Model of Search Unemployment." *Journal of Political Economy* 92 (October 1984): pp. 824–40.

Arrow, Kenneth. "The Theory of Discrimination." In *Discrimination in Labor Markets*, eds. Orley Ashenfelter and Albert Rees. Princeton, N.J.: Princeton University Press, 1973. Pp. 3–33.

Barron, John M., John Bishop, and William C. Dunkelberg. "Employer Search." *Review of Economics and Statistics* 67 (February 1985): pp. 43–52.

Barron, John, John Bishop, and Kevin Hollenbeck. "Recruiting Workers: How Recruitment Policies Affect the Flow of Applicants and the Quality of New Workers." Unpublished paper, National Center for Research on Vocational Education, Columbus, Ohio, 1983.

Becker, Gary S. *The Economics of Discrimination.* Chicago: University of Chicago Press, 1971.

Boudreau, John W., and Sara L. Rynes. "Role of Recruitment in Staffing Utility Analysis." *Journal of Applied Psychology* 70 (May 1985): pp. 354–66.

Breaugh, James. "Relationship Between Recruiting Sources and Employee Performance, Absenteeism, and Work Attitudes." *Academy of Management Journal* 24 (March 1981): pp. 142–47.

Bureau of National Affairs, Inc. *Selection Procedures and Personnel Records.* Personnel Policy Forum Survey No. 114. Washington: BNA, September 1976.

————. *Recruiting Policies and Practices.* Personnel Policy Forum Survey No. 126. Washington: BNA, July 1979.

Cain, Glen G. "The Challenge of Segmented Labor Market Theories to Orthodox Theory: A Survey." *Journal of Economic Literature* 14 (December 1976): pp. 1215–57.

Datcher, Linda. "The Impact of Informal Networks on Quit Behavior." *Review of Economics and Statistics* 65 (August 1983): pp. 491–95.

Dickens, William, and Kevin Lang. "A Test of Dual Labor Market Theory." *American Economic Review* 75 (September 1985): pp. 792–805.

Doeringer, Peter B., and Michael J. Piore. *Internal Labor Markets and Manpower Analysis.* Lexington, Mass.: D.C. Heath, 1971.

Dunlop, John T. "Policy Decisions and Research in Economics and Industrial Relations." *Industrial and Labor Relations Review* 30 (April 1977): pp. 275–82.

Globerson, Aryeh. "Probationary Employment—Objectives and Effectiveness." Unpublished paper, Tel-Aviv University, January 1968.

Hill, Raymond E. "New Look at Employee Referrals as a Recruitment Channel." *Personnel Journal* 49 (January 1970): pp. 144–48.

Holzer, Harry J. "Informal Job Search and Black Youth Unemployment." *American Economic Review* 77 (June 1987), pp. 446–52.

Hunter, John, and Frank Schmidt. "Ability Tests: Economic Benefits versus the Issue of Fairness." *Industrial Relations* 21 (Fall 1982): pp. 293–308.

Karren, Robert. "The Selection Interview: A Review of the Literature." Washington: U.S. Office of Personnel Management, August 1980.

Kerr, Clark. "The Balkanization of Labor Markets." In *Labor Mobility and Economic Opportunity*, ed. E. Wight Bakke. Cambridge, Mass.: MIT Press, 1954. Pp. 61–70.

Lazear, Edward. "Why Is There Mandatory Retirement?" *Journal of Political Economy* 87 (December 1979): pp. 1261–84.

Lilienthal, Robert. "The Use of Reference Checks for Selection." Washington: U.S. Office of Personnel Management, May 1980.

Lippman, Stephen, and John McCall. "The Economics of Job Search: A Survey." *Economic Inquiry* 14 (June 1976): pp. 155–90.

Malm, F. T. "Recruiting Patterns and Functioning of Labor Markets." *Industrial and Labor Relations Review* 7 (July 1954): pp. 507–25.

———. "Hiring Procedures and Selection Standards in the San Francisco Bay Area." *Industrial and Labor Relations Review* 8 (January 1955): pp. 231–52.

Marshall, Ray. "The Economics of Racial Discrimination: A Survey." *Journal of Economic Literature* 12 (September 1974): pp. 849–71.

McCall, John. "Economics of Information and Job Search." *Quarterly Journal of Economics* 84 (February 1970): pp. 113–26.

Mincer, Jacob. *Schooling, Experience, and Earnings.* New York: Columbia University Press, 1974.

Mortensen, Dale T. "Job Search, the Duration of Unemployment, and the Phillips Curve." *American Economic Review* 60 (December 1970): pp. 847–62.

Osterman, Paul. *Getting Started: The Youth Labor Market.* Cambridge, Mass.: MIT Press, 1980.

Pissarides, C. A. "Efficient Job Rejection." *Economic Journal* 94 (Supp. March 1984): pp. 97–108.

Rees, Albert. "Informal Networks in Job Markets." *American Economic Review* 56 (May 1966): pp. 559–66.

Reid, Graham. "Job Search and the Effectiveness of Job-Finding Methods." *Industrial and Labor Relations Review* 25 (April 1972): pp. 479–95.

Reynolds, Lloyd. *The Structure of Labor Markets.* New York: Harper and Row, 1951.

Schmidt, Frank, et al. "Racial Differences in Validity of Employment Tests: Reality or Illusion?" *Journal of Applied Psychology* 53 (January 1973): pp. 5–9.

Schwab, Donald P. "Recruiting and Organizational Participation." In *Personnel Management*, eds. K. Rowland and G. Ferris. Boston: Allyn and Bacon, 1982. Pp. 103–28.

Spence, Michael. "Job Market Signalling." *Quarterly Journal of Economics* 87 (May 1973): pp. 355–75.

Steffy, Brian, and James Ledvinka. "The Impact of Five Definitions of Fair Employee Selection on Long Run Minority Employment and Employee Utility." University of Minnesota, Industrial Research Center Working Paper 86-04, 1986.

Stigler, George J. "Information in the Labor Market." *Journal of Political Economy* 70 (Part 2, October 1962): pp. 94–105.

Stiglitz, Joseph. "Theories of Wage Rigidity." National Bureau of Economic Research Working Paper No. 1442, September 1984.

Taylor, M. Susan, and Donald Schmidt. "A Process-Oriented Investigation of Recruitment Source Effectiveness." *Personnel Psychology* 36 (Summer 1983): pp. 343–54.
U.S. Department of Labor. *Recruitment, Job Search, and the United States Employment Service.* R&D Monograph 43, Employment and Training Administration. Washington: U.S. Government Printing Office, 1976.
_____. *The Public Employment Service and Help-Wanted Ads.* R&D Monograph 59, Employment and Training Administration. Washington: U.S. Government Printing Office, 1978.
Willis, Robert, and Sherwin Rosen. "Education and Self-Selection." *Journal of Political Economy* 87 (part 2, October 1979): pp. S7–S36.

Chapter 8

Turnover, Employment Security, and the Performance of the Firm

By Paul Osterman[*]

Massachusetts Institute of Technology

This chapter is about turnover and its synonyms, and those synonyms—employment security, labor mobility, quits, and layoffs—demonstrate the problems with the topic. Turnover is a topic whose beauty, or lack thereof, very much lies in the eye of the beholder. Many economists extol labor mobility as the mechanism that drives the labor market toward equilibrium. In a similar spirit are the favorable comparisons of the fluidity and flexibility—and therefore high turnover—of the American labor market with the (supposed) rigidity of European markets. By contrast to these positive assessments of turnover is the fact that in much of the personnel literature—and in some variants of economic theory—turnover is seen as wasteful of the firm's investment in hiring and training its work force. The corollary of this perspective is the positive assessment accorded to employment security policies of nations such as Japan and firms such as IBM and the argument that renewed American competitiveness requires broad diffusion of these policies.

What is apparent is that there is considerable room for disagreement on the costs and benefits of turnover. This implies, of course, that the issue is not whether turnover is a "good thing," but rather how much is optimal under what circumstances. The difficulty with carrying off such an admirably balanced assessment successfully is that the literature on turnover falls into at least three broad categories and the points of contact among them are few.

[*] The author is grateful to Myron Roomkin and Christopher Ruhm for comments.

There are the human capital and job-match interpretations (which view turnover as flowing from the optimizing behavior of workers and firms), sociological models (which emphasize the determinants of job satisfaction and the role of social contact networks), and internal labor market models (which view turnover as flowing from strategic decisions by firms as to how to organize work). Each of these explanations implies somewhat different strategies for understanding the impact of turnover on performance.

In this chapter we will first provide data on patterns of turnover and employment stability in the U.S. We will then discuss, in turn, each of these three general approaches from both a theoretical and an empirical perspective. We follow with a review of what is known about the impact of turnover and employment stability on the firm's performance, and we conclude with a discussion of emerging issues and trends in practice and the public policy debates which flow from them.

Any effort to reach a conclusion about the relationship of turnover and firm performance is complicated by ambiguity concerning the proper measure of performance (see Kanter and Brinkerhoff, 1981, for a review of alternative measures). If profitability is the appropriate metric, then it is very hard to draw summary judgments since whatever costs and benefits are associated with a given turnover rate have to be weighed against other characteristics of the system—wages, for example—which the rate entails. On the other hand, if performance is measured as work-group productivity, then it appears possible to conclude that performance improves as turnover is reduced. Other measures, such as organizational adaptiveness, are difficult to quantify although tentative assessments are possible. Finally, many would argue that the social benefits of employment stability exceed private benefits.

Empirical Patterns of Turnover and Employment Stability

An inquiry into the empirical patterns of turnover and employment stability may be approached from either of two angles. The first employs quit and layoff data to address turnover directly. The second uses information on job duration and asks about the fraction of the work force which has spent a given period of time with an employer. We will take both tacks, starting with data on turnover. First, we summarize the main conclusions:

1. Turnover, both quits and layoffs, are very unevenly distributed by age, sex, industry, and occupation. Women have higher quit rates than men, young people have higher quit rates than older workers, and layoffs are concentrated in blue-collar manufacturing sectors.

2. There is no time trend in quit behavior. Although no pattern is entirely clear, there is some reason to believe that layoffs are becoming more broadly distributed with new groups of workers—white-collar and nonmanufacturing—becoming increasingly at risk.

3. When we ask about job stability, we do find a common pattern—frequent job turnover early in careers followed by long tenure on a "permanent" job. For many workers the "lifetime" employment model of Japan seems to be a reality in the U.S. However, there is substantial dispersion in this pattern, with only half of the men and far fewer women and minorities holding "permanent" jobs.

Table 1 provides data on the distribution of layoffs in 1982, a year of weak economic performance (the overall unemployment

TABLE 1

Layoff Rates by Industry, Occupation, Age, and Sex for 1982:
Percentage of Total Unemployment in Each Occupation
or Industry Accounted for by Layoffs

	Adult Men	Adult Women	Teenagers
Occupation			
Professional & Technical	15.7	10.3	—
Managers & Administrators	12.4	5.7	10.0
Clerical Workers	20.0	12.1	5.2
Sales Workers	12.2	11.2	6.5
Craft Workers	33.9	28.4	16.9
Operatives except Transport	39.8	37.0	21.9
Transport Operatives	31.4	29.8	13.6
Nonfarm Laborers	26.3	27.4	10.6
Service Workers	12.6	10.3	5.8
Industry			
Mining	43.6	30.2	12.5
Construction	32.2	23.4	17.3
Manufacturing	42.7	36.4	22.2
Transportation	33.9	23.2	10.5
Wholesale & Retail	13.4	9.8	8.1
Finance, Insurance, Real Estate	6.0	7.9	—
Services	12.3	9.3	6.1

Source: Bednarzik (1983), pp. 7–8.

rate was 9.7 percent). It is apparent that adult men face greater risk of layoff than do either teenagers or women,[1] largely due to the fact that the more cyclically sensitive industries are disproportionately staffed by men.

It is also clear that the incidence of layoffs varies considerably by industry and occupation, with workers in manufacturing industries and blue-collar occupations being much more at risk than other employees. The explanation is complex. One factor is that manufacturing industries are more cyclically sensitive than nongoods-producing industries. An additional issue is that unionization rates are higher in manufacturing, and unions appear to prefer to adjust demand fluctuations by layoffs rather than hours or wage adjustments (Medoff, 1979). We will explore the implications of this pattern later.

The greater vulnerability to layoffs of men, manufacturing employees, and blue-collar workers has long been accepted as the traditional pattern. But there is now some evidence of change. In particular, white-collar workers appear to be increasingly subject to layoffs. Large and visible companies such as Ford, CBS, Union Carbide, Kodak, General Motors, and New York Life have all recently announced substantial reductions in their white-collar labor forces, and *Business Week* recently reported that 89 of the 100 largest firms have established programs to reduce the number of management-level employees.[2] However, the aggregate unemployment data do not yet reflect a shift in the relative risk of layoffs.

An additional aspect of the layoff issue concerns the distinction between permanent and temporary layoffs. Roughly 70 percent of all announced layoffs end in recalls in the sense that the workers return to their previous jobs (Bednarzik, 1983; Lilien, 1980). This fact has played an important role in debates about the welfare interpretation of unemployment, with some arguing that, because most spells are short, unemployment is a voluntary and transitory phenomenon. In fact, although most individual spells may be short, most of the unemployed are experiencing long spells and their unemployment is best interpreted as their genuine difficulty in finding jobs (Clark and Summers, 1979). The issue for us is how to

---

[1] In this table the term "layoff" includes both temporary layoffs which end in recalls and permanent separations.

[2] *Business Week*, September 16, 1985, p. 34.

interpret short-term layoffs followed by recall. Is this turnover as the term is conventionally understood?

The answer depends on the certainty, from the firm's and the individual's vantage, that there will be a recall. From the individual's perspective, if what occurs is that he or she is laid off and goes into a lottery with a 70 percent chance of recall, then, although the chances may be good, the uncertainty is sufficiently high that behaviors on the job that might be associated with job security (e.g., willingness to quickly accept new technologies) may not be forthcoming. On the other hand, if the 70 percent to be recalled are identified in advance, then the layoff is really a kind of vacation. There are situations in which the latter perspective is accurate—for example, the August layoffs preceding retooling in the auto industry. However, in general, there does appear to be a high degree of uncertainty associated even with layoffs that eventually end in recall. Katz (1986) reports that only 15–25 percent of job-losers on what were termed "temporary" layoffs were actually given fixed-duration layoffs with instructions as to when to return. Bednarzik (1983) shows that of those on "temporary" layoff who were reemployed within a month of the layoff, 37 percent found jobs with other firms.

From the firm's perspective, the statistical fact is that it can lay off workers with a very high probability of recall. In effect this becomes a mechanism for adjusting hours of work in a world in which more direct adjustments (i.e., by reducing the workweek) are not common. Further, this mechanism is subsidized by the unemployment insurance system, as UI taxes are not fully experience-rated. Turnover of this sort should improve a firm's performance, given the other constraints it faces. The only complication is whether there is a bias toward losing the more productive workers while they await recall. To the extent that productivity is associated with tenure, this should not typically be a problem since high-tenure workers will be the first to be recalled.

The evidence with respect to quits is considerably less complex. Quits are strongly related to age, a pattern that reflects a mixture of what might be the emotional and the rational (Osterman, 1980). As a result of young people's relatively greater interest in leisure than in careers, they quit jobs frequently and their occupational and industrial distribution is typically in settings in which there are few returns to tenure. At the same time, and especially as they leave the teen years, their early work years are characterized by job-shopping.

Quit rates also vary by occupation and sex, as shown in Table 2. Occupational differences are typically understood, in part, in terms of the composition of occupations (young people who are quit-prone take unskilled work) and in part in terms of differences in specific human capital (skilled craftsmen have made greater investments than have unskilled laborers). The differences in specific human capital are also reflected in higher wages which, in turn, reduce quits.

Gender differences are more controversial. Women have historically had higher quit rates than men largely because they have been prone to quit and exit the labor force (Barnes and Jones, 1974). This behavior has been widely used to justify women's lower wage rates in human capital terms (Mincer and Polachek, 1974). However, there are more complex shadings in these patterns. Viscusi (1980) shows that while women's quit rates are, indeed, higher in their first year on the job, after that period their rates are no higher than those of men. Blau and Kahn (1981b), working with a sample of young men and women, estimate quit equations and argue that if male occupational and industry values are put into the female equations, then female quitting is no more frequent, and perhaps even less common, than quitting by men. Osterman (1982) shows that quit rates of women are lower in industries with a higher prevalence of affirmative action plans. Taken together, this evidence suggests that a substantial, though probably not the entire, component of the higher female quit rate is due to opportunity, not

TABLE 2
Quit Rates by Occupation and Sex

Occupation	Quit Rate	
	Male	Female
Professional & Technical	4.6%	14.9%
Managers, Officials, Proprietors	8.7	15.5
Self-Employed	7.4	15.0
Clerical & Sales	11.1	18.3
Craftsmen & Foremen	7.6	23.6
Operatives	10.1	17.5
Laborers	9.3	15.1

Source: Viscusi (1980), p. 391. The data are taken from the Panel Study of Income Dynamics and refer to 1975–1976.

preference. To the extent that this is true, this unequal distribution of quitting signals misallocation of economic resources.

Secular Trends

One might also ask whether turnover exhibits any secular trend. This is a question that in the past has engendered some intellectual sparks. Prior to the 1920s, employment, even in large firms, was remarkably unstable, and Jacoby (1985, p. 116) reports that annual turnover rates of over 100 percent were common. Arthur Ross (1958), examining whether the post-World War II era of benefits and security engendered a "New Industrial Feudalism," discerned a sharp decline in the quit rate in the 1920s and a more modest decline in the 1950s. His explanation for the 1920s trend is that "the employer decided to decasualize the whole employment relationship and to incorporate system into it" (p. 911).[3] In effect, this was the rise of the internal labor market. Ross attributes a slight decline in quits in the 1950s to an aging of the labor force and greater employment stability.

Whatever the historical record Table 3 suggests, and

TABLE 3

Turnover Rates by Year, 1969–1980
(Monthly Rates per 100 Workers)

Year	Capacity Utilization Index	New Hires	Quits	Layoffs
1969	86.3	3.8	2.7	1.2
1970	79.5	2.8	2.1	1.8
1971	78.5	2.6	1.8	1.6
1972	83.5	3.3	2.3	1.1
1973	87.6	3.9	2.8	0.9
1974	83.7	3.2	2.4	1.5
1975	72.9	2.0	1.4	2.1
1976	79.6	2.6	1.7	1.3
1977	82.2	2.8	1.8	1.1
1978	84.7	3.1	2.1	0.9
1979	86.0	2.9	2.0	1.1
1980	79.6	2.1	1.5	1.7

Sources: Data on new hires, quits, and layoffs from *Employment and Earnings*, various years. Capacity utilization index from *Economic Report of the President*, 1984, p. 271.

[3] Ross's explanation is supported in more detail by Jacoby, although Jacoby dates the innovation earlier than does Ross.

regressions with controls confirm, the past decade and a half have seen little secular change in turnover. This is consistent with Pencavel's (1970) analysis which found a decline in quits from 1947 to 1959 but no trend thereafter. Unfortunately, this series was terminated in 1981 and no comparable subsequent data are available. Also, the sample is limited to the manufacturing industry and is overly weighted toward larger and more stable firms (Utter, 1982). Subject to these caveats, it is apparent that while quit and layoff rates are sensitive to cyclical conditions, no secular trend is discernible (although there are dissenting views on this point).[4]

Job Tenure

A very different way of organizing the empirical evidence is to focus upon job tenure. If one could collect data on the length of time people hold jobs, what would this tell us about patterns of turnover and stability? The Current Population Survey periodically asks people about the length of time on their current job, and these data have been examined in detail in several recent papers (Akerlof and Main, 1981; Hall, 1982). Robert Hall provides the most useful organization of the data and we will focus on his results.

Hall takes data on current tenure on the job and calculates "expected tenure" by computing a series of age-based transition probabilities. Thus, although we do not observe actual completed tenure, by several assumptions (the most important of which is that the economy is relatively stable structurally over time), we can get estimates.

The modal pattern is that members of the labor force go through a period of extensive job changing during which they hold a relatively large number of jobs. They then eventually find a job which lasts quite a long time. For example, 20–24-year-olds in 1978 had held an average of four jobs and 7.4 percent were in jobs which would eventually last 20 years. By ages 30–34, the figures had increased to 6.7 jobs, and 27.7 were in jobs that would last 20 years or more. For subsequent age groups, the figures essentially stabilize at roughly 10 total jobs and 40 percent in 20-year jobs (Hall, 1982, pp. 722–23).

---

[4] One dissenting view is found in Ragan (1984) who enters labor force characteristics into a standard time-series quit equation and picks up a negative time trend. However, the total decline he finds amounts to a very modest 1.4 quits per 100 workers per month over a 30-year period.

Although 40 percent of the mature labor force eventually find long-term employment, the figures differ sharply by sex. For all age groups, 37.3 percent of the men are in jobs that will last 20 years or more, compared to 15.1 percent of the women. To give an age-specific example, although among all 35–39-year-olds (males and females) 35.5 percent are in jobs which will eventually last 20 years, for men alone the figure is 47.0 percent.

Despite the evidence, one is hesitant to call these long-term jobs "lifetime" jobs, although Hall does use the term. Although it is obvious that many workers who are in jobs that have lasted or will last 20 years do hold them for life, a substantial minority do not. For example, among 40–44-year-old men who have accumulated 20 to 25 years of tenure, 21 percent will leave these jobs sometime within the next 10 years. For the same age group, but for men with 10 to 15 years of tenure, 36 percent will leave their jobs within a decade (Hall, 1982, p. 724).

In short, the job-tenure data provide a somewhat mixed picture. A great deal has been made of the "lifetime" or long-run aspect of employment, and this is understandable given the conventional view that U.S. jobs are unstable and the contrast frequently made with the Japanese *nenkō* system. Long-term employment is the rule for a very substantial minority of men, although even for this group there appears to remain a nontrivial amount of residual insecurity. However, more than half of all men and the great majority of women are not in long-term jobs, nor will they ever be.

An additional point is that there are differences in job tenure by occupation (Sehgal, 1984, p. 20). In the 1983 Current Population Survey, the source of the most recent tenure data, the actual median tenure on the job for men (a figure which will be below Hall's estimate of "expected" tenure) varied from 8.1 years for "executive, administrative, and management" jobs to 4.1 years for "non-household and non-protective service" jobs. The distribution was tighter for women, ranging from 5.8 to 5.3 years in all occupations except four—sales, technicians, service, and private household.

Alternative Theoretical Perspectives on Turnover and Employment Stability

As we noted earlier, the literature embodies three broadly different approaches to an understanding of turnover and stability.

For the first two, the human capital/job-matching and sociological models, there is a vast amount of reported research, most of which develops slightly new twists, both theoretical and empirical, on basic themes. As several reviews are available (Price, 1977; Bluedorn, 1982; Parsons, 1973), we will make no effort here to cover the territory comprehensively. Instead we will describe the core models and orient the discussion toward drawing the implications of these models for firm performance. More effort will be devoted to elaborating the internal labor market perspective since it is less familiar in this context.

In working through these models there are two useful distinctions to keep in mind. The first is that turnover is composed of two flows, quits and layoffs, and the determinants and consequences of the two may differ. Although this might seem obvious, to a surprising extent the distinction is blurred in many models. The sociological literature on turnover seems to focus almost exclusively on quits; see Price (1977, p. 9) for an explanation of this orientation. In the specific human capital and job-matching models of microeconomics, the two phenomena are treated symmetrically; a worker quits if the wage is "too low," but the decision to lower that worker's wage can be interpreted as a layoff. However, for many purposes the distinction is quite important. First, of course, the welfare difference between quits and layoffs is substantial. Second, much of the recent public policy concerned with employment stabilization (for example, Work in America, 1984) centers on efforts to minimize layoffs.

The second cleavage is a bit harder to explain but is equally important. This is the difference between unintentional and intentional turnover. In models of the former, the aggregate turnover rate of the firm is the byproduct or aggregate of micro interactions between workers and firms. Ex ante, the overall turnover rate for the firm or the work group as a whole is not a matter of explicit concern, although there may be some consideration of the chances that a given individual will leave (if, for example, his or her wage is too low). By contrast, in the intentional models the aggregate turnover rate is an explicit policy variable. In structuring the employment relation, the firm (or the firm and the union) considers the firm's turnover rate to be an outcome variable whose value is of interest and, therefore, is taken into account.

Human Capital and Job-Match Models

The central notion in most microeconomic models is that turnover, and employment stability, are the byproducts of maximizing behavior by individuals and firms. At the core of these models is the idea that labor productivity or skill is a more or less continuous and measurable variable whose value varies depending on the joint investment decisions by the firm and the worker. These investment decisions can take the form of training (in human capital models) or job search (in job-matching models). Whatever deal is struck concerning the distribution of costs and rewards between the employer and the worker brings with it a given level of turnover.

In the human capital framework productivity is determined in part by the degree of firm-specific human capital embodied in the employee. Accumulation of such human capital is costly—presumably due to the expense of supervision, materials wastage, and the opportunity cost of using less than fully skilled workers—and the cost is shared by the two parties. In general, workers pay their share by accepting a wage below their actual marginal revenue product. Later in their careers this investment will pay off in higher wages.

This simple model contains a number of implications concerning turnover. As investment in specific training increases, both parties will have an incentive to reduce turnover since exit reduces the returns on the investment. Since tenure is likely to be positively correlated with specific skills, we would expect workers with high tenure to have low quit rates. Indeed, this is one of the most consistent findings in the empirical literature. The symmetry of the model also leads to the expectation that layoff rates will be lower for high tenure workers, again an expectation that is generally confirmed. We would also expect that factors which are negatively correlated with investment in specific human capital would be positively correlated with high turnover. In this literature a common explanation for the high turnover rates of women is that their shorter periods of labor force participation lead them to limit their investments in specific human capital (Mincer and Polachek, 1974).

What are the implications of the human capital model for the relationship between turnover and the performance of the firm? Most of the researchers in this area do not ask this question, but one did—Pencavel (1972). At first glance it would seem clear that high turnover is costly since the firm will lose its investment in the worker's skills and, indeed, Pencavel makes just this point. In his production function the partial derivative of quit rates upon output is negative because of the loss of skill and teamwork involved (the model includes no possible benefits of turnover, such as "new blood"). However, the analysis is deeper than this. The level of turnover will vary with the firm's wage level since higher wages imply that a greater share of the returns to specific skills are going to labor and this will reduce workers' incentives to search for better jobs. Firms are therefore optimizing over two variables—the wage rate and the turnover level. Pencavel shows that "the quit rate which is optimal from the point of view of the profit maximizing firm is that, at the margin, the harmful effects of turnover on productivity are just matched by the wage, hiring, and training costs associated with that turnover rate" (Pencavel, 1972, p. 57).

The implication is that firms with high quit rates will have low wage rates and vice versa. This, in turn, greatly complicates any conclusion about the relationship between turnover and performance since the *profit* rates of the high turnover/low wage and low turnover/high wage firms may not differ. Indeed, all else constant, they will not vary and therefore any empirical effort to detect the impact of turnover on financial performance will find no effect. On the other hand, if we choose to measure performance not by the bottom line, but rather by a direct measure of productivity, then the specific human capital model does contain a clear implication that turnover reduces productivity by an amount that varies directly with the level of specific human capital required by the production technology and embodied in the labor force.

An alternative interpretation of turnover has substantially different implications. Job-matching models (Jovanovic, 1979) view the process of worker attachment to the firm as one of shopping around for the best "fit." The key assumption is that the quality of the match will vary by individual and firm and that different people will have different productivity in different enterprises. The quality of the match is unknown prior to actually experiencing it, and hence workers will change jobs until the expected benefits of search fall below the costs. What drives these models is not skill acquisition in the specific human capital sense, but rather the (undefined) notion of fit.

In their purest form the job-matching models imply that the positive relationship of wage growth and tenure is not a function of skill acquisition, but rather an artifact of the statistical fact that a sample of individuals with long tenure will contain relatively more "good fits" than a sample with short tenure. What little empirical work there is has attempted to test this hypothesis by determining whether the return to tenure is a result of only this sample-selection phenomenon (Abraham and Farber, 1986; Altonji and Shakotko, 1985). The findings lend some support to the job-match model, but the tests require strong statistical assumptions since the hypothesized determinants of pay growth (specific human capital and fit) are both unobservable and, with respect to any given job, in effect identical (a good fit is equivalent to a dose of training given the first day of work). One might expect that the shape of the tenure/wage profile would differ in the two models (a one-time step function in the match theory and continuous increase in specific human capital), but there is no reason to expect this pattern in the data since, given long-term employment, the actual time path of earnings is variable depending on the incentives facing the parties and the contracts (actual or implicit) they reach.

The job-match perspective does provide a clear contrast to human capital theory when it comes to turnover. In contrast to the specific human capital model in which turnover is always costly to productivity, the job-match model would predict that a high rate of turnover among new employees might be optimal. It is in this initial probationary period that the quality of the match is explored by both sides and turnover by "bad fits" should enhance productivity. Subsequently turnover becomes costly to the extent that high productivity/good match employees leave the organization. What this analysis does, therefore, is to move us away from a focus upon *the* organizational turnover rate and suggest instead that the relevant variable is the turnover rate among employees of different job tenures. This is not, however, to argue that job-match models provide a superior understanding of the turnover process. Although it is clearly true that an initial period of "job-shopping" characterizes the careers of many young people, it is also true that turnover rates continue to decline with job tenure well after the early "get acquainted" period. The match model has difficulty accounting for this continuous decline and the specific human capital story remains important.

Sociological Models of Turnover

Sociologists have also invested considerable effort in research on quits; layoffs are generally ignored. Most of this literature is reviewed in a book-length survey by Price (1977), which is extended and updated in Bluedorn's (1982) review. In contrast to the human capital/job match models which focus on a single, readily identifiable (if not measurable) motivation or process, much of the sociological literature is characterized by lists of background variables and intermediate outcomes that are tied together in an order and structure dictated by the particular author's view and the patterns of the data. Thus, for example, Bluedorn provides a synthesis in which (1) demographic variables influence (2) expectations and (3) external opportunity; these two factors, in turn, interact with the (4) organization to produce (5) job satisfaction; job satisfaction affects (6) organizational commitment which, in turn, determines whether (7) job search occurs; the results of job search affect the (8) intent to leave, and this finally determines (9) turnover.

At this level of generality, models of this sort are unobjectionable in that they simply lay out in more detail the variables which any explanation of turnover must consider. It would not be difficult to play out the specific human capital or match models in this framework. However, it is this elasticity that makes characterizations of this sort ultimately frustrating. In the end, they seem to be nothing more than a list, albeit one with some temporal ordering. What is necessary to add some bite to the model and to distinguish it from previous economic theories is to understand what is distinctively "sociological" about turnover.

One major arena lies in understanding why some individuals are more movement-prone than others. If, for example, two people with the same skills, in the same setting, and facing the same external opportunities have different probabilities of quitting, then this would appear to provide an opportunity for a distinctive intellectual contribution. Some of the most interesting work along these lines has been done by Granovetter (1986) who argues that turnover is, in important part, a function of the social networks in which an individual is embedded. A worker with contacts in a broad range of firms is more likely to move than one whose contacts are more limited. This line of thinking can help explain patterns of movement by neighborhood and social class (Wial, 1987). It is also relevant to job-matching theories since the network interpretation implies that employees and firms have substantial information about each other even prior to a formal employment relationship.

A second distinctively sociological topic concerns the role of groups and institutions. Economists frequently think of individuals and firms as autonomous actors engaged in one-on-one bargaining. To the stereotypical economist, what might appear to the untrained eye as patterned behavior, or institutions, is really the result of these individual bargains repeated because of their optimality. By contrast, sociologists recognize that groups and networks play an independent and distinctive role in the production and allocation process.

In most settings production is dependent upon group interaction and cooperation, not on isolated workers. When groups are important, then a series of issues that are related to turnover become salient. The sociological perspective with the greatest relevance for assessing the impact of turnover on performance lies in research on work groups. Numerous studies have documented that productivity is a group, not an individual, phenomenon. To the extent that common experience, high morale, and shared expectations are important, then high rates of turnover can be expected to disrupt production. It is this line of thinking that undoubtedly accounts for the strong bias in the sociology literature for the belief that turnover lowers productivity.

Internal Labor Markets

In the human capital/job-match models firms and workers in effect engage in individual bargaining. In the sociological models interpersonal relations shape turnover and its consequences. In neither of these approaches is turnover and employment security explicitly regarded as a strategic variable—part of a larger set of personnel policies the firm manipulates to achieve its ends. However, in models of internal labor markets the extent of turnover and the role of employment stability are bound up with other decisions concerning wages and the allocation and deployment of labor.[5] In some models the firm (or the firm and the union, where

---

[5] See Kerr (1954), Doeringer and Piore (1971), and Osterman (1984b) for elaborations on the idea of internal labor markets.

there is one) explicitly considers and chooses the level of turnover along with other characteristics of the employment system.

Variants of internal labor market models bear substantial similarity to the human capital/job-match models in that they seek to explain observed outcomes as a result of microeconomic optimization. What distinguishes these models from others is that the firm is posed with what can be interpreted as a "personnel" problem and in seeking to solve that problem creates a "personnel" policy which involves, among other aspects, reduced turnover. The personnel problem is how to encourage maximum effort and to discourage shirking and other forms of self-interested behavior on the part of employees in an environment in which repeated monitoring is both costly and difficult. The solution in so-called bonding models (Lazear, 1979, 1981) is to shape the time path of the compensation stream (which includes pensions) so that it is costly for workers to quit or to risk being fired. Clearly, in such models turnover is reduced. An alternative solution is to pay an efficiency wage—that is, a wage which is higher than that which the worker could receive in the open market.[6] This wage premium induces effort and discourages turnover.

In these models turnover, assumed to be costly, is reduced by the appropriate compensation incentive schemes. As such, they appear to be a major step toward realism in formal modeling of employment relationships. However, except in a purely formal way (e.g., by positing that monitoring is easier in some jobs than others), the models do not do a good job of explaining *variation* in turnover and in internal labor market arrangements for different occupations. The models could also be enriched if the wage/turnover relationship were examined in the broader context of other internal labor market rules, e.g., those concerning job classifications and mobility within the firm. Finally, more work needs to be done on explaining why these patterns change—why, for example, an increasing number of firms are offering workers job security in return for work rule modifications. To understand these issues we need to be able to make our selections from a somewhat richer menu of internal labor market characteristics and types.

One way of addressing these issues is to make distinctions among alternative ways of organizing internal labor markets.

---

[6] Yellen (1984) reviews these models.

The core firms[7] in the American labor market have traditionally organized work according to a logic of one of two dominant models, which we will call the *industrial* model and the *salaried* model.[8] Our image of what work is like and how it must be changed are reflections of the strengths and weaknesses of these two paradigms.

The industrial model is the method of organizing blue-collar work which became the norm as a result of the unionization drives of the Great Depression and which was further refined in the era of postwar prosperity.[9] In this model work is organized into a series of tightly defined jobs with clear work rules and responsibilities for each classification. Wages are linked to jobs, and hence an individual's wage is determined by his or her classification. Management's freedom to move an individual from one job to another can vary from situation to situation, but the typical case is that both promotions and lateral shifts are limited by seniority provisions and by requirements that workers agree to the shift. Finally, there is no formal job security and it is understood that management is free to vary the size of the labor force as it wishes. However, when layoffs do occur they are usually organized according to reverse seniority. Although the structure of this model emerged from the spread of unionism, it should not be construed as being limited to unionized settings. Because of fear of unions, government pressure for uniformity, and imitation, the model spread throughout the economy.

The model has a strong internal logic and the parts fit together in a coherent way. Because wages are linked to jobs, the jobs need to be carefully defined so that there is common understanding concerning who is doing what work and, hence, is entitled to what wage. Similarly, while the system provides no overall job security (management can vary the size of the work force at will), individual security is based on a bumping system grounded in seniority, and careful job classifications are necessary for the system to be effective. For workers, the overwhelming value of the system is that

---

[7] This term is used loosely to exclude what might be termed the secondary labor market patterns. That is, we are not interested here in understanding the low-wage, high-turnover sector in which many youth, immigrants, and women find themselves. This sector is, of course, of central importance to issues of poverty and low incomes.

[8] Osterman (forthcoming) describes internal labor markets in these terms and analyzes the firm's choice among them.

[9] For a historical account, see Jacoby (1985), and for a description of a more modern version of the "classic" pattern, see Doeringer and Piore (1971).

it creates security in an insecure environment. Given fluctuations in product demand and management's unchallenged right to lay off employees, the job control model uses the organization of work as a shield. The tight definitions of jobs mean that management cannot reduce staffing by reorganizing tasks or combining jobs; hence, the volume of work is regulated (if not maintained) by the system. The job-based bumping system also means that if layoffs occur, they are implemented in an impartial way in which the only relevant criterion is seniority. The system blocks favoritism and enables workers to make reasonable plans and gauge their degree of security. There are, of course, costs to this model—notably the difficulty of altering the work organization in the face of changing technology or other pressures. This difficulty arises because of the logic of the system itself and because, over time, that logic takes on a moral legitimacy that adds to its weight. However, for a long time these problems seemed minor compared to the logic and stability of the industrial model.

Most research in labor economics and industrial relations has emphasized blue-collar work; consequently, the salaried internal labor market model is not easy to delineate. However, an understanding of the model is important for three reasons: it describes the employment pattern of large numbers of workers, it extends beyond white-collar work to a number of innovative blue-collar employment settings, and some of its characteristics indicate the direction which management is trying to push work in general.

The salaried model combines a more flexible and personalized set of administrative procedures with greater commitment to employment security. Although individuals have job descriptions, much as industrial employees have work rules, these descriptions are not intended to have legal or customary force; that is, they are subject to revision by superiors, and employees are prepared to take on new activities as demanded. By the same token, the clearly defined job ladders and promotion sequences that characterize industrial settings are absent here. For example, one observer, reporting on interviews, said that "[p]eople in the same position [in the same firm] disagreed among themselves about its place in the organizational career map. Twenty distribution managers identified seven routes to their jobs . . . and they imagined that there were three likely and seven rare moves from their jobs" (Kanter, 1978, p. 132).

The flexible career lines and job descriptions are consistent with another aspect of this employment system—the greater role of personal considerations in wage-setting. There is greater scope for merit considerations in determining pay and the wages of two individuals in the same job may vary considerably (see Osterman, 1984a, for evidence). Put differently, the pay system in industrial settings, in which the dominant consideration is job assignment, is far less prevalent in the salaried model.

What closes the salaried model is an employment security promise. In the classic salaried model individuals, once they pass a probationary period, can expect lifetime employment with the firm. Unlike the industrial model in which it is explicitly understood that the firm will adjust the size of the labor force in response to product market conditions or technological change, the implicit promise in the salaried system is either that layoffs simply will not occur or that the firm will make strenuous efforts to avoid them. This latter point—that absolute promises are not necessary—is important because without it the scope of the salaried model would be limited. What is crucial is that employees are sufficiently convinced of the sincerity of the firm's commitment to employment stability that they are willing to provide the degree of flexibility which is the firm's reward in the system.

The salaried model characterizes much white-collar work. The career patterns of most managers and many professionals who work in bureaucracies are accurately captured by the model. However, the salaried model is not simply another way of describing white-collar work. There have always been a few American firms that have stayed outside the mainstream industrial model for their blue-collar work forces. In the 1920s the exception was termed "welfare capitalism" and represented an effort to develop an alternative to unions. In the postwar period the alternative has taken the form of applying the salaried model in a blue-collar setting. In return for flexible work rules and a willingness to accept managerial prerogatives with respect to deployment, these firms offer their blue-collar workers a commitment that layoffs will be avoided whenever possible.

The industrial and salaried models each entail distinctive costs and benefits. The industrial model often implies considerable rigidity in wage structure and the deployment of labor. However, it provides firms with flexibility in terms of adjusting employment levels via layoffs. Hence, these systems tend to be characterized by relatively high turnover. On the other hand, the salaried model, with its attention to employment security, restricts the flexibility of the firm in determining the number of employees. But in return the firm gains a measure of internal flexibility and commitment that may be lacking in the rival system. We will see below that what is interesting about the current period is that firms' shifting valuations of these alternative strategies for organizing work have different implications for turnover rates in the firm.

Turnover and Performance

We have seen that it is useful to think about turnover from three different perspectives. Individual optimization models interpret turnover as the byproduct of decisions by firms and workers to invest in either information or human capital. Sociological models emphasize that the employee is part of a work group and a broad network of social relationships, and that turnover and its consequences flow from the nature of these interactions. Finally, the internal labor market models take a more global perspective and view employment security, or its absence, as a component of a package of rules which in the aggregate constitute the internal labor market. The firm organizes its work according to the package that makes the most sense given the constraints it faces.

What, then, is the impact of turnover on performance? Is turnover costly because of the expense of hiring, because the most skilled employees leave, and because the work group is disrupted? Is it beneficial because it enables the firm to maintain "lean staffing" and to bring in new blood? More to the point, since there is logic in both perspectives, under what circumstances does one tendency prevail over the other?

One line of thinking on these questions comes from the personnel literature. The basic approach here is to engage in an accounting exercise by listing and attempting to measure the out-of-pocket costs of turnover. Thus, for example, Thomas Hall (1981) provides a method for estimating turnover costs which include items such as advertising expenses, agency fees, relocation expenses, reduced productivity while new employees are learning, and so on. In response, Kesner and Dalton (1982) acknowledge these costs but note benefits of turnover. They list items such as displacement of poor performers, savings on unvested pension funds, and lower wages of new entry-level employees.

There is no question that these costs and benefits are real and that any organization must consider them in an analysis of its turnover rate. The difficulty is that, as a true measure of the costs and benefits of turnover, such an accounting is seriously incomplete. As we have seen, all theoretical perspectives on turnover view it as one element of a larger system. In the human capital literature the system consists of turnover/wage-level tradeoffs. In the internal labor market literature the issue is employment security and flexible internal deployment. It does not make sense to measure what are in effect the transaction costs of turnover without measuring the costs and benefits of the entire system which generates the turnover rate. On an out-of-pocket basis, for example, turnover may appear more or less costly, but this might overlook the benefits of a low wage level throughout the firm or the costs of rigid job classifications. Put differently, to understand the impact of turnover on firm performance we need to embed the analysis in a larger framework.

When we turn from the personnel literature we find that, with the exception of one important line of research discussed below (the Freeman-Medoff studies of quit rates and productivity), economists have had very little to say empirically about the relationship of turnover and performance. The reason probably is that they are more interested in measuring firm performance by profits than by such intermediate measures as work group productivity. As we have seen in the human capital/job-match models of turnover, there is in principle no expected relationship between profit rates and turnover rates in a cross-section of firms because each firm can choose the wage/turnover combination that maximizes profits. Whatever disruptive effects flow from a high turnover rate can be compensated for by the lower wage rate that is associated with high turnover. On balance, then, there is no predictable relationship between profits and turnover.

Although there is little economic research that directly examines the relationship between firm performance and tenure, it is possible to exercise some dexterity and draw upon a slightly different line of thought. A considerable amount of work has gone into studying the consequences of job mobility *for individuals*. This research can be applied to firm performance in the following sense: If we are willing to assume that wages reflect productivity, then we can ask whether the wages of mobile individuals rise or fall. If wages rise, then productivity increases, with presumably positive benefits for firm performance (although it is not clear to which particular firm these benefits accrue).

There are several studies (e.g., Borjas, 1981) which simply examine the impact of mobility on wage growth; some find no effect while others report a negative impact. However, it is more conventional in the literature to distinguish between mobility caused by quits and that caused by layoffs. Although this distinction seems to make sense, the basis for it is not entirely clear. In specific human capital models, for example, there is no substantive difference between a quit and a layoff. As Rosen (1977) points out, "[J]ob separations should occur if and only if productivity in the current job is less than productivity on an alternative job. Therefore, who initiates the turnover decision should be irrelevant to the outcome" (p. 3). A similar point might be made about job-matching models: Turnover may improve productivity, but whether the turnover is induced by a quit or a layoff should be irrelevant. In the context of neoclassical theory, for the distinction to be important there must be heterogeneity among workers which is not fully compensated by wage differentials.[10] Institutional labor economic models of wage-setting have much less difficulty with this problem since there is no presumption that wages are linked to individual productivity.

Theoretical niceties aside, the pattern of empirical results is clear. Virtually all studies find that individuals who voluntarily change jobs (quit) experience earnings increases relative to stayers, while those who are laid off experience earnings losses. It would therefore appear that voluntary job mobility is, on net, productivity- and performance-enhancing. On the other hand, turnover caused by layoffs is costly not simply in terms of lost output while unemployed, but also in terms of subsequent lower productivity upon reemployment.

As a final point, however, it is important to place several qualifications on this line of reasoning. First, the results do not distinguish between turnover in different circumstances. Because,

---

[10] See Ruhm (1986) for a thoughtful discussion of this issue. He also presents a summary of the studies in this area and some new empirical results.

for example, the average effect of quits is positive, it does not follow that any quit rate in any firm is a good thing. Second, the results report only private returns to individuals and we are forced to infer social returns to firms or society. A variety of factors might drive a wedge between the two and create a situation in which a private loss (or gain) has different social effects.

There is a richer sociological literature on the consequences of turnover. This work has been reviewed by Price (1977) and Bluedorn (1982), and we will draw heavily on their summaries. One strand of this research examines the impact of senior management turnover on the profitability of firms, but, with this exception, the studies have emphasized intermediate impacts such as work group productivity or the ratio of overhead to production labor.

Lieberson and O'Connor (1972) studied 167 firms for the period 1946–1965. They ran regressions in which the dependent variables were sales, earnings, and profit margins against a variable that measured whether there was a change in the identity of the president or board chairman. They found that executive changes were correlated with positive increases in profit margins. However, even if methodological problems were not troubling,[11] this research is of limited interest to us given its restrictions to a highly specific and probably idiosyncratic category of turnover.

There is also a surprisingly extensive literature on the impact of turnover on the performance of sports teams. Indeed, four of the nine papers on organizational performance reviewed by Bluedorn were sports studies. This topic has the advantage of having easily measurable outputs, but it is hard to believe that the results are generalizable.

Beyond these studies, the remaining relevant research emphasizes intermediate impacts. One such impact is whether the "best" people are the most likely to quit. If this were true, high quit rates would imply a lower quality labor force. Theory is skeptical of this effect. In specific human capital models, individuals with numerous outside opportunities are more likely to leave, and one might presume that these are the best workers. On the other hand, people whose firms have invested in their specific training are also less likely to leave, and again these may be the best workers. The

---

[11] There is no effort to explain the determinants of executive turnover; yet it seems likely that the causal arrows also run from profitability to turnover.

research findings mirror this uncertainty. Bluedorn (1982) reports that there is "no support for any consistent relationship between individual performance and separation. . . . [I]t seems likely that systematic relationships between individual performance and separations are a very organization specific phenomenon, and no general tendency is evidence from research to date" (pp. 100–101). Of course, as our earlier discussion suggested, even if the "best" people did leave, we would still need to know about their wages relative to those of less exalted performers before we could reach firm conclusions about the impact of turnover on profits.[12]

Another indirect approach is to examine the impact of turnover on the shape of the organization. Here the main finding concerns the effect of turnover on the ratio of supervisory staff to production labor, the argument being that the costs of administering high turnover will increase the fraction of resources devoted to administration. Price (1977, p. 93) reports that there is "medium" support for this proposition, but the two empirical studies (Kasarda, 1973; Carlson, 1962) are of school systems, not private firms. Furthermore, even in principle this relationship must be highly contingent on broader organizational issues and skill levels: a high turnover operation such as a shapeup of day laborers will involve less administrative staff than lower rates might entail in a traditional organization.

Finally, efforts to measure the impact of turnover on work group productivity also have had mixed results. Bluedorn (1982, p. 102) reports that in the aggregate the research suggests an inverted U-shaped pattern with productivity highest at moderate levels of turnover. However, this conclusion seems to be based on three studies—one of a basketball team, one of a kibbutz, and one of a group of scientists. Clearly, one must be cautious about accepting these results.

Despite these mixed findings, a very strong bias remains in the sociology literature toward believing that turnover is negatively correlated with performance. The origins of this bias probably lie,

---

[12] In a recent paper, Klein, Spady, and Weiss (1987) examine quit rates, in the first six months of employment, of semiskilled workers all paid the same wage, for whom physical productivity data were available. They find that the most productive are more likely to quit, which they attribute to the flat wage scale. It is not clear, however, how these results might be generalized given the special characteristics of the sample and the employment setting.

first, in the equating of performance with productivity, not profits; second, in the view that work group cohesion depends on stability; and third, in the view that the best workers are those most likely to leave. These assumptions are so potent that Price (1977), after reviewing much of the evidence cited above, writes (p. 119):

> "The author believes that successively higher amounts of turnover will be found ultimately to produce, more often than not, successively lower amounts of effectiveness at a decreasing rate. . . . This is not to deny that turnover in many instances clearly enhances effectiveness. These positive results must, however, be subtracted from the negative results to arrive at a net balance . . . and the net balance will probably be found to be negative."

However, the problem is, first, that the factual basis for this conclusion is shaky and, second, that the conclusion itself is so highly contingent as not to be very helpful. What are the organizational conditions that determine which direction will prevail? On this topic the literature we have reviewed is surprisingly silent.

What this implies is that in order to assess the relationship of turnover to performance we need to move toward models in which structural considerations explicitly enter. The internal labor market models clearly have this characteristic and we will return to them. First, however, we review a line of research that examines the relationship of turnover, unionization, and productivity.

In a series of recent papers and in a book, Richard Freeman and James Medoff have demonstrated that unionism has substantial impacts on turnover rates. They argue that unions have two effects on turnover. First, by raising wage levels, unions reduce quits in a manner that standard theory would predict. Beyond this, however, unions reduce quits through what, based on Albert Hirschmann's (1971) work, they term the "voice" effect—that is, the opportunity unions provide workers to express and resolve their grievances internally rather than by quitting. Freeman and Medoff (1984, p. 95) estimate that this effect reduces quits of union workers to levels 31 to 65 percent below those of comparable nonunion workers.

The second effect of unions on turnover is to increase the layoff rate. Here Freeman and Medoff argue that the structure of union decision-making, the median voter model, places junior workers at higher risk in union settings. The consequence is a much higher layoff (frequently temporary layoff) rate in unionized than in nonunion firms (Freeman and Medoff, 1984, p. 115).

Unions reduce quits and increase layoffs. What is the net impact on turnover? Freeman and Medoff do not net out the two effects; however, if we work with the data provided above on average quit and layoff rates, we can come up with a rough estimate. In 1979 the quit rate was about twice the layoff rate. If unionism reduces quits by 50 percent but doubles layoffs, then it would appear to leave turnover unchanged. However, most layoffs are temporary and end in a recall. If we either eliminate these cases or do not give them full weight, then the conclusion would be that, on balance, unions reduce turnover. Data provided by Freeman (1980) on the impact of unions on average job tenure support this interpretation. The actual figures appear to be sensitive to choice of data, but in each case the tenure of union workers is higher than that of nonunion workers. In regressions that include other factors that might influence tenure, the union coefficient accounts for roughly 50 percent of the raw differential. For example, in the 1972 Panel Study of Income Dynamics union members had 8.8 years of tenure and nonunion workers 6.6 years; the coefficient on the union variable in the tenure regression was 1.06 (Freeman, 1980, p. 658).

Finally, what does this tell us about the impact of turnover on performance? Freeman and Medoff argue that unions increase productivity through several mechanisms—by reducing turnover, by "shocking" management into improved processes, and by upgrading the general industrial relations climate. They make this point in a series of studies, but the one that speaks directly to the turnover issue is by Brown and Medoff (1978). They estimate a production function for manufacturing industries with a series of standard controls (plus a control for labor quality) and include a variable measuring unionism. In their equation that excludes quit rates, they find that unions increase productivity (value added per worker) by about 20 percent. When a control for the quit rate is introduced, the union impact falls to 16 percent. Put differently, about a quarter of the positive union impact on productivity appears to be due to a lower quit rate. For our purposes, of greater interest is the quit rate coefficient itself. Brown and Medoff's result (based on manufacturing industries) is that a 10 percent reduction in an industry's quit rate would improve productivity by 1.0 percent, which is quite substantial. In the same equations, a 10 percent increase in the capital/labor ratio increases productivity by 1.4 percent and a 10 percent increase in union density increases productivity by 1.6 percent. It is hard not to believe that the quit rate in these equations does not act as a partial proxy for other variables that impact productivity. Nonetheless, these results are impressive and are among the strongest evidence that high turnover has an adverse effect on firm performance.

Employment Stability and Macro Performance

At this point it appears impossible to reach a judgment about the net impact of turnover and employment stability on firm performance. A part of the difficulty is that there are alternative measures—profitability versus productivity, for example. In addition, it would appear that any answer would be contingent upon the particular institutional circumstances. Turnover of unskilled farm labor will have different consequences than turnover of skilled scientists. Obvious as this point is, it is a distinction that tends not to be made in the literature.

But there is an even more serious problem. In most theories of turnover, be it quits or layoffs, the rate is in effect an accidental byproduct of more fundamental social processes. Thus, in the microeconomic literature individual judgments about job search and allocation of training imply a turnover rate, while in the sociology material social networks and perhaps psychological disposition lead to a given level of turnover. The consequence is that the turnover rate itself is not a decision variable. Thus, it makes little sense to talk about the costs and benefits of turnover when no one is making the actual turnover decisions. This might also explain the absence of cogent conclusions, or even frameworks for conclusions, in the literature.

Yet turnover has been the subject of a good deal of public discussion in recent years. The debate over the merits of employment security and continuity has developed on several fronts. In collective bargaining unions seem to be increasingly interested in trading work rule changes for employment security pledges, which can be seen as evidence of a shift toward the salaried internal labor market model described earlier. Positive expert reaction to employment stability—notably that of the Work in America Institute (1984)—perhaps kindled by the seeming success of the Japanese lifetime employment system, has also stimulated interest in the topic. Japanese internal labor markets are seen as flexible, with broad job descriptions and widespread willingness by workers to accept redeployment. In other words, these internal markets are in effect organized along salaried lines. Finally, on the other side of the debate, the labor market problems of European economies have led some commentators to conclude that employment security in those countries creates serious distortions in the functioning of their labor markets.

Much of the recent public discussion of employment security has consisted of recommendations that firms should adopt one or another variant of an employment security pledge. The argument proceeds by listing the benefits of employment security (typically defined as security within a firm, not specific job security or income security), followed by a discussion of the steps a firm needs to take to implement such a policy.[13]

There are two problems with arguments of this sort. First, the discussion is typically one-sided, with little attention being given to the costs of the policy. To the extent that costs are considered, they are generally administrative (the costs of planning), not the potentially more substantial costs associated with a fixed, inflexible labor force. Second, it is frequently unrecognized that employment security is but one aspect of a large set of employment relationships which we summarize by reference to an internal labor market. It does not make sense to focus on the benefits of one component of such a package; rather, the strengths and weaknesses of all components and all systems need to be weighed, one against another.

A more fruitful way of casting this debate is in terms of alternative employment systems in internal labor markets. The earlier discussion suggested that one of the broad models, the salaried model, explicitly includes employment security as one of its components. Although layoffs are limited, this employment security component does enable the firm to attain considerable internal flexibility in the deployment of labor, the introduction of new technologies, and other aspects of employment relations. We also saw that the salaried model is applied in blue- as well as white-collar settings, although it is clearly not the most common mode of

---

[13] For a more balanced analysis, see Dyer, Foltman, and Milkovich (1984).

organizing blue-collar employment. The most common form is, of course, the industrial model with its higher layoff rates but greater work rule rigidity.

The industrial and salaried systems do have common features: employees spend the bulk of their careers within the firm, with training and socialization provided by the company. The chief difference lies in the kinds of flexibility each model provides. The industrial model permits firms to reduce staffing levels almost at will in response to changing product market conditions. The price of this freedom is the narrow job classifications inherent in the system. When job classifications correspond reasonably well to the requirements for accomplishing the task, the cost is small. However, when the work is variable (as in much managerial employment) or when the technology changes, then the cost may be high. The salaried model, as we have seen, is a system that provides much greater flexibility in job assignment and job definition, but there is a cost: firms cannot easily reduce staffing levels, and this commitment to employment security may be costly. For example, one high-tech firm we have studied, when faced with the need to reduce staffing levels, went through an extremely lengthy and expensive process of retraining some workers, moving others to different parts of the country, and buying out still others—all in the name of maintaining the implicit job security pledge. Perhaps even more costly for the company was the delay before any action was taken, and the company also had a hard time convincing its middle-level personnel of the legitimacy of its action. A firm organized along industrial lines would not have delayed; it simply would have laid off workers.

Indeed, among the serious difficulties confronting any advocate of transforming an industrial internal labor market into a salaried system are the costs which the firms perceive as associated with commitments to employment security. One such cost has to do with perceptions about the effects of such a system on worker incentives and management power. Many Americans enjoy de facto job security. We have already seen that job durations for the currently employed are often very long—typically more than 20 years—and there is also good evidence that firms resist layoffs (or hoard labor) over the business cycle (Fay and Medoff, 1985). We have argued that an absolute promise of job security, of the sort provided by IBM and a handful of "model" firms such as Lincoln Electric that have adopted job security, is not a necessary component of the salaried model. What is important is that job security be an important "value" and that the work force not only perceive this value, but be convinced of it via a series of company actions to stabilize employment and eliminate or reduce layoffs. However, even this level of security implied by the salaried model may pose problems, as illustrated by the explanation provided by a Polaroid manager for the *abolition* of its security pledge and the subsequent layoff of thousands of employees: "A lot of people thought working at Polaroid was like having a government job. That just couldn't go on."[14]

Put less vividly, the costs of explicit job security—even when product market conditions permit it—are perceived to be loss of initiative by the worker and loss of control by the firm. Whether in fact this is true is, under present circumstances, almost beside the point, so widely shared is this perception.

It is worth noting here that the Japanese system, which is often celebrated for its "lifetime employment," did not simply emerge either from an alternative cost-benefit calculus by firms or from an alternative cultural tradition. Rather, it grew out of a period of very heated labor unrest and in many respects was forced upon employers. Andrew Gordon (1985, p. 155) notes that in the 1920s:

> "Bad times, combined with the . . . weakness of unions . . . gave managers the power to almost fire at will [and many did] but negotiations over layoffs and union willingness to strike over jobs, even in a depression, remained characteristic of Japanese labor relations. In the late 1920's this tension over job security led some companies to exercise caution or even moderation when faced with the need to fire, so as to avoid labor disputes. This sort of interaction would eventually produce far greater job security when the balance of power shifted to favor labor two decades later."

This shift in the balance of power came with the American occupation at the end of World War II and the reestablishment of unions under occupation decrees. Two watershed events occurred in the late 1940s when management at the Japanese National

---

[14] *Business Week*, May 29, 1985, p. 51.

Railways and at Toshiba announced large layoffs, followed in both instances by major strikes (the one at Toshiba lasting 55 days). The companies were forced to retract their plans and issue no-layoff pledges. Yet even these union victories had no lasting effect. With the early 1950s came a management offensive which, combined with a restrictive macro policy, succeeded in remaking the Japanese industrial relations system. Management accepted and broke major strikes, including a 113-day mine strike and a 173-day strike in the steel industry. A series of layoffs (including a 20-percent layoff at Toshiba) were announced and carried out. More importantly, however, union shop-floor job control (along American lines) was destroyed and union rights (e.g., union/management councils and large numbers of union officers within the plants) were eliminated. The wage system was also changed from one based on need (age and family circumstances) to one more linked to productivity, seniority, education, and sex. However, when firms established increased flexibility and the principle of management control, they in turn compromised on the job security issue, and that compromise became what we now think of as the "timeless" Japanese system (Gordon, 1985).

The Benefits of the Salaried System

It is true that many employers perceive substantial costs associated with employment security and, by implication, the salaried system. At the same time there are also benefits. The major benefit of the salaried model is that internal labor markets are considerably more flexible than under the industrial system, and this flexibility brings with it cost savings with respect to staffing levels, training requirements, and the introduction of new technology.

There are two broad categories of evidence along these lines. The first is the effort of some American firms to transform their blue-collar work in the direction of the salaried model and to do so by offering employment security in return for reforms on the shop floor. Examples of recent agreements along these lines include the Saturn contract between General Motors and the United Auto Workers, the National Steel contract, and the American Airlines contract with the Machinists' union. It is clear that the trade of job security (to some degree) for work-rule reform will continue to be a major theme in collective bargaining.

A second source of evidence comes from the experience of other nations. We have already touched upon the Japanese system of lifetime employment. The job security provided by the *nenkō* lifetime employment system seems to buy a great deal of internal flexibility. Workers receive extensive training and are willing to accept reassignment as the firm requires. Consider, for example, this description of work at a Japanese steel plant (Koike, 1983, p. 43):

> "There are three large blast furnaces, each of which is operated by four work groups in three shifts. Each group, consisting of about a dozen workers, has to cover approximately ten positions. . . . [J]ob assignments are made in an egalitarian way. . . . Every half-day workers rotate jobs, regardless of seniority. . . . One or two workers are exchanged yearly among the three blast furnace workshops. . . . In addition the worker normally also moves to the maintenance workshop which services all three blast furnaces. . . . As a consequence, within ten years or so, a worker will have had experience in more than 30 positions."

Of course, it is well known that another component of this flexibility is Japanese management's extensive use of temporary and part-time workers. We will return to this factor below, but for now the key point is that job security buys flexibility.

The Japanese example is important because it counters the common view that job security introduces so much rigidity into the labor market that overall economic performance lags. However, with this point made, additional evidence on the link between employment security and flexibility can be drawn from Europe. In Sweden, for example, employment security comes from several sources. First, under national employment security legislation, the number of temporary layoffs is reduced dramatically, although the rates of permanent separations from firms are not very different from those in the U.S. Second, the extensive welfare state and job training programs reduce substantially the risks inherent in job loss. The consequence is that despite the conditions—strong legal regulation of the labor market and high unionization rates—which Americans would expect to lead to rigid internal labor markets, Swedish internal labor markets are, in fact, very flexible.

This flexibility is apparent in a number of ways.[15] First, as we noted above, there are few job classifications and those that do exist are very broad. Thus, for example, at Volvo, the largest Swedish industrial firm, blue-collar workers are effectively classified into one of six groups (in U.S. auto firms there may be over 100 job classifications), while at the largest high-technology firm, Ericsson, there is a four-level job classification system for blue-collar workers. Second, management faces few restrictions on the deployment of the work force. The codetermination legislation requires consultation with the union (or, as a practical matter, with the work group organization) prior to moving a worker from one job to another, but, if anything, this improves efficiency since the representatives provide management with information on the relative abilities and skills of different workers. As a practical matter, with this information in hand and with the consultation requirement fulfilled, management is free to promote whom it wishes and to reassign job responsibilities as it sees fit. Seniority plays a very limited role. Indeed, no manager we interviewed felt seriously constrained from promoting the person whom he or she regarded as best qualified or from redeploying labor as dictated by production requirements. All of this is in sharp contrast with the U.S. system of posting, bidding, and seniority.

What price is paid for this flexibility? The greatest cost is borne by the government in the form of an expensive labor market policy, but firms do not escape entirely. They seem to accept without serious complaint the codetermination requirements, but vary in their views on the solidarity wage policy and the employment security laws. For companies which are contracting, the security laws require not simply advance notice (which, despite the fuss raised in the U.S. when suggestions along this line are made, is not an issue in Sweden), but layoffs based on reverse seniority. This latter requirement may be a problem for firms which believe that their most skilled workers are found in groups with lower seniority. The most common solution (negotiated on a case-by-case basis with the unions) is early retirement through government-subsidized "disability" pensions. The complaint about the wage policy rests on

---

[15] The information in this paragraph and the entire description of Swedish internal labor markets are based on personal interviews I conducted with Swedish employers (in manufacturing, finance, and service industries), union leaders, academics, and government personnel.

the belief that it makes the recruitment of skilled workers more difficult. There is, however, little evidence to support this belief, and the employer complaints tend to have a certain ritualistic tone. The major exception to this generalization appears to be the recruitment of engineers, but the cobweb model of boom and bust applies in the United States as well as in Sweden.

The lesson, then, from Japan and Sweden is that a promise of employment security generates considerable benefits with respect to internal flexibility. This has growing relevance in the United States where new flexible technologies are increasingly leading management to expand job duties which, in turn, is in conflict with the rigidity inherent in the industrial model. Even more telling, however, is that the flexibility demanded by new technologies, combined with increased market competition and shorter product cycles, will lead to repeated pressure to reorganize work. One can imagine that the industrial model might respond once to such pressure, but that continual changes in job classifications would not be forthcoming. For this reason many firms will find that the salaried model, with its flexibility, offers considerable advantages. The question, discussed below, is whether it will be possible to provide the degree of employment security implied by the model.

Future Developments

We have already seen that there is no discernible secular trend in the quit and layoff data. Thus, there is little basis to expect that the future will look any different than the past. However, if we ask about structural changes, then there is reason to believe that job security and employment continuity will emerge as increasingly important issues.

One force pushing in this direction is demographic. The American labor force is aging, with fewer young people and more who are middle-aged. Youth account for most job mobility and labor market adjustment is typically accomplished via job changing of young workers. The larger middle-aged labor force, which will dominate the labor market in the next decade, is likely to be unwilling to accept a high degree of job insecurity. The political pressure from this group will keep employment continuity on the political agenda.

More and more of the recent collective bargaining agreements have placed a high premium on job security. For example, both the

GM and Ford contracts with the UAW and the Communications Workers' contract with AT&T contain innovative job security/ retraining programs. Although the details vary, the basic idea is that employers set aside a sum to be used to retrain incumbent employees for new occupations. Although absolute job security is not promised, the thrust is to limit layoffs to the extent possible and to rely on retraining. In return, the unions accede to more flexible work rules and an easing of restrictions on internal deployment. Agreements of this sort are likely to become more common. It remains to be seen, however, whether in the aggregate they have a very substantial impact. One limiting factor, of course, is that the unionized sector appears to be shrinking. Second, anecdotal evidence suggests that many similar agreements have in the past simply funded training which would have occurred anyway and that layoffs have not been successfully reduced. A practical difficulty has been that decisions to change a technology have remained entirely at the firm's initiative and by the time they are implemented extensive retraining is often difficult.

These qualifications aside, it is also true that if there is follow-through on job continuity/retraining agreements, they are a potentially innovative and important response to the pressures of technical change and uneven labor demand. A significant practical research question is how to manage the selection and retraining process effectively and equitably.

A second possible direction for change lies in public policy. One might imagine, for example, passage of legislation comparable to European laws on job security. These laws range from simply requiring advance notice of layoff to requirements that works councils approve layoff plans (Gennand, 1985). Although poor European job growth is often blamed on these policies, the factual basis for such charges is unclear and a case can be made that a number of benefits flow from the more moderate versions of these laws (Piore, 1986; Osterman, forthcoming). One might imagine American policy moving in this direction in the long run, but it is very hard to see anything happening in the foreseeable future. To the extent that job security is a public policy concern, it lies in court considerations of employment-at-will doctrines and affirmative action limitations on layoffs.

The third force is the employers themselves, and it is reasonable to expect the most action here. This is not to argue that employers will take the sort of "employment security" pledge that many advocates have called for. Rather, the nature of the evolution of a firm's internal labor market will be the stimulant for the new pattern of employment security. For some workers this will imply greater job security, but for others turnover is likely to increase.

As we have seen, firms are in a bind. They want to shift to a salaried model for blue-collar work. However, macroeconomic uncertainty and unwillingness to permit labor to become too great a fixed cost leads them to fear that employment security is too high a price to pay. In the case of white-collar employment, they want to maintain the salaried model but at lower employment levels. It is as a resolution of these dilemmas in both white- and blue-collar work that we can understand the increase in nontraditional employment patterns. In both cases a possible strategy is to offer job security (or a commitment to make every effort to avoid layoffs) to a core of more or less permanent employees and to surround this core with a "periphery" of temporary, contract, and part-time workers who enjoy less protection. The workers in the core will be willing to work under the salaried model and to provide both flexibility and commitment to the firm. The peripheral labor force will provide the firm with a buffer against either macroeconomic (cyclical) downturns or labor force reductions necessitated by technical change. In a sense this "core/periphery" model is a strategy for having it both ways. It enables firms to achieve substantial internal flexibility with a highly trained and committed labor force while at the same time maintaining management's ability to adjust employment levels at will.

Given these advantages, one would expect the number of firms adopting the core/periphery model to increase and, indeed, that has been the case. The growth in the amount of temporary employment and in the number of firms supplying temporary workers have been widely noted (BNA, 1986). In addition, collective bargaining agreements now include explicit provisions for core/periphery models. In the Saturn contract, rigid job classifications are traded for job security; the contract contains specific language to that effect:

> "Saturn recognizes that people are the most valuable asset of the organization. It is people who develop new technologies and systems, and people who make these

systems work in order to meet Saturn's mission. Accordingly, Saturn will not lay off Saturn members [regular employees] except in situations arising from unforeseen or catastrophic events or severe economic conditions."

There is other evidence that the employment relationship at Saturn is organized along core/periphery lines. The contract establishes a category of employee termed "associate member" and states that "up to 20% of the workforce may consist of associate members. While every attempt will be made to avoid layoff of associate members, they will not be covered by the Job Security provision." In effect, the firm is establishing a class of employees outside the core, and this group will bear the brunt of insecurity.

Saturn remains a goal; the plant has yet to open or produce one car. As such, it is best interpreted as an ideal toward which the industrial system may be evolving. However, arrangements similar to the Saturn pattern are found in some of the so-called "two-tier" agreements generated in recent rounds of concession bargaining. Under two-tier plans the wages of newly hired employees are lower than those of incumbents. Other examples of two-tier agreements are the American Airlines contracts in which incumbents received lifetime job security while new hires did not. These contracts also permitted the airline to employ part-time and temporary workers who receive no protection at all under the agreements.

Although the previous examples are drawn from collective bargaining relationships, the core/periphery model is hardly limited to that setting. IBM, for example, protects its core work force with a number of buffers. Up to 10 percent of the staff may be hired on temporary contracts, and these people are the first to go in any downturn. In addition, the company uses subcontractors not simply to achieve production efficiencies, but in order to maintain a smaller work force. Again, in downturns the subcontracted work is brought back in-house.

For white-collar employees, extensive anecdotal evidence as well as field research suggest that firms are increasingly employing temporary staff help, outside consultants, contract workers, and the like. These employees, who work at all skill levels, provide a peripheral labor force that protects the job security of the core. For example, in interviews with 12 large white-collar employers in Boston, we found that eight had recently established in-house temporary work pools, in effect internalizing the profits of outside agencies while maintaining the same flexibility by creating a work force outside normal personnel rules. The same interviews revealed that the use of such temporaries is not limited to clerical workers, but includes occupations such as engineers, computer programmers, and draftsmen (Osterman, 1984a). The same point was made forcefully by Mangum, Mayall, and Nelson (1985, p. 603) in their report of interviews with 74 San Francisco employers:

> "These interviews showed that if the 'Kelly Girl' image of the [temporary help service] industry as primarily a clerical phenomenon was ever accurate, it is no longer. Electronics firms used temporary draftsmen and assemblers. . . . Mechanical engineers, technical writers, and programmers were also hired through [temporary help service] firms. Chemical firms . . . hired temporary computer programmers and chemical engineers. In finance and insurance . . . switchboard operators, data-entry operators, and accountants were evident as well. . . . Trucking firms deployed temporary workers as both drivers and warehouse help. . . . At hospitals . . . demand was primarily for nurses, but some technician occupations were also required."

Despite this evidence of the spread of the core/periphery model, there are also good reasons to doubt that employment systems in the United States will evolve totally toward the Japanese model. The core/periphery model can work only if a sufficiently large number of people are available and willing to accept the often unstable and inferior working conditions associated with employment on the periphery. That this labor force would be available is problematic for several reasons.

The total peripheral labor force might include women looking for part-time work, undocumented workers manning production lines, young people just entering the job market, and skilled workers who, for "life style" reasons, want to maintain flexibility in their work attachment. It is obviously difficult to generalize about supply trends for such disparate groups. On balance, however, the trend seems to be in the direction of a supply growing more slowly than it has over the past two decades.

No one would dispute that women have historically formed the largest group of peripheral workers, but there are indications that the growth of this pool will slow. First, female participation rates will not continue to rise as rapidly as they have in the past. In 1960 the gap between male and female labor force participation rates was nearly 50 points; in 1983 it stood at just over 20 points. But there are limits as to how much this gap will continue to close over time; even in Sweden, the nation with the most generous family support program in the West, the participation rate gap between men and women remains at 10 points.[16]

Even more significant is the changing character of the female labor supply. Women are increasingly less interested in peripheral work. A strong signal of this is that although women's voluntary part-time employment increased sharply during the 1960s and most of the 1970s, it leveled off in the early 1980s. Between 1982 and 1985 full-time employment of women over the age of 20 increased by 11.9 percent, while part-time employment for the same age group increased by only 4.4 percent.

Another potential source of peripheral workers, young people, is shrinking due to demographic shifts, and this is especially significant since available surveys suggest that the overwhelming majority of temporary workers are young. This leaves basically only two other possible sources. One group might be middle-aged people who are interested in working as contractors or temporaries in order to maintain their independence or to be able to work at home—or for other similar reasons. Although much is made of this group in the business press, it is difficult to believe that this source would produce a substantial number of people. Indeed, all of the hard evidence suggests that as people age, they become more interested in security, not less. The second possible source are older workers, but this would require a reversal of the presently declining trend in their labor force participation rates.

None of the foregoing is intended to argue that the use of peripheral labor is not likely to expand somewhat. Expansion can occur if and when firms can find people who are willing to work in peripheral jobs; expansion can also occur if the number of good jobs shrinks and people are forced to accept peripheral jobs involuntarily. However, limitations on the core-periphery strategy also flow from the likelihood that a substantial expansion of peripheral

---

[16] In 1984 the Swedish male labor force participation rate was 0.76 and the female rate was 0.67. See McMahon (1986), p. 6.

employment will lead to a revived union movement which, in turn, will seek to alter the terms of employment.

Conclusion

Much of our discussion has had an uncomfortably equivocal quality. We saw that the theoretical literature reaches no clear conclusions about the relation of turnover to firm performance. The empirical material did little to sharpen our assessment, although we are on firmer ground with respect to productivity than we are in terms of profits. Finally, we sought to place the discussion in broader terms by viewing turnover as one element of a larger set of employment questions. That perspective provided us with a way of thinking about emerging issues of job security and employment stabilization. Because of demographic changes and heightened demand-side shocks, these issues are likely to be of increased interest to the labor force. From a firm's perspective, the topic is also relevant because their efforts to achieve greater internal labor market flexibility raise the question of what, if anything, they are willing to offer their work forces in the way of employment security in return.

It is far from clear how these issues will play out. One possibility is the employer militance and concession bargaining strategy. This is a clear tactic and one which has been widely practiced in recent years. However, it entails several limitations. It is unlikely to be successful on a repeated basis in the same firm, yet the nature of new technologies seems to require continual shop-floor flexibility, not simply a one-time adjustment. In white-collar settings employer militance may undermine the commitment already present under the salaried system. We saw that a second strategy, the core-periphery pattern, holds some promise but appears to be limited in the extent to which it can expand. The third possibility, which we have not discussed, is a set of public policies aimed at encouraging the diffusion of the salaried model and providing the labor force with the requisite security via externally based employment and training programs. In short, it is very unclear what the future holds with respect to turnover and employment stabilization. We hope that we have at least highlighted some of the nuances and complexities of the topic.

References

Abraham, Katharine G., and Henry Farber. "Job Duration, Seniority, and Earnings." National Bureau of Economic Research Working Paper No. 1819, January 1986.

Akerlof, George, and Brian Main. "An Experience Weighted Measure of Employment and Unemployment Durations." *American Economic Review* 71 (December 1981): pp. 1003–11.

Altonji, Joseph, and Robert Shakotko. "Do Wages Rise with Job Seniority?" National Bureau of Economic Research Working Paper No. 1616, May 1985.

Barnes, William, and Ethel Jones. "Differences in Male-Female Quitting." *Journal of Human Resources* 9 (Fall 1974): pp. 439–51.

Baysinger, Barry, and William Mobley. "Employee Turnover: Individual and Organizational Analysis." In *Personnel and Human Resource Management*, Vol. 1, eds. Kendrith Rowland and Gerald R. Ferris. Greenwich, Conn.: JAI Press, 1983. Pp. 269–319.

Becker, Gary S. *Human Capital*. New York: Columbia University Press, 1972.

Bednarzik, Robert. "Layoffs and Permanent Job Losses: Worker Traits and Cyclical Patterns." *Monthly Labor Review* 106 (September 1983): pp. 3–12.

Blau, Francine, and Lawrence Kahn. "The Causes and Consequences of Layoffs." *Economic Inquiry* 19 (April 1981a): pp. 270–95.

—————. "Race and Sex Differences in Quit Rates by Young Workers." *Industrial and Labor Relations Review* 34 (July 1981b): pp. 563–77.

Bluedorn, Allen. "The Theories of Turnover: Causes, Effects, Meanings." In *Research in the Sociology of Organizations*, ed. Samuel Bacharach. Greenwich, Conn.: JAI Press, 1982. Pp. 75–128.

Bolt, James E. "Job Security: Its Time Has Come." *Harvard Business Review*, No. 6 (November 1983): pp. 115–23.

Borjas, George. "Job Mobility and Earnings Over the Lifecycle." *Industrial and Labor Relations Review* 34 (April 1981): pp. 365–76.

Brown, Charles, and James Medoff. "Trade Unions in the Production Process." *Journal of Policital Economy* 86 (June 1978): pp. 355–78.

Bureau of National Affairs. *The Changing Workplace: New Directions in Staffing and Scheduling*. Washington: BNA, 1986.

Carlson, R. O. "Executive Succession and Organization Change." Midwest Administration Center, University of Chicago, 1962.

Clark, Kim B., and Lawrence Summers. "Labor Market Dynamics and Unemployment: A Reconsideration." *Brookings Papers on Economic Activity*, No. 1 (1979): pp. 13–60.

Doeringer, Peter B., and Michael J. Piore. *Internal Labor Markets and Manpower Analysis*. Lexington, Mass.: D. C. Heath, 1971.

Dyer, Lee, Felician Foltman, and George Milkovich. "Employment Stabilization." Unpublished paper, New York State School of Industrial and Labor Relations, Cornell University, 1984.

Fay, Jon, and James Medoff. "Labor and Output Over the Business Cycle." *American Economic Review* 75 (September 1985): pp. 638–55.

Freeman, Richard B. "The Exit-Voice Tradeoff in the Labor Market: Unionism, Job Tenure, Quits, and Separations." *Quarterly Journal of Economics* 94 (June 1980): pp. 643–73.

Freeman, Richard B., and James L. Medoff. *What Do Unions Do?* New York: Basic Books, 1984.

Gennand, John. "Job Security: Redundancy Arrangements and Practices in Selected OECD Countries." Paris: Organisation for Economic Co-operation and Development, September 1985.

Gordon, Andrew. *The Evolution of Labor Relations in Japan: Heavy Industry 1853–1955*. Cambridge, Mass.: Harvard University Press, 1985.

Granovetter, Mark. "Labor Mobility, Internal Labor Markets, and Job Matching: A Comparison of Sociological and Economic Approaches." In *Research in Social Stratification and Mobility*, Vol. 5, ed. Robert Robinson. Greenwich, Conn.: JAI Press, 1986. Pp. 3–40.

Hall, Robert. "The Importance of Lifetime Jobs in the U.S. Economy." *American Economic Review* 72 (September 1982): pp. 716–24.

Hall, Thomas E. "How to Estimate Employee Turnover Costs." *Personnel* 58 (July-August 1981): pp. 43–52.

Hirschmann, Albert. *Exit, Voice, and Loyalty.* Cambridge, Mass.: Harvard University Press, 1971.

Jacoby, Sanford. *Employing Bureaucracy.* New York: Columbia University Press, 1985.

Jovanovic, Boyan. "Job Matching and the Theory of Turnover." *Journal of Policital Economy* 87 (October 1979): pp. 972–90.

Kanter, Rosabeth Moss. *Men and Women of the Corporation.* New York: Basic Books, 1978.

Kanter, Rosabeth Moss, and D. Brinkerhoff. "Organizational Performance: Recent Developments in Measurement." *Annual Review of Sociology* (1981): pp. 321–49.

Kasarda, John D. "Effects of Personnel Turnover, Employee Qualifications, and Professional Staff Ratios on Administrative Intensity and Overhead." *Sociological Quarterly* 14 (Summer 1973): pp. 350–58.

Katz, Lawrence. "Layoffs, Recall, and the Duration of Unemployment." National Bureau of Economic Research Working Paper No. 1825, January 1986.

Kerr, Clark. "The Balkanization of Labor Markets." In *Labor Mobility and Economic Opportunity,* ed. E. Wight Bakke. Cambridge, Mass.: MIT Press, 1954. Pp. 92–110.

Kesner, Idalene, and Dan Dalton. "Turnover Benefits: The Other Side of the Coin." *Personnel* 59 (September-October 1982): pp. 69–76.

Klein, Roger, Rachel Spady, and Andrew Weiss. "Factors Affecting the Output and Quit Propensities of Production Workers." National Bureau of Economic Research Working Paper No. 2184, March 1987.

Koike, Kazuo. "Internal Labor Markets: Workers in Large Firms." In *Contemporary Industrial Relations in Japan,* ed. Taishiro Shirai. Madison: University of Wisconsin Press, 1983. Pp. 29–61.

Lazear, Edward. "Why Is There Mandatory Retirement?" *Journal of Political Economy* 87 (December 1979): pp. 261–84.

———. "Agency, Earnings Profiles, Productivity, and Hours Restrictions." *American Economic Review* 71 (September 1981): pp. 606–20.

Lieberson, Stanley, and James F. O'Connor. "Leadership and Organizational Performance: A Study of Large Corporations." *American Sociological Review* 37 (April 1972): pp. 117–30.

Lilien, David M. "The Cyclical Pattern of Temporary Layoffs in U.S. Manufacturing." *Review of Economics and Statistics* 62 (February 1980): pp. 24–31.

Mangum, Garth, Donald Mayall, and Kristin Nelson. "The Temporary Help Industry: A Response to the Dual Internal Labor Market." *Industrial and Labor Relations Review* 38 (July 1985): pp. 599–611.

McMahon, Patrick J. "An International Comparison of Labor Force Participation, 1977–84." *Monthly Labor Review* 109 (May 1986): pp. 3–12.

Medoff, James L. "Layoffs and Alternatives Under Trade Unions in U.S. Manufacturing." *American Economic Review* 69 (June 1979): pp. 380–95.

Mincer, Jacob, and Solomon Polachek. "Family Investments in Human Capital: Earnings of Women." *Journal of Political Economy* 82 (Part 2, March/April 1974): pp. S76–S108.

Osterman, Paul. *Getting Started: The Youth Labor Market.* Cambridge, Mass.: MIT Press, 1980.

———. "Affirmative Action and Opportunity: A Study of Female Quit Rates." *Review of Economics and Statistics* 64 (November 1982): pp. 604–12.

———. "White Collar Internal Labor Markets." In *Internal Labor Markets,* ed. Paul Osterman. Cambridge, Mass.: MIT Press, 1984a.

———. *Employment Futures: Reorganization, Dislocation, and Public Policy.* New York: Oxford University Press, forthcoming.

Osterman, Paul, ed. *Internal Labor Markets.* Cambridge, Mass.: MIT Press, 1984b.

Parsons, Donald. "Quit Rates Over Time: A Search and Information Approach." *American Economic Review* 63 (June 1973): pp. 390–401.

Pencavel, John. *An Analysis of the Quit Rate in American Manufacturing Industry.* Princeton, N.J.: Princeton University Press, 1970.

————. "Wages, Specific Training, and Labor Turnover in U.S. Manufacturing Industries." *International Economic Review* 13 (February 1972): pp. 53–64.

Piore, Michael J. "Perspectives on Labor-Management Flexibility." *Industrial Relations* 25 (Spring 1986): pp. 146–66.

Price, Joseph. *The Study of Turnover.* Ames: Iowa State University Press, 1977.

Ragan, James. "Investigating the Decline in Manufacturing Quit Rates." *Journal of Human Resources* 19 (Winter 1984): pp. 53–71.

Rosen, Sherwin. "Human Capital Theory: A Survey of Empirical Research." In *Research in Labor Economics*, ed. Ronald Ehrenberg. Greenwich, Conn.: JAI Press, 1977. Pp. 3–40.

Ross, Arthur M. "Do We Have a New Industrial Feudalism?" *American Economic Review* 48 (December 1958): pp. 903–20.

Ruhm, Christopher. "Heterogeneous Workers, Wages, and Labor Mobility." Working Paper, Department of Economics, Boston University, June 1986.

Sehgal, Ellen. "Occupational Mobility and Job Tenure in 1983." *Monthly Labor Review* 107 (October 1984): pp. 18–23.

Utter, Carol. "Labor Turnover in Manufacturing: The Survey in Retrospect." *Monthly Labor Review* 105 (June 1982): pp. 15–17.

Viscusi, W. Kip. "Sex Differences in Worker Quitting." *Review of Economics and Statistics* 62 (August 1980): pp. 388–98.

Wial, Howard. Untitled Ph.D. dissertation, Department of Economics, MIT, 1987.

Work in America Institute. *Employment Security in a Free Economy.* New York: Pergamon Press, 1984.

Yellen, Janet. "Efficiency Wage Models of Unemployment." *American Economic Review* 74 (May 1984): pp. 200–205.

CHAPTER 9

Industrial Relations
and the Performance of the Firm:
An Overview

By RICHARD N. BLOCK
Michigan State University

MORRIS M. KLEINER
University of Minnesota

MYRON ROOMKIN
Northwestern University

SIDNEY W. SALSBURG
Arbitrator

The impact of industrial relations on firm performance is of increasing interest to industrial relations scholars. Traditionally, the field has focused primarily on the employment relationship and factors that influence it, and the governing paradigm, implicitly if not explicitly, has been John Dunlop's *Industrial Relations Systems* (1958). In this view, the industrial relations system is composed of employers, workers and their representatives, and the government, all sharing an ideology and all operating with economic, technological, and political constraints. When such a model is used, the industrial relations system of a plant, a firm, an industry, or a country is viewed as the dependent variable to be studied. The researcher then attempts to identify what determines the attributes of the system.

At the time that Dunlop conceived this model, and for several years thereafter, it was logical to try to explain variations in the system and its rules in terms of differences in the environment. Although much was known about the environment that affected the industrial relations system, the systems themselves were new.

Modern American trade unionism developed as a phenomenon of the early years of the 20th century. In the first third of the century, scientific management and the human relations school evolved as a way of organizing employee relations in the absence of collective bargaining. The modern private-sector collective bargaining system emerged in the period between the mid-1930s and the 1950s (Jacoby, 1985). Meanwhile, starting in the late 1950s, there was increased interest in personnel/human resource management. Thus, the entire industrial relations system was in a state of ferment, with many new initiatives and new subsystems to study.

At the same time the environment was essentially stable. Between the end of World War II and the late 1970s, the United States experienced reasonably consistent economic growth, with the downturns relatively mild as compared to pre-World War II troughs. The United States was, in essence, a sheltered market, with its manufacturers experiencing little foreign competition. Also, during this period the important communications and transportation sectors were highly regulated, insulating their industrial relations systems from market pressures.

As a result, the industrial relations system operated in what was basically a highly controlled environment, experiencing few exogenous shocks. The product markets were domestically rather than globally driven. Although there was a wave of labor legislation in the mid-1960s, most notably Title VII of the Civil Rights Act of 1964 and other antidiscrimination legislation, this did not alter the fundamental stability of the economic, technological, and political environments.

In this paradigm researchers were aware that wage structures and other firm human resource policies were, in part, shaped by demand considerations. It has always been accepted that the ability of firms to pay different wages, adopt different strategies, and implement different employer policies is based on the fact that product market conditions differ across firms.

For example, product market concentration, product differentiation, governmental barriers to entry, regional differences in worker attitudes toward collective bargaining, and unique access to special resources (Levinson, 1966) may provide firms with access to economic rents in which workers may share. These rents, then, provide firms with some degree of freedom to follow different industrial relations/human resource policies.

Renewed interest in the impact of the product market on industrial relations systems was associated with the instability in the environment in the late 1970s and early 1980s (Block and McLennan, 1985). The deregulation of the airline and trucking industries brought competition to industries that had never truly experienced it. Foreign firms took advantage of the lack of trade barriers to U.S. markets and began to take larger and larger shares of the markets in such basic industries as steel and automobile manufacturing.

These and other structural and economic changes had serious implications for corporate performance, and firms often looked to their industrial relations system as a vehicle for improving corporate performance. This new source of pressure on the industrial relations system then made it necessary for industrial relations scholars to turn their attention to those aspects of the product market that might influence the industrial relations system.

The product market had changed, and firms that had previously been successful found themselves with new competitors. There was no guarantee that the management practices that had resulted in successful performance in the sheltered markets of the previous 30 years would continue to work. Corporate management had to search for efficiencies. At least in some firms and industries where differences in labor costs were important, companies began to look to their industrial relations systems and their human resource management practices as a source of contributions to enhanced firm performance. These changes resulted in a recognition that the overall performance of the firm, and in the aggregate of the economy, had a substantial impact on employment and the industrial relations system. Thus, the extent to which the industrial relations system enhanced or weakened the economic performance of the firm was an important consideration.

Because national and state economic performance can be thought of as the aggregate of the economic performance of the firms within their borders, policy-makers at the federal and state levels, although primarily concerned about the employment effects of poor firm performance, also began to be concerned about employee relations and how different systems affected the performance of firms within their jurisdictions. The federal government launched workplace initiatives through the Federal Mediation and Conciliation Service and the Department of Labor.

Among the states that committed some public resources to workplace initiatives were Illinois, Indiana, Kentucky, Michigan, Ohio, West Virginia, and Tennessee (Cleveland, 1987). Public officials in the federal government and at the state level began to express the view that to the extent that firm- and establishment-level industrial relations affected economic performance and jobs, it had an impact on the public and therefore was an appropriate arena for policy-makers. This was a substantial departure from the traditional view that industrial relations systems were generally private matters so long as no laws were violated.

These public initiatives sent a message to the industrial relations system that it was necessary to rethink the notion that the government should not intrude in the workplace except to assure that none of the practices were illegal. The view expressed in these initiatives was that the governments had an interest in employee relations practices to the extent that these practices were seen as impairing the efficiency of firms within their jurisdictions. While none of these programs could force changes in legal industrial relations practices, the degree of government encouragement in this area was unprecedented.

The development of human resource management in the firm, with its focus on the employer rather than on the multiple actors in the industrial relations system, also contributed to the growing interest in industrial relations and firm performance. Practitioners and academics in human resource management had generated numerous practices that have become associated with modern employee relations systems. Presumably these practices were adopted, at least in part, because of their impact on firm performance.

This interest in industrial relations and firm performance has added a new dimension to the study of industrial relations. We continue to be concerned about how the web of rules is shaped by the success of the corporation. But we are also interested in relationships that go in the opposite direction: How do the practices of industrial relations contribute to or detract from organizational performance?

The chapters in this volume represent the first attempt of which we are aware to bring together in one place research on the relationship between firm performance and industrial relations. In commissioning these chapters we were aware that firm performance, although a popular topic, is not a precisely defined concept. The authors, therefore, were free to define performance in ways appropriate to their topic. The measures they identified can be grouped as follows:

Labor Quality	Intermediate Outputs	Outputs	Outcomes
Job satisfaction	Increased product quality	Sales	Capital market assessments
Employee participation		Revenues	
	Increased productivity	Profits (pre- and posttax returns on investment, returns on assets, stock price)	Market share
			Stature and reputation

No attempt is made here to test the claim that improvements in labor quality or intermediate outputs do, in fact, result in improved outputs or outcomes, nor do we try to disentangle the complex relationships that link these various measures.

The chapters fall into four categories: the impact of direct costs of employment on firm performance (Ehrenberg and Milkovich; Allen and Clark), the impact of indirect costs of employee relations practices and related employee behavior on firm performance (Ichniowski and Lewin; Gershenfeld; Holzer; Osterman), the impact of unionism on direct measures of firm performance (Becker and Olson), and the relationship between human resources and corporate strategy (Lewin).

The Impact of Direct Labor Costs on Firm Performance

The chapters by Ehrenberg and Milkovich and by Allen and Clark examine what is probably the most straightforward and obvious question: How do differences in compensation and pension policies—policies that involve direct and continuing costs to firms—affect firm performance?

Ehrenberg and Milkovich tell us that, despite the voluminous literature on compensation, very little is known about the impact of different compensation policies on firm performance. In general, the literature addresses the effect of compensation policies on intermediate, human-resource-related measures of firm performance—productivity, absenteeism, etc. Although there are simple univariate results that suggest a correlation between some compensation policies, these authors do not believe that this is convincing evidence that such a relationship exists.

The strongest correlations are between executive compensation and firm performance. The change in executive compensation, rather than its level, is correlated with improvement in measures of firm economic performance. While this is what would be expected if the incentives presumably built into executive compensation policies had their intended effect, Ehrenberg and Milkovich tell us that more of the improved economic performance of private-sector for-profit firms is associated with executives' learning their jobs than with incentive effects of the compensation system. They also found that golden parachutes (the large severance payments awarded to executives if the firm is successfully taken over) do serve their purpose of aligning management and shareholder interests. Finally, they found that incentive effects also seem to exist in the public and private nonprofit sectors.

These authors found that the relationship between nonexecutive employee compensation and firm performance was more difficult to discern than that between executive compensation and firm performance. They note the consistently strong correlations between firm size and differences in intraindustry wages. These have usually been attributed to advanced technology, the disutility of working in a large firm, the greater degree of unionism in large firms, and the greater costs associated with employee monitoring in large firms. There is no indication, however, that these high-wage practices affect a firm's economic performance. Indeed, although there is evidence that suggests a systematic relationship between employer characteristics and relative compensation across firms, there is no evidence to indicate that these differences affect firm performance. Finally, when this matter is viewed in the other direction, industry profit levels generally are not a good explanatory variable in wage equations, which suggests that just as the evidence does not indicate that wages affect profits, neither does it indicate that profits affect wages.

Attention has focused recently on variable compensation systems that link employee pay or compensation with some measure of employee or firm performance. Although these plans are adopted because they are thought to enhance performance, the evidence on their impact on employee performance is weak, and there is no evidence concerning the impact of these plans on firm performance. Ehrenberg and Milkovich attribute the weak merit pay–employee performance relationship to the fact that merit plans affect pay increments rather than pay levels. They did find some indication that profit-sharing and gainsharing plans enhance employee productivity and performance, although possibly with a plateau effect after an initial increase, but there is no evidence as to how these plans may affect firm performance.

In interpreting their results, Ehrenberg and Milkovich make two important points. First, they remind us that compensation systems are endogenous. In other words, changes in compensation policy are not likely to be random; rather they are driven by the actors in the system who are most affected. Second, these systems are primarily designed to influence intermediate employee relations outcomes and costs. Thus, the measures of final outcomes may have too much noise to enable scholars to assess the impact of these policies.

The Ehrenberg and Milkovich review suggests to us an important point in analyzing the impact of compensation systems, or any other industrial relations practice, on firm performance. Although each of these practices can be successful in isolation, success may not be discernible in firm performance if other nonemployee-relations practices are not successful, or if the final performance measure is a function of factors only marginally related to the employee relations practice.

The foregoing suggests that the impact of compensation systems must be viewed at the margin. What is the marginal benefit or cost associated with changing an employee relations practice, taking into account the effect of other internal firm practices? Given the influence of executives on organizational decision-making and performance, and the cost to the corporation of their errors or misalignment of interests, one would expect there to be a relationship between changes in their compensation and firm performance. On the other hand, the marginal benefit and cost to the organization associated with changing an employee relations practice that does not apply to executives may not be great.

Allen and Clark examine the impact of one of the many types of employee compensation, pensions, on firm performance. Based on a review of the literature plus some new empirical work, their major finding is that pensions seem to reduce employee turnover, possibly through minimum vesting periods, a minimum length of service in order to obtain 100 percent vesting, and benefit formulas based on final (presumably maximum) earnings. A reduction in turnover is generally thought to have positive effects on efficiency.

They also asked whether pensions result in added costs to firms that have them, or whether there is a tradeoff between pensions and wage rates. In general they found that there were no negative compensating differentials; that is, firms with higher wages had a higher percentage of the work force covered by pension plans.

Allen and Clark point out that pensions still may not add to the cost of doing business if they are shown to increase productivity, possibly through reducing turnover. Their results on the relationship between pension coverage and turnover were inconclusive, however. On average, they found no pension coverage–productivity relationship, although pensions were associated with higher productivity in nonunion industries with high wages, low new-hire rates, and younger workers. There was a similar pattern of association between pensions and profit rates. They found no evidence of an effect of pensions on productivity growth. Overall, Allen and Clark believe that pensions have their principal impact by decreasing turnover rates among younger workers and increasing retirement age.

As was the case with compensation, it may be that it is difficult to find any direct impact of pensions on intermediate measures of firm performance, much less on the direct measures. It is possible that the additional costs associated with pensions are not so great that, by themselves, they would affect firm performance. It may also be that the firms that have pensions are the ones more likely to have market power and the ability to pass the costs through to their customers. This would be consistent with the data that show that workers in larger firms are more likely to be covered by pensions than are workers in smaller firms, and that workers under a union contract are more likely to be covered by pensions than workers not covered by a union contract. Both of these characteristics tend to be associated with concentrated industries.

Employee Relations Practices, Employee Behavior and Firm Performance

Although it is difficult to measure their costs directly, employee relations practices and the behavior of employees are important to industrial relations. A firm has a number of options from which to choose each of the employee relations subfunctions. Employees, in turn, can react to these practices in different ways. In theory at least, firm practices and employee behavior can make a difference in firm performance. The chapters by Holzer, Ichniowski and Lewin, and Gershenfeld address the impact of specific employee relations practices—recruitment, grievance procedures, and employee involvement. Osterman examines in detail a crucial cost component that we have discussed elsewhere, employee turnover.

Holzer's chapter on recruitment and performance represents an important step in attempting to bring together two heretofore separate strands of work in the literature—the work of economists on job search and labor demand and the work of scholars in human resource management on recruitment. He makes the important distinction between "efficiency outcomes," from the point of view of the firm, and "equity outcomes," from the point of view of society, and he points out that hiring and employment have a social as well as an economic component. A firm uses the recruitment and selection process to bring to its attention productive workers who are willing to accept jobs at the wage and benefit level the firm is willing to offer.[1] From society's point of view, the recruitment and selection process, which results in a job, is the worker's entry into the economic system. Thus, society has an interest in making sure that access to the system is open to all.

Holzer uses this notion of an efficiency-equity tradeoff as the basis for his analysis of firm recruitment techniques, and he notes some evidence for at least the perceived existence of such a tradeoff. His results indicate that those recruitment methods that

---

[1] In his chapter Holzer implicitly discusses the situation in which the employer allocates resources to recruitment because the costs of poor selection are, presumably, greater than the costs of recruitment. It is possible, however, that there are positions for which the costs of poor performance and turnover are so low that it is irrational to allocate resources to recruitment.

result in higher perceived productivity also result in a larger percentage of older male workers being hired. But the coefficients are neither very large nor very significant, suggesting that any positive effects of recruitment procedures on efficiency outcomes are more than outweighed, on balance, by the negative effects of these procedures on younger, female, and less experienced workers. The coefficients suggest that employers are gaining little in the way of efficiency by using these methods, while society is losing more in the way of equity. On the other hand, it is important to realize that an individual employer bears even the small costs of recruitment techniques that result in less efficient workers, unless these costs can be passed on to others.

Holzer's chapter is a move in the direction of developing a methodology that will enable us to learn whether or not recruitment, screening, and hiring practices matter for firm performance. The preliminary question he is attempting to answer is: Do they matter for employee performance? If so, then they might matter for firm performance.

Holzer's work may provide insight into the impact of Equal Employment Opportunity (EEO) requirements on firm performance. What is more equitable for society may not be more efficient for the firm. More generally, to the extent that the industrial relations system is viewed as the entire range of governmental restraints on employers, Holzer's contribution may be that it alerts the field to the necessity of examining the impact of the regulation of employee relations on firm and, therefore, on economic performance.

While Holzer considers the effects of measures to bring employees into the firm on the performance of that firm, Ichniowski and Lewin as well as Gershenfeld discuss the impact on firms of different voice and work organization mechanisms available to employees after they have been selected. Viewing a grievance procedure as a formal voice mechanism within a firm, and as a partial alternative to exit, Ichniowski and Lewin first attempt to model the incidence of grievance procedures among firms and the determinants of employee preferences for grievance procedures. They say that employers will adopt grievance procedures when the information and dispute-resolution benefits derived from them outweigh the administrative costs associated with them.

If we assume that employers make such a benefit/cost calculation, then employer attributes that would be associated with a positive benefit/cost ratio for grievance procedures include the number of layers between the covered employees and top management, the presence of rigid and fixed work rules and practices, high costs of turnover, and high costs of a work stoppage or slowdown. We would note, however, that the fact that a majority of large nonunion U.S. companies have implemented their own grievance procedures, albeit without arbitration, indicates that the costs of the procedure are not sufficiently great as to have any substantial effect on firm performance. To the extent that these unilaterally promulgated grievance procedures are created, at least in part, to reduce the probability of unionization among the firm's employees, they appear to be an inexpensive method of accomplishing this goal.

Under the assumption that there is a tradeoff between wages and the availability of a grievance procedure, the following attributes will be associated with employee interest in the procedure: a preference for stable employment and a relatively small number of superior external job opportunities. Ichniowski and Lewin attribute the universality of grievance procedures in the unionized sector to the greater incidence of fixed work rules and practices there and the greater probability of a work stoppage or strike.

They then turn to an analysis of the impact of grievance procedure availability and grievance activity on intermediate measures of firm performance. Their results show that the availability of grievance procedures reduces turnover in both unionized and nonunion companies. We would point out, however, that while a reduction in turnover may, on balance, enhance efficiency, it is not entirely costless if its availability discourages less productive workers from quitting and finding a better match between their skills and their job or makes it less likely that firms will discharge people whom they might otherwise discharge.

Ichniowski and Lewin's results on the relationship between grievance procedure use by individual employees and the turnover of those employees indicate that grievance users and grievance losers are more likely to leave than are nonusers and nonlosers. We would note that the implications of these results for firm performance are unclear. If the users/losers who are leavers are using it and losing because they are poor performers and are responding to company pressure on them because of their performance, then the grievance procedure is performing a useful function. On the other hand, if they are leaving because they believe the grievance procedure is not providing them with an effective voice, the procedure may be costly in terms of reducing the firm's credibility, thus causing the firm to incur reputational costs among its employees associated with a procedure that is not performing as intended.

Regarding the effect of the availability and use of grievance procedures on strikes, Ichniowski and Lewin note that outside of some work in the coal mining industry, which indicated that the greater availability of grievance procedures reduced strikes in that special, conflict-prone industry, there has been no research done in this area. We should mention, however, that one would expect the presence of a grievance procedure to reduce strikes in the unionized sector. Almost all grievance procedures in that sector are associated with no-strike clauses, and strikes in violation of a no-strike agreement can be enjoined.[2] In addition, one would expect that the quantity of strikes in nonunion firms is close to zero. Of course we have no way of knowing about slowdowns, or even how to formally identify one.

Finally, they note some indirect evidence that would be consistent with a positive productivity effect for grievance procedures. On the other hand, grievance procedure usage in unionized plants is associated with lower productivity in those plants. These results suggest the need to analyze grievance procedures in more detail in order to determine precisely what is meant by "voice." Is the voice used to provide the employer with useful information, or is it used as a device to obstruct the employer? If the latter, to what extent is the "voice" telling the employer about problems in its industrial relations system that need to be addressed?

Gershenfeld examines the impact on firm performance of newer types of employee participation in decision-making, usually called employee involvement (EI) or quality of work life (QWL) programs. Although these methods of work organization are difficult to define, it seems that they can best be described by

---

[2] *Boys Markets, Inc.* v. *Retail Clerks Union*, 398 U.S. 235, 74 LRRM 227 (1970).

contrasting them with what they are designed to replace—hierarchically-based management decision-making that provides for little questioning and is all from the top down. The terms that are continually used in this context are "participation," "joint," "problem-solving," and "cooperation."

Many of these nontraditional methods of organizing work were adopted as a means of permitting firms to adapt to changing markets and were designed to contribute to enhanced firm performance. Indeed, the assumption underlying them was that one of the factors adversely affecting firm performance was the hierarchical nature of work organization and decision-making. To the extent that this could be changed, firm performance, and overall economic performance, would improve.

The evidence with respect to the impact of employee participation on firm performance is meager. Gershenfeld's review turned up some indication that employee satisfaction increases and that, in general, firms that have adopted employee participation schemes perceive them to be successful. On the other hand, widespread improvements in productivity seem to be difficult to identify. Indeed, it may be that the aggregate of all these studies may best be summarized by the findings of Kochan and his MIT colleagues (1986), reported by Gershenfeld, that suggest that although employee involvement and quality of work life processes may have an impact on the organization of work, they operate at the margin of the firm's functioning and may be dropped when more fundamental product issues affect them.

More interesting, however, is that while these processes may not have a substantial impact on intermediate or direct measures of firm performance, their costs are not particularly great. They seem to provide worker satisfaction at a minimal monetary cost. Despite this, many firms and unions seem to be hesitant about EI/QWL. Why? It may be because the benefits, in terms of employee welfare and firm performance, are marginal and the costs in terms of the sacrifice of the internal integrity of the parties and what they view as their legitimate responsibilities are great. Management is held accountable for corporate performance, so they want ultimate control over it. Union leadership feels it is responsible for the welfare of the membership and they do not want to share that responsibility.

332   HUMAN RESOURCES AND FIRM PERFORMANCE

Thus, EI/QWL seems to be an option that is often considered and tried when the traditional systems do not seem to be working. But it may be contradictory to the relationship between the parties that derives from their respective legal statuses: management represents the stockholders/property owners who control the corporation, and the union, where it exists, represents employees, who are normally not property owners and whose status, constrained by a collective agreement, is at the will of the owners/ managers.

The Holzer chapter analyzes entrance into the firm, and the Ichniowski-Lewin and Gershenfeld chapters address practices in the firm. The Osterman chapter completes the cycle, in a sense, by examining the impact on firm performance of exit from the firm. Unfortunately, the data do not permit us to measure the true costs of turnover on firm performance. Osterman does tell us, however, that individuals who quit have higher earnings on their new jobs and that individuals who are laid off have lower earnings on their new jobs, usually after a spell of unemployment that imposes costs on society. On the other hand, we should point out that it is also clear that layoffs, especially those associated with redundancy, enhance at least short-term firm performance by reducing costs. In short, then, employees benefit from quitting and stockholders benefit from layoffs.

The most important contribution of Osterman's work, however, may be his attempt to focus on the effects of employment security for overall (macro) economic performance. Thus the distinction he makes between the two models for organizing work—the industrial and the salaried—seems particularly useful. The industrial model (at least the one developed through collective bargaining) is characterized by generally rigid job classifications, with management making labor force adjustments through varying the size of the work force (i.e., through layoffs). Security, to the extent it exists, is obtained through seniority and a reduction in management's discretion. The system minimizes employee uncertainty concerning the internal environment.

The salaried model, on the other hand, involves a flexible, personalistic set of rules for determining work. Supervisors and superiors are continually revising the organization of work as the needs of the firm change. Thus, there is substantial management discretion. In return for their discretion and the imposition of internal uncertainty on employees, management promises (but does not guarantee) job security; firms will make necessary adjustments through internal reallocation of resources rather than through variations in the size of the labor force.

Osterman believes that there is a growing interest in the salaried model of work organization. If this is true, it may be because firms are recognizing societal pressure to provide their employees with some kind of security. In this sense the firm, as a supplier of employment, may have a social function to perform (a view not unlike the European). An important contribution of the Osterman chapter may be that it focuses attention on the social aspect of employment, as much of the societal concern about firm performance is due to the presumably positive impact of firm performance on job security.

An inherent problem with this model is that layoffs do usually enhance firm performance, at least in the short run. To the extent that this is the case, the system is working in reverse. The argument, however, that layoffs and job losses would be greater without an improvement in firm performance begs the question, since society is still bearing a cost of unemployment. Moreover, the argument that a few layoffs prevent larger scale layoffs by enhancing firm performance has not, to our knowledge, been tested empirically. Indeed, it might be interesting to examine firms that imposed large-scale work force reductions in the early 1980s to see if they performed better than comparable firms that did not make such reductions. Clearly, in the short run raw cost-cutting will enhance performance, but the impact of such cost-cutting on long-term performance is unclear. Ford is an example of a firm in which severe corporate cost-cutting combined with astute strategic decisions has resulted in a very strong firm performance.[3]

Finally, it must be noted that the case for internal flexibility and the salaried model implies a low level of employment, possibly at about the same level as those who have lifetime employment. To the extent that this is true, then the increase in the number of employees who have job security, in a real sense, would be negligible. Similarly, the core-periphery notion may partially address the turnover problems of the firm, but not of society. The

---

[3] See, for example, "Can Ford Stay on Top?," *Business Week*, September 28, 1987, p. 78.

"core" work force, at least in terms of numbers, may be equivalent to that part of the work force that would not be laid off in any event. To the extent that this is the case, the salaried model does little but "formalize" what already exists and has existed for years.

Labor Relations and Direct Measures of Firm Performance

Of the authors of chapters in this volume, only Becker and Olson attempt to analyze the impact of labor relations on direct measures of firm performance. Their question is a simple one, but fundamental to addressing the issue of industrial relations and firm performance: Do unions and events related to unions affect the performance of the firm, however measured? In so doing they expose the field to the methodology of "event testing," which is an estimation procedure that has been accepted by academics in finance, accounting, and related business disciplines. The assumption with this technique is that the capital market has accurately valued the stock of a firm and can appropriately revalue that stock based upon new information about the firm. Becker and Olson start with the assumptions, therefore, that the market has access to information on firm-level industrial relations and is capable of accurately evaluating the impact of industrial relations news on the financial condition of the company. In addition, as in any other empirical investigation, they have the burden of identifying and controlling for all other factors or events that might also explain the stock market's appraisal of the firm at the same time.

Their central hypothesis is that unions and events associated with enhancing unionism in the firm will have a negative impact on the value of the firm. This results because the employees, as agents of the employer, have an incentive to shirk. Unionism, in turn, increases the costs of monitoring the employee agents.

Becker and Olson's thorough review of the literature and their own new empirical work result in a clear conclusion that the market does not like unions and reduces the value of firms, at least in the short run, whenever something happens that enhances unionism in firms. Thus, in their discussion they refer to Ruback and Zimmerman's (1984) study of the effect of union elections on stock prices of 253 firms involved in elections in units with 750 or more workers. Ruback and Zimmerman found some decline in stock prices associated with the occurrence of an election and some, although not conclusive, indication that the declines were greater when the union won than when the union lost the election.

Other reported findings include Becker's work showing an increase in shareholder equity associated with concession bargaining, work by Neumann (1980) showing a decline in shareholder equity for a 29-day period surrounding a strike, research by Abowd (1987) showing redistribution of cash flows from stockholders to workers associated with negotiated settlements, and a finding by Becker and Olson of an average decline in stockholder wealth of 20 percent during the 14-month period from March 1934 through April 1935 for firms presumed to be most affected by the passage of the National Labor Relations Act. An analysis of risk allocation in 1,006 companies between 1970 and 1981 showed that unionized firms are associated with greater risk for workers than for stockholders. In addition, their new analysis of returns of 1,000 firms indicate that investors in unionized firms earn lower risk-adjusted returns than do investors in other firms.

The Becker-Olson chapter, combined with other work on the impact of unionism on firm performance,[4] raises important questions about the nature of unionism and the relationship between unions and employers. Becker and Olson state that agency-type problems arise in the employment relationship because employees have better information than employers about the nature and magnitude of their current and future efforts, and employer monitoring is costly and, therefore, imperfect. Since the interests of employees and shareholders are not identical, imperfect monitoring provides employees with an incentive to shirk and appropriate firm resources for their own use.

But do employees have an incentive to shirk? Much of the traditional view of industrial relations assumes that there is a conflict of interest between employers and employees. But there is a new literature that assumes a general similarity of interests. If this literature is correct, then not shirking will make the profit pool larger than it might otherwise be. Similarly, lower expenditures on monitoring will increase the size of the profit pool. Becker and Olson take the divergent-interests approach, viewing the union as a potential appropriator of a greater portion of the firm's cash flow for the employees than they would be able to capture absent the

---

[4] See also, for example, Clark (1984).

union. Given the response of the stock market to unions, it would seem that the market shares the Becker-Olson view.

The Ruback-Zimmerman results on elections suggest that the market responds negatively to any firm's new association with unionism. The mere occurrence of an election is seen as a negative signal, even if the employer ultimately wins the election. The market may assume that the best union organizer is the employer, and if there is sufficient union support even for an election, then the firm may not be doing as good a job as it might in its employee relations—thus the reduction in the stock price. In other words, where there is smoke, there is fire. If there is a greater decline in stock price associated with the union win, then the market may simply be reducing the firm's stock price further for truly poor human resource management and for the decrease in management's flexibility. This begs the question, however, of why the market does not have sufficient knowledge about the company's (presumably) inadequate industrial relations practices at the time of the event. Some recent reports of the results of stock analyses for nonunion firms with so-called "good human resources practices" suggest that the market does take human resources factors into account when valuing stocks.[5]

Regarding strikes, Neumann's results suggest that the market does not like strikes. But what are the long-term results? If a company wins a strike, presumably long-run shareholder equity should improve. Thus, it is crucial to carefully take into account the time frame being considered.

We should note that although the message is clear—the market does not like unions—the rationale for this message is not. One possibility may be that the market values flexibility in resources. The more discretion management has to pursue the interests of stockholders, the better the market likes it. To the extent that management has less discretion in the presence of unions than when unions are absent, the market places a lower value on the firm than it otherwise might. It may also be that union activity is seen as an indicator that the firm's management is not managing its human resources well. To the extent that this is the case, the market places a lower value on the firm.

---

[5] Most of these reports have appeared in the press without supporting data or sources being identified.

Finally, in evaluating the Becker-Olson event-testing results, we must realize that the methodology does have its limitations and its critics. It is not well suited for separating out simultaneous events, those with either unclear beginnings or endings, or those that are embedded inside another or bracketed by other significant events. It should also be noted that event-testing uses the stock of the company as the unit of analysis, whereas the industrial relations event in question may be pertinent to only a portion of a corporation or one of a company's several facilities.

Industrial Relations and Corporate Strategy

Unlike the other seven chapters, which take what may be thought of as an empirical view of the impact of industrial relations on firm performance, Lewin takes a broad strategic look at the industrial relations/human resources function. He critically reviews the emerging literature on industrial relations policies as a strategic variable.

In Lewin's view, the notion of industrial relations as a strategic variable for the firm implies that the industrial relations policies and practices of firms are rational and predictable. He claims that much of what has been called strategic in industrial relations is not that at all, and he says that changes in industrial relations practices and policies are not the result of broad-based strategic decisions by firms based on matters over which corporate management has control. Rather, he contends, these changes are simply the result of firms reacting to their economic environments. They are attempts by management unilaterally, or by managements and unions together, to adapt their industrial relations policies and practices to changing circumstances.

Thus, Lewin sees the recent increase in management resistance to trade unionism, if it is only recent, as an attempt by management to adjust to a changing economic environment. He points out that union-avoidance policies are consistent with a standard neoclassical view of management decision-making; environmental pressures have changed the benefit/cost calculus associated with the old, less adversarial practices.

Lewin also considers the focus on union-avoidance in plant-location decisions as unnecessarily narrow, and he claims that no attention was paid to other factors such as capital costs, land costs, distribution channels, transportation costs, etc. In this regard he argues that the authors of these studies have usually labeled any management choice as "strategic," thereby stripping the notion of strategy in industrial relations of any substantive content.

His view that management's industrial relations decisions are reactive rather than strategic is reinforced by his analysis of the literature on airline industry collective bargaining, changes in collective bargaining structures in Britain, and the increase in labor-management cooperation and worker participation. All of these changes, he contends, are indications of management reaction to the environment rather than strategic behavior on the part of management.

Lewin is looking for something predictive rather than descriptive; we should be able to predict when a particular change in practice will occur and when it will not occur, and the nonoccurrences should be just as strategic as the occurrences. He also believes that a strategic-choice theory of industrial relations should be able to explain dualism between cooperation and adversarialism. He also distinguishes between strategic choice and reactive behavior models. In his view, strategic decision-making implies power and control over events, and this type of decision-making has been absent when changes in industrial relations practices have been made over the past decade.

Even if one does not agree with much of what Lewin says, it does remind us to be cautious when labeling management behavior as strategic, and his chapter also reminds us not to confuse what may be a short-run management dominance in industrial relations with management's strategic decision-making. In other words, the fact that management may have an enhanced ability to do what it wishes does not mean that what it wishes to do is necessarily strategically motivated. Indeed, it may be that management dominance, to the extent it exists, represents a manifestation of the fundamental economic notion that the demand for labor is a derived demand—derived from the product market. Thus, when markets were sheltered or regulated and product demand was essentially price inelastic, unions were strong because employers had little incentive to resist them. Now, since markets are competitive and employers must make different strategic decisions, they are the dominant actors. If this is true, then Dunlop's market constraints may be what is most relevant. The focus should be more on the product market rather than primarily on the employment relationship.

All of this suggests that industrial relations may not always be a strategic variable. Whether or not it is may depend on the nature of the industry and the firm's strategic response. Thus, for example, industrial relations was important in the airline industry because labor costs often provided the margin of profitability. Labor costs were important in autos, but they were not necessarily the only variable that required manipulation. In basic steel in the United States, an industry faced with a world-wide oversupply of its product and outmoded facilities, the industrial relations system was not a major factor in the decision of a number of companies to diversify. And it may be that the rubber industry's decision to invest in capacity to produce radial tires can be called strategic in that it involved a major resource allocation since, presumably, if it invested in radials, it would not invest elsewhere. Once the decision was made to invest in radials, then the firms decided to place their radial capacity in nonunion facilities, in essence deunionizing the industry (Block and McLennan, 1985). These four examples suggest that it may be misleading to focus too much on industrial relations as a strategic variable to the exclusion of other factors.

It should also be observed that, while Lewin tells us what strategic decision-making in industrial relations is not, he does not tell us what it is. In other words, Lewin has not provided us with a definition of "strategy" or "strategic behavior" in industrial relations. It does seem, however, that industrial relations becomes strategic when it is the major basis, or one of the major bases, on which the firm establishes or maintains its competitive position in the product market.

Finally, it should be noted that while Lewin's chapter addresses the notion of the industrial relations/human resources system of the firm as a variable that management can adjust to meet the strategic needs of the firm as defined by management, there have been recent instances in which the industrial relations system adjusted its tactics and influenced the direction of the firm. In the cases of Wheeling-Pittsburgh Steel Corporation and the Allegis Corporation, the industrial relations system had something to say about the strategic direction of the firm, rather than the other way around.

In 1985 the United Steelworkers of America, using as a weapon the necessity of its agreement prior to the approval of a bankruptcy reorganization of the Wheeling-Pittsburgh Steel Corporation, in essence forced the resignation of the chairman of the board before agreeing to terms that would save the company from bankruptcy.[6] In 1987 the bid of United Airlines pilots for Allegis's United Airlines unit signaled a lack of confidence in the Allegis strategy of becoming an integrated seller of travel services. In essence, the bid put United into "play," with the result being the resignation of the chief executive officer and a market repudiation of the strategy.[7] Thus it may be that a firm's industrial relations system can have an independent influence on corporate strategy.

A Final Word

The chapters in this volume suggest the difficulty and complexity of the task of understanding the impact of industrial relations on the performance of the firm. There is debate as to the definitions of both the dependent and the independent variables. What is this phenomenon that we are trying to explain, and what should we examine that might conceivably help us to explain it? While it would be helpful if we had a uniform accepted definition of firm performance to use, we have not yet reached that point in our field. Accordingly, we are forced to use a variety of measures and to evaluate the evidence from dissimilar studies.

As regards the dependent variable, it is clear that most of the work done to date has addressed intermediate measures of firm performance—productivity, waste, etc. Although Becker and Olson do examine direct measures of firm performance—market valuations of the firm—they are limited by the short-run nature of

---

[6] See, for example, "A Watershed Strike at Wheeling Pitt," *Business Week*, August 5, 1985, p. 26; "Wheeling Pitt: A Battle to the Death," *Business Week*, September 9, 1985, p. 35; Thomas F. O'Boyle, "Wheeling-Pittsburgh's Chief, Carney, Has Agreed to Resign, Directors Say," *The Wall Street Journal*, September 19, 1985, p. 3; Helen Fogel, "Ex-Ford Executive May Head Steel Firm," *Detroit Free Press*, September 20, 1985, p. 68; Terence Roth, "Steelworkers' Paul Rusen Seeks to End Strike Against Wheeling Pittsburgh," *The Wall Street Journal*, September 24, 1985, p. 4; and Roth, "Wheeling-Pittsburgh Employees Are Set to Return to Work Under New Contract," *The Wall Street Journal*, October 28, 1985, p. 2.

[7] See, for example, Laurie P. Cohen and Scott Kilman, "UAL Inc. Takeover Talk Is in the Air," *The Wall Street Journal*, April 9, 1987, p. 6; Robert J. Cole, "Why Allegis Reversed Course," *The New York Times*, June 11, 1987, p. 29 (and related stories); "Allegis Shakeup Came as Shareholder Ire Put Board Tenure in Doubt," *The Wall Street Journal*, June 11, 1987, p. 1; and "United's Pilots Are Inching Closer to a Coup," *Business Week*, August 1, 1987, p. 32.

the event-study methodology. While they find that certain aspects of industrial relations that are associated with unions affect the market valuation of the firm in the short run, we do not know whether industrial relations really matters over the long run. Given the availability of intermediate measures of firm performance and the fact that industrial relations practices are often designed to address these intermediate measures, a useful research path to follow might be to examine whether these intermediate measures (such as productivity and absenteeism) influence firm performance. If they do, then we might be able to measure, or at least infer, the effects of industrial relations practices to the extent that they affect these intermediate outcomes.

Regarding the independent variables, the authors of chapters in this volume have looked at a variety of industrial relations phenomena—direct costs of employment in the form of compensation and benefits; employment relations practices in the form of recruitment, grievance procedures, and labor-management cooperation; and employer reactions to employee turnover. The notion of corporate strategy as a useful way of looking at industrial relations and firm performance has also been examined. The protean manner in which the authors addressed the question posed suggests that we might be able to move forward if we had broader formulations of the issue. Specifically, we might ask: How important is industrial relations practice to different firms and different industries? This is a basic question that must be answered.

It is also important to note that the authors of the various chapters in this volume usually isolated one industrial relations practice and attempted to determine the impact of that practice on firm performance. Yet we know that firms implement a multitude of practices simultaneously. Moreover, they generally follow patterns and organize these practices into clusters in accordance with a company's culture. Thus, some firms take pride in minimizing layoffs, while providing training for employees and putting great weight on time with the company as a criterion for advancement. Other companies place more pressure on employees to produce in the short run and do not hesitate to terminate employees who do not produce, instituting reward systems consistent with this philosophy. Recruitment, compensation, pension, and voice practices in the firm may reflect these differences. Therefore, it would be misleading to look at one practice in isolation from other, complementary practices.

When we move beyond the realm of industrial relations, it is important to realize that industrial relations practices, even if they are important, are not the only firm decisions that affect performance. Firms make a series of decisions in the context of other corporate functions (i.e., marketing, finance, etc.) that also affect firm performance. While the industrial relations system may be important, it cannot be divorced from the other functions it supports.

Thus, perhaps a broader model is in order. Firm performance may need to be viewed as a function of internal firm policies and practices as well as of the environment. Attempts to examine for the marginal effect of an organization's industrial relations/human resources while controlling only for the environment and not controlling for other internal policies may misspecify the model by omitting important variables.

Finally, although this volume has focused on the firm as an entity, it still must be kept in mind that the unique contribution of industrial relations as a field is that it views the employment relationship not only as a factor of production and as a means of meeting the goals of the employing organization, but also as a means by which people earn their living. The recent, important, and well-founded interest in the industrial relations field in firm performance should not cause us to disregard the interests of employees. Balancing these interests has always been at the heart of the field.

References

Abowd, John M. "Collective Bargaining and the Division of the Value of the Enterprise." National Bureau of Economic Research Working Paper No. 2137, January 1987.

Block, Richard N., and Kenneth McLennan. "Structural Economic Change and Industrial Relations in the United States' Manufacturing and Transportation Sectors Since 1973." In *Industrial Relations in a Decade of Economic Change*, eds. Hervey Juris, Mark Thompson, and Wilbur Daniels. Madison, Wis.: Industrial Relations Research Association, 1985. Pp. 337–82.

Clark, Kim B. "Unionization and Firm Performance: The Impact on Profits, Growth, and Productivity." *American Economic Review* 74 (December 1984): pp. 893–919.

Cleveland, John. "Common Ground . . . Mutual Gains: A Business Plan for Fostering Productive Work Relations in Michigan." Lansing: Michigan Modernization Service, Michigan Department of Commerce, June 1987.

Dunlop, John T. *Industrial Relations Systems*. New York: Holt, Rinehart, and Winston, 1958.

Jacoby, Sanford. *Employing Bureaucracy: Managers, Unions, and the Transformation of Work in American Industry: 1900–1945*. New York: Columbia University Press, 1985.

Kochan, Thomas A., Harry C. Katz, and Robert B. McKersie. *The Transformation of American Industrial Relations*. New York: Basic Books, 1986.

Levinson, Harold. *Determining Forces in Collective Wage Bargaining*. New York: Wiley, 1966.

Neumann, George R. "The Predictability of Strikes: Evidence from the Stock Market." *Industrial and Labor Relations Review* 33 (July 1980): pp. 525–35.

Ruback, Richard S., and Martin B. Zimmerman. "Unionization and Profitability: Evidence from the Capital Market." *Journal of Political Economy* 92 (December 1984): pp. 1134–57.